The Politics of Truth

to

MARGARET

The Politics of Truth:

Toward
Reconstruction
in Democracy

by

HOLTAN P. ODEGARD

THE UNIVERSITY OF ALABAMA PRESS
University, Alabama

Parts of chapter 13 were previously
published in the periodical *Main Currents in
Modern Thought* by permission
of The University of Alabama Press.

Preface

> *If you will tell me why the fen*
> *appears impassable, I then*
> *will tell you why I think that I*
> *can get across it if I try.*
>
> MARIANNE MOORE

THIS IS A PACKAGE OF THOUGHTS FOR A TIME OF BEGINNING that should have started long, long ago. It is therefore hypothetical and open-ended, ripe with questions, much in need of help, and calling for the courage to break out yet newer leads. Its hope is that others, carrying less well lashed and adhesive loads of cultural baggage, will be stimulated to take the intellectual leaps that I could not.

Since the new monsters of science can no longer be crammed into the old pickle jars of "power politics" or the comfortable cracker barrels of the democratic process, and since the voice of God no longer effectively thunders out of the polling booth, the search is on for new social inventions that can make government democratic and convert it into an instrument of knowledge and intelligence.

There are those who are satisfied to castigate "technocracy" and cop out, claiming (ab)solution in a new spirit for the age, a change in the temper of the times—but apparently not intruding far enough through personal contact to discover that the "technocrat" is mulling over the same problems and sharing the same concern. Spiritual revival, yes, but throw in a leading measure of scientific attitude, and enlist all the inside help in sight! As Utopia and Uphoria vie for honors in pointing paths out of present discontent, we champion the first, pre-ferring determination to resignation; preferring to seek the objectivity of maximum clarity and not to wander off into the dark, trailing lizards; choosing justice over peace when the chips are down. Only insist that the ideal world be usable as a guide, make no pretense to finality, and have room for both right and wrong!

So many people's ideas have gone into this book that I almost think of it as a group project. Were it not for the memory of painful and lonesome effort, putting word after word, I might nearly be persuaded that a host of illustrious men joined directly in. Yet, if any of them should accept responsibility, it is Horace Fries, and he died before it was begun. His influence pervades.

I am delighted to be able to report that Max Otto read the manuscript before its last revision and approved. This touches my pride.

The encouragement of James McCamy and John Gaus has been of surpassing importance. Their comments were many and excellent, and can only have provoked quality throughout. The book has also been much improved by Ordway Tead's perceptive suggestions.

Roy and Elizabeth Larsen have been critically helpful in bringing the book to life and presenting it for public test. But for the enlightened personnel policies of my wife and two great public administrators, Richard E. Arms, urban and regional planner, and Raymond T. Olsen, city manager, the book would not have been written at all.

HOLTAN P. ODEGARD

St. Croix Cove,
Wisconsin
April, 1971

Table of Contents

viii

ix

CLOTURE

xi

Introduction

CHAPTER ONE

Democracy in a "Pig Pile"

> The scientific revolution has imposed
> an abrupt end to traditional history of
> mankind; ... what we are witnessing
> now are the last spasms of power
> politics, relegated to the fringes
> of Western civilization.
>
> EUGENE RABINOWITCH

THE WORLD IS SELDOM READY FOR ITS INVENTORS, THOUGH they never seem to catch it enough off balance to tip it out of orbit. So far the universe has held sufficient tolerance to accommodate all of human creativity.

How long this fortunate standoff is likely to last no man knows, but it is clear that human creativity becomes more powerful with each passing hour. And with each creation comes an anxious backward look at the foundations of social sanity. Albert Nobel, after the invention of dynamite, and the nuclear physicists after the atom bomb, took panic and developed unwonted social conscience in awe of the potentials they had unleashed. The atomic scientists in addition recognized that there were dangers inherent in government too poorly organized and informed to act wisely in the age of science.

There are perils more portentous, however, than even the explosive and fall-out achievements of the physical scientists. Present day forms and procedures of political and social organizations are perfectly unprepared to handle the sort of decisions and agreements that will be demanded by changes in biological inquiry and social development already under way. It is now being predicted, for example, that within two hundred years the biological sciences will know how to twist the tail of the gene and control the hereditary aspects of human character from chromosome to grave. Evolution will be at the mercy of mankind. Obviously the decision, or even the possibility of deciding, to mint a new issue of ten thousand Einsteins, Leonardos, or Mozarts cannot be left to private discretion. Would not a thousand Helens launch the earth out of orbit? When someone, by adding a new turn to the chromosome, learns to quadruple the memory or the inventiveness of a select population, is there not an earth-shaking potential that must be tightly and jealously watched?

Neither midnight cabal, benevolent society, nor doting parent can be handed the privilege of stamping the future character of the race, or of selecting the character of a superhuman race to displace mankind. (Though, it must be admitted that society, to a very minor—but eventually cumulative—extent, has already unintentionally bent the course of evolution by perpetuating the unfit for procreation through the "humanitarian" efforts of medical science.) On the other hand, would anyone want to turn the decision as to the future character of human character over to any existing government? Or to any two, three, or one hundred of them? If present patterns of social behavior persist, there will be grand manipulation of the human brain, perhaps irreversibly affecting the course of evolution, well before there is understanding of what it is all about.

The one simple point of this excursion into the always surprising future is that when the chips are down no form of government is self-government enough so that anyone feels completely at home and at ease.

Is it not possible that a systematic seasoning of truth could make all the difference in the world? The old line democracies are, if not out of step, then out of tune with the times. Science has invaded field after field, transforming the very basis, transposing the old harmonies, on which government, politics, and power rest. The new truths of science have altered the face of the earth while the old "truths" of politics have been turning into fantasy.

As if to accentuate the point, political science is suddenly faced with a doubt that it knows what it is talking about at all. After many years during which politics was analyzed in terms of power, the fashion built up to avalanche proportions before the revelation broke forth that the term "power" had lost precise definition. Thinking about power, instead of providing a useful tool for political analysis, quickly collapsed to "a great sloppy, gelatinous mass, pitted here and there with an agitated insight." [1]

The situation is intensified by the recent transformation of physical science from a respectably academic, progressive, self-effacing, cooperative endeavor, ultimately aiming at human betterment, into a compulsive mechanism reaching far beyond human betterment, becoming—inner driven—a relentless urge before the stride of which human betterment scrambles and scatters as best it may in its stumbling ignorance.

Science can, apparently, no longer progress under private auspices alone, but demands financing by public funds—in result upsetting traditional government-science relationships. In the mad turmoil, old ties have been broken and old meanings have been lost or rendered useless.

Meanwhile, just when new thought is needed in political and social philosophy, the old is given a shot in the arm. Computer machinery is developed that permits unimagined extension, refinement, and extrapolation of old formulas based on old Newtonian and Cartesian concepts; and much talent, beguiled by refinement, is diverted from creative thought. This is like suddenly discovering how to build higher walls after the invention of gunpowder.

Perhaps the greatest technological threat of all is the offer that by 2006 A.D. we may telephone a vote to the Capitol Computer on every or any pending bill to enact it or defeat it by direct popular action, without danger of subversion.

To match the creativity of science, to channel the social scramble for betterment, a little emulation of the disrupting spirit is to be prescribed, a taste of the experimental search for truth. Politics must become self-consciously allied with the search for truth. Science in politics must become experimental. In the process politics will become a part of social experimental inquiry and inquiry will become a part of politics. And, hard as it is now to imagine, political science will resume, in the trans-computer era (when the computer's magic spell is spent), its bygone role as master science.

In place of the vast political and social effort to manipulate man and nature, is to be envisioned a democratic, self-governing, self-controlling reorganization, with participation and scientific experiment developing through administrative reorganization—knowingly and humanly to control instead of blindly and brutally to force.

1911 AND ALL THAT ADMINISTRATION

In addition to threats from scientific and technological achievement there is the overburden of currently culminating trends demanding administrative democracy.

The "pig pile" of progressive technological complexity finally mounted high enough to give rise to a new dimension in government at a date that may conveniently, though roughly, be set in 1911. That was the year Cannonism was overthrown.[2] The Speaker of the House of Representatives was thenceforth a crippled contender for effective leadership of governmental policy. Until then, Speaker had vied with President for top billing, and leadership had swung from Speaker to President to Speaker, alternating—at least so we are told—with the strength of personality and the capacity of the individuals involved.[3] Great men had risen to brilliance from one vantage or the other; Clay, Reed, and Cannon had traded the limelight with Jefferson, Jackson, Lincoln, and Cleveland. Whatever the explanation behind this almost cyclic phenomenon, it came to a symbolic end in the 1911 revolution. Since then the weight of administrative activity has tipped the scales, apparently irrevocably, to the glory of the Executive.[4]

It is easy to recognize in the post-1911 rise of the administrative heap much of the eager contagion that sweeps up the impulse to pile on when two boys knock themselves to the ground and the "Pig pile!" cry arises from the playing field.

But 1911, as a symbolic date, emphasizes only the political turning point. Widespread change was occurring all over the place both before and after 1911. When radical change takes place in ways of organizing government in a democracy, fundamental changes are sure to be found in many, if not all, other aspects of society as well. The patterns of transactions making up society are in constant flux. During the present era their groupings and regroupings have arisen to sheer acrobatics. Organizational patterns throughout the social fabric have undergone radical transformations to accommodate the machinery, the technology—ultimately the system of scientific knowing—that developed over the last few centuries and has been promoted at a frenetic rate in the last several decades. Poetically enough, it was 1911 that saw Rutherford lay out the basic organizational pattern of the atom: a small nucleus surrounded by electrons.

People no longer seem to have the time or the capacity to take care of their own affairs. Where they used to perform as working groups, they hire specialists and staffs. Where Robert's Rules of Order used to preside at the center of activity and to moderate associational activities, a hired expert has taken over. A local Chamber of Commerce finds its many committees ineffective, if not also apathetic, and engages a crew headed by an Executive Secretary, to feed the committees with information, ideas and, eventually, leadership. A downtown businessmen's association discovers that the urban problems in which it is involved are too broad and too detailed, too specialized, to be met by the intermittent, day's-end efforts of its members—and hires a retiring member of the group, or a "public relations man," to fill the gap, and, if he has the personality and ability, to dominate the downtown. A city planning commission wangles the funds to hire a young planner only to find that its accustomed procedures are no longer pertinent because the new man has a ready "technical" answer which obviates discussion, eclipses their experience, and promotes him from the title to the literal function of Planning Director. The membership of a labor union retires in "apathy" as open debate is given over to a situation where The Office proposes and the membership ratifies.

Many activities that were once independently pursued by individuals are today organized, administered, staffed. Mammoth insurance agencies, state and federal unemployment and social security offices, old age and retirement schemes, and poverty programs attempt to furnish the security that used to be preserved on a family scale in the form of land and equipment, supplemented by very modest cash savings. Young Americans, instead of, as formerly, spending their leisure hours "messing around" or taxing their individual ingenuities, are eagerly welcomed into the plans, games, and programs arranged by the administrative personnel of the city's park and playground system. Even charity, the erstwhile Christian personal virtue, has been organized to the teeth, becoming transformed into something new and strange, where its heart and spirit become welfare councils, boards of directors, publicity managers, advertising experts, and social worker teams— or swarms.

Even more impressive, however, have been the number and size of new tasks assumed by administrative organizations in response to inventions,[5] to the proliferation and perfection of machinery and its abundant fruits: gigantic industrial organization, extreme division of labor, urban concentration of population, complex financial structure and monetary systems, institutional paper shuffling, mass "communication," universal education.[6] A newly complex society, faced with unprecedented work, has characteristically turned to what may, very generally, be called administrative organization.

The administrative, in this broad sense, is probably the oldest, most venerable mode of coordinated action—as old as the human species itself. Present day constitutionalism, with its heavy reliance on legislative control, resulted from efforts to curb the unrestrained administrative autarchy prevalent in the eighteenth century. But in our time administrative organization has again pushed to the fore—even within the context of constitutionalism—to become all pervasive. It has become the accepted form of social organization as never before. While it formerly assumed prominence at selected points—the Church, the army, the King's Household—it now preempts the field. It has become a "way-of-life." Even farm organization has assumed the administrative pattern.

We live in the "administrative state"—that is to say, in a country where the preponderance of institutions is administrative. Yet we cling to a theory of republican government and democratic politics that matured while government was mostly made up of representative, legislative institutions—the "legislative state." The vision and ideal of democracy still current after many years of de facto administrative government depicts the rule of the people through their elected delegates in representative assembly. Can the people also rule in an administrative state in any meaningful sense? When the administrative way of life begins to eclipse in scope and importance the legislative way of life, it is time to look, not only at what it is, but at what it can be and what it should be; not only at what it does, but at what it can and should do. Can it be equipped to cope with the thumblessness that is so widely deplored in society? Can it be specifically democratic? Some sort of democracy in administration *must* be a genuine option, for the best administrative alternative is a soul-sapping benevolence.

A NEW DEMOCRATIC SEQUENCE

Meanwhile, the world has moved out of the climate that bred legislative democracies. Since World War II half a hundred new nations have been created, but only a few can be called democratic by any stretch of the imagination. Yet many of them grew out of years of tutelage (of various sorts) in the ways of the Western democracies. Many other existing states have been reconstituted; new constitution, new regime, new faces—but not more democratic for all that. After the American and French Revolutions, there was a time when the countries in the community of nations seemed to be headed, one by one and however laggardly, toward legislative democracy. There has now apparently been a change in the course of the development of nations.

Before the 1911 revolution, the historical growth of the most highly developed systems of government had proceeded in three stages. Woodrow Wilson described them as (1) absolute rule with a corresponding administrative system, followed by (2) constitution-framing to substitute popular control for absolute rule (with administration neglected for higher concerns), followed by (3) development of administration under new democratic constitutions.[7] This put administration at the end of an historical line, to be polished and perfected within the established purity of democratic legislative forms.

The twentieth century, however, has established a new pattern, first dramatically demonstrated by Russian, then Chinese, experience and now also visible in African development, as well as in many other parts of the communist and non-communist world. The new sequence of stages moves from (1) agrarian society (with absolute rule) to (2) administrative state to (3) industrialization. This new pattern puts administration in a strongly entrenched position that is different from its position in the days of the old absolute rule monarchies. It is now too complex to be so absolute as it was, and it is in command of too many technical complexities to be so easily replaced by legislative hegemony.

Now that administrative organization has become so prominent among social organizations as to vie with the family, to overshadow the town meeting, and to promise more effectiveness than either in terms of stabilizing and improving the fortunes of men, the less highly developed systems of government can no longer be expected to pass through the three periods of growth experienced by the old line democracies. Society is now so complex, so technical, the executive is is vast, so encompassing (even in the less developed sections of the world) that the process of developing constitutionalism and substituting popular control or a balance of power for absolute rule can no longer be expected to follow the pattern of comparatively simple or relatively non-technological eighteenth and nineteenth century societies. Comparatively speaking, legislative democracy was the sustained performance of an agricultural-mercantile society. It has survived the onslaught of industrial technology because it was, in some countries, entrenched in social habit well in advance, and has proved highly adaptable as well.[8] It is doubtful that legislative democracy can develop as it used to, if at all, *after* the fact of extensive technological sophistication. At least there is no clear evidence that it can.

The problem of democracy for developing countries is one of accommodation to the twentieth century pattern so that, having passed from agrarian society to administrative state, they do not rest content with the polishing and perfecting of industrialization, but also lead on to "democratic" government. Apparently many Latin American, African, and Southeast Asian countries will be unable to pursue the historic legislative path to democratic institutions, but will have to take a route through administrative bypaths instead. Having arrived prematurely (according to old expectations) at a comparatively high stage of administrative competence—or at least at a stage of development crying more insistently for such competence than for Robert's Rules of Order —the most promising route to democratic institutions would appear to be through drawing out and perfecting whatever democratic attitudes, attributes, and tendencies are to be found in the administrative way of life, and, in states where there is no hint of democracy, through importing or inserting it deliberately into administration.

Woodrow Wilson's advice as he launched the study of administration in 1887 was for old line democracy to improve its administrative system by learning from the more advanced systems of the enlightened absolutisms of Europe (Frederick the Great, Frederick William III, Napoleon) which had, at a late date, organized administration "to subserve the general weal with the simplicity and effectiveness vouchsafed only to the undertakings of a single will." [9] Wilson's suggestion was important for his day as an attempt to widen administrative horizons. But in terms of the twentieth century sequence, a new prescription is needed.

Today, democracies with the most highly developed systems of administration should be asked to inquire as to what can be done to make administration itself democratic. And when they have learned the basic secrets, they should be expected to urge the exportation of administrative democracy, as they used to urge legislative democracy —in the spirit of the American and French Revolutions—as antidote to international communism.

It has been a serious mistake to assume that administration can have the same excellence in different countries regardless of the prevailing system of government, and that administration is politically (in the broadest sense) neutral. This assumption has been current ever since guidelines for the study of administration were first charted in Woodrow Wilson's classic essay published in 1887, near the beginning of the proliferation of administrative organization. [10] (The Interstate Commerce Commission was created in that same year.) It is a direct corollary of the idea that a clear distinction can be made between policy and performance; that the two can be institutionally separated —policy being a legislative function and its execution a function of the administration. "The field of administration is a field of business," Wilson said, "it is a part of political life only as ... machinery is a part of the manufactured product." [11] This over-simple division of labor between legislative and administrative organizations is, however, not in fact to be found. And it has ceased in theory to be particularly prized. Almost everyone now knows that administration is a vital participant in the forging of policy and almost everyone has accepted this fact as a necessary feature of modern government. Unfortunately, the corollary—the idea that good administration is the same for all governments, from democracy to dictatorship—has not been discredited. [12] It has scarcely been questioned. It is equally false.

Wilson contends that,

> So far as administrative functions are concerned, all governments have a strong structural likeness; more than that, if they are to be uniformly useful and efficient, they *must* have a strong structural likeness. A free man has the same bodily organs, the same executive parts, as the slave, however different

may be his motives, his services, his energies. Monarchies and democracies, radically different as they are in other respects, have in reality much the same business to look to. . . . For all governments alike the legitimate ends of administration are the same.[13]

And he clinches it with a preposterous analogy:

If I see a murderous fellow sharpening a knife cleverly, I can borrow his way of sharpening the knife without borrowing his probable intention to commit murder with it; and so, if I see a monarchist dyed in the wool managing a public bureau well, I can learn his business methods without changing one of my republican spots.[14]

It must be admitted that Wilson's point is well taken. His characterization of administration, his general comparative description, has fit appearances. It must *not* be admitted that the past should be continued, that it is normal or proper for democracy to continue with an administrative system indistinguishable from that of a despotism, or even one that bears "a strong structural likeness." [15] The development of administration (Wilson's third historical period) under constitutional democracy should be expected to take a self-consciously democratic turn—particularly since development after 1887 has put administration in a more persuasive political position.

The theory of administration has for some time taken direction from a refutation of the classic separation between policy and performance. It is time now to refresh the new direction by hearty disagreement with the sterile corollary to that separation, and to insist that administration can become democratic, as distinguishable from both American administration of the past and administration of non-democratic countries of today. In entering the realms of policy, administration has passed through the portals of the moral. It can itself be specifically democratic.[16]

There is no political theory that can give the new African the service that the "social contract" theory gave the new American of colonial and revolutionary days. Even the doctrines of communism are far behind the times and remote to the realities of the administrative state.

In effect, the new African, still responsive to tribal organization and folklore, has only the rituals of science and technology. Nothing else is current, guiding, honored, or inspiring. He seeks to find his place in the United Nations through a tangle of tribal thought and primitive custom, with no working political theory to sail by. Many Latin American, Near Eastern, and Southeast Asian governments, as well—not to mention communist governments—are simple administrative autarchies. Unfortunately, since the Western European pattern of displacing absolute rule with constitutional legislative democracy was once successful, expectation and effort continue to be oriented in that direction. The Western world continues to encourage alien cultures to follow its historic trail. However, it is no longer possible to *virtually* dispense with administration while leaving the legislative way free to entrench itself into social habit as a principal participant in policy determination. The underdeveloped countries, unlike the old line democracies in the early years of industrialization, must depend on government and its administrative strength for economic and social advancement. Legislative-administrative relationships must, therefore, necessarily develop along new and different lines.

Practically speaking, if the United States or the United Nations had a workable (and perfectible) theory of administrative democracy, it could do a lot of good among the nations upon which aid is being lavished and frequently wasted. It has been observed from many perspectives that the major blocks to effective aid programs have come from administrative deficiencies in the aid-receiving, or host countries. There are administrative problems due to lack of efficiency, faulty scheduling, inadequate budgeting, poor personnel coordination, lack of proper equipment, and failure of resourcefulness in leadership and in a dozen other overlapping administrative skills. But an important part of the administrative deficiency also has to do with responsibilities, freedoms, roles, participation, vision, and the other dozen overlapping features that nudge administrative skills into self-conscious democratic expression.

True to form, which is to say, true to discarded theory—only showing how stubborn theory is, how persistent even when renounced—America proclaims the principle of self-determination for others—and in fact gives evidence of sometimes acting on that principle—so far as elections, constitutions, popular assemblies, and courts of law are concerned. At the same time she brazenly steps forth with administrative assistance—as if administration were "purely" technical, separable from policy, from the moral content of government. Administrative assistance is desperately needed; there appears to be little question about that. Indeed, a realistic approach, it seems, would push a much greater percentage of aid in that direction, for without adequate administration other technical aid is feckless. But if policy and performance are as intertwined as has been said, it is sure that effective administrative aid impinges on self-determination and makes foreign interference as real as if the "aid" were in influencing elections. This is something the leading communist countries can be relied upon to understand—in terms of their own authoritarian systems—and to exploit in trying to shape new countries after their own images.

The eventual objective of democratic countries in extending aid must be self-government for the people of the receiving country. The effective route to this goal is the careful conversion of foreign aid to self-help. Aid is quickly brought to naught without local participation. This was learned long ago by the American federal government while trying to extend aid to states and localities. And such self-help—involving, incidentally, changes in understanding, attitude, and perception—given the persuasive fact of the importance of technology, must be found in the growth of administrative capabilities. Again, the major need is for coordination, guidance by a theory of self-government, a theory of democracy explicitly fitted to the fact of administrative centrality.

APPEAL

After all the above comments about foreign governments, this book will hazard few terse recipes for direct export. Export should await at least some experimental success in organizing democracy at home, and then should be adapted in light of differing cultural circumstances. The substance of what has been said about foreign aid may also be said, *mutatis mutandis*, about federal aid to local governments within the United States. When America learns how to convert its own system into what can be called administrative democracy, and to apply it between its own partly coordinated governmental units, then other nations can be asked to emulate it, to study it with a critical eye to improving it and adapting it to their particular situations, environments, and problems.

What is most critically needed is a little thinking that can run ahead of the doing, theory that can project enough to play the guide—but, by all means, theory that is also sensitive enough to be improvable by the course of events. This is an appeal for utopian thought; that is to say, for thought based on the realities of human nature. And it is an appeal for scientific thought—thought that is couched in cooperative and improvable terms.

The subject of government has become too extensive for detailed mastery by a single mind, since in its theoretical connotations it subsumes human nature, thought, and environment. To start a book with an apology for ranging through diverse fields so vast that they are obviously beyond the competence of any one man is poor form. This book, therefore, opens with a challenge. The author shares with the rest of the individuals of his species the plight of becoming more stupid and superficial by the minute. It is doubtful that any man today can claim the wisdom of his father in terms of available knowledge. The world has passed into an era in which wisdom has become a function, not of the individual, but of the community of men. Instead of pretending to omniscience, the most that the present treatise can do is urge more powerful thinkers to join in an experimental inquiry in politics.

The cooperative effort of scientific investigation is the effective way around individual limitations. The most practical approach, some of the first steps of which are hazarded in this book, is to start laying the foundation for a theory of science in administration. If truly scientific, it will be testable, objectifiable, and improvable—rapidly perfectible when pursued with determination by a group of dedicated scholars. As will be shown, this is bound to involve mankind in a "politics of truth"—self-government, self-correcting, an experimental laboratory organized for the creation of truth—a merging of the social reformer with the social scientist. It is to be hoped that the advance of learning will, in short order, reduce this present pre-scientific treatise, as well as matters of chromosome control, administrative-technological pig pile, and democratic sequence in national development to the level of merely curious historical interest.

CHAPTER TWO

Theory is to Think Ahead

> *I have no doubt that later generations will look back at many of our political systems with the same feeling as a modern astronomer studies an astrological book or a modern chemist an alchemistic treatise. . . . In our political actions and our political thoughts magic still holds its ground.*
>
> ERNST CASSIRER

TO BE EFFECTIVE, A THEORY OF PUBLIC ADMINISTRATION must either grow out of an adequate theory of government or else provide, within its own scope, for the whole of political life. In addition, it must intimately relate to a respectable theory of human nature. At the present time there is no adequate theory of government in general, and most of what there is relates to and depends upon obsolete ideas about human nature.

This chapter will point up, in a schematic way, some of the theoretical problems and deficiencies in traditional ways of thinking about representative institutions. Then it will lead on to the suggestion that a theory of public administration, to be effective, must strike out on its own from the basis of a fresh and improved understanding of human nature; it must make room, within its scope, for thinking about government on the very broadest, most general level.

REPRESENTATIVE DEMOCRACY—THEORETICAL PROBLEM OF LEADERSHIP

The theory of representative democracy, in the soil of which administrative theory took root (as witness Wilson's theoretical attempts), has become a thing of rags and patches. Perhaps there never was an internally consistent theory, free of holes and raveled edges. Better understanding of human nature has rendered pretty well obsolete the picture of man upon which the idea of representative government was orginally superimposed. Over the years this original theory of representative government has been tinkered with, adjusted here and there to fit new facts, accommodated by refinement and distinction to altered social circumstances, and "perfected" by incorporation of explanations of the unanticipated novelties that have emerged. As a result, the current condition of political theory resembles pre-Copernican astronomy, a basic structuring set about with epicycles.

Graham Wallas put it point-blank when he observed that "the democratic movement which produced the constitutions under which most civilized nations now live, was inspired by a purely intellectual conception of human nature which is becoming every day more unreal to us. If, it may then be asked, representative democracy was introduced under a mistaken view of the conditions of its working, will not its introduction prove to have been itself a mistake?" [1]

Representative institutions came into the field under the banner of high-minded rationalism, to the strains of atomic individualism. The corporate Middle Ages had long since crumbled. Its social organization, held together by personal relationships, feudal rights and duties, had been unable to withstand the assaults of technological change; its peculiar bonds of union had snapped. Neither it nor its administrative systems were equipped to cope with new and accelerating problems as they emerged. The new substitute for the unitary doctrines of the Church—the Cartesian mind-matter dualism—pervaded the realms of knowledge in the eighteenth century, even as it today pervades the realms of common sense. [2] The kingdom of mind, morals, and soul had been violently wrenched from that of body, motion, and matter, and the corporate, cohesive medieval oneness was displaced by a relationless twoness.

With particularism rampant, with unrelated individuals freed from the all-encompassing older order, social problems still cried to be solved, and theorists proceeded to describe new types of social organization that related men to each other in the only fashion the rigid dualism would permit. Since matter was classed as inferior and turned over to the eager hands of science, and since the body, emotions, and feelings were correspondingly disparaged, organizations were theoretically propounded in which men were interrelated on the level of reason. A spate of social contract theories (theories of union through rational agreement or assent) ensued, and, as a part of this epidemic, the basic theory of representative government.

A chapter of this story is the rational faith to be found, for example, in John Milton, who celebrated his belief by assuring the world that in a free market of ideas the truth would be victorious. This is perhaps a close approximation to the way things in fact work out, but it is also an oversimple reading (compatible with the Cartesian dualism) of the nature of truth. Who is to say how much of the success of this maxim has been due to popular belief that it is true?

Another chapter of the story revolves around John Locke's rational faith that men are good judges of where their interests lie and are moved to act on these judgments. The fact remains that, Locke notwithstanding, men do not always act according to their own self-interests and are not necessarily the best judges of where those interests lie. Men do not identify their interests apart from social process; this is the very simple meaning of the observation that they are social animals. As a matter of fact, if political processes do not also help in discovering, developing, making, or creating interest, their services in reflecting or expressing interest are pathetically superficial.

A third episode centers about Adam Smith's decree that the division of labor resulted from the economies of production—a rational calculation—that it effected. But it must now be recognized that, contrary to Smith, men must first have turned to specialization of function (if indeed there is sense in such speculative pre-historical sally) as much for the non-rational reason of job satisfaction, emotional or aesthetic, as for any consideration of efficiency. Because of their basic reliance on these now apparent deficiencies in Locke and Smith, majority rule and the factory system, in their theoretical inceptions, display very cursory relation to what we now know as human nature. The three errors of rational faith—here attributed to Milton, Locke, and Smith—continue to echo down the legislative halls of time.

The inauguration of the representative system may be said to mark the final institutional flowering of the Age of Reason. Whereas representation had been used to a limited extent among the Greeks and the Romans, and within the Church (notably in the monastic orders), it required the widespread acceptance of a Cartesian dualism before it could flourish. Medieval representation attempts were inhibited and finally and fatally disrupted because of their incompatibility with the strong bonds of personal loyalty so important to the social organization of the time; they were defeated, in a sense, by the oneness of the age. Indeed, William of Occam's conciliar theory for Church government based representation, as did the medieval parliaments, on corporate bodies, instead of on individuals. It should be noted in passing that the same corporateness and personal loyalty continue to militate against the development of representative institutions in many Latin American countries.[3] Representation became the dominant pattern of political organization only when organic organization had broken down, when a need to interrelate particularized individuals was felt, and when the theorist had successfully (for a time) relegated the body, the personal, the organic, the emotional, to inferior status while raising the mental, the moral, the rational, to the prime level of ultimate significance. Representation was essentially a technique for interrelating *rational* men so that they could better deal with their common problems.[4]

Advocates of representative government once expected, indeed there are those who still expect, a legislative body to constitute a composite of a country's opinion. The theory was that constituencies would send to the *deliberative* assembly able, well-qualified individuals seriously chosen to *re*present the opinion of the electors and to legislate for them, to decide matters of state, not in the way the electors themselves would have decided, but after careful deliberation and on the basis of their own superior judgment and reasoning. Job insecurity in the form of periodic elections was established to insure the "responsibility" of such delegates. In American constitutional organization, the representative institutions formed a cornerstone of a carefully balanced system constructed to avoid both the hasty judgment of the mob and the impulsive coercion of the tyrant by a judicious "balance of powers." The American version of the Age of Reason hoped institutionally so to divide the emotional components of associational life— the struggle for power—as to assure the ascendance of wisdom.

History, however, soon gave the lie to neat expectations in behalf of the representative system. The discretion of legislative delegates has perhaps never in fact been unfettered. The death a-borning of the Electoral College's originally intended discretion is an outstanding case in point. Legislators have very seldom been free to pursue higher wisdom in matters of state, unencumbered by strings of local loyalty and chains of indebtedness to particular demands or popular whims. Holding a limited, perhaps an ignorant, view of responsibility, the electorate has time and again reduced its delegates to the humble and bitter role of merely reflecting constituents' interests. Too concerned with deliberation, too disdainful of the body, the Age of Reason had failed to encompass in its theory of representative government a theory of leadership—at the most crucial place—between delegate and constituency.

Perhaps leadership theory was not just omitted, but could not have been provided at the time. There was, in the period of the American

Revolution, a reaction against English authority and the leadership it entailed. Indeed, we get the feeling from *The Federalist* that leadership was synonymous with intrigue. Would not a general characteristic of revolt against administrative autocracy have been to fail to distinguish continued need for leadership? For failure of theory and its institutionalization to provide a place for leadership within representative government, the representative was constrained to followership as he, in fact, reflected the interest of his constituents and listened to the marketplace reverberations of free speech. (It would seem that the original assumption expected that the truth would rise out of the deliberations of the men of superior quality elected to office, and that this truth, having in turn gained its due recognition, would lead forth in a triumphant march through the marketplace of ideas.) The legislative caucus in the United States and the political parties eventually tried to fill the gap. But that is another story—an illustration of practical adjustment to a break in theory, subsequently reflected in revised theory.

THE REFINEMENT OF REFLECTION: STILL NO LEADER

John Locke fashioned the basic theoretical material out of which the first major refinement of representative government theory was later wrought—the refinement that converted representation into reflection, keeping theory honest by bringing it to terms with practice. While perpetuating the Cartesian dualism in gross terms, his theory of perception provided a novel linking between matter and mind, challenging Descartes' belief in "innate" ideas, and so channelling the theory of knowledge that it is today the only recently questioned view of common sense. Locke is frequently said to have developed a democratic theory of knowledge in contrast to the aristocratic theory of innate ideas.

Under the influence of Newtonian science, Locke postulated two worlds, one an external world of things—atoms and action—and the other an intimate world of thoughts; and he then linked the two by means of a representative theory of perception. He proceeded to invert the Stoic, Scholastic, Cartesian custom of deduction from self-evident laws or thoughts, by teaching that knowledge derived from experience. While maintaining that men were intimately acquainted only with their own ideas, he proceeded to insist that these ideas were mere reflections of the material world (including the operation of minds). Through a chain of causal sequence, conforming strictly to laws of Newtonian physics, external objects and events were said to become represented in the immediate presence of man's thoughts.

Conversely, thoughts were, supposedly, only "representative" of the stimuli impinging on the senses. Thus knowledge became an indirect or filtered product of "experience." [5]

It is significant that Locke's primary qualities (extension, shape, solidity, mobility) all relate to the sense of touch (and kinesthesia), to Newton's pushy Nature. The other four senses (including sight—the source, according to Russell, of the fundamental notions of relativity science) furnish only secondary qualities—color, sound, flavor, odor.[6] If anyone wants a cue to the real meaning of our inherited (but very current) "power" concept, he should look into this Lockean distinction between primary and secondary qualities.

There is no necessary antipathy between a belief in innate ideas and the concept of majority rule. Innate ideas are not inevitably aristocratic in tendency. In contrast, the empiricist's theory of knowledge, based on a representative theory of perception, almost of its own momentum extends on into a statement of majority rule. It clears the way for an impartial, impersonal appeal to the mediation of factual or "outside" information. It finally dissolves, *in theory,* whatever remains of the interpersonal organic bonds posited in the organic thought that went before, leaving, in place of personal ties, a multitude of discrete receiving sets. It opens the gates of the marketplace of ideas to all perceivers, not just to believers. And, so long as the distinctively human, the mental and moral, is held aloof from an experimental scientific method, it leaves the test of truth, the determination of the correctness, the accuracy of a perception to a statistical calculation.

Thus, after the period of constitution-making, as constitutional government was being democratized,[7] the first refinement of the theory of representative government was devised. Pressure from the electorate to make representatives reflect constituency opinion was appended to the theory. This refinement of the representative theory still has tremendous popular appeal; we even hear of legislators briskly taking straw polls and counting letters and telegrams—shifting their responsibility into the gears of their computing machines.

As reconstituted to meet the demands of majority rule, however, representative government still presents no adequate theory of leadership. It serves no better than before to link legislator and constituent in an effective, working, leader-led relationship. As between matter and mind in Locke's theory of representative perception, so it is between elector and legislator in the democratic theory of representative government: provision is made for only one-way interaction. Majority decision at the polls determines the accuracy with which a delegate represents his constituents—through perceiving their opin-

ions—but there is no corresponding formal institutional device, either in practice or in theory, by which his wisdom can modify their opinions; though it cannot be denied that this sometimes does occur—for example, by means of the representative's practice of having a local office and appointment hours.

The function of the representative in the legislative halls is reduced from deliberation to calculation. His job becomes one of utilitarian computation, a process through which opinion is *ascertained*. Its fatal defect is that it does not involve him in a process by which opinion is *created*. The basic assumption, in the spirit of John Locke, is that discrete individuals are capable of determining what is to their own best interest, entirely apart from any social process of deliberation. (Unless, of course, the eclectic free market of laissez-faire speech is considered a social process of deliberation.) How computation can resolve conflicts is a mystery; its best bet is to freeze them, to hold them at bay, in the hope that they will be, not resolved, but rendered pointless and impertinent by the attrition of time. The legislature becomes the unseen hand in a leaderless laissez-faire "market" of ideas.

The process of reasoning, deliberating, considering, is not a process of computation (especially not of quantities). It is preeminently one of creation. If governmental organization is to be patterned after the thinking process, as representative democracy has assumed, it will have to be radically reorganized to reflect what is now known and is being learned about knowledge and human nature.

COMPROMISE, THE PRODUCT

In place of creation ("invention," if you prefer) representative government emphasizes compromise. Conflicts that come up for legislative resolution are seldom, if ever, treated in a purely deliberative fashion. To the extent that majority rule and tendencies to reflect constituency or group wishes have displaced *representation*, compromise has more and more displaced rationalistic "deliberation" as the legislative group process. It is now frequently praised as the traditional and habitual mode of the legislative way of life. The exaggerated dogma of limited government that attended the organization of American legislative institutions has tended to stabilize compromise as the primary legislative way of handling conflicts. The revolt against authority *per se*—in also revolting against leadership—in effect arranged to avoid the need for coming to political decision, by insisting that there should be as little government as possible. How else than by compromise (coercion aside) can a nation handle conflicts that have been

permitted to rise—unattended as the lines of division harden along the way—up to the level of policy decision, before a serious attempt at resolution is made? And how much more surely is the compromise pattern fixed when government is limited to attending to only the most general aspects of interrelating men—especially when the citizens are regarded as self-contained, free-wheeling independents. "In those days there was no king in Israel, and everyone did exactly as he pleased".

Compromise does not resolve conflicts. It only "handles" them. The Three-Fifths Compromise and the Missouri Compromise of American history are classic illustrations. Compromise is a decided improvement over domination and sacrifice as a way of handling disagreement, but it does not, as a rule, get down to treating and transforming the rudimentary germs of discord. Compromise temporarily resolves discord by taking a part of this viewpoint and a part of that, and asking for the suppression of the rest of each. Since nothing is done to accommodate, reconcile, or transform the fundamental factors behind disagreement, the success of compromise tends to be temporary—unless matters are tempered by time—and a new form of the old controversy bounces back at a later date.

As limited government becomes a thing of the past and more and more functions and duties are piled on administrative backs, compromise becomes less and less justifiable. The indefinite extension of the compromise pattern and mentality into the comprehensive workings of the welfare state would be fatal. But the workings, the modes, of the bureaucracy in the administrative state have developed within—and grown out of—the dominant context of legislative democracy and have accordingly, to a very serious extent, already come to share its pattern and philosophy. Since administrative processes become daily more all-encompassing, it is the undue extension into the pervasive administrative state of outmoded ways of thought and their attendant ways of doing that must be guarded against. As will be explained in later chapters, there are alternatives to compromise that respect new understandings of human nature and probe deeper than rational compromise, in order to work out creative and lasting resolutions to conflicts. Such alternatives will be shown to be particularly appropriate, if not endemic, to administration.

MURKY CONCEPTS: POWER AND PUBLIC OPINION

Political theory has also been unfortunately limited by two of the concepts upon which it has heavily relied for analysis of political phenomena: "public opinion" and "power." These are vague con-

cepts at best, though with much currency. Any theory that sets "public opinion" as the final governor of any state is hopelessly confusing because of the purely imaginary character of its central concept. The "power" that theory would "balance," while less ephemeral than "public opinion," is likewise inadequate to the realities of today. They both derive their existence from an antique way of thought. They are translations into social terms of the push-pull of the Newtonian physical universe.

Taking its cue from the lop-sided reliance of Newtonian science on interpretation in terms of the tactual (and kinesthetic) senses, social theory has conceived of "power" in oversimple terms of force. The balancing of power in social engineering follows the same fashion as the equilibrating of forces in designing bridges. Social engineering thinks in the same terms; stress, vectors, parallelograms of force. In gross terms of theory, the political party assumes a key role in balancing the pushes of social forces and pressure groups, just as the structural engineer accommodates into a stable whole the gravitational pushes of the material components of a bridge. In actual fact, any social balancing that occurs relies on the calculations of an imaginary slide rule, on the largely ineffable social judgment of men of affairs. And so it must be until there is a viable theory and concept of social power. Simple, straightforward Newtonian billiard table theory is no more likely to be negotiable among the complexities and sensitivities of social life than among the space-time geodesics of the universe.[8]

The practicing politician is accustomed to treat public opinion as a moral imperative, with some justification, since votes are tenuously involved at some remove. The failings of the concept, when used in this limited way, are only those of its association with the idea of discrete individualism: it ends in a utilitarian calculus of dissociated opinions, uncoordinated in the process of formation and correspondingly unamenable to coordination at the pollster's end of the line. However, when viewed as the controller of democratic destiny, as the ultimate maker of broad policy tendencies, that is, as a causal determinant, it gathers a bright sheen of unreality. Not only is it thingified, but it is also transformed into a force acting at a distance. It becomes a social gravity correlative to the gravitational force that Newton assumed to be acting between stars and their planets. Half a century ago John Dewey appropriately wrote:

> The principle of magic is found whenever it is hoped to get results without intelligent control of means; and also when it is supposed that means can exist and yet remain inert and inoperative. In morals and politics such expectations still prevail, and in so far the most important phases of human action are still affected by magic. We think that by feeling strongly enough

about something, by wishing hard enough [by having an opinion held in common with enough other people, I add,] we can get a desirable result, such as virtuous execution of a good resolve, or peace among nations, or good will in industry. We slur over the necessity of the cooperative action of objective conditions, and the fact that this cooperation is assured only by persistent and close study.[9]

The idea of public opinion as sovereign, governor, controller, is partly, too, an echo of Milton's market-place theory of truth. Milton asserted, it will be remembered, that, given freedom of speech, the truth would in the long run triumph in an open market of public scrutiny. Public opinion pops up as this same sort of buoyant, self-raising, self-contained elemental force.

Perhaps the love of power should be reinterpreted in terms of geodesics. Perhaps stray "opinions" should be brought to terms with what is known, since Einstein's special relativity theory, of instantaneity. In any case, the condition of current political theory is deficient to the considerable extent that it relies on such loosely, vaguely, or archaically formulated basic concepts.

EMOTIONAL THEORY

Comparatively recently a new epicycle has been superimposed on the simple orbit of discrete individualism by the psychoanalytical acceptance of the emotional. The practicing politician has long recognized the importance of emotions to his trade, the value of a handshake, the votes in a smile, the strength of a fear, the persuasiveness of a public relations manager. And the *evil* due to emotion or mob or faction in politics has been long deplored—and loudly. But theory has just now begun fully and systematically to recognize and specify the non-rational, the emotional dimensions of all participation in politics.

Almost a complete about-face from the direction taken by the early theory about representative government is entailed, for example, in the intriguing psychoanalytical approach of D. W. Winnicott.[10] According to this view, democracy is not a matter of reason, but of morality, of character, of the wholeness of men. Winnicott defines democracy as "society well-adjusted to its *healthy* individual members." If a man is mature, or "healthy"—as psychiatry indefinitely defines this term— he can, without personal distortion, internalize the cultural, political cleavages of society and arrive at solutions to social divisions through internal struggle. Such solutions can then be expressed in his vote. Thus Winnicott maintains that democratic machinery exists "for the illogical election and removal of leaders," and that "the essence of democratic machinery is the free vote (secret ballot)," which "ensures the freedom of the people to express deep feelings, *apart from conscious thoughts*. . . . The vote expresses the outcome of the struggle within [the voter], the external scene having been internalized and so brought into association with the interplay of forces in his own personal inner world." This view, to illustrate its remoteness from rank rationalism, characterizes proportional representation as anti-democratic "even when secret, because it interferes with free expression of *feelings,* and is only suitable for specialized conditions in which clever and educated people wish for a test of conscious opinions." [11]

Winnicott nicely rounds out his representative theory by insisting that legislators must be chosen as individual persons, according to what we usually speak of as character. "As a whole (healthy) person the legislator has the total conflict within, which enables him to get a view, albeit a personal one, of total external situations. He may of course belong to a party and be known to have a certain tendency. Nevertheless he can adapt in a delicate way to changing conditions." [12] Winnicott feels that in contrast "the election of a party or a group tendency is relatively less mature. It does not require of the electors a trust of a human being. For immature persons, nevertheless, it is the only logical procedure, precisely because an immature person cannot conceive of, or believe in, a truly mature individual. The result of the vote for a party or tendency, a thing and not a person, is the establishment of a rigid outlook, ill-adapted for delicate reactions." [13]

Here then is a theory, for whatever one might think of it on other counts, that would set Locke on his head and relegate political parties to an ornery stage in the infant growth of democracy. It illustrates to perfection the fact that political theories have had very little to do with representative institutions since the time of their inception, except in retrospect. They have, for the most part, been after-the-fact "explanations"—patchworks devised to make rational sense of developments in the world of practical affairs. As such, they betray the true function of theory.

THE PROPER JOB OF THEORY

The true function of theory is not *mere* explanation. Theory must explain, of course. It must comprehend, without contradiction, as many relevant facts as possible. But it can be more than a well-organized understanding. It can be a perfectible guide, and it can be a fountainhead of fruitful, testable hypotheses.

The political theories that have formed the environment for thinking about administration are now inadequate in very crucial respects.

They have been founded almost without exception on what are now known to have been quite erroneous accounts of human nature. They have been molded of poorly chosen concepts that by their one-sidedness (power) or imprecision (public opinion) evade the ardors of operational definition. They have been after-the-fact rational accountings for stray happenings, unguided by theoretical discipline.

Instead of continuing in the ways of Ptolemy—adding orbits on orbits, qualifications on qualifications—the productive way to proceed is to break out a fresh effort, deriving theory from more adequate understanding of human nature and letting it run on ahead, leading the way in the true tentative fashion of theory and hypothesis. Given the circumstances of chaos, patchwork, or vagueness in political democratic theory, and given the current primacy of administration (stressed in Chapter 1), the conviction grows that the usual procedure of deriving administrative theory as corollary, if not afterthought, of legislative theory must be abandoned in favor of an inversion. First, a theory of public administration should be developed in accordance with the most reliable information available about human nature; then what is left over that can be called political theory should be allowed to fit where it will in the remaining nooks, gaps, or crevasses, as the case may be, that remain.

But first it must be seen that administrative ways, while hampered by the heritage of theories about representative government, nevertheless show promise of a new lease on life and a new lease on politics.

ADMINISTRATION'S ANTIQUE HERITAGE

Transported intact from political thinking about the representative system of government, the same discrete individual populates and dominates the usual ways of thinking about the administrative scene. Again he is, Locke-like, the great judge of his own socially unprocessed self-interest and is rationally impelled to act in accord therewith. Again he is joined to his fellow only at the "upper" or rational level; his person, his character, is studiously slighted. Organic relating of person to person is avoided among a welter of rational "principles" and schemes for "chain of command," "span of control," or "rationalization of procedure"—the usual run of which is devoted to and extracted, Smith-like, from over-simple conviction that the proper social patterns can derive from the rational organizing of labor after the economies of production. (Always there are exceptions. Important recent thinking about administration, and discerning descriptions of the inner workings of administrative groups have reached beyond the antique ideas that have hedged traditional thinking about representative democracy.) Again there is no regular or effective provision for leadership. Within the organization, disembodied directive takes its place; and between citizen and administrator (the President excepted) stands the jealous legislator, the great Policy maker.

Implicit in the one-time-imagined clear-cut break between policy and performance and in the exclusion of character from organization or from contribution to administration, was the reduction of the individual worker to the status of mere means. Here, again, is the Cartesian dualism: where the hierarchy is rationalized the doer (even, curiously enough, if his job is thinking) becomes a tool. American civil service systems demonstrate this bias by overemphasis, in recruitment, on subject-matter or skill proficiencies and by obtuseness in providing and protecting individual security by tenure provisions at the cost of group functioning. Does any civil service code adequately protect a municipal street department crew from disruption by an "individualist" who "does his job" but refuses to become a compatible group member, thus innocently but effectively disrupting the morale and undermining the efficiency of the crew? Even the "scientific" management philosophy, in some of its exaggerated forms, while never in practice carrying public administration to the ruthless extremes found in private industry, was cynically tempted to value the individual as a complete human rather than an inanimate thing, an impersonal "hired hand," for the wrong reason: the success of such recognition in improving the production rate.

Public administration also accepted as basic theoretical tools the limiting concepts of "public opinion" and "power" from representative government theory. The tapping of public opinion is now a highly respected activity of administrative agencies, in some cases very gravely undertaken, in others very uncritically. Acceptance of power is equally uncritical. The executive, of course, participated in the constitutional division of power between the three branches of government. But, in addition, administration has variously participated in the pressure group power struggle (e.g., Corps of Engineers) and helped in the engineering of compromises by balancing power. Indeed there is increasing indication that Congress and the Parties, finding it inconvenient or distasteful to force particular compromises or to establish particular balances, are turning the function of settling group conflicts over to the administrator in the form of skeleton legislation or vague and/or self-contradictory laws to be "interpreted" in enforcement.[14] The contagion of the compromise mentality becomes a mounting peril. If administration is infected as seriously as are representative institutions, society can expect eventual accumulated violence from the temporarily dormant dammed up germs of discord, tranquilized by temporizing compromise "solutions" to real problems.

Administration's subscription, Milton-like, to the market theory of truth is pointed up by discovery that communication, far from automatically or ultimately transmitting truth, is blocked for the reason that no one listens to the fine products of "free speech" in administration or its interminable communiques.

PROMISE IN ADMINISTRATION

Theory seems more likely to depart from the tradition of after-the-fact description at the point of contact with administrative than with representative institutions. Hampered as it has been by allegiance to outmoded concepts, criteria and philosophies, the practice of public administration and some of its unsystematized thinking nevertheless show promise of being able to lead the way toward new patterns of theory. Where representative government theory has formally recognized the emotions and the totality of character only in the belated shadowy admission of an inscrutable, ineffable vote, public administration has been eagerly stimulating and trying to assimilate the revolutionary implications of the findings of the social sciences. There is much experimenting and much new thinking taking place within the realms of administration. And there is the wide possibility that, should this thinking and experimental testing be seen to be fruitful, theory may regain its proper role of guidance.

Instead of simply asking, as has been our wont in the antique fashion of division of powers: "What effect will the increasing implementation of the power of the chief executive have upon the status and power of representative assemblies?" [15] instead of looking for a reconciliation between "administrative power and democratic government," [16] we must inquire into the fundamental realities behind this fiction of pushy power and this conviction that representative assemblies are the embodiment of democracy. We must ask how governmental activities, apart from how they happen to be historically allocated among agencies, can be handled democratically for our day.

Thus, at the outset it seems certain that the solution will not be found in integrated hierarchical administrative organization under the President's command and, through him, fully accountable to Congress (as proposed by the President's Committee on Administrative Management and the Hoover Commission). Neither will the solution be found in legislative guarantee of administrative responsibility and accountability through control over objectives, methods, and structure of administration (as suggested by Hyneman in *Bureaucracy in a Democracy*,[17] and by such others as Dahl, Macmahon, and Finer).[18] Even the idea that administrative agencies can themselves become representative and therefore responsible cannot be expected to carry very far. Such responsibility might be arranged (1) through administrative integration with the power and purpose structure of the state, relying on prior development of a responsible two party system; (2) through improving and clarifying representation within the administrative hierarchy itself by means of advisory committees, citizen, and interest group participation in administration and the like; or (3) through a total interdependent process of government as described by Paul H. Appleby.[19] However, these devices do not penetrate to the root difficulties behind the formulated problems; they rather tend to hide them under a patchwork of outmoded representative government theory.

The electoral system is preeminently not a process through which to develop public wants, values. It records what people *say* they want, but it shies clear of the creative process of integrating (recreating) ideas, feelings, experiences, and conflicts into publicly significant or coherent form. *It neglects the process by which opinion is created.* The lack of provision for leadership in the theory of representative government seems to point up this deficiency. There is a great gap between the life, the person, of the voter and the macrocosm. This gap has become particularly apparent in technological society as excessive specialization has segmented the business of associated living to the point where only the rare individual can see more than a few of the trees in the forest or is able to relate what he does see (and do) to the wild dithyrambic life beyond.

Possibly no more should be expected from the electoral system than it currently affords. What should be sought is a democratic device to take the place in administrative government that the vote takes in legislative government—but a creative device. Very likely a large part of the felt inadequacy of modern democracy lies in the absence of intermediate, multipurpose institutions of encompassing character between the citizen (or the particular or specialized interest group) and the government. An attempt to fill the need for such an intermediate structure—for which the Swedish Ombudsman is a preliminary effort—can be made within the administrative branch of government. This may be where leadership of a genuine give-and-take variety is today institutionally most possible, and where a process for the *creation* of public purposes, wishes, wants can be most effectively inaugurated.

CONCURRENCE—GOVERNMENT BY AGREEMENT

Calhoun's theory of the concurrent majority, stripped to the bone, to the simple statement of sectional veto, has proved to be a remarkably accurate general description of the operation of American national institutions. American government has turned out—even without the constitutional reform (including dual presidency) advocated by Calhoun—to be extremely sensitive to constituent groups and interests, requiring their concurrent consent (the constituting of a concurrent majority) in legislation affecting their interests. Applied through the mediating services of administrative organization and reoriented within a deeper understanding of human nature, the kernel of the idea of concurrent majority may provide an effective element of a useful guiding theory.

A hint for improved theoretical formulation is to be found slightly below the surface of a not uncommon mode of operation of conservative, democratic local government in America. Picture a city council composed of men of no particular competence, indeed rather clearly unprepared for the job of directing a multi-million dollar enterprise— at least in comparison with their counterparts heading business or industrial establishments of equivalent size, complexity, budget, and capital investment. It is possible that such a council—though funded with ignorance, whimsy, partisanship, and a dominating drive for re-election—may nevertheless be adequate to the role of lawmaker when in partnership with a professionally competent administrative staff.

It is no longer surprising when an alderman votes against a proposal which he admittedly approves but which is loudly opposed by a handful of misinformed constituents; for example, when he votes against funds for preparation of a land use plan because some of his constituents imagine it to be a slum clearance program. "Sure, a land use plan is OK with me," he explains, "but *they* don't understand what it is. What else could I do?" Or, "I know it would be good for the city, but they think it's slum clearance. So I had to vote against it." Such a happening is clearly not *representative* government at work. Nor is it even the "representative" government that attempts to mirror the opinion of the majority. It may appear to be (and in some instances may actually be) a miscarriage or malfunctioning of legislative government. But at the same time it may be only a perverse detail from the working veto of concurrent majorities in local government. At the peril of stagnation, at the cost of unnecessarily prolonged misery, city councils of a particular conservative stripe will refuse to take action on a given matter because a group they fancy in some fashion significant registers displeasure.

The same city council that enacts a push-power struggle with a view to eventual compromise when allocating street lights and paving jobs among its various wards or when distributing annual appropriations between fire, health, and sewer departments, reacts in an entirely different way when the matter at hand is new and so complex as to be beyond the competence of the aldermen—given the very limited time they have to allocate to the serious business of understanding what they are doing.[20] This is not to imply that a budget is a simple thing or at all understood by its makers. Perhaps it once was. At any rate, it is the new legislation, as contrasted with the traditional functions, that tends to be treated in a fashion potentially outside of the traditional push-pull compromise pattern. A city council hesitates to establish policy. Its members, while believing they should be representative, know full well—perhaps inarticulately—that they are not and cannot be, no matter how conscientiously they try. They are therefore reluctant to act on general matters in areas without precedent.

Amid rampant public apathy, a conservative[21] aldermanic tack avoids avoidable stir. A ward alderman particularly tends, as a rule, to concern himself chiefly with superficial appearances, with appeasing purely local (contrasted with municipal) demands, with satisfying constituents' personal wants. He is accustomed to treating with and honoring individual complaints, individual appeals for help, and is correspondingly hyper-sensitive to the drag of minority disapproval. It is especially interesting to watch a new mayor, who has served an apprenticeship as alderman, begin to notice that there are such wide horizons as community or general welfare.

The vote, the electoral system, the political party, and the city council, even in our more successful experiments, fall far short of reflecting what the people want—simply because "what the people want" cannot be reflected. It is not something simply built up of independently self-discovered (Lockean) self-interests. It is not something preexistent, to be sought, to be identified, but rather something nonexistent, to be wrought, to be created. Therefore, when a city council throws up its hands in fear and confusion upon a show of opposition to a much needed complete revision of an obsolete building code, it says, in effect, "Take it back boys and see that you agree with each other before bringing it in again. Show a little leadership!" It is not necessarily belying its function of advancing the general welfare; it may be only insisting that the people's "want," which it cannot reflect, be created—under leadership it cannot itself provide.

This built-in aldermanic sensitivity to minority disapproval can throw the administrator into the delicate though spotlighted position of coordinator of popular "want," preliminary legislator of general weal.[22] With the city council concerned more about agreement behind "their" legislation than about its substance, the function of resolving conflicts and integrating values and purposes falls to the public executive—when it isn't left to the collusion of private groups (the electricians, the plumbers, the carpenters, the masons, the real estate board, the architects' association). The quality of his success becomes the mark of the democracy involved.

SUMMARY

This chapter has run through great spans of time and has skimmed great ranges of thought. It has claimed to find inadequacy and chaos in much of the basic thinking that bolsters the institutions of representative democracy—the basic thinking that was thought to provide adequate working tools with which to make a way out of social problems. The familiar terms that have been briefly commented on—free speech, self-interest, power, public opinion, compromise, the function of theory, the vote, leadership—will turn up in their proper turns in later chapters where efforts will be made to find substitutes, alternatives, or improvements.

But the chief fault of traditional democratic thinking has been said to be its preoccupation with explanation, its after-the-factness, its failure to play bird-dog, to point, to guide in the fashion of hypothesis. Could it be that there is an interrelatedness between the failure of thought to assume leadership over practice and the failure of representative democracy to encourage an effective leadership relation between government and citizen?

It is further observed that, though presently still boxed in by the preconceptions and limiting theories of representative democracy, administration nevertheless shows promise of providing the lead for future democratic government. If theory is to look ahead, to become properly hypothetical, a new start is recommended with its focus on administration instead of on representation. If administration is to accept the leadership being forced upon it by events, it correspondingly needs a theory with the guiding quality of leadership. Let us begin by grounding it in scientific findings about human nature!

Part I

THE MAKING OF TRUTH

CHAPTER THREE

Foundations of Utopia

> *Where politics, morals or philosophy*
> *are concerned, I view with suspicion*
> *the judgment of those who know*
> *nothing about their own composition.*

> JEAN ROSTAND

UTOPIA BY TRADITION IS FOUNDED IN REALITY. IT IS BASED upon and extrapolated from human nature as in fact upon occasion observed. This, at least, is the legacy from Sir Thomas More, whose ideal is said to have built upon first-hand accounts of visitors to Inca Peru.[1] The aim of the present work is to follow a similar course, starting with the realities of human nature, not, however, as discovered in some remote corner of the globe, but as uncovered by contemporary findings of experimental science.

In a way this is what Locke tried to do too when he patterned representative democracy after the representative theory of perception. However, the science behind him avoided human reality, resting on a philosophy that in fact defied human nature by artificially disrelating the mental and moral from the rest of human nature, and exempting the distinctively human from investigation by experimental science. Locke's instinct was good: government, in a very general sense, must be structured after the patterns of perception. But as it was, strange disjunctions between the realms of practice and theory arose from stubborn adherence to unreal theoretical formulations.

Democracy, however, developed by a sort of trial and error process in disregard—almost disdain—of the attempts at systematic theory that ranged around it. When fine theories leave fundamental factors out of their reckoning or deny the existence of compelling relationships, it is only to be expected that what men do will sometimes do violence to what they say. The degree of social control sired by a successful theory does not depend only upon its habitual acceptance or on the intensity of belief it inspires. It depends crucially on its relation to the truth, to the reality of the situation in which it finds itself.

When they are at their best and rise above the level of vain imaginings, ideas (theories) are only tools—structured instrumental processes for facilitating the business of living. Promoting life, they must work among the live and hard, personal and strange components of emerging situations, by interrelating and integrating them, and, as we say, making them meaningful. Therefore, to function successfully they must be served with sensitive perception of the concrete components they face, and their interrelations and interdependencies—not forgetting their dependence on thought.

It can be said that the practice of democracy has shown more sense, more realism than has the theory of republican institutions. Note as examples the penchant for voting for person before issue and the long-standing practice of setting policy by administrative decision or through administrative participation in decision. Both of these clearly contradict the tenets of recently dominant faiths. They also demonstrate the need for repair of prevalent political theory.

There have been similar practical breaches of faith with the representative theory of perception and the half-and-half theory of human nature. For instance, in contravention of the representative theory of perception, illusions (for example, momentarily mistaking a stray lady on the street as an acquaintance, or dodging an angry bee that on closer inspection becomes a frightened fly) are quite commonly attributed to a personal contribution to the content of perception, not to what's "out there." They are generally explained away as "mere" illusions not "really" perceived. Likewise, the half-and-half theory is quite commonly belied by the practice of extracting moral imperatives from scientific findings and by deriving rational profundities from ineffable feelings. Each of these violates a still-cherished belief, demonstrating the need for repair of perceptual theory.

Fortunately for the future development of administrative institutions, the futility of theoretical pipe dreaming as a technique of practical, democratic organization is finally becoming apparent—at the very time when work in the social disciplines has provided sufficient background in thought and technique to begin to flower into effective scientific achievement. At last it is possible to shake free from the age-old practice of deriving theory of perception from prior beliefs about human nature supported with gross (over-general, imprecise, unquestioned, untested) observations about the perceiving situation. Now there exists a usable background—a veritable abundance—of revealing information, derived from sensitive scientific experimentation; though much of it also can be extracted from ordinary everyday experience that is commonly overlooked, if not denied. At long last the table can be turned and a new start can be made toward constructing a viable and perfectible theory of human nature from tested evidence produced by scientific inquiry. A part of the end product should be a package of *guiding* thoughts for government, in particular for public administration.

PAUSE FOR TRANSACTION

The experimental approaches to perception that have been recently so productive did not spring unheralded and unanticipated from the aseptic depths of a "scientific laboratory," untarnished and untouched by prior thought. There were ideas, attitudes, and a whole spectrum of philosophies in the air. As has been the case with every scientific start or advance, psychological experimentation has been conditioned by its immediate environment of thought. Antecedents included basic research in optics, in addition to a rich heritage of general psychological investigation, but productive experiment has flourished under a host of differing philosophies.

It is of particular interest here that some of the important segments of experiment in the psychology of perception have drawn strength from the viewpoint of instrumentalism, the work of John Dewey in the logic of scientific inquiry,[2] and the collaborative efforts of Dewey and Arthur F. Bentley in establishing the transactional approach to social problems.[3] Indeed, there is a group of psychologists now referred to as "transactionalist."[4] In a sense, these experimental developments in the theory of perception rely upon these particular philosophical formulations, though it may be more accurate only to say that they relate to these formulations. What is most important, however, is that the psychology of perception has risen, in these and other critical experiments, above the level of deduction or speculation, and has attained the perfectible stature of scientific hypothesis. While the psychology of perception is broken into a number of schools of thought, with varying interpretations of the experimental findings, critically revealing experiments are appearing from many diverse corners of ongoing inquiry.

It is important to take a careful look at transaction, at this point, not only because this concept has nourished some of the great experimental advances in perception, but also because it philosophically grounds the further argument of this book. The present work will attempt to adopt the transaction viewpoint with some consistency.

"Transaction" stems from Dewey and Bentley's attempt to stand-
ardize terminology in "an effort to extend observation under pos-
tulation." [5] Here are their definitions:

> *Self-action:* where things are viewed as acting under their own powers.
> *Inter-action:* where thing is balanced against thing in causal interconnection.
> *Trans-action:* where systems of description and naming are employed to deal
> with aspects and phases of action, without final attribution to "elements" or
> other presumptively detachable or independent "entities," "essences," or
> "realities," and without isolation of presumptively detachable "relations"
> from such detachable "elements." [6]

To describe a situation as "transactive," then, is to say that neither
self-acting agents nor inter-acting forces (fitting the pool-table picture
of the world) are to be detected—anywhere. Man and environment
are not clearly and cleanly distinct or distinguishable from one another. Indeed, everyday language is daily suspect because it continues to
speak in terms of discrete essences, as if men could be meaningfully
considered apart from environment. The tyranny of inherited language, imposing patterns of interaction on ways of thought, is almost
unbeatable. Inquiry that would hope to penetrate very deeply into the
mystery of human affairs must therefore make special efforts to shake
loose from the old cobwebs of inter-connection and inter-action, and
search out the nexus of transactional statement to find the truths that
are operative behind the language barrier of push and pull, behind the
language of "loosely speaking" that suffices for practical purposes
where population is sparse and life is simple.

In transaction the focus of reference is the total situation, organism-
and-environment-as-a-whole. Order and focus are found, not in the
organism or in the environment, but in the transacting organism-
environment. The parties to a transaction are only aspects of the
"field," so to speak; they are not atomic actors but phases of a whole
in action. Hermann Broch speaks of "the obduracy of a circumstance
that is more complete than the human being, although he himself is
the one who builds the walls, who carves and hammers, who braids
the lash and forges the chains." [7] P. W. Bridgman says, "it is a simple
matter of observation that the observer is part of what he observes
and that the thinker is part of what he thinks. We do not passively
observe the universe from the outside, but we are all in it up to our
necks, and there is no escape." He believes "that the final solution
will have to carry further the consequences of the insight that quantum
theory has partially glimpsed, namely, that the observer must somehow
be included in the system." [8] Another way of approximating this
description is to say that the Self emerges from out of the situation,

from experience, rather than that experience is an attribute, adventure or expression of a pre-established self-organism, something tailored to fit upon or dress up a fully fashioned entity. I like the way Dewey put it many years ago: "Speech and honesty . . . are things done by the environment by means of organic structures or acquired dispositions." [9]

A fairly close analogy can be seen in any economic transaction. It is clearly senseless to consider either a seller or a buyer by himself without reference to the other or to the commodity or to the "market." Dewey and Bentley clarify the concept very nicely by reducing it to the simplest case: "Suppose a man engaged in but one transaction and that with but one other man, and this all his life long. Would he be viewed in distinction from that transaction or from that other man? Hardly." [10] But he wouldn't be a man in the first place. It takes as many transactions to make a man as swallows to make a summer.

Self with a capital S, already used immediately above, will continue through the pages of this book to specify the social Self that is the reality of transaction, the intimate Self extending on beyond a man's skin. The intention is to imply quite the opposite of unchangeable essence—not transcendence but scope—using the word in the sense that a pianist's Self includes "his" piano, or a mother's Self includes "her" child, or Frankie's Self includes "her" man, or a man's Self includes "his" reputation. For some purposes, it may even be said that the furthermost bound of the Self is a man's imagination.

For particular and small-scale occurrences, where the context is simple and the relevant factors few—as, say, a description of a tennis match—the old inter-action way of analysis suffices, as Newtonian physics suffices for problems of automechanics. But when social problems of far-reaching importance are encountered—even when an exhaustive psychological and sociological analysis of the tennis match is desired—it is necessary to go beyond the limitations set by thinking in terms of fictional forces, to a transaction analysis viewing man-and-culture-as-a-whole. Especially where life, and, most dramatically, human life, is involved, every action generates not simply an equal and opposite reaction, but a transaction.

SIGNAL PERCEPTION

"Perhaps," remarked Sir Arthur Eddington, "reality is a child which cannot survive without its nurse illusion." [11] He referred to the vast difference between the bare surface we experience in everyday life and the intricate molecular substructure projected in the theories of physics. Today, following the accumulation of experimental evidence in the psychology of perception, this statement can be reaffirmed in more general terms and with less of a "perhaps"—provided only that we do not assume, as did Eddington, an eternal verity that is only waiting to be discovered. Through perceiving man creates the changing reality in which he participates.

Reality is no longer a crystal clear, symmetrical manifestation to be captured in picture form. It has been ground into a muddy suspension, stirred round by the transactions of life. Revised characterization of reality will emphasize doing instead of being. It will, correspondingly, be perfectible, supporting the virtue of not pretending to solidify a final statement.[12]

Reality lies neither in the middle of my head nor "out there" beyond my skin. It lies between Berkeleyan solipsism and Lockean mechanistic materialism, and is found in a synthesis that resolves the dilemma in the usual way: by returning to, grappling with, and winning out over the root assumption common to both horns—the physical-moral, objective-subjective dichotomy. Though there are many situations in which description in terms of subjective-objective separation, in terms of what is seen corresponding to or representing what is "out there," admirably serves practical purposes (when there is no apparent evidence that the perceiver contributes anything to that which he perceives), it has become apparent that this way of speaking does not serve to describe other situations (where there is no correspondence and that which is perceived is contributed in part by the perceiver). Furthermore, it has been systematically interfering with the advance of scientific inquiry into perception phenomena. Any fixed correspondence between a perceived and an assumed ontological object is purely *ad hoc*.

One of the most arresting illustrations of the merging of the subjective and the objective is shown in the revolving trapezoid exhibit developed by Adelbert Ames, Jr. Bentley describes the demonstration as follows:

> A rectangular window of conventional appearance can be seen slowly revolving on its vertical axis. A trapezoidal window, comparable in size, and similarly revolving alongside, cannot be seen to revolve, and cannot even be plainly seen as a trapezoid. Persistent efforts by experimentors to see complete revolutions of the entire frame have failed. Even when a long rod touching the window is used as an aid by the observer, he makes little progress, and that little is lost by the following morning. Headaches and nausea may mark his disturbance. What the observer "sees" ... is an apparently rectangular window of changing length, oscillating at changing speeds to right and then to left in a total arc of about 100° (if degrees of arc can be injected at all in a case like this), and then returning to its starting point, just as the rectangular window completes its full observed revolution.[13]

Apparently habitual assumptions (if not some more primitive mechanism), in the form of vertical-horizontal, rectangular orientation, establish extensive control over what is seen. This trapezoid demonstration differs in effect from many, many other demonstrations only in being more simple, direct, and dramatic. It dispels, once and for all, the idea that there is a one-to-one correlation between an independently existing environmental object and one's dependable perception of "it."

Robert Livingston makes an equivalent observation after reviewing many recent neuropsychological studies. They have shown, he says in the old interactional way of speaking, "that the sensory data on which our perceptions necessarily depend are being contaminated during the earliest input stages by our past experiences, expectations and purposes."[14] As for purpose, isn't it the man who most desperately wants to get ashore that first sights land—or gives the most false alarms before land is reliably sighted? The familiar fact that light rays from an object strike the retina of the eye in the form of an inverted image, gives another illustration of control by habit, assumption, experience, expectation, purpose, or by something perhaps even more deep and dark. In spite of the inverted image we see things right side up. Moreover, if glasses are worn to invert the inverted image, the world (though it looks all wrong for a while) turns right side up again after a time of adjustment, despite the glasses—only to turn upside down again (for a while) when the glasses are removed. In a similar fashion, we learn to see in nature the landscapes that the great painters—Cezanne, Hobbema, Constable, Grant Wood—have taught us to see. Nature's landscape did not look the way it does until these men created it. Which is to say that the landscape is not nature's. Nor is it man's. It is a transaction between the two.

Walter Lippmann's classic statement must also be noticed in the present context. In a summary of wisdom from William James and John Dewey, he says,

> For the most part we do not first see, and then define, we define first and then see. In the great booming, buzzing confusion of the outer world we pick out what our culture has already defined for us, and we tend to perceive that which we have picked out in the form stereotyped for us by our culture.[15]

The staged murder, first performed in Germany and since run round the world, again points in this same direction. This "murder" is a psychology classroom demonstration in which a fake murder is enacted in full view, under the noses of an unsuspecting student audience. The "observers" are afterwards invariably found to have perceived widely divergent sequences—pursuant to widely different definitions, habitual assumptions, purposes. Richard L. Gregory, retaining the ancient inside-outside dualism in his description, summarizes in the language of data processing:

> Perception seems to be a matter of looking up information that has been stored about objects and how they behave in various situations. The retinal image does little more than select the relevant stored data. This selection is rather like looking up entries in an encyclopedia: behavior is determined by the contents of the entry rather than by the stimulus that provoked the search. We can think of perception as being essentially the selection of the most appropriate stored hypothesis according to current sensory data.[16]

Unfortunately, this statement is too clean and easy with its inside-outside dichotomy. It misses the additional fact that sense data, itself, is "contaminated" from the "inside."

Perceptual abilities develop only through arduous, painstaking practice. Once a discovery or a creation is made, or a problem is solved, the world never again looks the same. One's very eyes physically change in response to expectation and purpose.[17] A number of laboratories have recently reported that an animal's sensory reception can be modified by previous experiences, even by its expectations and purposes—as the vigilance of the antelope's ears atrophies in captivity. In one experiment, electrodes implanted in the brain of an animal trained to expect a ten-beep-per-second signal continued to record ten beeps per second, even after the signal was changed to six.[18] The sleeping mother of a newborn child can tune her ears to signal the faintest whimper of her baby, while cutting out the unimportant heavy noises that could disturb her sleep. Part of the mechanism behind this purposive concentrating of attention includes an altering of the actual sensitivity of the ear nerves by the brain.[19] The effect of expectation on sensory reception is so very fundamental that, as Livingston says, "modification of sensory signals occurs within the sense organs themselves and continues all along the ascending transmission pathways to cortex and wherever signals go beyond the cortex." [20] He draws the conclusion that "perception is thus contaminated from the outset and can only be made more objective by elaborate and time-consuming techniques that education, and particularly science, have developed for changing our world view." [21] But such a statement begins again to imply a transcendent "Reality" behind appearances. Science and education are indeed increasingly objectifying —but they need not necessarily be presumed to relate to a purified pre-existent Objective.[22]

The intimate involvement of purpose, thought, assumption in perception is easier to appreciate when thought is seen to be borne along on the main stream of unnoticed sensory reception. Constant contact-pressure of the environment appears to play a necessary part in thinking. It has now been observed that men may begin to develop hallucinations and delusions—unordinary shifts in perception and thought—when isolated from all sensory stimuli for a space of only a few hours (for example, submerged, soundless and lightless, in warm water with a snorkel tube for breathing).[23] The unnoticed sights, sounds, and touches normally in constant flow are apparently an important support to thought (the ability, for example, to add and to subtract) and memory. Perception, not as event reception, but as unperceived body-contact with the world, every nerve quietly groping for the reassurance of intimacy with the universe, such contact-perception, relating to the whole, is a signal for sanity. It indicates how much man is part of the world and how little he can separate out his own thinking. The high mortality rate of infants in foundling homes is attributed to lack of handling; that is, to sensory deprivation of a sort. Brainwashing of American prisoners during the Korean war employed sensory deprivation as a "conversion" device. And the penal practice of solitary confinement demonstrates that the effects of isolation were known long before scientific psychological experimentation began. Does this human need for basic transaction with the universe help explain why the idea that blindness is a part of evil has been such a recurrent theme in human history?

It becomes evident that perceiver and perceived cannot be ontologically separated, just as a walker cannot be divided by a picket fence from the walk he is taking. The old frame of reference tries to formulate it with these terms: "I can never know how much of what I perceive is what I am looking at out there and how much is my doing." Perceiver and perceived can be distinguished only instrumentally. Perceptions carry out transactions between thoughts and things.

The subject-object dichotomy is finally beginning to heal through recognition of the subjective factors in perception and the crucial perceptual factors in thought. Not only is there an interdependence between perception of where a thing is, perception of what it is and when it is perceived, but where, what and when interdepend on the habitual assumptions, the past experiences, the "values," the desires, the expectations, the loyalties, the purposes of the perceiver—in short, upon "character." "Fact" and "value" are inherently related, completely interdependent (trans-dependent). What is directly presented by the transaction of perception is the conjunction of a knower and a known. Indeed, it is partly because of the complexity of statement in interactional terms that some of the psychologists working with these new discoveries have turned to the simplicity of the transaction approach. "An investigator could study the interdependence of various aspects of a perception forever," it has been said, "and never get at the reason for such relationships until he asked himself what function such an interrelationship of phenomena served in the transaction of living." [24]

Instead of *being* a disclosure (or a representation) of reality, a perception (perhaps better called a perceiving) *functions as* a signal. A worm-seen is a signal to a fish for successful action, it hopes. To a fearful two-year-old child, a half-dead housefly may be a signal to scream and run; to his five-year-old brother, it may be a signal of harmless prey for sadistic pleasures. The test of a perceiving is, not its accuracy, not its "representativeness," but its success; that is, whether, functioning as a signal, it leads to satisfactory or more satisfying action or choice. This signal understanding of perception immediately helps clarify the human condition—for example, why it is that the same scene yields different appearances or impressions at different times. The perplexing change in a scene of fond memory on revisiting it in later years is accounted for by a switch in signals. The perception itself changes because it serves a signal function in a new situation altered by accumulation of experience and transformation of purposes. If the extraneous assumption of absolute distinction between out-there and in-here, between public and private, is rigorously expunged, the living reality can be seen to be a never-static process of creation through perception, a production of transaction.

THOUGHTS AND PERCEPTIONS

Though the absence of sensation can seriously alter thought, ideas are not immaculately conceived out of pure sensation. They are rather wrought out of live situations from the myriad participating environmental, habitual, assumptive, purposive, expectative, physical and conceptual aspects involved in the transactions of life. [25] Ideas, what is known, cannot be separated from the process of knowing. A cue should be taken from the Egyptians who thought with their hearts, they thought, and the Old Testament tribesmen who were instructed by their reins. It would be easier to understand thought as an accessible, malleable, influencible, transactional aspect of life if we did not try to keep it contained so cleanly in the skull. There's the old adage "Hard seats make spare thoughts" to point up the fact we've known all along that heart, reins, liver, spleen, bowels, blood, phlegm, choler, and melancholy tamper at times and in vast measure with thought. It is now quite firmly established that such purely physical events as hormone injection (not to speak of brain surgery) can cause changes in thought—even in character.

The testing and tempering of ideas, as of perceptions, is by satisfactory action or choice. This is clearly indicated by the Ames demonstration with the "distorted room." This room is carefully constructed with one wall twice as high and twice as long as the opposite wall. From a particular viewing point, however, it produces the appearance of a familiar rectangular room. It looks normal and the observer thinks it is normal until he begins to take action. As he becomes successful in moving the end of a pointer from place to place about the room or throwing a ball at a target in the room, he gradually sees and conceives it in its distorted form, correcting his thought and perception.[26] In the process of reorientation, thinking seemingly takes the lead out of illusion, helping, by successive approximations, to bring thought and perception to square with action.

Conceptual structures function instrumentally in creating the changing reality of which people are passing parts. Human thinking appears to have sprung out of the mindless gropings of evolution in efforts toward improved or more adequate realization of nameless aims or purposes. Ideas, thoughts, concepts are abstract instruments (tools) used among the writhing realities of live situations to secure control of change.

What is particularly strange is that men should have strayed so far from the reality of mutual dependence as to imagine themselves discrete. But this illustrates an important facet of the human condition: that in running on ahead to anticipate outcomes, to test effects of actions in advance of performance, the mind of man is able to elaborate whole systems of nonsense—particularly when it runs on into areas so far unguided by methods of test. Why have men seen themselves disassociated but for contract as in the seventeenth century contract theories of the state, when in fact they are involved in transaction, of which contract is only a phase? It is because the creativity in man can fashion griffins and unicorns, because abstractions can be played with, juxtaposed, and permutated for the fun, fear, and fancy that can be extracted in the process.

While ideas are instruments for dealing with reality and controlling change, it should be noted that the guiding capacity of an idea is limited. It varies in relation to the other aspects of the total situation in transaction. A man may "know," for instance, that his headaches or his ulcers are due to tension, but he has to reeducate his habits, attitudes and expectations through a careful process in order to do something about it. He may "know" that he is watching a three-dimensional screen, but still duck when a hammer appears to fly in his direction. He may "know" that the revolving shape he is watching is a trapezoid, yet never be able to achieve a simple, direct perception of it as such.

Actions are determined by perceptions, in first instance, not by knowledge. Unless successful action involving realization of purposes is brought in as reinforcement, however, habitual assumptions take precedence over mere information, and even accurate perception cannot be achieved. It has been reported, for example, that, after a day or two wearing the special image-inverting glasses mentioned above, subjects continued to see the world upside down, so long as they sat passively looking around. But they would see it "flip over" right side up when they reached out to touch the things they were looking at.[27] Perception and action should not be kept distinct as separate processes. Perceiving is a way of acting, a mode of transaction. It is man's orderly engagement with environment.[28] It is through doing (that is, through skills, through the integrating or artistic service of successful performance) that illusions are dispelled and perceptions are brought in line with a more adequate understanding of reality. A man's total organism may often be wiser than his awareness; he may often be more right through the way he lives than through the way he thinks.

The Eskimos, it is said, have many different words for ice and snow, to our mere handful. What to a man of the temperate zone is just plain ice can be to an Eskimo any of a number of different things. It's a matter of vision. He sees different "ices" as directly as we see different colors. He lives in a different reality, with another rainbow. This extra sensitivity comes through the necessities of arctic life. Successful action has undoubtedly, in many situations, been synonymous with survival, and the signal reliability of a perception a matter of life or death. Yet, strictly speaking, it cannot be said that acute perception was forced upon the Eskimo by his environment—as if man and environment were separable existences.

Herman Melville found that Polynesian islanders had developed at least twenty different terms for coconuts in different stages of growth—perfecting perception with little encouragement from demands for survival. "Many of them," he testified, "reject the fruit altogether, except at a particular period of its growth, which, incredible as it may appear, they seemed to me to be able to ascertain within an hour or two. Others are still more capricious in their tastes; and after gathering together a heap of the nuts of all ages, and ingeniously tapping them, will sip first from one and then from another, as fastidiously as some delicate wine-bibber, experimenting, glass in hand, among his dusty demijohns of different vintages." [29] Clearly there is here an elaboration of sensibility, a creative refinement of aesthetic enjoyment that goes beyond gross evolutionary explanations.

Perhaps if we were referring to the house mouse as a species, simple description in terms of survival of the fittest could suffice— though even that is questionable. No doubt, perception processes as well as ideational processes are extensions into the human race of the dim purposes in the evolutionary processes that saw the fish rise from his belly in the mud to walk on two fins and eventually to call himself man.[30]

Functioning instrumentally, as tools to improve the human condition, ideas help to organize and reorganize perception so as to perfect it in its creative signal role. But within the matrix of transaction, thought takes its place as only one of many aspects; it too grows out of transaction. If it is *the* leader out of chaos, its dependence on the other aspects is extreme. In first instance, for example, signal perception directs the course of action. It is the total reference of man-in-environment that calls the tune in the end, though the tune may be elaborated "beyond reason" in delicate refinement of purpose.

PURPOSE

The aspect that seems to arise to crucial prominence out of the human situation as transactionally viewed is purpose. Perception may be interpreted as direct, unreasoned estimation of the impact of foreseen consequences on purposes. Purpose performs a sort of traffic control function in determining the specific assumptions that will be elicited in a given situation. For example, the chips of stone in a gravel pit may function as identities or as similarities depending on the purpose that relates them, whether that of laying roads or that of collecting specimens. Gold functioned one way for Aztecs, another for Spaniards, relating to associated purposes. The delicate refinement of perception of Melville's Polynesians attended refinement of purpose, through a process of progressive specification, purpose and perception alternately affecting and occasioning refinement in each other. Hindu and Moslem, with divergent purposes (projected ends) see distinctly different things in a cow. No landscape of Van Gogh, Watteau, or Sesshu depicts what is "out there," except as filtered by purposes —however inarticulate. An effective action, a successful choice, always relates to a more or less identifiable purpose. To use Hadley Cantril's general terminology, "perception itself is part and parcel of purposive activity. It is an emergent co-product of purposive activity and can not really be understood except in that context. We may define a perception, then, as an implicit awareness of the probable consequences an action might have for us with respect to carrying out some purpose that might have value for us." [31]

Special sensitivity to the portents of hostile surroundings, as in the Eskimo's ice perception, can be described as an unthinking cultural adaptation to the "purpose" of survival. The identification of purpose can even be pushed back into the dark shadows and grand generalizations of underlying evolutionary purposes and tropisms—so dim is our understanding of purpose at all. Consider, for example, the fact that many of the vigilance mechanisms of an animal species atrophy after it has been domesticated for a while. Here are biological changes apparently responding to the reorientation of purpose or something very close to purpose. The captive situation of security from natural enemies permits release from instinctive alertness. The purpose of protection gone, a particular group of perceptions becomes meaningless, unreal. The signal (perception) unneeded, its specialized agency —the twitching antelope ears of anxiety—atrophies. In the end the new biology will say that life itself *is* purpose.[32]

It seems almost as if one sees only what he is prepared to see; as if purpose permits perception. If this strong a statement is to be made, however, the preparation for perception must be conceived in its broadest biological sense.[33] The fact remains that some sights obtrude themselves on the individual. Ability to perceive some things, simple forms for example, has been shown to be innate.[34] But this may be attributed to the fact that every man subsumes all evolution. Purpose at an earlier stage in the development of the species can have raised a perception readiness to the level of rote. The organs of perception have been bent by pressure of survival to perceive the world in ways that have been found useful.[35] This may be why the working of perception is felt to be beyond chance. At this end of the course of evolution, sights do indeed obtrude, preparation having been long since laid by primordial, prehuman purpose.

Purpose, however, is not immutable, and it cannot be *separated* out of transaction. In particular it should be noted that, while purposes are more stable than perceptions, new purposes can be communicated through perception. This is one of the important functions of the artist. (See chapter 13.) And where creativity is at hand, it may be that perception and purpose merge for the moment.

Purposes, "values," morals, character—the "subjective" aspects of situation—have been mistakenly held immune to experimentation, to be described, but, because of their "ultimate" status and their inaccessibility, not to be subjected to scientific inquiry. The purposes appearing as determinants in transaction are not fixed and unmalleable. They too, change, grow, re-form amid the myriad other dynamic factors involved. "The doctrine of fixed ends not only diverts attention from examination of consequences and the intelligent creation of purpose, but, since means and ends are two ways of regarding the same actuality, it also renders men careless in their inspection of existing conditions." [36] Purposes are most clearly related to other "subjective" items, such as habitual assumptions. However, it has been discovered that they can, and furthermore must, if progress is to be made in psychology, be handled as variables and be progressively specified in experimental operations.[37] As will be seen in chapter 6, scientific experimenting with purposes must constitute the core of moral science. It must also provide part of the basic patterning for administrative organization, constructing, out of the developing truths of human nature, the basic reality upon which, in turn, to lay the foundations of a progressive utopia.

END TO ILLUSION. INTEGRATION

In general, illusions are not affected by knowing about their duplicity. On the other hand, successful practice in situations characterized by illusion tends to remove the illusion. (This was illustrated above in the experiments with the image-inverting goggles and the distorted room.) That is to say, successful practice tends to set up perceptions that can be directly successful in realizing the purposes involved—successful practice being, in respect to current sights, the daily counterpart to survival of the species, in respect to yesteryear's sights now readied in innate ability. Immediately, however, there follow the question of the success, the satisfactoriness, of the purpose or purposes behind the successful perception and the successful practice, and the question of the satisfactory handling of conflicting purposes.

It is, of course, not at all rare to find that purposes pursued were after all quite unworthy. Voltaire's *Candide* is the perfect illustration. Nor is it rare, unfortunately, to have chosen poorly between purposes (for example, marriage vs career). The fortunate fact is that men need not have inadequate or unworthy purposes. They can and do change them in response to the aggregate of factors involved in each live situation. And, in time to come, as purposes (values), under the prodding of thought, are progressively and instrumentally specified through scientific procedures, techniques, and findings, men will be able to do better jobs in setting adequate and satisfactory purposes.

There is power and potential for perfecting purposes, for seeing that they are progressively more satisfactory, in integrating procedures enacted in full awareness of the freedoms stemming from transactional understanding of the human condition. It is particularly by recognizing the impermanence of all aspects of the transactional situation, and by putting them in kinetic relation with each other, that growth is facilitated—in purpose as in prosperity.

The viewpoint of transaction helps break down the rigidities that bar effective integration. Transaction contradicts the conception of organism and environment "interacting" within a mechanistic framework, with the participating entities preserving unchanging structural identity through thick and thin of the process. First it discards as deceptive the concept of "entity" and replaces it by a more pliable term, such as "instrumentality." William James went so far as to suggest that "the word 'I' is primarily a noun of position, just like 'this' and 'here.'" [38] Then it admits the thoroughgoing creative, recreative, or, perhaps, destructive aspects of every event. For, every transaction to some extent modifies all the instrumentalities involved. Even billiard balls are structurally modified, albeit minutely, by the friction and attrition of a game of billiards.

This recognition of the priority of function over structure is basic to progress toward ever more satisfactory human conditions. It goes beyond a mere ranking for precedence. Structure must first be interpreted in terms of function before inquiry can proceed beyond mere classification or description. The way is led by a child's untrammeled definitions in terms of function—" a floor is so you don't fall into the hole your house is built on"—or in terms of purpose—"a hole is to dig." The structure of a tooth, to illustrate, is interpreted in terms of what it does—stresses, strains, abrasions—, and, as well, in terms of its relation to the other teeth in the same mouth, to the working of the stomach and its digestive juices, to the purposes to which it will be put—whether pulling nails or straining soup—and to social customs or artifacts—including everything from the roasting of pigs to electric blenders.

Within the transactional approach, the test for the adequate functioning (satisfactory action) of all the instrumentalities, including purposes and ideas, involved in any situation, is in the integration of these factors that is from time to time achieved or created. An aim, for example, can be judged by the ease with which or the extent to which it can be incorporated into a plan of action. Ideas and concepts, functioning as instrumentalities within transaction, can take on the task of promoting integration. In result, the total transaction will assume from the inside a mystical aspect—a bootstrap, self-levitation sort of thing—while it assumes from the outside the appearance of a creative process. In order to perform the integrating function successfully, ideas must call upon perceptual sensitivity to the dynamics involved in transaction—starting around once more in the complex round of interrelations now described as transaction.

Integration is almost always more than an intellectual affair; as was said above, there are severe limitations to the promotional capacity of ideas. For example, the stretch of personality needed to appreciate new music, say Schoenberg in the first half of the twentieth century, is more quickly achieved when reinforced by kinesthetic pleasures or accomplishments, through patterns in the skilled joints of performance. Notice how an artist will sometimes "appreciate" a new painting by spontaneously acting out its structure with form-fitting gestures of arms and wrists. In teaching children to read, the Montessori method uses sandpaper letters to hasten visual recognition through the aid of touch.

An excellent illustration of the effectiveness of integration in improving performance and satisfaction is afforded by the Flash Technique developed by Hoyt L. Sherman at Ohio State University.[39] This is a technique deliberately designed for systematic, in-situation integration of personality—chiefly on a touch-kinesthetic and visual level. Through practice, drawing pictures in the dark, after they had been flashed momentarily on a screen, football and basketball players improved their games and dental students increased their operating skills. Practice in coordinating muscular movements with flashed visual impressions resulted in measurable increases in peripheral visual acuity. Perception was altered by action and purpose. In Horace Fries' description, the resulting

> integrated response is provided by the football passer who throws the ball upon seeing at a glance the deployed players. He does not have to move his head or eyes about in an effort to concentrate on different focal points. On the other hand, the untrained passer has to depend more upon the co-ordination of several separate acts of vision into a hurried idea of the disposition of the players and then make his pass in accordance with his idea. The Flash training unified the total visual field with the muscular requirements of the situation, thus cutting down the intervening process which otherwise would be necessary to complete the act.[40]

It should be noted that values and purposes are involved in this illustration from the world of practical skills. Evaluations, choices, orientations toward purposes, participate in the selection and employment of means—which, when looked at from below, are tentative or stepping-stone ends. "Cutting down the intervening process" is an integrating of purposes (evaluatings) and ideas (choices) into an aesthetic perception. Perception is displayed as a creative process leading to richer successes and satisfactions.

Any one of the dramatic psychological demonstrations with illusions can lay the groundwork for integrations to cure the fact-value cultural personality split patiently suffered by most people today. Here at hand is shock therapy with which to treat anyone afflicted with the clouded "picture" of reality symptomatic of our culture's schizophrenic subject-object split. The dispelling of illusions is, itself, restorative. If only everyone would participate directly in one of the most disturbing of the demonstration experiments! And he can, of course. The trapezoid experiment, for one, can be set up in anyone's living room for his own special emancipation. Facing up to unanticipated dimensions of reality in carefully selected revelation situations can be socially significant as it weakens the cultural wall separating fact from value. A major advance toward more successful perceptions, ideas, and purposes is felt by people experiencing the shock therapy of facing up to their illusions.

Through perception man creates and recreates his changing reality. Through integration he improves it, bringing partial patterns into more complete patterns—of purpose, thought, perception—putting pieces of the Self together.[41] In some sense, the integrated organism is considered normal—a smoothly functioning organization of tissues and organs. In transactional sense, the integrated organism is a Self, man-in-nature-as-a-whole in motion. As balance is upset, new levels of integration are arranged.

Even with the restorative aid from the revelations of psychology of perception experimental shock treatment, however, the whole story of reality is not told. The final say for the social animal, as will be expanded on at length in coming chapters, is in public test.

SUMMARY

Distant generations will not proclaim that the twentieth century pierced very deep into the fog of fantasy surrounding human nature. Discovery, however, has not subsided. Experiment is continuing on many fronts. Only a few stray examples have been mentioned here, enough merely to point out that there is now a beginning of scientific evidence that can be substituted for the crude representative theory of perception and its partner, the half-and-half interpretation of human nature.

The new reality that emerges from inquiry into perception turns out to be moving, changing, growing—so kinetic, in fact, that the human enterprise might be better off if the term "reality" were simply dropped and forgot, since it will be such a struggle to strip it of its mind-vs-matter connotations. This new reality is best and most conveniently described in terms of transaction. It is found to be characterized by a merging of the subjective and the objective, so that there is no longer a fine-line boundary separating the two. Instead, what is found to be useful and describable is a unity of perceiver and perceived, where each is considered simply an aspect of the transaction that subsumes them.

Perceptions come to be interpreted as signals, indications as to how to act, rather than as representations of what is "out there." And thinking becomes a tool, an instrument for establishing control and pointing changes in directions that come to be desirable. The key term in the transaction "transformation equation" of reality is that mysterious aspect labelled "purpose." Coming from out of the old "subjective" side of the human situation, purposes can be found to be changeable and perfectible in context, as are all the other factors involved in transaction. Progressively more satisfactory functioning of all the aspects of a situation may be had through integrations promoted by ideas and concepts, and aided by perceptual sensitivities. For now, at least, one of the invaluable products of experimental integration is in bringing the reality of transaction to direct experience by the shock of liberation from the cultural tyranny of objective-subjective, fact-value dichotomy.

A full characterization of the nature of human nature is impossible. Not enough is yet known. Needed more than anything has been the scientific beginning now offered by findings in the psychology of perception. Such a beginning can be expanded on, tested, modified, improved in self-corrective inquiry. Knowledge can now be expected to leap eagerly forward in this opening field, as it has in other fields of scientific inquiry.

Next, administrative theory (and political theory) must be squared with what is being learned about human nature. If knowledge in the basic disciplines investigating human behavior is to expand at the rate heralded by all indications, administrative theory (and political theory) must also establish itself scientifically—so that it too may be tested, modified, and perfected in a self-corrective, incremental fashion. In alternative, it will simply turn somersaults each time a new dimension of human nature is revealed.

The further effort of this book will be to develop a substitute for the seventeenth century theory of representative democracy that was patterned after the representative theory of perception. The new will be based, in the tradition of utopia, on the realities of human nature newly revealed in signal perception. The Self, the use of ideas as tools, the creative handling of purpose, and the mark of success in integration, these topics of present discussion, in particular, will be further developed in broader moral and governmental contexts.

CHAPTER FOUR

The Growth of Character

Codes that are meant to embody ideals
have a way of embalming them.

T. V. SMITH

Life has become second nature to us.

JEAN ROSTAND

GOVERNMENT IS A MORAL ENTERPRISE; IT DEALS IN PUR-
poses and conflicts of purposes. The backdrop to politics is the systems of
morality that have been hung up from time to time.

This chapter will devote itself to analysis of the rise and fall of
ethical codes. It will announce their origin and their function in social
control,* using historical reference as an instrument of heuristic exposition, more as a technique of exegesis than as an adduction of
proof. And it will emphasize the insufficiency of today's inherited
moralities. In a sense it will be an attempt to indicate how it is that
men sometimes act in defiance of the human nature observed in
chapter 3, and how it is they have arrived at the present stage of
development. In short, it will recount the story of the growth—with
its ups and downs—of human character.

MORALITY AND SOCIAL PERCEPTION

Man's rich heritage from the experience of the race accompanies
him in even the simplest transaction with the inanimate world. The

---

*As used in this book, "social control" is deliberately stripped of the totalitarian
and Machiavellian connotations that cling so stubbornly to it. These are rather
relegated to the category of coercion and compulsion. While this arrangement is not
entirely satisfactory in view of old associations, there seems to be no better alternative, because "social control" makes such an appropriate counterpart to "physical
control," and because, as will be seen in later chapters, it so inevitably takes
strength from the reciprocal controls of experimental science.

measured cadences of Isadore, Hythloday, and Zarathustra strike the ear of Peter the Hermit in the song of the desert thrush. They are omnipresent in, omni-party to any transaction into which he mixes. They are part of the habitual assumptions, the expectancies, and also the purposes involved, alone in a cave though he may be.

Out in the very real world, there is an added dimension to transaction. In addition to the voices of the past and the voices of nature are the voices of each other. The new dimension accrues when a second person becomes party to a transaction. In place of one set of habitual assumptions and purposes there then are two.

Of all the things that need to be seen, it is the purposes of the other man that are the most stubbornly inaccessible. This is rather strange since he has a tongue with which to talk and he shares with the rest a most elaborate language. Indeed, the gift of speech is crucial to man's social nature. One would think that, in view of the transactional condition of human nature, as described in chapter 3, the capacity for social perception would flow "naturally" from the nature of the beast. However, this may be less a case of failure than one of inordinate expectation. Perhaps we seek to see a special depth and detail in the character of our own kind that we have not demanded in our view of sheep or atoms—until recently. At any rate, social perception (perception of the purposes of others) is especially important because of man's social nature, his innate gregariousness.

As human problems are studied with a transaction approach, difficulties in social perception may diminish. It remains, meanwhile, an everyday complaint that the judging spectator signally fails to perceive the world of reality the person he observes is encountering. As one of C. P. Snow's characters says, "We are none of us men of flesh and bone except to ourselves." The subject always knows more and feels more deeply than the spectator can appreciate.

> He seems to thee a little less living than thou; his life is dim, it is cold, it is a pale fire beside thy own burning desires. . . . So, dimly and by instinct hast thou lived with thy neighbor, and has[t] known him not, being blind. Thou hast made [of him] a thing, no Self at all.[1]

I suspect this persistent blindness appears deceptively exaggerated in its everyday occurrence; we pretend to a perception of our own purposes far beyond warrant. We fail to perceive our own purposes with any great clarity, I suspect, just as we fail respecting those of our fellows. Once a man forms his own picture of himself, he actually cannot clearly detect, if he can detect at all, the feelings, purposes, reactions, and experiences that would distort that picture.

When a situation is complicated by the participation of a second person, two purposers are present and the situation becomes potentially moral. Morality is conceivable whenever a conflict of desires, interests, purposes arises.[2] Morality takes off from such small beginnings—from the insubstantial spark that flies off when purposes rub together—to be elaborated into grand and disembodied ethical codes, but also to preside over the way men act, to establish sensitive and detailed arrangements of social control, merging into and comprehending the aspect called "government" or "politics." The very elementary inception of morality sets out from perception of the purposes of others, from the question of the adequacy of social perceptions functioning as signals. This is what determines in first instance the satisfactoriness of action in a moral situation and what determines in first instance the structure or quality of the emergent morality and the integration of purposes. Morality grows out of social perception, it happens only as men develop the special sensitivities—an evolutionary achievement—that makes social perception possible.

MORAL AWAKENING

When the personal history of one man varies noticeably from that of another, it becomes apparent in a divergence of purpose. Reflective morals begin with the perception of these differences.

Differences of purpose, "value," desire appear as "subjective" attributes at a comparatively recent stage in the development of the race.[3] Early peoples were very closely knit and controlled by mores, customs, tabus. Fruit of the hunt and the field were shared unquestioningly, habitually. Ownership was a matter of use; a tool was "personal when used but communal in potentia."[4] The problem of divergent purposes had not yet arisen; there had not been enough variety in personal history for it to become visible or to be formulated. In the ideal type folk society, as Robert Redfield abstracts it, "patterns of what people think should be done are closely consistent with what they believe is done. . . . What is done in the ideal folk society is done not because somebody or some people decided, at once, that it should be done, but because it seems 'necessarily' to flow from the very nature of things."[5] As long as one man is doing much the same thing as another under severe restriction by uncontrolled physical surroundings, he is not free to develop character.

It was only yesterday, so far as we have any record, that the important question of right and wrong was first asked. "Is the end worthy?" Five thousand years ago, after the "forces of nature" had been brought considerably under control, the Nile had been tamed, and great feats of engineering performed, the first stirrings of moral awakening were felt. By then a great, complex, and stable governmental administrative organization had developed. Specialization had resulted in widespread and fairly detailed division of labor. (Caste divisions and slavery apparently were insufficient in themselves to contribute the variety in activity that would lead to perception of divergence in purpose.) The self, elaborated and specified by individual appropriation of tools, had been consolidated from amorphous tribal existence. In turn, personality had begun to extend beyond a man's skin, eventually to flower as character. It was apparently only after many centuries of this successive development and many centuries of social stability that men were able to sort themselves out from their fellows, disentangle themselves from the enveloping blanket of primitive custom, and perceive variety of purpose as a dimension of life in need of deliberate human control.

According to James H. Breasted, the earliest known discussion of right and wrong is found in a drama celebrating the supremacy of Memphis and dating from the middle of the fourth millenium B. C. At first reflective morality is scarcely distinguishable from the advanced stage of morals as custom, in which stage conduct is approved or condemned as "what is loved" or "what is hated." [6] The source of law in this very early period of ethical development was evidently the Pharaoh who, through his administrative organization, greeted "loved" conduct with life and meted out death for "what is hated." Under the favorable conditions brought about by the stable, seemingly eternal, great administrative state governments of the First (4000 to 3500 B.C.) and Second (3500 to 2500 B. C.) Unions, "the realm of family life reached a high development as a world of tender emotions, inevitably inclining to become those of approval and disapproval, and leading to notions of praiseworthy or reprehensible conduct." [7] Gradually the word "Maat" came to signify "justice," "truth," "righteousness." Conduct (purposes) became a matter of reflection.

"Having arisen as an individual and personal matter, as a designation of right conduct in the family or immediate community, Maat had then gradually passed into a larger arena as the spirit and method of a *national* guidance and control of human affairs, a control in which orderly administration is suffused with moral conviction." [8] The Memphite drama, hinting at the earliest achievements in reflective morality, was the product of a group of priestly temple thinkers. This moral discernment began with the temple priesthoods and the aristocrats of the royal court, only later to descend gradually to the masses. Right and wrong were in the beginning decreed by the Pharaoh and discussed in royal circles—becoming first a means of control over the actions of the royal court and then of the provincial nobles and of the masses.

Religion in the most primitive stage of human development was an awesome endeavor of ancient man to control his environment and the gods he saw in it. As a part of Egyptian life it evolved from stage to stage. At first having nothing to do with morals, it culminated in a highly refined ethical idealism, an instrument of social control. The first battle, a major struggle to gain a moderate control over nature, was won, leaving the nature gods somewhat less than terrifying. The second battle, which we are still fighting, the struggle of men to control themselves (as contrasted with the struggles to control each other, as through tribal or imperial warfare) was only to begin after centuries of social experience had brought about the perception of human conduct and the invention of right and wrong. In the meantime the imposing fabric of the administrative state, which, because of its size and its endurance beyond the memory or imagination of living men, attained the stature of a natural wonder, impressed its structure on the imaginary constructions of religion. The Sun-god was remade in the image of the Pharaoh. "The forms of the state began to pass over into the world of the gods, and an important god would be called a 'king.' " [9] A celestial morality ensued which was, so to speak, a reprise of the narcissism of the race.

Fifteen hundred years after the Memphite drama, during the Feudal Age, moral stirrings, "conscience," which had entered at the top, with the wealthy recognizing the common bond of humanity in spite of their sharp separation from the lower classes, grew to a concept of social justice.[10] Society came to be perceived as a whole. Family approval of conduct was no longer sufficient; the whole of society was brought under the sway of ethical ideals which were quickly reinforced by being attributed to the dispassionate judgment of the Sun-god. Even the Pharaoh was subjected to the supernatural requirements of social justice. "Ideas of social justice, as they found practical expression first in the idealised kingship, and then in the actual character of its incumbent, were thereupon quickly reflected into the character and activities of the Sun-god, the ideal king. The obligation to maintain social justice, which men felt within them, became a fiat of the god, their own abomination of injustice was soon believed to be that of the god, and their own moral ideals, thus becoming likewise those of the god, gained new mandatory power." [11] Where once religion had sought to control the conduct of nature and the nature gods, now it attributed perfection to God and sought to control the conduct of men. Thus reflective morality, through its alliance with the supernatural, shows in dramatic form its true function—that of social control.

With the shift in emphasis from pyramids to prayer, from wealth to virtue, from acts of propitiation to subjective attributes, from judgment in terms of immediate appreciations to questioning of the worthiness of ends or purposes, and with the discernment of society as a whole, together with its complement, the individual self as an independent, comes the beginning of the age of character. An age began that even now, so many centuries later, is still brand new. In the words of the Sage of New England, "we think our civilization near its meridian, but we are yet only at the cock-crowing and the morning star. In our barbarous society the influence of character is in its infancy." [12]

MORALITY—INSTRUMENT OF SOCIAL CONTROL

Individual character arises when family morality is extended on into national ethics. Character, as we have seen, first appeared at the top in the form of an idealized king, soon to be projected into the perfections of a moral god. But with the overthrow of custom and the elevation of ideal morals to the throne of social control, particularly in league with supernatural sanctions, democratization of responsibility was practically inevitable. The floodgates to the hereafter were opened. Where formerly only Pharaohs sailed, now anyone passed who could float his conscience. [13]

In most general terms morality is a tool mankind has invented for controlling human conduct and human nature. It is *the* instrument for attaining ever richer satisfactions out of a mass of conflicting purposes (desires, interests, wants, values). "Not every ideal can be realized. Many must go down. But the fundamental problem of morality is to secure the richest total of satisfied desire." [14] Morality is much more than a particular moral ideal such as freedom or equality, more than any or all sets or codes of perfections or oughts. It is the process, method, instrument of adjustment among such ideal imperatives.

Moral ideals and ideas are instruments, as are ideas of any sort. In any given situation they provide and indeed *are* the intellectual structuring (guiding) of the purposes, values, etc. involved. Generally they are borne to the situation by the individual in the form of conventions or stereotypes which summarize the funded experience of his life *and* inheritance. They serve as essences of the wisdom of ages of human relations, as concentrates of the social experience of the race, relieving the individual of the need to derive, through personal experience, private directives for reliable conduct.

Morals can, however, be revised, recreated or even created, sometimes seemingly *ex nihilo*, as a product of transaction. They are continually emerging in the form of personal codes. They also can be and continually are judged for their success in terms of the integration they facilitate or frustrate, that is, in terms of moral achievement, the attainment of more accurate perceptions and richer satisfactions. This was the subject of the end of the previous chapter.

Even today, in our sophisticated and recently skeptical age, this plastic and functional character of moral ideals is not widely appreciated. Changes of purpose and desire (the very "stuff" of morals), reevaluations of what is prized, are among the most frequent and familiar of daily occurrences emerging from common and ordinary transactions. They are accepted as matters-of-fact, without an afterthought—sometimes they are called "education." Even those changes in purpose and direction which reach deep down into the soul, mounting to complete reorientation of character, to liberating and glorious moral rejuvenation or rebirth are greeted with phlegmatic credence. They may inspire awe, wonder, or hysteria, but there is no questioning of their occurrence. The simpler of such changes are known as aesthetic, the more violent and radical as religious experiences. Yet we live under a curious primitive taboo: morals it seems must be left inviolate, untouched; their alteration, revision, development, progression, test must be left to chance. We may sermonize, we may moralize, we may moot paradoxes and pit the ethics of Ikhnaton against those of Tom Paine. But we may not initiate a deliberate system of human control (science) in respect to morals.

The Egyptians began this taboo, no doubt for solid and sufficient social reasons of their own. Religion was so intimately joined with all aspects of their life that it would have been truly miraculous for their greatest creation—the human conscience—to have evolved in worldly purity. Very likely, with conscience dawning first on the peaks of intelligence, among the pyramids, the governors of society, supernatural sanctions were felt needed to buttress this new way of social control invented by the genius in man. At any rate, here is the start of the Teleological ethics that must be applauded in inception though deplored in undue extension.

TELEOLOGICAL ETHICS

All morality is teleological in that it pertains to the control of human purposes. And human conduct is teleological to the extent that it is regulated by purposes or ends-in-view. The Teleological ethics, however which have had such a long and respected life on earth, project or postulate Purpose in the Universe and succeed in controlling or compelling human purposes, whether through hope, through fear, or through conviction, by exacting homage to celestial intention.

Nevertheless, despite Teleological ethics, morality has undergone continuous development and evolution. Different groups at different times have raised new ideal (moral) types of conduct—appearing in succession: warrior, sage, stoic, saint, gentleman, citizen, comrade. There has been progress in the forms of social organization, from the kinship of the tribe to the authority of the king to the citizenship of the modern state. With all its faults of class pride, group exclusiveness, and secular demeaning of labor, the Middle Ages (again the upper classes) bequeathed a legacy of rich ideals—courage, loyalty, a sense of honor, consideration for others, protection for the weak, courtesy. New ideals were brought in by the industrial revolution and by town living. Town life saw expansion of wealth, comfort, knowledge, and skill and with them the important ideals of honesty, as the trader settled down and became dependent on steady customers, of liberty, as men gained independence from feudal lords and as they were freed from petty group tyranny through blessed urban anonymity, and, eventually, of the dignity of labor, as labor became an independent variable on the economic and aesthetic markets. It may be that even today under our very noses a full-bodied social ideal of intelligence[15] is developing in response to practical need.

In each instance these ideals have performed wondrous feats of social control. It is impossible, for example, to conceive of the development of our present vastly complex and intertwined financial system in the absence of the controlling ideal of honesty. A certain level of similar public honesty may have been prerequisite to the institutionalization of the vote and majority rule as cornerstone of constitutional democracy. Nor would our democratic states be possible without the control over purposes exercised by an ideal of liberty.[16] Consider how the exercise of discretionary powers by public officials is now left largely to be controlled by "inner" checks.

Important as such moral ideals are in any age as social instruments for the control of purposes and ultimately conduct, Teleological ethics may be said to have hit its Western heyday in the Middle Ages. Buttressed by a pervasive religion and by long-standing working relationships, moral ideals were probably as comprehensively effective then as during any other period in recent Western history. Details of social relationship, ways of doing, were worked out and established over many generations during which there was relatively little disruptive social change. Moral strife, social unrest and the conflict of character were automatically reduced to a minimum by the unquestioned acceptance of encompassing folkways. Character tended to be restricted to types by this detailed superposition of moral control. Social perception reached a high level of common accuracy, the perception of purposes being greatly simplified by the social control, the structuring, imposed. And correspondingly, it was possible for a man, particularly for a governor of men, to act and to make judgments in ways that would be felt to be just, by simply remaining within the bounds of the accepted folkway structure. The age was remarkable—so, at least, goes the stereotyped interpretation usually given of it —both for the success of its social perceptions and the success of its moral ideals, in terms of the integrations achieved.

For our day, however, Teleological ethics is unable to give satisfactory service as an instrument of social control. During their initial period of development from basic needs in society and for a varying time thereafter, such ethics no doubt successfully guide purpose and conduct. But there comes a time in the career of any moral ideal when the social situation to which it orginally applied has slipped out from under it, conditions have so changed that, while it may still regulate conduct, such regulation no longer results in integrations. The wisdom embedded in the historical experience of the race does not automatically project reliable guidance into situations outside all experience. Just as the precise instincts of lower creatures may fail under a shift of environmental conditions, so the cultural beliefs, customs, codified moralities of the invisible world which man, the creature of dreams, has devised as instinct surrogate may play him false in novel situations. "Old time religion" is an example recent enough to be still understood if approached with a little effort at sympathetic appreciation. It was once effective on the American frontier as a social control, gathering converts and helping lead settlements from gambling, drinking lawlessness to quiet, decent, orderly living. In the urban America of atomic energy, however, it becomes at best an anti-intelligence influence and a breeder of guilt-filled emotional cripples. In an age that is finding a desperate need for educated and dependable citizens, the regulation of conduct by such beliefs or moralities runs directly counter to hopes of integrative results; it becomes a regulation by coercion instead of one of control.

In times of rapid and radical change, ethical obsolescence is most especially the rule. But furthermore, to ethics that postulate Purpose as their guardian other metaphysical beliefs almost invariably accrue, and men find themselves fettered by convictions, for example, that "human nature can't be changed," that "evil is necessary," that "poverty in some form or other is unavoidable," or that "there will always be wars and rumors of wars." Ideas and actions are then unfortunately restricted. Ethical obsolescence is also intensified by the part of the joy of living that consists of spinning dreams and elaborating symbol systems, running them on and on to unneeded and extravagant lengths. This, too, tends to perpetuate the hegemony of time-voided codes. Teleological ethics sing a long and disembodied swan song as they degenerate to propaganda and preachments.

With the scientific revolution a chain reaction was started. Technological innovations that followed one upon the other, together with the scientific knowledge that gradually cracked the comfortable anthropocentric universe and dislodged its philosophical and theological accretions, destroyed the folkways of the Middle Ages, leaving nothing comparably effective in their place. At the same time the new science, which threatened not only the economic and social status quo but also the conceptual and moral order, was accommodated by being assigned a special province of its own. The universe, and each individual soul therein, was split into two unequal parts, one being forfeited to science and the other preserved for Purpose—meaning, in final analysis, for chance. [17] Here entered what has become known as the Cartesian dualism.

The organic personalism of the Middle Ages gave way to contractual particularism. It became the fashion to imagine that morals were completely separable from physics, minds from matters, that mind didn't *really* matter to the physical world and that matter didn't *really* matter to the spiritual world. Purposes were retracted to a defensive position behind or within the horny battlements of man's skin; they were believed to be purely "subjective." It was as if purposes revolved in an orbit of their own, casting their shadows on events but remaining themselves imperturbable, self-validating—as if justice were the product of faith.

DEMOCRATIC RIGHTS

The much cherished democratic rights of Western democracy took as their point of departure the feudal system of rights, duties, privileges and statuses of the Middle Ages. The significant relation that obtained between the earlier and the later is perhaps most clearly to be seen in the English experience of historical continuity between aristocratic privileges and democratic rights.

Two important faults attached to the growth of democratic rights: (1) While privileges, for example, had been an important strand in the organic fabric of society, the "rights of man" came to embody an essential separateness between men and permitted the myth of opposition between fictitious entities called "the individual" and "society." (2) While statuses, for example, had been attributes of persons-in-society, characteristics of a social situation, accretions to function, the "rights of man" became attached to the human organism aspect of the transactional situation, to the disconnected "man" independent of function.

Society became fluid as the folkway structure of the medieval world dissolved. But status, instead of also becoming fluid, and flowing smoothly from situation to situation, event to event, transaction to transaction, stiffened its backbone and set about to shore up society in the easy way left open—through establishing an artificial hierarchy of human organisms. There was, it seems, considerable continuity or carry-over from medieval organic institutions into later and looser life. But the inheritance was not healthy, for the reason that the new fluid society was essentially incompatible with the static forms that were sought to be preserved. The life that was thus sought to be perpetuated adhered in the form of moral ideals to the subjective aspect of subsequent life, and correspondingly twisted it askew.

To be sure, patterns of respect and authority have changed. Noble, knight, and prelate have been displaced by capitalist, manager, and movie star. The fault is that status clings tenaciously and blindly to subjective organisms, through thick and thin, through kaleidoscopic changes in events, indifferent to the character of the particular situation at hand. Thus we have movie stars campaigning in behalf of presidential candidates, to illustrate the irrelevance of static-status customs. There has been an approach to the democratization of status in the realms of representative politics where "stature" has threatened to displace it, and where the respect a legislator receives tends quickly to collapse with loss of function. Yet even here seniority senselessly rules and "Senator" is an honorific title. In place of status as a moral ideal for social control a more flexible term, like stature or standing, should probably be developed as being more fruitful for a rapidly changing world.

The French Revolution and the American Declaration of Independence fell short in the attempt to counterbalance an obsolete hierarchy of statuses with an absolute ideal of equality. The absolute ideal, deriving from theological dicta about equal or non-privileged status before the judgment throne of God, referred, basically, to an equality of status. All men were posited equal in the sight of God. Equality was not a challenge to status *per se*. The contest was rather between equal status and privileged status. Equality was a status rather than a stature concept.

The theological background to equality highlights the attachment of equality to the abstracted "subjective" aspect of the individual—the soul. Granted, equality is a more suitable ideal than is status for directing social control under conditions of fluid social forms—where there is a high degree of social mobility from class to class, job to job, function to function. Nevertheless it lacks a certain realism because of its relation to a fictitiously separable entity. Partly for this reason it has been variously reinterpreted as "equality of opportunity," "equal treatment," "equality according to ability." Or it is restricted to separated fields: equality before the law, political equality (one man, one vote), social equality.

Perhaps no one now subscibes to a literal interpretation of the assertion that "all men are created equal." The doctrine nevertheless tends toward a simplistic denial of the value of the individual, of the rounded Self which is the transacting organism-and-environment, the contributor of novelty, of "value," to society. For a man to feel that he is "just as good as" the next man no doubt liberates him from the depressing effects of hierarchical statuses imposed without relation to function or event. However, it also tends to relieve him of respect for genuine functional or situational differences. Whether in the form of equality, privilege or respect, a teleological ideal of personal (meaning half of a Self) status tends to set up an attitude of intolerance which is an unwillingness to seek and abide by public verification.

The ideal of freedom meets with like difficulties. It again projects an idyllic goal for a mythical half-a-Self. The British and American ideal does better than does the Continental approach which boldly proclaims the Cartesian dualism in terms of rational freedom from the frailties of the flesh. Our idyll of freedom from coercion lays its great emphasis on opposition of an atomic individual to organized methods of control, becoming in its enthusiasm a revolt against authority in any form.[18] While it does not leave men susceptible to organic spasms of subservience to law as does the continental variety, it nevertheless accepts the same basic separation between mind and body.

In its early and pure version, freedom from coercion was nicely buttressed by fantasies of social contract as bridge from what now seems an incredible State of Nature. Following the crumbling of the medieval universe, Social Contracts had been needed to give theoretical coherence to the effort at recreating the social fabric destroyed by release from medieval organic coercion. Coercion may be taken as an indication that social structure, or some aspect of social structure has crumbled. Medieval authority had become coercive as it attempted to deal in traditional ways with unprecedented situations presented by movement and invention. The Social Contracts, were, in effect, attempts to provide a theoretical basis for morality so that social control could be stabilized, made reliably effective. But that Contract approach was severely limited by the Cartesian partition of human nature, on which it relied. The Contract was a rational construct devised to organize, to unite social structure on the basis of ungrounded and disembodied intelligence rather than through comprehensive mutual adjustment of whole men. The freedom it supported could correspondingly be partial, at best.

A jealous pursuit of freedom from the mandate of others can culminate in entirely unrealistic insistence upon minimum government— even where the self-control features of republicanism are present. Pitting an abstract freedom against an abstract authority tends to leave government too impoverished adequately to perform some of its essential functions. Furthermore, the authority that is permitted to government under this arrangement remains one of status and is almost automatically mistrusted by men beset with a status-ideal of equality. Besides, modern institutions of self-government are too remote—individual control, participation, consent too tenuous—for this sort of authority to be felt to be self-imposed. Republicanism is not yet an adequate institution of self-control.

Very likely the impoverishment of authority is also partly due to failure very notably to wring solutions or decisions, that can be felt to be just, out of emergent conflict situations. No smoothly viable moral method now fills the role once played by the folkways of the Middle Ages. It is dimly sensed, however, that authority, to be effective under fluid social conditions, must gain release from the rigidity of status. There are intimations of authoritative effectiveness in the fluidity of ways of doing, the fluidity of perfectible methods.

THE WITHERING OF MORALITY

Once upon a time justice was a clear process of punishment or reward, meted out for violation or observance of recognized rules. The deed alone was considered; the act alone judged.[19] Following the discernment of purpose, a distinction began to be made, and a qualitative difference noted, between intentional and involuntary misdeeds. Motive came to be considered. And judgment was related to deserts. This was undoubtedly an important advance in the evolution of morality. But the development, on the other hand, that saw motive become purely "inner" while retaining a crucial role in justification is a prime instance of moral backsliding. Any motive is only a element, only one of many dynamic parts, in a particular situation. In itself it provides no more valid justification than does faith. "Integrity" is not enough today, not, that is, the "integrity" of the atomic individual. It is not sufficient to be wrong with the best of intentions. There is something bitter about doing harm with the "right motives" in mind. Perhaps this is close to the core of what is meant by irony.

To honor motive above consequences is to champion ends— "inner" ends at that—at the expense of means. It is to deny the conjugal relationship between ends and means. The twentieth century is peculiarly tempted to this vice because of the breakup of experience, the aggravated spread between deeds and their consequences. Between the two extend vast mysteries of machinery, both physical and social; so that, from the vantage of the deed, results cannot be detected, and to the sufferer of consequences their author is anonymous. If you toss an innocent apple straight into the air, you will find that it does not descend on your head as it would have in Newton's day. Instead, it is caught up in a vast and invisibile machinery, to fall on the unexpecting in a hail of bullets. No wonder men are lost, anxious, purposeless, faceless! (Rebecca West argues that the breakup of cause and effect is a cause of treason in our day.) A great educational loss has accompanied the change from rural to city living. The obvious feedback from actions in respect to animals and plants is no longer a daily teacher in dramatic and sympathetic terms of the essential roundness of experience. Even a village store no longer knows where its cheese comes from, so divided is life by specialization. As John Gaus points out, a farmer used to be judged by the care he took of farm equipment— covering the mowing machine to protect it from the rain etc.—but how judge a broker by his fortieth story office? In highly industrialized society, the simple, direct situation of transactional man-nature relationships becomes obscured as nature disappears behind the sheer mass of human fellowhip. From such a context, the man of the century is easily inclined to deny the transactional character of his existence and to claim justification for his deeds from the purity of his intentions —particularly since he is not commonly aware of the unspanned gaps between doings and their final products.

To apologize on the strength of "meaning well" becomes, under these conditions, a badge of irresponsibility. It is a mark of either refusal to deliberate or failure to understand, to perceive. At the present time such failure is facilitated, almost dictated, by cultural inheritance of the habit of motive mooting, making it difficult for the individual to see that deliberation, consideration, correlation may be demanded by the situation.

The respect in which motive is held testifies to the fragmentation of morality. Morality can obviously go off in all directions at once if something so private as motive is guiding the helm. Correspondingly, the effect of morality in social control is neutralized. Once weakened by the autonomy of the "individual," however, it has been further diluted by group processes.

Contemporary ethical theory is so weak that it is forced to grant autonomy or near-autonomy in fashioning ideals of right and wrong to businessmen, scientists, lawyers, educators, even artists, politicians, and morticians, within their various fields of specialization. Increasingly, division of labor is the phenomenon directly responsible. Those who spend their lives in remotely related or unrelated occupations, unless suffused with an unusual amount of imaginative sympathy, tend to constrict their moral horizons within the physical boundaries of their primary groups. Indeed, what a man sees is so closely related to what he does that detailed division of labor cannot help but point toward grouped variety in perception (Contrast the farmer's with the speculator's attitudes toward selling lots in a flood plain.) and ultimately toward group differences in projected moral ideals. (Such divergence in perception may in part account for the mid-century outcropping of group interpretations of politics in America.) The resulting meagerness of community, of understanding based on beyond-group relatedness, furthers the withering of morality to sportsmanship or good manners. This is sometimes all that is left over after groups, particularly professional groups, have appropriated ethics as a means of group protection against demands of the rest of society and as a means of controlling or disciplining intra-group activity.

Division of labor, in addition, is beginning to set the stage for a coming scene of character climax in which humanity, the whole of the human group, will stand out as the primary group, both in morality and loyalty. Occupational specialization—even professionalism—in its moral function of group control is bound to be increasingly less effective as increasing division of labor makes it clearer and clearer that the individual job is less and less important and that the "individual's" importance will have to be found in broader realms of citizenship and creative use of leisure. In America this basic weakness of parochial groups—the tenuousness of their authority, the poverty of their certainty, and the looseness of the loyalty they inspire—is evidenced by the failure of labor organizations to become the organic groups once expected. They have become merely matter-of-fact, special purpose business agents. The basic weakness of inferior groups is also apparent in the comparative position of federal over local government in the acquaintance, esteem, and understanding of the citizenry.

Meanwhile the scale of moral problems has broadened immeasurably. To a great extent, the fundamental problems of politics, economics, culture are ignored by narrowly limited moral codes. (Overpopulation has been a prominent example.) And where they are not ignored, they are either treated—as is poverty—by an inapplicable ethics drawn from a less fluid society of the past, or approached—as is property or the directing of genetic development—from the partial perspective of particular group ethics. Moral criticism is not focused effectively on social institutions. Impersonal machines, markets and institutions seem to be deciding the more significant questions in profound independence of, and indifference to, human moral control. In fact, they are in turn manipulated to an extent by autonomous or semi-autonomous governmental instrumentalities; but these in further turn so pervasively disregard each other that the product almost amounts to the suzerainty of chance—to the ascendance of disrelated autonomous moralities—or, occasionally still, to the overlording of the general inheritance of customary morality. And the failure of men to assert control, to broaden the horizons of morality, to attempt at least to span the unsounded depths between individual activity and social impact, to wrest the direction of affairs from chance, is the very essence of irresponsibility. The impotence, anxiety, purposelessness, thumblessness that is purported to characterize the present age is not beyond repair. But it will take much moral effort and the assumption of responsibilities we have in the recent past even refused to perceive.

The other face of freedom is supposed by many to be responsibility.[20] The new meaning brought into life by the ideal of liberty was that men should be not only free but also law-abiding, for the reason (among others) that they were now free to make their own laws. The responsibility to make good laws and to obey them was thus thrust into the hands of the free as an adjunct of their liberty. It is true that the ideal of freedom cannot be very productive unless accompanied by some degree of responsibility somewhere. It may even be that freedom is proportionate to the degree that men recognize their responsibilities. However, the tendency is to see the two, not as coordinate aspects of living, but as antitheses which must be deliberately balanced to arrive at a golden mean. With a fixed ideal of freedom as freedom from any-authority, and with the ingrained habit of thinking in terms of status, men do not easily accept responsibility as an ordinary aspect of transaction but tend to resist it as homage to a status-authority. The ideal of freedom, as it is held, does not, in other words, subsume responsibility as a built-in feature.

Responsibility is not an ideal. It is not a part of Natural Law, as are equality, life, liberty, and property. It is not assumed to be self-evident. So long as men are believed to be essentially separable from their fellows and from the world beyond their skins, inalienable rights may be bravely championed in behalf of fictional individuals, with some internal, theoretical coherence of meaning. On the other hand, responsibility in such an environment is a trumped-up, contractual affair, an attempt to hold together what has been put asunder, left to chance, using as binding the very root assumptions that divide.

The irresponsibility for which modern man may be indicted is directly related to the obsolete Teleological ethics, to the unnatural Rights he embraces. It is not simply failure to relate deeds to outcomes, or readiness to leave the larger institutional questions to chance. It is failure to replace an outgrown system of moral ideals with a system that can adequately and creatively fulfill the true role of moral ideals, that of social control.

SUMMARY

From the very beginnings of life in a cluster of successful catalysts, through eons of evolutionary development, past the slithering creatures who crawled out of the mud, blinked at an unaccustomed sky, and bailed a chancy atmosphere in and out of new-made lungs, down to the culminating achievement of the twentieth century—battling humanity—there has been a process of natural selection at work, we are told, factoring out the fittest for survival. Current interpretations of biological evidence explain in addition that this fitness has been a grouped affair. At least from the time when non-seasonal sexuality was brought into play and father anthropoid was brought into lasting alliance with mother and child to form the family—from the time this permanent group was established to make it possible to carry children through longer infancy to survival—at least from then on fitness has been a grouped affair. Some such stable grouping must have been necessary for the development of language. And language, in turn, for the development of societies that could rise to the fine discrimination of right and wrong—the beginning of morality and the dawn of character. The group is genetically and evolutionarily prior to survival, language, morality, and character.

Associated survival is, however, much older and deeper than the human species. It seems to be the rule rather than the exception that living things strive for interdependence rather than independence. Multi-cellular organization itself may be described as the trend setting variant from life-or-death competition between separate cells. Ashley Montague insists that the evidence shows cooperation to be more dominant and biologically more important than either aggressiveness or non-ruthless competition, and that without it the improvement of the individual and the strengthening of the species would be incomprehensible. He quotes P. R. Burkholder:

> The most important basis for selection is the ability of associated components to work together harmoniously in the organism and among organisms. All new genetic factors, whether they arise from within by mutation or are incorporated from without by various means, are accepted or rejected according to their cooperation with associated components in the whole aggregation.[21]

There is support for this position—that people are primarily social; that dog-eat-dog survival of the fittest is not the evolutionary fact—in Money-Kyrle's conclusion that people with authoritarian and people with humane personalities differ in the accuracy of their perception of the "outside" world, the first sometimes perceiving with distortion, the last invariably more realistic.[22]

Alfred Adler's fine definitions of vice and virtue also reinforce the transactional understanding of Self. He says, "When we speak of virtue, we mean that a person plays his part; when we speak of vice, we mean that he interferes with co-operation. I can, moreover, also point out that all that constitutes a failure is so because it obstructs social feeling, whether children, neurotics, criminals, or suicides are in question. In every case it can be seen that a contribution is lacking." [23]

It is not necessary to pursue adaptation analysis into the fine detail of human social organization, though it is interesting, and perhaps eventually fruitful, to speculate in the realms of grand design. Does thought, the evolutionary newcomer, represent a resting point in the development of the human species via modification of flesh, blood, and bone through unconscious processes? Or will human evolution henceforth take the form of leaps of thought, new inventions, creative integrations terminating in novel aspirations? Is new experience in thinking evolution itself? Does "survival of the fittest," acting in the marketplace of ideas, preside as an "unseen hand" over the elimination of thoughts whose divergence from parent background is too extreme?

Whatever the ultimate product of such speculation, there is assurance, if anything can be assured, that thought will not inhabit an alien realm, but will have a direct effect on the evolutionarily more ancient aspects of the Self. The more that is learned about how men think and about the full impact of thought, the more certain becomes deliberate human control of blood and bone evolution. In the not distant future, the major evolutionary advance of the blood and bone variety will be a conscious step: control of genetic mutation and liberation from the painfully slow process of chance-arrived variation.

At that time we will be able to say without ambiguity that the purposes astride in the universe have led out of adaptability to freedom, culminating in creativity. Character, in a very real sense, will have come into its own.

Excursion into evolution and biology leads around from a different perspective to transactional description of the human situation, giving an added depth to the idea of Self. The sort of outside purpose that acts as an extra force to keep the isolated pieces of the living universe running, spinning, and fighting can be dispensed with. Selves transacting in environment manifest, for direct observation, what can be described as purpose. Until scientific investigation brings a closer understanding of the anatomy and properties of purpose, its rudiments can be tentatively identified in the quality of discontent with what *is*—called the "radical bent" in later chapters. This quality is displayed by all forms of life. It is the pervasive, ever renewed outreaching of life probing and extending into the more and more remote corners of the expanding environment to make a niche for itself by hook or by crook, adapting itself to the most hostile, preposterous, and uninspiring of surroundings. Here is something that is more than survival, leading to preliminary indentification of life itself as purpose at its very broadest and most general. Do we call it "purpose" at the near, intimate end and "evolution" when separated by time?

In an evolutionary setting that shows the human Self a survival success in and because of its group—a situation satisfactorily described only by transaction—the importance of social perception is appropriately accentuated. Only a group that had risen to the height of sensitivity necessary for the control of the easy aspect of situation— environment—could further "adapt" to the exalted sensitivity necessary before Selves could begin to perceive purposes as entertained by other Selves.

The biological basis for morality, as here described, does not lend encouragement to the idea that character grows to freedom through a process of emancipation wherein men become more and more individual, separable, finally dropping the capital S of the Self to become blithe spirits of independence. Rather does it sturdily support a socializing process that produces tremendous variety among members of the human group (more variety than found in other animal species) —so much variety that "individuals" eventually come to perceive the divergence of purpose and the dawn of developing character—within a nexus that ties the Self more and more securely to society—the way a child as he develops diverges more and more from his playmates, becomes a person in his own way, but in the process becomes more and more firmly bound to society. The Self produced, the character under way is then in fact a set of walking social relationships and the mythical individual has disappeared—so completely as to raise doubt that his separate existence has been anything but an arbitrary assumption, even from the physical and physiological standpoints.

This chapter has seen the beginning of character—how it rose out of social perception, began to develop during the early elaboration of systems of morality as tools of social control, and hit a premature end of growth while still in its infancy, as morality hardened into Teleological ethics. Only when purposes are perceived is concern about conflict of purposes—the elementary moral situation—possible. Moral prescriptions, systems of morality, codes of ethics then come into play as uniquely human instrumentalities for group survival through control over the warfare of conflicting purposes. Stalled for millenia on plateaus of Teleological ethics, mankind may now be ready to resume the climb toward character.

It is possible that there will always be a rift, or at least a difference, between saying and doing, profession and performance, theory and practice. At any rate, this is what men have come to expect. It is indeed to be expected during the dawn of character building, while rigid systems of Teleological ethics hold sway, one after the other. There was, however, a great turning in history when the scientific revolution liberated a profound and irreversible disquiet. Since that time, the disjunction brought about by firmly established separation between mind and matter, moral and physical, has undermined the traditionally rigid moralities at a faster and faster rate (urged on in the last 50 years by the increasing disjunction—most evident in the rural to urban shift—between person and place, between human organism and non-human environment), accentuating the rift between profession and performance, but also cancelling the social control that might be expected from viable morality. The popular view of human nature (the half-and-half man) did not contain control concepts capable of coping with the full dimensions of reality. Thus we are left with moral commitment to ideas of equality, freedom, and responsibility that, because of their inadequacies, leave us thumbless for lack of social control.

The search for social control will lead, in the coming chapter, to a look into the operating of the culprit disquieter itself, the disrupting cultural factor—experimental science—to see what can be derived from this major revolutionary yet sensitive process, that may lead to revolutions in sensitivity of social control.

CHAPTER FIVE

Control in the Search for Truth

Science may not have all the answers,
but it is supplying the remedies.

AN EXPERIMENTAL ATTITUDE TOWARD MORAL CODES AND social arrangements has been slowly developing—at least in some specialized outposts of civilization. At these points, the expectation of correspondence between doings and professings has steadily grown.

If, after centuries, even millenia, character is to get off dead center and resume a steady climb out of the wasteland of Teleological ethics, out of a condition of arrested development, it should seek the aid of experimental science. One of its best hopes is in the cues it may find in this great revolutionary event that exaggerated the spread between thinking and doing in the social realms, and dramatized the undermining of social control, at the same time that it closed the ranks between theory and practice in the more strictly environmental realms. This scientific revolution perfected a basic system of self-control within inquiry that can now be generalized and used to rejuvenate social control, elaborating moral devices appropriate to the fluid social conditions that experimental science itself has brought about.

By looking at experimental science as a transactional inquiry and in this light reviewing the sort of reciprocal control engendered between its theoretical and practical or applied aspects, a vantage is available for new perspectives on social control. In the process, special emphasis will fall on the importance of sensitivity and emotion to inquiry; the peculiar intimacy between science and morality; what it means for experimental science to be a collective enterprise; the special value in a non-dualistic understanding of objectivity; the crucial function of deliberate change in experimental science, in the enstatement of control; how it is that prediction retires into the shade when purpose is accorded its proper social recognition either in inquiry or in more pedestrian day-by-day situations of life.

SCIENCE AS TRANSACTION

There is a popular stereotype that depicts science as a ruthless activity of cold reason pursuing an "objective" course toward pure knowledge in sublime indifference to moral considerations. The prototype of the scientist of this view came to earth in a flying saucer some years ago, a science fiction monster from outer space. Playing the title role in the movie "The Thing," he proceeded to strike terror into the hearts, souls, morals, and intellects of the brilliant scientists (human) of an isolated government weather experiment station in Alaska, as I remember. His most apalling attribute was not his revolting appearance or his appetite for mammalian blood, but his unearthly "intellect." He was, "scientifically," centuries in advance of his meager human adversaries. His "mind" was capable of running circles around the scientists'. It seems he and his breed held the initial supreme advantage of being vegetables. Being nothing but rational turnips, they were nothing but "reason." They had not been retarded in "mental" development by the irrelevancies of pain, pleasure, fear, love, pride, desire, greed, joy, and the rest of what we usually lump under emotion and feeling; they had not been distracted from scientific achievement by moral diversion.

Well, in fact, this high-minded turnip is more than fiction. Minus the deformities and blood-sucking, he represents the absurd logical extreme of the belief that minds can be sorted out from morals and that science is a disinterested activity of mind. The error of this modern-traditional view of scientific activity becomes quickly apparent when the picture is thus pushed to extremes. The fact is that reason, mind, even of the coldest, highest, most scientific variety, is an evolutionary development that cannot be divorced from the concomitant development of physical, emotional, moral, and aesthetic sensitivities. Pain and suffering are maximized in quantity and intensity at the highest level of evolution—man as a member of an organized polity.

Man is not at all a denatured monkey. On the contrary he has reached new heights of sensitivity. He sports a magnificent matchless gift for suffering—as dazzling even as his creative genius. Suffering has crept out of the vast seas of evolution, taking refuge in the hearts of individuals and species in proportion to the demise of instinct and the ascendancy of thinking. It culminates for now in *homo sapiens*. Is thinking the most painful sort of growth—with, perhaps, release in moments of generalization? Could it be argued that suffering in some refined way figured as exquisite index of evolutionary advance? At any rate, the wretched lord of the planet owes his extraordinary capacity for social perception, for sympathetic understanding, to his special sensitivity. Without it, it is certain that scientific curiosity would never have come into being, much less the ability to perceive or experience hitches or blocks to ongoing activity and to formulate them into scientific problems. The chief virtue of scientists is that *as scientists* they are not turnips.[1]

Scientists are like everyone else. "Ideological bias, compulsive inattention to facts that later seem obvious, the failure to draw implications that are there, and the repeated drawing of implications that are not there—all these are part of the physical scientist's life as well as of the historian's or sociologist's." [2] No one really expects them personally to rise above the very human penchant to err, always to refrain from injecting their temperaments, their foibles, into their work. But, on the other hand, the long-standing mythology is that Science itself (a dangerously thingified abstraction) has an abstract existence in a rarified atmosphere far above the smoke of human hopes, desires, values.

In the words of Julian Huxley, "Emancipation of natural science from considerations of value is a fiction, approximated by the possibility of temporarily and artificially isolating scientific activity from other human activities." [3] The fiction should have been shattered beyond repair by Einstein's use of Riemannian geometry. Ever since Descartes' unification of mathematics and geometry, ever since his infectious genius sparked the search for precise correlation of physical phenomena by means of mathematical formulas, the mainstay of this fiction has been the *apparent* correspondence between mathematics and reality. Einstein's brilliant stroke was to intuit a general solution to the theoretical problem he was facing and *then* to search around and find a mathematical language that could express his until then ineffable solution.[4] Mathematics by this event became as relative as everything else. Scientists are now free to pick and choose between the various systems of mathematics until they find one appropriate to the particular purpose at hand. It should now be evident that mathematics, like most human thinking, is a tool. It is not the essence of reality, but an instrument for dealing with reality. When there is correspondence between the two it is because a system of mathematics has been invented to deal with the realities man has made. It is not at all a matter of uncovering the way reality fits into mathematical forms, with the expectation that all of reality will eventually be found so to conform. There appears, in addition, to be an imprecision in reality that contradicts expectation of perfect alliance with the rigors of mathematical precision. This looseness, "give," or tolerance in reality is what is called "uncertainty" or "chance."

There is no special reality that can be termed scientific in contrast to the reality of everyday life. That we sometimes think there is, is the unfortunate product of the disjunction that exists (due largely to perverse habits of thought) between science and the moral life. Reality for the physicist as for the common man is found in *trans*actions involving minds and matters. So that we can say with Dewey and Bentley: "What one can investigate a thing *as*, that is what it *is*, in Knowledge and in Fact." [5]

Reality in any instance comprehends "subjective" and "objective" aspects. "What one can investigate a thing *as*" involves morality, whether the investigation centers about crime or cosmic rays. Attach the "as" to Science and in place of the mythical thingified abstraction an ongoing human activity appears—a way of knowing that would better be served by some such title as *sciencing*. And it becomes clear at once that morality is involved, not just in the application of garnered know-how, but in the very heart of the know*ing*-how process itself.

It should hardly be necessary to point out that any scientist is engaged in purposive activity. If he is an applied scientist, he is trying to solve problems, inherited or newly formulated. If he is a pure scientist, he is trying to improve the conceptual tools which the applied scientist uses and tests.[6] Attitudes, interests, assumptions, loyalties, awarenesses, expectations, abstractions, desires, both conscious and unconscious, are directly involved in the most fundamental judgments, choices, decisions of scientific research or experimentation. They are so intimately involved as to be incorporated in scientific method itself, far from being neutralized by method as private bias and peculiar individual limitations are neutralized by application of a "personal equation." Most notably they are present in the awakening to consciousness of what John Dewey has named the problematic situation. The feeling of inadequacy in a system of ideas or a theory, the doubt as to the relation of action and outcome, the sensing of a hitch, a snag, a block to purposes or tropisms in the process of ongoing development, the perceiving which distinguishes facts of scientific interest from those which are not—these precursors to a formulated problem grow out of the network of attitudes, interests, motives, and so on that form the fabric of a man's being. And the next step, problem formulation, equally emerges from the marrow of his bones, being essentially an aesthetic achievement. It is not, however, just the beginning, but the whole of inquiry that is affected. Personal attitudes and interests are, as O. J. Herrick concluded,

> the key factors in all really original scientific investigation. . . . These interests and the attitudes of the inquirer shape the whole course of the investigation, without which it is meaningless and fruitless. To neglect these components of scientific work and the satisfactions of a successful outcome is to sterilize not only the process but also the results of the inquiry. The vital germ of untrammeled imaginative thinking is thrown into the discard, and too often we seem quite content with the dead husk which is so easily weighed, measured, classified, and then stowed away in the warehouse.[7]

Throughout the process of scientific inquiry, from the uneasiness, the feeling of cross-purposes that marks its inception to the elation, the feeling of integration that consecrates a successful terminal test, the elaborate and largely unconscious and aesthetic process of weighing, adjusting, and integrating, called "value judgment," plays a crucial role. Formulating a problem out of a snag in ongoing experience; or perhaps choosing to investigate this problem instead of that one; designating or perceiving, from among many, the elements or aspects of the situation that are possibly strategic to the problem and eliminating the others; designing an hypothesis that will be worthy of test; or deciding which of competing hypotheses to test first; selecting standards to be used in experimentation;[8] deciding which kind of apparatus to use for experimental purposes; designing an experimental procedure that can bring an hypothesis or a standard to test; defining what can be considered evidence for the solution of the problem; deciding that the action initiated has not only solved the problem, but also resolved the experienced difficulty that the problem sought to formulate—in all these scientific activities the play of value judgment is manifest. And to the list must be added the choosing of the scientific method itself.[9]

Wherever, in this whole scheme, resolution of a conflict between desires, values, interests is involved, the situation becomes specifically moral. Morality is, quite simply, and at its broadest, the shepherding of such conflicts. Even in pure scientific research such moral decisions can be of crucial (if sometimes hidden) importance. Alone in his laboratory a man can enact in "internal" (private) struggle the war of competing social interests. But, alone in a laboratory or a library, just as much as crowded among straining shoulders or aching knees, men make moral decisions under the exacting benevolence of morality. The making of moral or value judgments is an integral part of scientific method. The trouble is that a benevolent morality is not enough. No viable procedure is now at hand for determining what moral judgments ought to be made.

A PROTOTYPE: SCIENCE WEARS THREE HATS

Science wears three hats. It can be considered as (1) a body of accumulated knowledge, (2) a method of arriving at truth, and (3) a collective enterprise—a structured system of social transactions. These three aspects are critically and thoroughly interdependent. But the dependence of the third on the first and second has been more apparent than has the reverse relation. The tendency has been to write off the collective enterprise aspect, to discount it, if not to deny it outright, in blind insistence upon the "objectivity" of science. Yet this is especially where the moral element joins in with greatest insistence. Morality spreads a cloak of social control, if not coercion, over any collective enterprise of human beings, inevitably casting its shadow on the method and product of such enterprise.

Where nothing better is at hand, the customary morals inherited from a simpler world are ready to assume direction. And, to the extent that they are not debilitated by the unprecedented fluidity of modern conditions and therefore superseded by the hegemony of chance or the manufacturing of public opinion, customary morals are exactly what remain to guide the public relations of science (as contrasted with its methodological or housekeeping activities) as well as a good part of the evaluative scientific decisions referred to above. The post-bomb conscience struggle of the atomic scientists presents an obvious case in point. On a more mundane level, the creating and stimulating of wants or interests for the sake of the profit of the want-maker, and the diversion of scientific knowledge to invention of such profit-yielding items is characteristic of twentieth century America—most crassly displayed in the advertising activities of the great pharmaceutical houses and the cigarette manufacturers.

Science does, however, have a morality that can justifiably be called its own. This morality is very largely restricted to the inner working of scientific inquiry, but it also inevitably tends tentatively to extend into the broader social workings of democracy. Unfortunately, the men well trained in the morality of science have also been trained, or at least convinced, to mind their own business and to keep that morality within the confines of specialty. At the same time, the practical men of government, the politicians and generalists, have been educated apart from the scientific and technical activities which are reshaping society. They are accordingly accustomed to ignore the controlling inner morality of scientific inquiry while themselves contributing to the shaping or the warping of the social framework within which scientific inquiry, with all its disrupting by-products, operates. One of the deepest tragedies of the world today is that the morality of science has been narrowed to a group ethic and restricted in scope to internal professional affairs. Nevertheless, there is hope. The return wave from science has inevitably brought about changes in the moral tone of everyday life; it has pervasively mediated conflicts in desire and transformed simple purposes, judgments, affections, preferences, aversions. Even the professional morality of science shows signs here and there of belatedly breaking ranks to preside over decisions among social doings.

The morality of science is succinctly expressed in C. H. Waddington's words as a "recognition that one belongs to a community, but a community which requires that one should do one's damnedest to pick holes in its beliefs." [10] Far from being a monolithic or single party organization, science is a pluralistic system built upon an ethos of criticism. The inverse view of the scientific attitude is given in epigram form by Jean Rostand when he says, "I am anyhow not witless enough to be altogether sure of my certainties." [11] The worker in science learns very early and very clearly the possibility of error.

The morality of science puts special emphasis on truth or, in other words, on the ever better solving of problems. This is an outgrowth of the ideal of scientific progress, the spirit of cooperation that seems to have originated among the superior artisans of the fifteenth and sixteenth centuries and that leads a man to think of his findings and inventions as contributing to a growing store of knowledge, with the expectation that others to come will add to, and perfect upon, his efforts.[12] Emphasis on progress and truth in turn places a premium on curiosity, on freedom of inquiry, on clarity and rigor of thought, on full and abundant discussion, on patience and perseverance, and on continual effort to perceive anew. In contemporary physics, J. Robert Oppenheimer says,

> we learn, so frequently that we could almost become accustomed to it, how vast is the novelty of the world, and how much even the physical world transcends in delicacy and in balance the limits of man's prior imaginings. We learn that views may be useful and inspiriting although they are not complete. We come to have a great caution in all assertions of totality, of finality or absoluteness.[13]

An important corollary to the idea of progress has been the constant concern with the way scientific ideas and facts are formulated and displayed. They should, for one, be couched in terms that permit their further improvement or refinement. This is, for example, why Lavoisier preferred his new system of chemistry to the old phlogiston theory which he thought too vague and in consequence too readily accommodated to any explanation into which it was pressed.[14] Into this expectation of refinement of scientific theory is built a healthy dose of tolerance.

Scientific theories should also be, as Henry Margenau suggests, logically fertile.[15] For example, the gaps in the periodic table implied untouched elements—later found or made. The laws of planetary motion led through logical analysis to a search for explanation of the eccentric behavior of known planets in terms of the influence of unseen planets—later found. The neutrino, discovered in 1956, was a product of the implications of $E=mc^2$ from 1905. Scientific theories should be so designed that further ideas and possibilities can be derived from them. This is why personal or inscrutable gods can have no place in scientific theory. Into this open-endedness is built a disbelief in finality, a modesty before ultimates.

Scientific theories, furthermore, should—indeed they always do—reject the attitude and practice of compromise in pursuit of truth. In place of the middle way, opposing hypotheses are selectively championed in proportion to evidence—or else both are endorsed in deference to evidence supporting contradictory positions, as in the current use of both wave and corpuscle descriptions of light. Into this refusal to compromise is built a spirit of determination not slavishly to follow the easy course, not to settle for what is less than right. This spirit will be called forcefully into play in coming chapters.

Science insists on a novel and thorough alliance between validity and freedom. In organizing social relationships within the sweep of the spirit of progress, it humbly subordinates fame and personal advantage to the cumulative effort, completely obviating authoritarianism; it hedges ambition and the desire for prestige within the mutuality of collective enterprise; it champions experimental verification in place of authority; and, for all its exacting discipline, it favors the individual, as a unique phenomenon, for all his diversity.

The power in the social relations of science is perhaps best illustrated in its control of prejudice, vanity and ambition.

> Would it be too much to say that in the natural sciences today the given social environment has made it very easy for even an emotionally unstable person to be exact and impartial in his laboratory? The traditions he inherits, his instruments, the high degree of specialization, the crowd of witnesses that surrounds him, so to speak (if he publishes his results)—these all exert pressures that make impartiality on matters of *his* science almost automatic. Let him deviate from the rigorous role of impartial experimenter or observer at his peril; he knows all too well what a fool So-and-so made of himself by blindly sticking to a set of observations or a theory now clearly recognized to be in error.[16]

It is certainly a mistaken viewpoint that seeks to find morality apart from the free-ranging pursuit of truth. Not only freedom but all morality must be intimately tied to validity. After all, the truth is a prime ingredient in the resolution of any conflict of desires or purposes. It is distinctly possible, as many have suggested, that the prototype of the Good Society—the organization of the relations of men, the institutionalization of their behavior, and the participation in the solution of their problems—is to be found in the organization, method, and substantive findings of science.

Two cautions must, however, be made against over-eagerness to find moral prototype in science. First, it must not be forgotten that knowing is transactional, that the minds and matters it subsumes encompass such phenomena as emotions, appreciation and purposes. This is a caution against the oversimple reading of science, the search for truth, as the life of "reason." Second, it must be clearly understood that the morality of science has no sure ring of final authority, no more than customary morals. No one can say with any show of assurance that the morality of science is scientific. Unquestionably the ethical advances, the new ethical standards it has embraced, have proven remarkably productive in the neighborhoods of life to which they have been extended. But suppose a true social science is finally, though tardily, brought into being. Suppose a moral science with which to attack moral problems wherever they arise is finally brought about. What then?

May not experimental moral inquiry go beyond the work of arranging moral uses for the findings of the environmental and life sciences? Might it not, by providing the vehicle for determining the "ought" of moral judgments—even inside the halls of the non-moral sciences—in time incorporate the non-moral sciences within its horizon-wide ambit? We like to ponder the audacity of a brain trying to understand itself, analyzing its own action of which the very analysis is a part, a system trying to deal with itself, to lift itself by its own bootstraps. But man, in dealing with anything, is an aspect of a system dealing with itself. This is the condition of reality.[17]

OBJECTIVITY IN SCIENCE

It should be no surprise, after all that has just been said about science and morality, now to announce that the objectivity for which scientific endeavor is justly famous has been very poorly dramatized. Entirely the wrong emphasis has been made. The traditional and erroneous approach has been dualistic (referring to Locke's perception and to Descartes)[18] in terms of a dramatic contrast between a "subjective," connoting the emotional, the sinful, the conscientious, and an "objective," connoting the inhuman, the eternal, the perfect, the "rational." Such an "objectivity" is distinctly illusory.

"Physicists are composed of electrons and chemists of molecules, and biologists are notoriously organic," says C. E. Ayres.[19] They have *seemingly* been able to detach themselves from themselves. And so the jumped-at conclusion is that they have somehow transcended themselves and humanity. What they achieve as scientists, however, is not a denial of their own humanity, but an appeal to social, to public test. Collective test, of course, is something larger than the perspective of any individual, and it is impersonal in the sense that it waits upon a multitude of persons. The objectivity of science is operational; it refers "to the use of accepted rules of empirical research *after* the problem, the variables, and the experimental design have been decided upon." [20] It is more arduous than the mere collection of social opinion or "common" consensus. "When we attain objectivity it is in the course of organized inquiry itself, and is a result of the internal controls and self-corrective methods of inquiry." [21] This sort of objectivity harks way back to Galileo's method of systematically objectifying through experiment.[22] Impartiality (objectivity) must come from methods, not motives.

As physical science is not so "objective," the way that term is usually used, so social science is not so hamstrung by the curse of "subjective" subject-matter as is generally supposed. With objectivity understood to be found in scientific methods of public test, there remain no a priori reasons why a moral science cannot attain the same objectivity as physics. It will take a bit of doing, however. The maxims of Jesus, for example, may turn out to be the scientific equivalents of phlogiston. As John Dewey has said,

> Matters that are distinctively human and moral . . . will continue to be matter of customs and of conflict of customs until inquiry has found a method of abstraction which, because of its degree of remoteness from established customs, will bring them into a light in which their nature will be indefinitely more clearly seen than is now the case.[23]

To say that the social scientist has a particularly difficult task because he is "inside his material" [24] is to distort the situation with false abstraction. Neither social nor physical scientist can possibly get outside of his material. Man is an aspect of nature viewing itself. As Heisenberg says, "natural science does not simply describe and explain nature; it is a part of the interplay between nature and ourselves; it describes nature as exposed to our method of questioning." [25] The scientist's only hope is to be objective within the terms *possible* to him: the terms of a validating social method.

Nor is there an "exact" science. "Exactness" in science is a part of the mythology of "objectivity" as relating to the Perfect, and a part of the belief, which should have been done in by Hume's analysis, that the universe is somewhere written down in mathematical formulae that are only waiting to be discovered. In Max Born's explanation, "The matter stands as follows: Even the simplest mechanical process—a turning wheel, a swinging pendulum—starts with a small inaccuracy, and there is always a critical moment when this gets greater than the whole range of the movement.... If the original inaccuracy is reduced the critical moment is delayed; but it exists all the same. An absolutely accurate measurement would be a demoniac, not a human, achievement. It is not only conceptually an abstraction which may well be called nonsensical, but it also contradicts the laws of physics, namely the kinetic theory of heat ... which it would be absurd to doubt." [26] As Bridgeman puts it, "physical happenings are never mathematically sharp, but are always surrounded by an instrumental haze." [27]

The imprecision of the social sciences is imposed by the very structure of the universe. But it is aggravated because the social sciences are still in a primitive stage of development and, more importantly, because moral science is more intimate than are the physical sciences. There is nothing so personally one's own as one's purposes. Mature human purposes, desires, aspirations will be the material of a moral science.[28] The detailed nature of this subject matter helps hold back the development of such a science. No biologist can control the learning capacity of a rat and breed one capable of mastering a maze just so complex and no more; no chemist can control the alliances and configurations to be made by a given ion in a chemical soup; no physicist can control the leap of a particular election to see that, with the addition of energy to the atom, it jumps to this "ring" instead of that. Yet this seems to be exactly the refinement of detail that the moral scientist will have to confront in his field. There is a dim recognition of this behind the often expressed doubts as to the future of social science due to the "unique" character of the phenomena with which it deals. For example, Graham Wallas complains that "the chemist can make sure whether he is using a word in precisely the same sense as his predecessor by a few minutes' work in his laboratory. But in politics the thing named is always changing, may indeed disappear and may require hundreds of years to restore." [29]

The present state of the social sciences is ironically ambiguous. As Robert E. Park points out, "It appears that the more scientific psychology and the social sciences have become the more they are restricted to the study of those aspects of human life that are neither characteristically human nor social." [30] The trouble is that the social sciences have been slavishly aping the physical sciences and have thereby so far missed their golden opportunity. They have sought to treat the human, the social as material they could observe and manipulate from the "outside," when in fact they could be delving into the heart of what used to be called "the subjective," into character itself.[31] The social sciences have yet to capitalize on their great advantage over the physical sciences. Their supreme good fortune, challenge though it is, is that instead of rats, ions or electrons they have people to study, and people, notably, talk—more than that, they "express" themselves by action and inaction and through their unspeakable arts. Indeed, social scientists can study themselves.

Potentially, at least, all men are social scientists. They are supremely "inside" their material, if you will. It is the democratic aspect, in the sense of participation, that must be added to make social science social—or human.[32] The newly recognized reality in transaction will be accorded its proper deference when objectivity is worked out of the "subjective," intimate material of morality through an objectifying method involving the participation of the "inside man."

THE IMPORTANCE OF CHANGE AND PURPOSE IN EXPERIMENT

Much of the confusion about science and morals is due to a failure to perceive their essential relatedness. The congruity of science with morality is frequently challenged by the suspicion that the two fall in quite dissimilar categories. "Isn't science a way of knowing, an attempt to understand and explain the universe, to explain why it is as it is?" it is asked. "And isn't morality a governing sentiment or attitude that tries to organize humane relations among men? Isn't the term 'moral science' thus as incongruous as, say, a 'lavender geometry'?"

The answer to this question can be framed in terms of minds and matters, and the dualism between thinking and doing can be quite simply denied. A transactional understanding of the human enterprise, as has been said, contradicts belief in the mutual impenetrability of these two aspects of the worldly scene.

The nature or aim of the scientific method, however, is also in question. Care must be taken not to overemphasize the first of the three defining frames of reference for science (the body-of-knowledge interpretation) to the disregard of the second (the method-of-inquiry interpretation). The view accepted in the above question—that science is purely a body of knowledge accumulated for the sake of wisdom, to answer the Greek question, "Why?"—must be shaken before the mutual compatibility of "moral" and "science" can be recognized.

Briefly put, when science became experimental, "How?" came to displace "Why?" Scientists may unceasingly seek to push back the seemingly endless curtains shrouding a final "why?" But in fact their endeavors are supported by society only because they keep discovering "how." They have found, not being, but doing. Besides presenting a general method of how to solve problems, science describes how to *do*, what concrete steps to take to accomplish particular purposes. In chemistry, for example, each scientific fact can be traced back step by step to some worthwhile end, result, or activity, or at least to some promising (or once thought to be promising) connection with practical use. And, within the realms to which science has been restricted, it, in the process, presides over the refinement of purposes and makes possible the generation of new aims. This is well illustrated by the burgeoning of the plastics industry as a direct outgrowth of the chemistry lab.

Morality, meanwhile, having been almost totally excluded from scientific inquiry, remains in the do-nothing land of "why?". In John Dewey's words, "The great trouble with what passes for moral ends and ideals is that they do not get beyond the stage of fancy." [33] The "how" is missing. It has not yet been supplied by science.

The Greeks conceived of science mostly as a matter of aesthetic appreciation. They were keen observers and built up from direct perceptions magnificent speculative systems to provide descriptive answers to their great question. Such a construct as Empedocles' "effluence," for example, can even now be appreciated as a penetrating description of the finer mechanisms of perception. It describes the visual process in terms of a thin sheath or film flowing to the eye from off the surface of an object—as the slippery serpent sheds his skin. Alien though this is to us in the wake of waves, frequencies, and amplitudes, its aptness can still be directly felt with a very little effort and imagination—and quantum theory gives it a renewed imaginative respectability. It is especially at hand in the experiencing of beauty, as when absorbing the visual immediacy of an inspiring landscape. Empedocles' experience is still available to all who will take the time away from their stereotyped responses. The keen edge of his descriptions can be felt as truly profound observation. An "effluence" inflow can be directly experienced, restful and regenerative. Have you ever seen a small child shield his eyes from the "effluence" of your studying gaze at him?

The Greeks could hardly have anticipated twentieth century understanding of the nature, operation, and function of perception. The scientific achievement of the twentieth century has been a product of growth, a product of step by step refinement of technical instruments (lenses, valves, clocks, scales, microscopes, cyclotrons) used in experimental validation of hypothetical speculation. The Greeks took the material of perception "as is" (even in the case of perception itself, as illustrated above), as grossly presented to the senses, without attempting to alter or affect it, and proceeded on that basis to construct descriptive copies of the universe. They thereby grossly underrated the need to make allowance for the human purposes or procedures involved.[34]

Galileo wandered among the artisans and munitions workers of his day and united the activity of the artisan with that of the abstract system maker, deriving, or creating, therefrom an experimental method. The origins of modern science, including interest of scholars in technics, began in the thirteenth century, but it was Galileo who first used the new methods with real maturity and true effectiveness.[35] His success was the culmination of ten generations of inquiry into scientific methodology. Thenceforth scientific theorizing was no longer to stem from raw, unquestioned perceptions. Scientific thinking about things was to be done, not in the context of things watched, but in the context of things affected. Human purposes and procedures were incorporated into the process of knowing. Science became experimental and the backbone of its method became the deliberate changing of the subject-matter of direct perception through the use of tools, through the use of apparatuses. It has taken several centuries to understand that the instant inquiry is pursued by way of performing operations to see what will happen (rather than by settling in patiently to record and process data), at that instant inquiry is reoriented from what is to what does, and becomes charged with human purposes.

Social science has not yet notably achieved the transition from Ancient to experimental standing. In administration, for example, there has been an expectation that principles could be extracted by distillation, through classification and analysis of great quantities of individual case reports. In the days before the computer, however, efforts at such accumulation did not mount to such results, clearly indicating that a science could not be built up of such material.[36] The computer cannot be despised, however, and its service should not be discounted. It may, hopefully, bring forth a performance in the social field akin to the empirical tour de force of Kepler, summed up in his three laws of planetary motion—a brilliant achievement of compilation and correlation.

But, social science has not, on the other hand, taken the experimental alternative either. It has not made the liberating leap from fact-finding to fact-changing.

The transition is not far off, however. Thanks to the generosity of the Federal Government, educational institutions, and the Philanthropic Foundations, with their financial support of mass ("team," they call it) research, it will not be long before the social disciplines are so hopelessly and bewilderingly buried beneath the amassed debris of miscellaneous, eclectic information, before they are so overwhelmed by the free-form "pig pile" of scrambled facts, that the fabulous computer of the future will fail to dig them out. A new approach will then be embraced for the sake of the sanity of the inquirers if for no other reason. The ascendance of the computer, the giant descrambler, has apparently raised hopes in some quarters that trivia may be elevated to respectability by the sheer brawn of inanimate "thought." Very possibly automatic data processing may put off the day of reckoning —but not for long.

Search should be intensifying right now for the new approach. Soon the incredible frenzy for accumulating research detail must abate as men begin fully to understand the potential in experimental social science, to understand that perceptions, since they are human creations, can be made progressively more efficient, more and more capable of separating significance from trivia. An open-ended opportunity inheres in the experimental perspective—that of tampering with the universe instead of merely watching it—as a way of sharpening perception and understanding. The ability to perceive and rope out what is manifestly trivial, as well as what is manifestly false, is chartered by meaningful experimental framework. As men advance in knowledge, facts are ever more made than found.

We learn what something is, that is, what it does, by deliberately changing it or, which almost always comes to the same thing, by changing its intimate setting. Deliberate change is the novelty that transports us from the stage of relating qualities of direct observation to that of dealing with relations between such qualities; it marks the inception of experimental science. As John Dewey has said,

> *The* method of physical inquiry is to introduce some change in order to see what other change ensues.... Physical science did not develop because inquirers piled up a mass of facts about observed phenomena. It came into being when men intentionally experimented, on the basis of ideas and hypo-

theses, with observed phenomena to modify them and disclose new observations. [37]

As the key to experimental science, deliberate (that is, purposeful) change constitutes the essential difference between knowing as aesthetic enjoyment and knowing as a means of control—the sort of knowing that a moral science may hopefully yet evolve.

SELF-CONTROL IN INQUIRY

Intentionally introducing changes to alter the course of events permits the establishment of control relations within experience. Learning the effects of doing teaches *how* to do. Correlation of changes permits the insertion of purpose so that men can control results, so that they can determine consequences—in the sense of determining to read a book. A three-minute egg, as example, is a product of control following upon correlation of chemical changes with changes in temperature and changes in time. Any event, phenomenon, or happening—such as honesty, neighborliness, pride in workmanship, efficient performance, atomic bomb, negotiated wage formula—fits within a vast system of related events, as an aspect of transaction. When correlations between events are sufficiently known, the possibility of control is at hand. Scientific statements of these correlations become the instruments of control. By means of them future occurrence of the desired experience or event can be controlled. Obviously every time a new relation is established, additional possibilities of control are immediately at hand.

Control contrasts fundamentally and sharply with the haphazard, the logically accidental, with chance, drift, blind trial and error. To wrest a matter from the arms of chance is to gain enough know*how* that it may be subjected to the direction of human purposes. So a canoe is controlled by an Indian who knows how to control his muscles and his paddle; so a stew is controlled by a camper who knows how to tend his fire, or by a suburban housewife who knows how to manipulate the "control" panel of her stove; so the product of committee action is controlled by a group that knows how to think together. It should be noted that where tools—the paddle or the stove—are invented, some of the knowhow is built into the instruments of control and correspondingly less and less skill is involved. Once the engineer has built the dam and power house, or the atomic scientist has constructed the atomic pile, or the chemist has produced an all-purpose fertilizer, relatively uninformed people can control the conversion of mechanical to electrical energy, the conversion of matter to energy, the conversion of lawn to luxuriance. If ideas are understood to function as tools in the continuing life process of surviving and improving, control can be described simply as the mediation of tools (instruments) in bringing about desired results.

Control is not simply a product of knowledge, however. It is rather an aspect of the continuing and complex process of knowing. The reason we talk the other way around is that we continue to suppose purpose to be pure, to arrive from outside the process of knowing. Even the very language we use is an automatic carrier of this presupposition. So much so that inquiry only too easily accedes to the demand that its "product" be party to extraneous purposes.

Within scientific inquiry "control" refers to an organizing, a directing of trial procedures. Scientific inquiry is characterized as "controlled inquiry" when as a way of knowing it is no longer eclectic, haphazard, but has become instead a self-correcting, self-directing system.

The self-corrective character of modern experimental science results from the instituting of a two-way system of controls. Experiments are controlled by theory and theories are reciprocally controlled by experiment.

An experiment, to be theoretically controlled, must be conducted within a theoretically set framework. Since it must then test the solutions to problems *as* the solutions are presented and *as* the problems are formulated, its conduct and construction are necessarily very closely controlled by the theoretical formulation—the detail of control running *pari-passu* with the fineness of the theoretical construction. For example, a problem formulated in terms of blood, phlegm, choler and melancholy does not lead to answers in terms of microbes or to experimental search for microbes. The phlogistic theory of heat does not lead to recognition of the relatedness of combustion and respiration. In more recent theory, it is well known that quantum and wave descriptions have separate languages and different corresponding controls over experimental construction. The control of hypothesis over experiment is not unlike the control of a central theme over a set of musical variations. Perhaps, except in terms of simplicity, clarity, directness, systematics, and deliberateness, this sort of detailed control is only an extension of the familiar fact that ideas and images are conditioners of action—as prejudices and stereotypes affect social behavior—as belief in original sin short circuits inquiry into the anatomy of evil.

Scientific descriptions, once established, serve as immediate instruments of practical control. The formula CH_3CH_2OH, for example, permits a host of practical transformations in industry and laboratory that the word "alcohol" does not. First, however, the control of concept or theory over the organization of experiment must be had before the practice of manufacturing can carry on.

If experiment were not kept orderly, related, and precise by effective theoretical control, the reciprocating control of experiment over theory could not provide a shining pinnacle to the success of the scientific method. Scientific theories are tested, not by being laid alongside of and compared against sensed or experimental data, but by way of their deductive consequences. It is to experiment that modern science accords final control: a theory must abide by the determinations of experimental test. The "control" set up alongside the "demonstration" in a high school physics course, being identical with the "demonstration" set-up but for one simple difference, illustrates quite simply a deliberate organization of experiment to achieve control of theory. Evidence from experiment continuously and progressively controls the formulation and reformulation of theory—as more and more returns come in.

Theory is also controlled, and perhaps more subtly, through deriving much of its subject matter from prior experiment. It must formulate problems out of the difficulties, incongruities, discoveries encountered in experiment. Thomas Young's first production of interference bands by shining a beam of light through two closely spaced holes, and Philipp Lenard's discovery of the photoelectric effect are excellent illustrations of how experiment can furnish food for theory and problem reformulation. In addition, experimental control over theory is established by the necessity that problems and solutions be formulated in such fashion as to permit experimental corroboration. Here is an area of continual struggle, the fight against gremlins, unicorns, and thingifications.

The mounting spiral of reciprocal control raises thought to greater refinement of effectiveness, under control by the results of experimentally induced change, while it lifts change out of the haphazard practice of indiscriminate trial and error, bringing it under careful theoretical control. This is a way, then, of setting two instrument-of-control packages (ideas: changes), (theory: practice), (thought: action) off against each other in a special kind of transaction (a dialectic?) come to be known as "experimental scientific inquiry." Under such intimate control, theory is tightbound to the world of deliberate change that is experiment, in a spiraling system of mutual aid. Experimental science is thus an extension of the evolutionary process of self-betterment. In a sense, men have learned how to stand on their own shoulders.

The spiral characteristic of the process is a matter of historical, and in some cases prehistorical, fact. For example, the hammer can be described as having its start in the stick an early man used as improvement over arm and fist. At a later date the idea or vision of improving the stick with an attached stone, or, still later, with a metal head, stimulated experiment with improved design and materials. As new needs were related to new ideal possibilities, the old tool was used in fashioning the new, both indirectly by participating in the expansion of thinking and directly by use in the process of manufacture, pounding the head into shape and place both figuratively and forcefully. Crude tools or instruments confirm ideas or laws that enable development of better tools that are useful in refining ideas—and so round and round. The same circularity can be seen in the long history of growth in understanding of time and motion. Measurement of time in terms of motion has been very painfully and gradually refined, moving through the centuries from heartbeats to sun dials, water clocks and hour glasses, to pendulums and springs, to astronomical clocks with compensating pendulums, as progressively more precise techniques and instruments became available. As timing instruments were sharpened, the theory of motion was refined in a spiralling swirl of transaction between man and environment, measuring time by motion but understanding motion only on the basis of the idea of time—until relatively recently, following the rounding of twentieth century theory, there are machines that can show time in its turn to be affected by motion.

It should, further, be noted that somewhere in this self-corrective, bootstrap self-levitation way of improvement is the kernel of creativity.[38]

The system of circular controls becomes scientific—that is to say, it becomes experimental inquiry—when the reciprocal arrangement is made systematic, deliberate, and self-conscious. Many are the ideas that unilaterally influence practice, arrive by chance, and are apparently immune to kickback from practice. And many are the practices that persistently condition thought without further refinement or repercussion. What is added to make inquiry experimental is the free operation of kickback and repercussion, and the observation of it in transaction. In other words, what is added is an interest in improving the theoretical and practical instruments of control.[39]

It should be pointedly emphasized that human purposes within the pattern of inquiry are controlled very much the way theories are. Science does not simply discover ways of fulfilling antecedent human purposes. Some it furthers. But others it destroys as a mathematical proof of impossibility does in a yen to square the circle, to trisect the angle, or (as in the wake of Gödel's theorem) to prove from within a logical system that it is free of self-contradictions. For the most part, science neither affirms nor denies but rather alters and creates. Finding better ways and better opportunities is the surest path to transformation of purposes.

Control, as opposed to accident, is an aspect of knowing, an aspect of the knowing transaction which extends appropriate recognition to emotions, habits, sensations, purposes—in short, to character. A man, in scientific activity and purpose, is controlled, not by the facts or organization that limit him but by his knowings of those facts or their arrangement. Any understanding that describes science as progressing through a series of "crucial" experiments (in which new theories are conclusively and rationally demonstrated to be superior to old ones which thereupon are speedily and unambiguously displaced by the new) disregards the transactional condition of life.[40] Scientific inquiry involves the total man; it is rational, aesthetic, emotional, religious, and much else. Science continues the painful process of sorting understanding out of the booming, buzzing confusion, but tidiness and absolute efficiency, even in the accepting or rejecting of demonstrable experimental results, is more than can be seriously expected of human scientists—by anyone with a beginning acquaintance with the complexity of the human condition. In the scientific enterprise, what the system of reciprocal controls, of self-correction, does is to promote progressive improving of knowings so that, through control over action, purpose and thought, encountered difficulties of life may be overcome.

Reciprocal control within scientific inquiry (the integrating of theory and practice, par excellence) does not, without, as Joseph Ratner says, "cooking the facts," predetermine the final success of an experiment. Careful organization of experiment is extremely important, however. A well organized experiment, even if it fails, may bear fruit by indicating direction for further experimentation. Correspondingly, a well designed off-track hypothesis can, in a sense, be credited for all that has to be learned or discovered to discredit it. But it is the result of the experiment that really counts.

> If there are any methodological ultimates in scientific inquiry, then this is one of them: the outcome of the laboratory test is *not* determined by the apparatus as organized in the experiment *taken by itself*. When the outcome is thus determined, you have either the honest manufacturing of contrivances or machines—which is not a case of *inquiry;* or else you have the dishonest manufacturing or faking of evidences.[41]

The final control is the outcome of the experiment—which is a finding, a discovery, perhaps even a creation. (See p. 323.)

Since Einstein repealed the Newtonian wont of according mathematics absolute charge over theoretical development and turned that authority over to experimental findings, reciprocal control now amounts to transactional self-control of the situation itself—in which the scientist, the subject matter, the instruments, and the theories are only distinctions. In place of mathematical precision is left whatever uncertainty experiment uncovers—perhaps, incidentally, involving more contradiction within reality than men like to tolerate within thought, public or private.[42] But there is also left increasing opportunity for control over the fortunes of mankind.

The Cartesian scientific world of cause and effect was essentially timeless. It was curiously otherworldly in its insistence on inevitable sequence of effects resulting from prior states, quite as unworldly, in inversion, as the Platonic view of things goal-oriented toward ideal archetypal Forms. The calculus only surface-solved the problem of motion—by the clever device of breaking events down into segments infinite in number and infinitely small to be run across the macrocosm like a cartoon motion picture. It might well be said that the Cartesian world in fact avoided the reality of time by devious ingenuity. It projected a comfortable environment where events were precisely determinate. Doubtfulness, apart from human ignorance and failings, was not admitted as a possible condition of the universe. Prediction was said to be the goal of science.

Up through the nineteenth century this was a workable way of looking at the universe of the physical sciences. There was a quiet revolution, however, the day it was realized that in sub-atomic realms of inquiry the experimenter's acts of observation affected his subject matter or his observation of it.[43] (Abstractly speaking, this should not have been surprising since man so obviously swims immersed in his environment—and his observation plays a decisive role in any event. It would not have been surprising except for the perpetuated myth that essential man existed independent of and separable from environment.) Not only was the Cartesian mind-matter partition rendered meaningless by this symbolic discovery, but the idea of causality as the unifying order of the universe was undermined—because purpose, character, could no longer be blinked. Quantum physics has shown that the causal mode of description is only a very special way of interrelating natural occurrences. The progress of physical science itself has pushed on beyond the idea that everything is ultimately determinate in a great chain of causation. The imprecision of reality can be seen behind the fine mesh of exacting mathematics. Science has broken its old bounds, burst its own bonds. Now it may spread out into the full light of purpose, and, in receiving it, quantum by quantum, rejoice in a new dawning of character within the system, the fraternity of inquiry.[44]

It is not only we who are doubtful; it is the total situation, the very universe. So far as we know, we cannot escape our transactional condition. Something in the line of indeterminate causation seems to be the order of the future,[45] because neither free-will nor determinism is control oriented. Pure free-will theory does not make theoretical provision for any continuity in human decisions or actions—much less in their consequences—that can be relied upon. It thereby denies significant control over the future. Strict determinism arrives at the same rejection of control by leaving humanity to be unmercifully coerced by an imaginary inevitability. The prediction in which it glories is a magical idea of inevitable occurrences. In the Cartesian order of causality, prediction is as timeless as the mathematics which governs it.[46]

Prediction does have a place in today's science. It has proved particularly apt in astronomy where the simplicity of repetitions almost of itself promotes a prediction-based reading of the universe. Yet even here predictability is far from complete and its future not at all assured, for example in connection with the birth and death of stars. After a sufficient length of time the infinitesimal margin of immeasurability may produce discernibly erratic behavior even among the eternal constellations. It is worth noting that the field most acclaimed for success of prediction—astronomy—is the least conspicuous when it comes to control. Perhaps primary emphasis should be put, not on disparagement of prediction but on outgrowing prediction mentality and on the importance of learning how to bring purpose to bear so that prediction can be surpassed by control. Even astronomy ultimately aims in this direction.

With the beginning of thermodynamics in mid-nineteenth century, physical science set forth in a new direction away from prediction and determinism. Quantum physics has since consecrated probability description, forcing the abandonment of the predictable universe of Newton—although the old causal desriptions of classical mechanics remain as a limiting form of the quantum formulas when the number of quanta or particles involved is extremely large. The future is sometimes *practically* determined by the past, but it is never *completely* determined. There are still great regions of the universe that for practical purposes can be treated on the basis of the old causal laws. But strictly speaking there are no repeaters, now called "replications," in scientific experiment. While the business of repeaters is cause-and-effect, the business of experiment is consequences and corroboration. In scientific experiment there are repetitions of the same kind of process or with the same kind of subject matter, but there can never be identity. In science each experiment logically ends, as did the first experiment of the sort, in a discovery. A probability formula can have a measure of predictive reliability, but prediction on-the-average seems a rather weak echo of the resounding assurance we used to hear. As Robert Oppenheimer has observed,

> We have got back into physics with complete rigor, with complete objectivity, in the sense that we understand one another, with a complete lack of ambiguity and with a perfectly phenomenal technical success ... this notion that the physical world is not completely determinate. There are predictions you can make about it but they are statistical; and any event has in it the nature of the surprise, of the miracle, of something that you could not figure out.[47]

Prediction as an attempt to foretell is no longer a touchstone of scientific method.

In the place of the prediction of nineteenth century billiard ball science, the twentieth century reads "control." Prediction is when men's ideas, judgments, purposes are not mixed into the situation and are not instrumental to the outcome. Control is when they are. In other words, control is the substitute in transactional statement, recognizing the involvement of purposes in the natural world, for the prediction of the Cartesian mechanical universe. Today it must be clear that scientific laws "are means of *prediction* only as far as they operate as means of *production* of a given situation, through transformations of antecedent problematic material brought about by the operations to which they give direction." [48] If prediction is understood in such a restricted sense it becomes equivalent to a statement of control. The general form in which it appears is: "If you do so and so, such and such will happen." "If you perform this operation, institute this change, that consequence will follow." [49] Purpose (at one remove] is injected into the situation: "If you hit upon the purpose of lighting this fuse, and then carry out your purpose, we shall have a fine explosion!"

SUMMARY

When experimental science becomes scientifically involved in the real world of transacting human being-doings, it sheds the sham of purity and aloofness. Under broad-brimmed hat number three it assumes the aspect of collective enterprise and becomes therefore directly involved in the live world of moralities. As a collective enterprise science has a morality of its own which insists upon seeking truth with deep commitment while ever trying to prove its own findings at fault. As a collective enterprise it seeks objectivity in ability to communicate without ambiguity.

Experimental social science will enjoy the superb advantage that it may work from the "inside" at the detailed nature of human purposes before submitting to the rigor of objectivity—the collective test. In the end it may advance so far as to present the environmental sciences with scientific basis for or improvement upon the morality they call their own but dare not yet label "scientific" in itself.

The first experimental step of social science must stretch from what is to what does, from fact collecting to fact changing. The deliberate use of deliberate change, marking the beginning of an experimental science, is what permits control. When change experimentally arranged is presided over by theory tentatively held, a two-way system of reciprocal control between the concrete material under investigation and the conceptual instruments employed may be established. At this point in time the magic of prediction gives way to the miracle of control.

It needs only to add that control in inquiry is not *merely* a closing in on truth. When inquiry into morals is experimental it becomes, by the very transactional nature of the scientific inquiry itself, what has been sought since the dawn of conscience—genuine social control. And it meshes particularly appropriately into a rapidly changing world.

CHAPTER SIX

Social Control and the Third Scientist

*What makes man so interesting to study
is that he can see himself as a product
of nature capable of seeing itself as a
product of nature capable of. . . .*

ALMOST EVERY DAY SOMEONE PIOUSLY, AND AS PUBLICLY AS
possible, pronounces the central problem of the world to be, not
science, the father of bombs and untold other wonders yet unborn,
but the control of scientific discoveries—not inquiry but the leashing
of its product. To be sure, the mastery of causal connections in nature
—the product of scientific inquiry—has presented the human race
with tremendous moral dangers. But the reason is that the causal connections in human nature have not been mastered at the same time.
This is to say that science itself is the central problem. The problem is
in the imbalance of science, that science has not been extended beyond nature study to take in the universe of morality.

Science has left the push-buttons of the atomic future under thumbs
still guided by whatever purposes just happen to lurk in the minds of
the men of position before the "control" panel, purposes informed by
old and, most frequently, out-of-touch or obsolete moralities. Wisdom
or knowledge that leaves off in mid-passage is only half-wise. A way of
knowing that can carry only half-way to fruition, that is, to human
betterment, is in desperate need of fundamental reconstruction.

Every society has ways of fixing its members' beliefs, setting their
purposes, and bringing them into workable agreement on important
matters and basic facts. The one common feature that has characterized this building of consensus has been uncritical, unquestioning
acceptance. The individual is led to agreement through anti-enquiring
devices (folkways, traditions, customs, Teleological ethics, revelation,
charismatic leadership, oracular pronouncements of old men) and,

more often than not, an admixture of coercion. Never has the reaching of agreement been systematically self-critical and self-correcting—except to a minor degree (and then only for short periods in special areas) in political democracies practicing free speech.[1]

Modern science, on the other hand, has very recently begun to substitute a radically different way of fixing beliefs and gaining agreement on basic facts. In the root inquiry into physical matters there is now a steady, deliberate and established way of criticizing, questioning and thereby correcting both consensus and the way of arriving at it. The radically new self-correcting institutions of modern science mark the crucial turning point on the path out of the dark history of coercion. It is nothing less than a revolution in the way men fix their beliefs and achieve agreements. The coming task is to see that this self-correcting way is not forsaken, dissipated in the upper atmosphere of human nature among moral, social, political encounters, but instead is made into a systematic, wide-awake and intended way of achieving moral beliefs and agreements through the criticizing and questioning of assumptions, facts, and philosophies.

Having first selected a perspective stemming from the transactions of science, it now becomes clear that the experimental way of reciprocal control that has worked in environmental inquiry can also extend into social areas and lead on to social control. The next step will be to explore differences between social and environmental sciences and to suggest that because man is naturally transactional, knower and known being undissociable, the reciprocal controls of social science must come to life among the moral Self-controls of practical life and must evolve into a decisively democratic way of progressively enriching human life, projecting the promise of an Osiris-like rebirth of character—character to be put together by the Isis of deliberate effort.

EROSION OF SOCIAL CONTROL

By the time of the first perception of purpose and the discovery of character—roughly five thousand years ago—men had already, through common sense discoveries, brought appreciable segments of environmental conduct within the province of human control. Indeed, exercise of purpose in control of natural events was an important, and probably an indispensable, forerunner of the perception of purpose itself. The reflective morals begun by the Egyptians, again the product of common-sense discovery, led to the beginnings of deliberate human control over human conduct. Unfortunately, Egypt soon slipped backward into sacerdotalism, not far removed from the magic spells and organic customs which reflective morals had arisen to displace.

Environmental control has not, so far as we know, been subject to the periodic reverses that have been the fate of moral control, although there are still areas where it has not been effectively asserted and magic holds sway. Severe droughts, for example, are still exorcized by prayers offered in the churches—no doubt because science has not learned to control the occurrence of rain, to turn it on and off. The ineffectiveness of prayer is more easily blinked when there is no working substitute at hand.

Once an effective control of environment has been developed, it is seldom, it seems, lost or abandoned; it is rather, if anything, doggedly extended and improved. In clear contrast, social control—human control over human conduct—is marked by a history of periodic reverses.

This may in part be explained by two basic complications that have left moral inquiry in circumstances distinctly less favorable than those surrounding environmental inquiry:

(1) Moral control is eroded by the sands of time. Purposes (a central concern of moral control), constituting as they do the very sinews of time, as will be asserted at greater length below, are brought taut as time stretches relentlessly on, and are finally strained beyond the elastic tolerance point of no return. Ways of controlling human conduct, the product of moral discoveries of common sense, become coercive with age because time is a genuine and intimate aspect or dimension of the moral "equation." Moral life is beset with creations, fraught with emergents, apparently studded with indeterminants. In contrast, physical discoveries have, until roughly the twentieth century, dealt with material too stodgy, too inert, too macroscopic to be discernibly affected by time. Physics, after three hundred years of scientific inquiry, has only now confronted problems analogous to our everyday moral problems where the dimension of time is seen to be appreciably involved. The analogy between the discovery behind the principle of uncertainty (that if we try to ascertain the position of a particular electron its velocity becomes indeterminate, and vice versa) and the difficulties encountered in the study of human being-doings is too apparent to be missed.

(2) The ineffectiveness of coercion (false efforts at control) is less immediately apparent in dealings with people than in dealings with environment. To hark back to an earlier statement, every action involving people generates a transaction, not simply an equal and opposite reaction. But more, there is a special tolerance involved. The tolerance apparently built into the universe and now found in physics to be focused in the extremely large and the exceedingly small, seems to have established a special beachhead in moral realms. Abuse environment and it strikes right back; abuse human nature and it sulks for a time

before retaliating, sometimes in subtle ways. Try to control a river with a whip and it rises to drown the credulous; try to control a race of men in an institution of slavery and hundreds of years elapse before the credulous are immersed in civil war. A faulty dam is soon destroyed; an obsolete moral maxim lives relentlessly on and on and on.

Perhaps this tolerance can be traced to man's special place in evolution, to the fact that, as Erich Fromm points out,

> man, in contrast to the animal, shows an almost infinite malleability; just as he can eat almost anything, live under practically any kind of climate, and adjust himself to it, there is hardly any psychic condition which he cannot endure, and under which he cannot carry on. He can live free, and as a slave. Rich and in luxury, and under conditions of half-starvation. He can live as a warrior, and peacefully; as an exploiter and robber, and as a member of a cooperating and loving fellowship. There is hardly a psychic state in which man cannot live, and hardly anything which cannot be done with him and for which he cannot be used.[2]

Such tolerance is very much like an ability to live with defect or disease, dormant yellow fever or incipient tuberculosis, without actually succumbing to it or becoming sick. "Apathy" is the name sometimes given to one of the special shielding cushions man raises to deflect need for immediate reaction.

Unless we are to assent to continuation of the history of periodic moral reverses, these two circumstances—the erosion of moral control by time, and human tolerance of moral coercion—must be squarely faced. Genuine moral control will entail coming to terms with them.

MORAL RELATIVITY—NO PLAYTHING, MORALS

The study of environment gradually arose, through a number of centuries, from the level of common sense, finally attaining the full stature of experimental scientific inquiry in the seventeenth century —thenceforth achieving ever more and more effective environmental control through a reciprocal control system of self-correcting knowing. The moral disciplines, however, have continued to limp along on the level of ancient common sense, leaping here and there to new discoveries of social control but lagging lamentably between leaps.

The present era seems to fall into such a period of lag. The system of Natural Law, which once gave conspicuous service, as for example in the control of international behavior during the time of Grotius and his immediate followers, and in the control of American behavior during and immediately following the American Revolution, has now degenerated to lip service and has not been supplanted by any system of moral control of comparable generality or acceptance. In recent times there have been occasional instances of moral progress, as evidenced by the Point Four program, the Marshall Plan, the Status of Forces agreements, the voluntary abandonment of empire and exploitation, the Supreme Court's end-of-segregation ruling, the "one man, one vote" decision. But for the most part we have fallen into a condition of moral relativity characterized by a great variety of jarring orthodoxies, beliefs, and creeds, each with its following, but none pursued with much assurance or commitment, except by a small and intense band of ardent partisans.

A condition such as this calls, as has so often been said, for the creation of a moral science. Perhaps, indeed, society had to come to a state of moral relativity before development of a moral science could be possible because socially acceptable, before experimentation would be permitted. One of the notable things about Teleological ethics—ethics tied to immutable ends—is that when they cease to control they begin to limit or to coerce. Breaking loose from the coercive straightjacket may well have been prerequisite to the instituting of experimental procedures.

Ironically enough, in view of the pervading reluctance to launch into a self-correcting scientific effort in moral inquiry, the alternative, the common-sense approach to knowing, is peculiarly unsuited to the realm of morals. Trial-and-error playing with things just to see what will happen—the chief common-sense or non-scientific way of stockpiling information—is not appropriate to moral affairs. Men do not light-heartedly toy with their own purposes—purposes are too intimate, too personal and thus too precious—though people have not been notably scrupulous about playing with the purposes of others, in evidence whereof we have an army of advertisers and public relations experts. The fact remains that the trial-and-error approach to purposes has never been freely espoused—at least, never since the discovery of character. We simply do not take purposes, desires, interests, values, and turn them over, shake them, thump them, bounce them, bite them in random succession to see what will happen, to see what a change in perspective will reveal them to be. They are too dear.

> To play is to let purpose wander free;
> Who play with purpose court insanity.

Reflective, common-sense moralities are generally extracted or compiled more or less after-the-fact from gross everyday experiences that have just happened to happen. Growing out of direct experience, they tend to begin as effective systems of social control. As they age and harden into traditional morality and Teleological ethics, however, they become more and more unreal—except during periods of extreme social stability—since times change and the reality to which they originally related inevitability slips out from under them. Their control thereupon silently shades into coercion. A vivid example is the degeneration of the once bright virtue of charity from a controlling and socially stabilizing moral institution to a coercive relationship marked by resentment on one side and hypocrisy on the other.[3] In this case, as in the many others, the coercion becomes manifest in the form of felt injustice. Incidentally, who is to say with firm assurance that such fine virtues as trust, good faith, respect for the dignity of man . . . may not be encumbrances in the world of tomorrow, or perhaps even traits of suicidal propensity and proportion? (Trust and good faith, by the way, are part of the equipment of gangsters, bootleggers, spies, and dope peddlers.)

The obviousness of coercion is to a great extent concealed by the ponderous tolerance of social life for moral abuse—a tolerance not found in environmental events. Our common failure to appreciate the fact that we can improve upon the obsolete moralities we inherit further helps to conceal their coercive effects. In the present day the coercive aspect of outmoded moralities is also hidden by their very multiplicity. When they are rendered ineffectual by enervating competition with each other, their coercion sometimes reduces to a simple failure to control where control is badly needed. Coercion is then naively blamed on happenstance.

It may be that current conservatism and sobriety about things moral stem from the traditional moralities which oppress mankind and which give a jealous and inordinate value and pride to personal dignity, to character continuity, to possession of one's own soul. However, neither pride in self-identification, respect for inherited traditional moralities, nor reluctance to trifle through trial-and-error with precious human purposes should be permitted to interfere with the development of an experimental way of knowing in the realm of morals. The cornerstone of such a moral science will be the deliberate, controlled changing of purposes. Moral science will differ from trial-and-error methods in that change will be related to hypotheses that are not play but are rather the serious business of trying to resolve stubborn problems through knowing. It will differ from traditional moralities in that through the self-corrective trait characteristic of experimental science it will avoid the peril of obsolescence and consequent coercion.

SOCIAL SCIENCE IS GREEK

We do, of course, have social sciences today. They are, however, for the most part, still Greek. They have not remarkably risen above the observational level of Aristotle's *Politics*, for example. It is possible that someday his *Politics* will appear to be the same clearly fanciful nonsense that his *Physics*—based on binary combination of hot, cold, wet, and dry with earth, water, air, and fire—today appears to be. Even Hippocrates, whose theory and practice of medicine was far in advance of intervening epochs until close to modern times, pursued—as it appears to us—an oddly passive procedure. For all his accurate information about bones, muscles, the general structure of the eye and ear and the chambers of the heart, he derived his wisdom without dissecting human cadavers and with scarcely a thought to chemical experimentation on animals. Systematic human dissection came much later. Aristotle apparently did practice vivisection in his zoological studies—not, however, with an experimental attitude, but only the better to observe.[4]

Descriptive rather than experimental in character, today's social sciences still deal with the material of perception as directly offered, immediately available to the observer. Except in rare instances, they have not yet got behind the gross qualitative characteristics of things as commonly, originally, observed; they have not become engaged in changing, transforming the subject matter of direct perception. Instead, they seem committed to accepting what is directly observed as final, elemental, and are prepared to treat their gross material only in thought—by way of description, classification, explanation, disquisition, logical analysis. This begins to explain why in the last twenty years political science, for example, in sharp contrast to physics, astronomy, or biology, has produced no new discoveries so clearly fundamental that all professionals in the field must know about them and try to adjust to their impact.

Experimental inquiry, in contrast, treats the values and qualities of direct perception as the raw material of problems. It seeks to uncover the relations underlying their occurrence, the relations by means of which their occurrence can be controlled. The relations upon which depend occurrences perceived as "water" or "lightning," for example, are not themselves directly observable. They are ascertained by experimental instigation of observable changes—chemical reactions, keys on kites. Deliberate inauguration of change is the foundation of the modern scientific method of determining the significance of directly observed qualities. As studies in the psychology of perception have amply shown,[5] there is a wealth of material behind the direct social perceptions (perceptions of other people's purposes) and illusions of daily life that can be brought within a system of experimental scientific inquiry.

Today's social sciences have not yet become involved in the scientific business of deliberately initiating change in order to find out "what makes things tick." They are sciences only in the Greek sense of organized bodies of knowledge accumulated from experience in particular fields. We hear from Lisle, France that a consultant to manufacturers has obtained a ninety-five percent success in selecting executives and engineers by relating the length of their thumbs to the length of their ears. It will be noted that as sciences sociology, anthropology, and politics are not finely distinguishable from such organized bodies of knowledge as embalming, horse racing, or philately. Even when people are studied in the gross like a solution of ions in a chemical soup (for example, the statistical work in many corners of economics, public opinion research or attitude surveying, much ethnological and sociological research, linear programming and other extensions of the theory of games in administration, space and location studies of the young regional science), unless change is experimentally instigated for the purposes of inquiry, all that is achieved is a refined Greek science of immediate qualities, with a little mathematical incantation thrown in for good measure.

Sometimes, when they tire of mere description, classification, logical manipulation, and construction of would-be universal propositions, today's social sciences do foray into the field of social change. Unfortunately, however, this typically happens at the end instead of the beginning of inquiry. There is occasionally a limited follow-through as a social scientist lingers to observe the consequences of policy change. The significant question, however, is whether these changes are tied to hypotheses that are in turn tied to higher level generalizations with strong enough logical knots (the way of science) that the testing of an hypothesis can result in improving or correcting the broader generalizations. And this is the question seldom asked by the social scientist. The Michelson-Morley experiment was, in contrast, well knotted into abstract generality, with the result that failure to measure the absolute motion of the earth led to the downfall of the ether theory.

The scientific procedure is to develop hypotheses that are logically linked to high level generalities, or abstract concepts and then to begin the inquiry by deliberately changing some manageable element so as to test the hypothesis and, indirectly, through logical linkage, the abstract concepts. For example, experiments with particles that emit light with a specific period or that are radioactive and decay with a definite mean life time, have demonstrated that time does dilate with increase in velocity and have served to confirm the special theory of relativity. Most of the work of physics in the last fifty years has been of this nature —filling in the implications of relativity and quantum theory. These latter have been, in other words, presiding over (controlling) the elaboration of detailed knowledge. If, however, the results of the experiments with oscillations at high velocity or of any of many others had been negative, or had turned in an oblique direction, there would have been important theoretical adjustment to make—as when Michelson and Morley dispelled the ether of nineteenth century theory or when, as the story goes, the simultaneous thuds of Galileo's ten- and one-pound spheres, landing at the foot of the Tower of Pisa, sounded the death knell of Aristotelian physics.

The social sciences have developed the habit of doing what is called "research"—sometimes very complex, computerized and all— then classifying and distilling and, in the end summarizing from a mass of collected information. At this point, at the end of inquiry, recommendations are made—but seldom in the form of hypothesis. And changes are made by someone else unconnected or remotely connected with the inquiry—a layman interested in solving a "practical" problem but oblivious to the abstract aspect. The change is therefore not sensitively controlled by hypothesis even if hypothetically propounded. The occasional pause of the social scientist to remark from the outside the consequences of policy change is more likely to follow in the spirit of verifying a research finding than in an effort to test an hypothesis and confirm an abstract concept. Such social scientific procedure is more akin to the empiricism of a Kepler deriving laws of planetary motion from painstaking analysis and correlation of keen astronomical observations rather than to the speculative inquiry, the axiomatic theoretic construction, of a Helmholtz or an Einstein.

Rarely can social inquiry be said to have been so arranged as to arrive at a significant test of hypotheses, much less of high level abstractions. Typically, the pattern is this: after extensive inventory, exhaustive research, and extreme analysis, the social science research team turns its findings over to the Department Head, the General Manager, the Congress and says, "We have looked at every possibility and counted all contingencies. Here is our recommendation. Do this and the world is your oyster. It will honor your memory as Oysters always do." Or it says, "We have studied this from the Left and from the Right—there being no Center. We have done our job and taken all perspectives into account. Now *you* must make a VALUE judgment. Here are seven things you can do depending on which one of the seven cardinal VALUES you endorse. And here are the seven corresponding consequences. Good luck!" The most the team has done is to gather a lot of common-sense. And where inquiry stopped it should have begun. Policy and planning can become crucial elements in the experimental instituting of change.[6]

THE LIMITS OF PREDICTION

Instead of prescribing changes in an experimental effort to discover the nature of things through observation of what happens under controlled conditions, the recipes of social science have characteristically taken the form of prediction. "My studies of the stockpiling of inventories indicate that there will be a major recession by next summer. Congress should do thus and so to avoid disaster." "Judging from past experience I can tell that the Federal Reserve Board will raise the rediscount rate in November. Get your loan now!" "I have asked a representative sample how they will vote. Too bad for Truman!" "My computer says the Twins will win the World Series." Well, we have learned to look with a doubting eye at the pretensions of social predictions as nowadays propounded, although there are still those who attribute inaccuracy only to imperfections in research techniques[7]—unfortunately in much higher percentage than those among the physical scientists who expect to resolve indeterminacy with patience and precision. Physicists have outgrown the "eternal" hope that was a byproduct of long steeping in causality, but it may be more difficult for scientists dealing more directly with people and their ways—because the habit of predicting human action is reinforced in each observer by the simple fact that he has a way of knowing what he himself is going to do. It is easy to forget to ask the other fellow about his choice.

The fact is that where people are involved the future can only be "predicted" when it can be controlled. And then only he can "predict" under whose control it lies. But this is cheating because predicting, by common usage, refers to the situation where the ideas, purposes, judgments of the prophet are not mixed in the situation and are not instrumental. It is like predicting "heads" when you have controlled the situation with a two-headed coin.

Judging from customary use of the term, much "predicting" done in scientific inquiry is cheating. The scientist predicts contingently: "If I do this, that will happen." But this is *control*!

The difference between prediction and control is illustrated in the following not unusual collective bargaining situation. In preparing to agree to change from piecework to an hourly rate pay plan, management suggests that the change should be accompanied by a slightly reduced wage-earning average because production can be expected to suffer somewhat when direct piece-work incentive is gone. (This is prediction.) Labor replies that the total of wages paid in the shop should remain unchanged and it should be up to the workers to see that production doesn't drop off. (This is control.)

It must take an extraordinary faith in nineteenth century determinism, or an extravagant disregard of the independence of individual human Selves to suppose that human affairs can be predictable. Generally speaking, the lower the form of life in the scale of evolution, the more reliable a contingent prediction (of the sort: If I do this, I will get hurt) will be. Almost any yellow jacket will try to sting when it sees that you are interfering with its movement; different snakes will tolerate different amounts of teasing before they will strike; some dogs bite in retaliation to a random gesture, others only for self-preservation. But with human being-doings, there is just no way of telling, except that it is easier to foretell the actions of highly irrational people— cases of advanced insanity, infants before the age of two, emotionally wrought mobs. It simply is not true that the actions of men are predictable, except perhaps where reference is to a condition of ironbound habit or to unthinking subservience to primitive custom conceivable only in remote tribes that have not yet seen the "dawning of conscience." Consider, for example, the complexities, injustices and impossibilities of the attempt of the loyalty security program of the 1950's to judge job fitness on the basis of predicted future conduct!

Physics has replaced cause (purpose) with colorless probabilities as the innate qualities of elementary particles. Having lost law abiding microcosmic individual detail, it has gained a pattern of probability in the mass. No longer laws of individual events; instead, laws of probability of events. Correspondingly, politics has turned from the laws of individual events, insisting on the freedom of purpose from the causal shackles of classical mechanics (now recognizable as the product of the imputation of human determination into nature), and has tried the probability approach of opinion polls (and later, but no less faultily, the approach of "attitudinal surveys"). But it comes up with the spectre of unpredictable man. Mindful matter makes its own laws. The erratic, firefly flashings of human purposes, the twinklings of indeterminate intentions—unlike the dithyrambic scintillations in unlawful sequence of colors emitted by atoms heated to incandescence —obey no permanent probability laws. They accept no unbreakable laws fixing frequency with mass action according to canons of a quantum theory. They accept no laws that are not the products of intention itself and therefore structured, formulated from within, from behind the secrecy that so far shrouds the elemental character of purpose, intention, from behind the uncracked sheath that guards the microcosmic stone of purpose and even now remains impervious to the probings of science.

SOCIAL SCIENCE IS AN "INSIDE" JOB

The "self-fulfilling prophecy" has many times now been raised as a final limit to the achievement of the social sciences. An instance of the "self-fulfilling prophecy" is clearly displayed in the impact of the prophecies of the FHA and American lending institutions on the prospects of urban renewal. Believing, in the fullness of their wisdom, that depressed neighborhoods will continue to deteriorate, these financial institutions have been reluctant to approve housing or improvement loans in deteriorating areas. By this reticence they, in turn, helped bring about the very results they predicted. A like mechanism, more properly called a "self-defeating prophecy," invalidates industrial personality tests. The predictions of the examiners are confounded when the job applicants become aware of the ideal personality that is sought and gain a fair familiarity with the construction of questionnaires. Unquestionably the generalizations of social scientists, as they are now coming off the presses, do tend to fulfill or destroy themselves. Of course knowledge of a "law" of social science by the people whose behavior it "predicts" may promote the "law" or, alternatively, render it inoperative! To understand this is merely to accept the fact that ideas have consequences. Knowing makes a difference. The fancy name for the phenomenon is "epistemological feedback." Didn't the Malthusian theory help defeat its own prophecy?

Notice the similarity to the situation of the atomic scientist when he finds that the attempt to take account of the disturbance he makes in a system under observation results in frustration of the means of observation as means of observation. There can be no observation that does not involve a transaction, and the effect on the object of observation is bound to show up in crucial cases. There can be no measuring device that does not impinge upon the matter measured, whether a yardstick is used or a photon of light. Physicists the world over have stoically accepted the impossibility of simultaneous exact measurement of, for example, the position and momentum of an "elementary particle." According to the quantum theory, the idea that what is observed would be the same whether it were watched or not, holds as an approximation only in the realm of large objects. The microcosmic world is quite a different matter. And this would include the world of purpose and introspection. But social scientists continue to cling, Sinbad-like, to belief in the magical possibility of determinism. It is only the Sinbads and the Sleeping Beauties, the fictitious and the overly-suggestive, who dutifully do, against their wills, what they know (because it has been foretold) they will do. This is sheer fatalism. It marks a failure to understand the transactional matrix of the human condition.

The fact that increased knowledge of human nature leads to unpredictable modification of human nature need not, however, be a cause for lamentation. Neither need it be the occasion for premature burial of social science in a fit of despair. The findings of an experimental science are not independent of the nature of its subject matter—and the subject matter of the human sciences inevitably includes the knowings and purposings of ordinary human being-doings. To deplore the "self-fulfilling prophecy" as a limit to social science is to regret the impossibility of an aristocracy of savants presiding over a sheepish populace with "scientific," dialectic cunning.[8] A true experimental science would have no need to manipulate people through maneuvers of propaganda and ideological appeal.[9]

A moral science will abjure the habit of prophecy, prediction as an essentially magical approach which attempts to treat subject matter disinterestedly from the "outside" while glorying in the false pride of "objectivity." Its hope and its eminent potential reside in the extension of control, not in prediction. Some day it will seem incredible that the twentieth century could have hoped to develop sciences in the realm of social affairs without dealing with purposes experimentally, without subjecting purposes to deliberate, on-purpose changes. We would not consider the astronomy of telescopes and interferometers a science if we could go out and tap the stars and drop them into test tubes. (Incidentally, the new neutrino astronomy has begun to do just that, literally placing pieces of the core of the sun into earthly test tubes.)

The environmental scientist's concern with the "human equation," his proper concern to eliminate or neutralize what for the purposes of his inquiry are considered irrelevancies, has been improperly carried over into the provinces of moral inquiry, which should be investigating not only experimenters' errors, foibles, and tendencies, but the full range of the impact of human purpose. There is a difference between prediction and control that becomes clear here. The former tries to anticipate, to obviate, to avoid, or balance out the impact of purposes; the latter to work with purposes toward an unknown future in the process of being created.

Note that this distinction holds equally well when the prediction is structured around the anticipating of purpose.

If the practitioners of present social disciplines insist upon calling themselves scientists, the only valid comment to make about them is that in their zeal to be amoral, "objective," they have avoided coming into experimental contact with an essential part of their material—human purposes. The fact that the moral scientist cannot escape being "inside" his material gives scope to unlimited creative possibility—provided his "inside" job is pursued objectively, in the sense of "publicly," "impartially," and without excluding environment. It particularly heightens the possibility of coming to close grips with problems of social control.

CONTROL OF PURPOSES

Purposes are the only determining phenomena we know. They prefix the results of conduct. They constitute the causal link between start and finish, between "cause" and "effect."[10] Indeed, the aboriginal beginning of the idea of determinism must have been an abstraction from human intent—from a savage's *determin*ation to crack a nut—rather than a deduction from metaphysical beliefs of destiny.

The earliest idea of causality seems to have come as an imputation of social organization into nature, the causal bond being thought of as a realization of justice.[11] The type-pattern is first to interpret the physical universe as a (cosmic) society, then to read back constraints of cosmic conscience, so to speak, in the name of "causality"—a sequence, incidentally, repeating the pattern, observed in chapter 4 where the sun god was seen to have been extrapolated from the ideal pharaoh of the super state and set loose to send back transcendental versions of moral code. Among the many specific illustrations of such imaginary construction are the many gods of history, the crystalline spheres of the Greeks, the luminiferous ether of the nineteenth century.

Behind the pattern and basic to it is the feeling that human purposes produce results[12] or that, as it used to be said, "by acts of our wills we cause phenomena to occur." What would be more natural than to take the only causing agent we know and extrapolate it to explain the happenings beyond our control?[13]

There has been a reversal in the direction of influence through analogy since the seventeenth century. After millenia of anthropomorphic interpretations of environmental conduct, a turnabout has taken place in deference to the authority of experimental science. Instead of deriving cosmos from purpose or from morality by analogy, men began to take morals by analogy from discoveries of scientific experiment about the functioning of the physical world—though it must be admitted that the analogy from science was sometimes, too, merely a return or rebound from an analogy originally received from social sources.

This change in direction of analogical indebtedness is partly described in terms of the "devalorization of being," the now classic partition of fact from value, the deliberate expulsion of such moral ideas as harmony, aim, perfection from scientific thinking. Cause, having been forced into nature in an early age, returned to morals with a vengeance at a time when men in the Western world were stirring anew, flexing their imaginations and causing the happening of important events. It came back reinforced from scientific speculation, in the form of determinism. Values were sternly restrained from interfering with the facts of science, so the story goes. But science in its turn was freed to exert maximum influence in the form of analogies freely projected.

The influence of this great partitioning event is so considerable that a scientist is able to admit indebtedness to social or political ideas only with a certain feeling of shame—for example, in recognizing the debt of evolution to the idea of progress, or the debt of the idea of force to the projection of "will" or sense of effort, or the debt of human pride to the assumption that nature is comprehensible. The other direction-flow of analogy, however, has been quite respectable for some time now—for example, in acknowledging the source of social Darwinism in evolution, or the source of social determinism in the determinism of classical physics, or the source of the social scientist's aloof, outside-observer approach to his material in the quantitative methods of the older physical sciences.

It is to be hoped that the modern direction in flow will continue just a bit longer before the next shift comes and analogies derive predominantly from moral science.[14] Perhaps, if it does continue, we shall be able to make a break from determinism in all realms of life, as has now quite cleanly been done in physics. Eddington says,

> If the mathematical argument in my mind is compelled to reach the conclusion which a deterministic system of physical law has preordained that my hands shall write down, then reasoning must be explained away as a process quite other than that which I feel it to be. But my whole respect for reasoning is based on the hypothesis that it *is* what I feel it to be.[15]

—or that it *does* what I feel it to do. For this reason, if for no other, an ultimate determinism *must* be denied. Behind the determinism of human intent is the indeterminism of man "making up his mind." Behind the determinism of Newtonian physics is the indeterminism of quantum mechanics. It is only very recently that science has freed us from the webs of causality spun out of human intention, oversimply imputed into nature, and then looped back to snare human intention itself. It is no longer necessary to violate the laws of physics in order to be free, purpose can be accepted as not a product of, but a link in, the great chain of being-doing.

If more minute sanction is felt to be needed than that given by the quality of direct experience which all men share with Mr. Eddington, it can be found in the current descriptions of modern physics—though one hesitates to make much of it because so much moral and religious nonsense has been produced by free-will boosters using analogy from the indeterminacy of the atom to justify supernaturalisms of all sorts. Photons are emitted by luminous atoms at erratic or random intervals. The fact that the human eye can detect the incidence of a very few photons would immediately imply that the biological organism is tuned to indeterminacy; it performs the amplifying function of a sounding board for random events. The physical basis of freedom may be small in first instance but a human multiplier may make mountains out of molecules—as a Geiger counter, triggered by a mere single radioactive "elementary particle," may make audible sound.

The analysis of perception with which this book began insisted that perceptions were as much man-made as man-found. Now we observe that perception of elementary processes is uncaused, undetermined. Between these two statements lies the role of purpose. Somehow human freedom is found in the conjunction of perception-making purpose and elementary indeterminacy.[16]

Purposes pop up as building blocks of consciousness. They support the stability which is human character. Through the continuity called "intention" they give structure to reality. Without them there would be no conscious sense of time.

Intentions are the cohesions, the sinews of time. They cannot be reduced to a mathematics of infinitesimals, to a calculus which is a succession of instants or locations. They span both duration and extension. They are the strings that draw character into coherence.[17] They are the link between cause and effect; and choice may be described as a node along this string of determination, a knot on the sinew of time.

It is the possibility of working with purposes to develop a system of social control that is exciting. Being themselves the immediate instruments of control, the antithesis of chance, of the haphazard, the instruments that smoothe the discontinuity of life, purposes are obvious candidates for incorporation within a reciprocal control system of knowing, within a system of experimental science.

Men are not born with purpose. They are educated to it. Purpose is a creation in, of, by, and for society. A two year old child, for instance, has not yet developed a bonafide set of purposes. Tell him, "Don't put those marbles in your mouth," and he agreeably answers, "I won't," seemingly with every intention in the world of obeying. Yet the next minute he pops one in. It isn't that he intends to "be bad," or that he is a slave of habit, or that he didn't "really" intend what he said. It is just that he hasn't matured enough for purpose to flower, to be the element of Self-control his elders expect it to be. It is even possible, parenthetically, that the biologist's maxim "ontogeny recapitulates phylogeny" describes the process of development well beyond the moment of birth, that the moral development of infant into man tends to repeat the moral development of the species.

Animal and even botanical processes may possibly some day also be legitimately described in terms of purpose. For example, the purpose of the plant as it turns its face to the sun, or the intention in the way a weed seed hitches a ride on man's socks to assault a virgin field. Perhaps what is seen from afar through the telescope of time as evolution is essentially purpose when viewed from near at hand. The polished refinement of human perception—the peak performance of evolution at its near end—may well be purpose-entrained, purpose-persuaded. All this may sound obscurantist, whimsical, or mystical for now. It is intended, however, to indicate the breadth of rethinking that is needed to accommodate the emerging understanding of human nature, coming out of transactional description and investigation, that will mature in the trans-computer world.

In a beginning study of purpose among men, we shall have to accept purpose as a social product. And this in the end may leave us not so far removed from the plants after all, if it is remembered that society is not contractual—as we Westerners so easily believe—and that the group is as primordial as humanity itself and the very condition of individuality.

When, as time goes on, the boy who sucked marbles without intention begins to develop a coherent set of purposes and runs athwart his grandfather, the old man remarks: "There's a stubborn little cuss. What a character!" It is this fact, the fact that we are continually building character, that makes an experimental moral science possible. A Self is a living, growing, changing thing, always in the business of making, creating, discovering itself through the transactions of life. There is no ready-made, pre-cast essential man behind the facade of becoming. There is instead a loose bundle of tendencies, attitudes, habits, beliefs, impulses, sometimes in mutual opposition, sometimes mutually inconsistent but balanced in mutual disregard, sometimes actively grouping themselves into patterns that make up character. As long as a Self is not mistaken to be a completed entity, a ready-made soul, Self-control can be genuinely possible. It becomes an adventure in quest of a grander character, a more satisfactory, more integrated Self yet to be. As Norman Cameron explains it,

> All that we mean by *self-control* is the regulation of an incipient or developing reaction by an organized self-reaction. Both the incipient (or developing) reaction and the self-reaction that regulates it arise, of course, in response to the same stimulating situation—excepting in those instances in which the incipient or developing reaction itself provides the stimulation for the regulating self-reaction. In both cases, however, we have clearly before us examples of the control of human conduct developing within human behavior itself.[18]

Morality as this kind of control has awaited transactional understanding of human nature and still awaits organization into a moral science. (Notice the close correspondence between Cameron's description and the description of the development of reciprocal control in physics given above, pp. 92–94.)

Our cultural heritage and our traditional moralities have carried the belief that purposes, values, desires, intentions are sub-rational occurrences. (The trick or dodge of converting distinctions into separations by thingifying them with names—for example, super-ego, ego, id—should be given the rogues-title of "Freudian Fallacy.") If a moral science is to be attained, purpose cannot be conceived in terms that accept a clean separation of habit and "subconscious" from intelligence. What a man is "really after" cannot be completely subconscious or totally unalterable. A man must be able to make what he is "really after" worthy, or honorable, or better, or something he is not ashamed of. He must be able to *control* it.

COERCION VS CONTROL
AND THE FORESHORTENING OF PURPOSE

Eduard Lindeman many years ago concluded that social research had come

> to resemble the plot of penny-dreadfuls: the investigator was the spy, the detective whose duty it was to run down and hunt out the secrets of the social

process. When they were all in, the indictment was published to the world in
the fervent hope that the prosecutor—public opinion—would step in and remedy the revealed evils. And curiously enough, this method was occasionally
successful. At any rate it sufficed to remedy certain social evils in a superficial sense. By this I mean that this procedure succeeded whenever it was
possible to enlist coercive measures on behalf of its cures. This is, of course,
superficial in the same sense that any coercive process is superficial.[19]

When morality degenerates into a system of coercion or limitation, it
ceases to be a method of social control. Control, as here understood,
cannot be got by coercion.

In physical, environmental affairs no one seriously hopes to coerce
results. A stone wall cannot be forced to stand up by kicking it when it
sags. You do not drive a straight nail by gritting your teeth and hitting
harder. A man who does these things we say has "lost his head."
This is the cue to what coercion essentially is—trying to obtain a *set*
result without *knowing how*. Genuine knowing, furthermore, refers
not only to the "how" but also to the setting of the result. For example, knowing about driving straight nails will convince most men not
to try driving them into stone.

In return, men are coerced by events (by "nature") only when
events are outside the process of knowing. What men don't know won't
control them: it will coerce. A chip in the eye from the abused stone
is the "natural" coercion of the event. (Note how swift the retribu-
tion!) Conversely, control in the sphere of practical affairs is knowing-
related doing—whether the knowing is of the common sense
trial-and-error variety, or the self-perfecting, reciprocal control variety of
modern science. And the return control exercised by events appears
only through the relationship called knowing. Thus it can immediately be seen that an installment plan, regarded as a modern device
for extension of intention, is controlling so long as the intention ex-
tender knows what he is about, but becomes coercive when "sold"
to him as a way of postponing till tomorrow the thoughts for today,
or when the full meaning of the arrangement for compounding interest charges is not conveyed as the intention is extended. A man's
actions and purposes are controlled by what he knows.[20] Control in
practical affairs, as in scientific inquiry (which also is practical), is thus
a two-way, reciprocal affair between knowing and doing. It is an aspect of the knowing transaction, not a mere applying of bundled
wisdom.

The current human condition is punctuated by a rash of parochial
group creeds, topped by only a very limited international humanitar-
ianism. And almost all of these diverse creedal clusters are, from the
perspective of society at large, more coercive than controlling. This is

clearly illustrated by labor's "featherbedding" practices or professional groups' attempts to restrict competition between members under the guise of "ethical practices," not to speak of the creedal coercions of Arab vs Israel or East vs West. If society could function while divided into separated little self-sufficient chunks, a multiplicity of moralities of control based upon specialized group knowings might be a workable option. But it cannot. These moralities, though apparently partially serving their purpose within the small group, inevitably reflect the fact that they are related to partial and limited moral experience, and fail by the extent of their restriction to secure control, achieving, if anything, coercion, instead. The break-up of experience[21] attendant upon the division (verging upon separation) of labor and the development of excessive specialism, has marked a retraction of common-sense moral knowing. Trial-and-error loses personal relevance when direct observation of consequences is lost in administrative organization or shunted off to analysis by specialist.

The locus of the difficulty is the foreshortening of purpose occasioned by this break-up of experience. Once upon a time, when the world was large and human organization small, a toy-maker or an alms-giver was in a position to see the end result of his doings. He could adjust his actions in terms of the far end, the satisfaction achieved, the need relieved, and the quality involved therein. Correspondingly victim, customer, and recipient could vilify or praise the author of his weal or woe, and negotiate for human betterment. There was fulfillment, completion available in gradual adjustment of work to greater satisfactions all around. The consequences of a man's small twentieth century doings, on the other hand, are lost in the transactions of middlemen and transport systems. And from the far end, the receiving end, the existence of the man with the work bench or the benevolence is but barely suspected. The self-breaking toy continues to be produced by the ton.

As results become so far removed by technology as no longer to be visible from the perspective of action, purpose—the link between cause and effect—becomes pointless; men become thumbless. Inevitably, with purpose foreshortened, social control breaks down. When the continuity of intention is blocked, stubbed to partial goals, to intermediate ends in incompleted transaction, control becomes a mere hope and terminates in coercion. When men find they do not know how to control a situation they tend, in despair, blindly to try to coerce it. Imagine an engineer trying to compel a river to give forth electricity, instead of controlling a transformation of mechanical into electrical energy!

The way out is not to resurrect an inclusive morality from the limbo of outmoded "shoulds." Its imposition would surely prove the blindest convulsion of despair. The rejuvenation of social control must emerge through the socializing of morality, through reconstruction built up from the moral knowings of mankind, not flagged down from transcendental speculations. It will emerge, in other words, from the only way of knowing that can transcend the parochial relativity of common sense experience; that is, from scientific moral experiment.

IMPOSSIBILITY OF MANIPULATION

Both moral science and the morality of social control, which latter will be anchored in scientific knowings, must necessarily begin with the multiple and minute subject-matter of moral life; namely, with conflicts of purpose (desire, want, aim, intention, value, etc.). They must begin at the moment when the determinism that would hope to erect a structure on prediction throws in the sponge and the determinism that is human determination, purpose, intention, takes over control. Here is the place where deliberate changes, as a part of the effort of experimentation, will be tried out—not in a trial-and-error spirit of play that is too volatile, too trifling for the gravity and intimacy of the subject matter, but in a serious endeavor (complete with hypotheses and high level abstractions) that aims carefully and systematically to smooth the path of associated living.

We shall have to forswear the habit of studying people from the "outside." Terminating as it does in precarious prediction of what people are going to do, this traditional method (borrowed from the nature sciences) is a dubious practice fruitless of scientific achievement. Not only from the perspective of the generality of mankind (contrasted with researchers and managers) but from the vantage of possible social control, learning all about a person's make-up, motives, "nature" and then trying to out-psych him—whether by propaganda, persuasion, education, threat, or force, and whether done for his own good, for the good of mankind, or for ulterior motives—is, in the long run, the cynical approach of manipulation—a tactic of coercion and a portent of failure.

When an attempt is made to distinguish policy formulation from social science by saying that the former deals with the setting and changing of values whereas the latter deals only with their observation, then, especially, do we arrive at a point where social science becomes a tool for the manipulation of people. Social science is reduced to finding how people react (stimulus-response), how their attitudes can be changed, how they can be sold something or made to vote this way or that. It becomes a source of and, by default, a sympathizer to manipulation of people by the managers of men. But this is just what is finally impossible, because people will not always react as predicted when they know the prediction.

There are unmistakable evidences of democratic tendency in the social relations of science. Science rises above hierarchy and status; it excludes fame and personal advantage as ultimate aims; it insists upon an equality in the face of experiment; it teaches the possibility of error; it fosters a freedom of criticism. The working scientist is not inhibited by precedent or authority as he attacks a specific problem; he is expected to follow any lead his ingenuity or creativity suggests. Additional evidence of democratic tendency is beginning to show among the products of science. Roger Money-Kyrle, for example, finds that under psychoanalysis patients always move toward the humane end of the spectrum, never in the opposite direction.[22]

Moral science, in addition, will have to be democratic since it will incorporate ordinary human being-doings—the people engaged in conflicts of purpose—into experiments involving deliberate change of purpose. It will depend upon, indeed, it will *be* their participation in experimental variation of purpose. For example, in eugenics the selective breeding of humans for perfection of the species—or to stem its deterioration—must be through such democratic Self-control. The purpose-er cannot be separated from his purposes in the process of knowing. A scientist cannot, from the outside, obtain sensitive enough contact with value, purpose, character to handle an experimental situation. The control in moral science must be an inside job, a reciprocal relating of hypothesis and purpose. Only when individual "characters" entertain both hypothesis and purpose can such intimate relatings be worked out into the light of public scrutiny.

An objective test of purposes through a validating social method of public scrutiny is, indeed, feasible only by way of the continuity of intention of individuals which Self-control alone can provide. Such continuity in turn immediately implies the whole-hearted and whole-personed participation of the citizen—the commitment of character—because it operates through his control of his Self. It also implies a level of citizen maturity and sanity that reluctantly excludes, besides children who have not yet become human enough for sustained intention, the mentally ill and unstable (however determined), the undeveloped and the retarded. Duration of intention must relate to the common observation that as a man ages time passes more and more quickly, that, as Jean Rostand says, man lives more briefly with his sons than they with him.[23] It is as if purpose, the sinews of time, contracted and tightened in process of maturing, and imposed corresponding constriction on time.

More than age is involved in the sustaining of intention. A background of experience in the transactions of living must contribute a complement of meaning. This is why "experience classes" in background broadening for underprivileged children, as conducted in some of our school systems, are so important. Intentions that are mature are the most completely meaningful. Among the signs of this maturity is increased assumption of responsibility for personal destiny and for a share in the destiny of mankind. Recent studies of chronic delinquents indicate that a disarming lack of concern for time is symptomatic of diseased, aborted, or ephemeral intention, and of immaturity and irresponsibility.[24] A pattern of active regularity, or at least the capacity for it, seems to be an important forerunner to the establishment of a mature Self. With it comes effective intention, the birth of purpose and honesty. As with so many other desirable things in life, the individual must practice with intention before he can have it; he must practice binding time before he can develop strong enough sinews to succeed as time-binder: this is a creative activity; the work of art must precede its appreciation.

The maturity we are seeking is found somewhere between the timelessness of random, free-wandering play and the timelessness of formfit Teleological ethics. On the one hand it brings continuity to moral life; but on the other it stops short of eternity. If the erosion of social control by the winds of time is to be stopped, a wind-breaking forest must be planted, a crop of morals adaptable enough to adjust to the ravages of time. In the soul of the citizen scientist will throb the maturity of intentions intentionally grow-up-able. Self-control on the part of mature human being-doings is prerequisite to intentions that can sustain the duration necessary for their validation—and therefore for science.

The mature citizen can be expected to resemble the freed and trustworthy individual Carl R. Rogers describes in the following passage:

> When we are able to free the individual from defensiveness, so that he is open to the wide range of his own needs, as well as the wide range of environmental and social demands, his reactions may be trusted to be positive, forward-moving, constructive. We do not need to ask who will socialize him, for one of his own deepest needs is for affiliation and communication with others. As he becomes more fully himself, he will become more realistically socialized. We do not need to ask who will control his aggressive impulses;

for as he becomes more open to all of his impulses, his need to be liked by others and his tendency to give affection will be as strong as his impulses to strike out or to seize for himself. He will be aggressive in situations in which aggression is realistically appropriate, but there will be no runaway need for aggression. His total behavior, in these and other areas, as he moves toward being open to all his experience, will be more balanced and realistic, behavior which is appropriate to the survival and enhancement of a highly social animal.[25]

Robert Roessler's quite similar description emphasizes the group characteristic of human nature:

If their own deepest feelings are available to them, [people] generally behave in ways we label "good"; if they have come to deny themselves, they sometimes behave in ways we label "bad." If they can permit themselves to experience any and all emotion, fully and consciously, they will—among other feelings—be sensitive to and respectful of the needs and feelings of others.[26]

He adds a very significant comment that brings around again the previously drawn distinction between coercion and control, which in turn suggests the interconnectedness of coercion, immorality, and immaturity or pathology:

when certain emotions are not accepted, they may express themselves in ways that are regarded as bad; conversely, when they are accepted they tend to be expressed in ways that are regarded as good. Persons who behave in "immoral" ways are not persons with too few controls, but persons who apply very strict controls with a false idea of their functions.[27]

The concern of social science will not be with pathology, except as old purposes or values appear "sick" after having been rejected and displaced by newer, fuller, more satisfying ones—although, on the other hand, the implications of the success of a stabilizing moral science growing out of the participation of mature citizens might be expected to provide new leads to encourage psychology, practical and research, to move out of a conceptual framework derived largely from pathology into a new emphasis on what is right with people. A moral science will have to be a science of the healthy in first instance. It will have to rest on mature individuals so that it will have a healthy, uncrippled, unscarred, fresh, spontaneous subject matter with which to work. A science dealing with the interests, purposes, values of mature individuals will have to be democratic and permissive or it will find its subject matter destroyed, distorted, or simply rendered inaccessible as a result of the experimental situation; it will find investigation systematically frustrated by the organization of experiment. [28]

If moral science is to set up a working system of reciprocal controls, with an ultimate aim of achieving progressive social control on political levels, it will have systematically to rely on Self-controls. Applying controls with a false idea of their functions is not control at all. Mistaken "control" is coercion—trying to attain a set end without *knowing how*, like kicking the stone wall to make it stand up. The controls a person applies to his emotions and behavior need, as Roessler's words suggest, a directioning from knowing how in order to avoid the pitfalls of "immorality." Granted, maturity and health are approximate descriptions. The distinction between control and coercion within the Self is not always finely drawn. Indeed, the line is continually being redrawn, and redefined. Part of the service of a moral science will be the developing of foundations in knowing-how. From understanding the function of controls will come what is termed in the next chapter "functional power" to displace the coercive might that is the pride and menace of today's civilization. But the foundations of control will come out of scientific moral inquiry. Although health and maturity of morality are refined with and created by or through the knowings-how of science, the Self-controls it must rely on will have to be those of people controlling their own desires, purposes, behaviors; and they must, therefore, to an extent be matured and whole before inquiry can take root. Moral achievement of social control, flowing from knowings about creating of Selves, integrating of character, can come about only through improved, more satisfactory intentions of mature citizens.

THE DEMOCRAT SCIENTIST

Moral science will ultimately complement and correct the physical sciences. Man does not really control his environment when he does not control himself-in-environment—the human environment. After all, man looking at nature is an aspect of nature viewing nature, nature taking its own measure.

It cannot be denied that the twentieth century has witnessed a new, profound indirect impact of science on morals. Modern warfare, for example, and the physical sciences trailing in its wake, have lost all semblance of humanity. Even fighting and soldiering with their strangely anomalous codes of behavior, are things of the past. The ideal for which warfare is now geared is the extermination of humans (even whole populations) on the same footing as rats or insects; it is too remote, too immoral even to be called cold-blooded.

In the present day, physical scientists seem to be more ready than the rest of the population to experience impatience at "higher" political, judicial, ethical, and social decisions. Part of the reason they are more poignantly afflicted with impatience is that they have been professionally trained to expect exactness and to search out precision.[29] Engineers suffer the same affliction. Another part of the reason is that they have a superior moral code to regulate some of their internal professional behavior—and the comparisons are invidious. It remains a fact, however, that, while daily engaged in making moral judgments in the round of scientific inquiry, environmental scientists have yet no viable technique for deciding what value judgments they ought to make.

The moral code developed in the social relations of the experimental setting of the physical sciences, while now perhaps serving as prototype of the fine and forward, will itself some day be drawn within the reaches of experimental morals. Someday there will be intimate and extensive interrelationships between the physical and moral sciences—as there are now between chemistry and astronomy.

Key concepts and discoveries of critical importance to the development of experimental moral science may yet arrive from deeper environmental inquiry. For example, much can be found out about thinking and about mental disease from brain dissection and from experimentation with lower animals. Or new concepts might possibly derive from study of the information coding, storing, and transmitting characteristics of some of the nucleic acids.

But the reverse relation, the gift of morals to environment, shows equal promise. Bridgman points out that

> whatever new way we devise to think about the microscopic universe, the meaning of our new concepts will have to be found back at the level of the large-scale events of daily life, because this is the scale on which we live our lives, and it is we who are formulating the new concepts.

He aptly adds that

> the seeds and sources of the ineptness of our thinking in the microscopic range are already contained in our present thinking in the large-scale region and should have been capable of discovery by sufficiently acute analysis of our ordinary common-sense thinking.[30]

Having learned from environmental inquiry, moral science may take the next step, sweep out the ineptness of thinking on the level of large scale daily events, and replace the external limitations on environmental science with the controls of social science.

As a method, as a collective enterprise, moral science will break out in a new direction, however. It will differ from physical science, as we understand it, in one fundamental way. It will add a new category of scientists to the division of labor accepted in physical inquiry.[31]

The pure scientist will remain and retain the job of perfecting, sharpening the conceptual tools of inquiry—ideals, theories, hypotheses. His function will be strictly analogous to that of his counterpart in environmental science.

The applied scientist will move into the laboratory of social transactions, probably as a *sort of* participant observer (administrator or engineer with a difference—without the cynical reporting to the factory manager on what the sheep do or can do), to take the lead in constructing apparatuses for testing hypotheses, and in bringing hypotheses to test in solving particular problems. The applied social scientist will not be an interloper. He will not, as he now sometimes does with interesting results, insinuate or finesse himself into the inner sanctum, into the confidential counsels of some group he wants to study, and attempt, through pretense of solidarity, to gain a grasp of group consciousness by a process of imaginative sharing. He will be more than an impartial observer. He will assume a distinct within-group function in full transaction with other group members. He will leave work with snake worshipers, occultists, and prophets of kingdom come to the therapists, the medical scientists, or the educators— those who work with correction of abnormalities or immaturities from what is essentially an outside perspective. He will certainly not merely concern himself with predictions about what the groups he is interested in are going to do. He will work as a specialist, honestly participating in group activities with mature individuals, but contributing particular competence along the line of organizing social experiment so that, as problems are solved by the people involved, progress is also made in test of their hypotheses concerning their purposes, and so that particular problems, experiments, hypotheses are productively related to general theory.

One of the reasons that the applied social scientist cannot be an outsider or an interloper is that he must work freely and cooperatively with the mature persons who furnish the practical problems and their solutions. These people will be the third kind of scientist, a special scientist not found in environmental experiment but essential to social inquiry. The material (subject-matter, participant, democrat, citizen) scientist will reign supreme at the bottom of the ranks in terms of philosophical speculation and methodological specialization. But he will be "on top" in terms of final scientific control—as an indispensable and integral part of the transaction of knowing within inquiry. It is the citizen, the man with the purposes, who must, through participation furnish the material, the subject-matter of experiment and, by joining the scientific team, democratize it.

The therapy of purge through confession may be what is needed before the first tottering step can be made toward a citizen science. Perhaps this is the time openly to admit that the social sciences do not yet offer any remotely satisfactory guide for the good life. As Lee Steiner says,

> If we would confide frankly to the public that we do not have sufficient validated knowledge upon which to devise reliable road maps to a good way of life, we might enlist the interest of the average person in cooperating with us, both in raising funds for further research, and in sharing whatever knowledge we do have.[32]

In any case, moral science will begin with the task of understanding how "participation" works and what its processes and ingredients are.

SUMMARY

There will always be weathering and scoring. Time, the great complicator of moral control, takes its inexorable toll. But the major moral waste, the erosion of social control, can be stemmed. Time will take a different sort of toll when purposes, intentions, are brought into the center of social scientific inquiry and experiment. Then it will be constrained to string along, to partake of and participate in the reciprocity of intentional control—the reciprocal control system of experimental social science—for intentions are the sinews of time.

Tolerance to moral abuse, the other complication in the way of social control, will give way to determined improvement in proportion as moral science demonstrates that inherited moralities can be improved upon through experimental contact with human purposes in a developing system of social control. When knowing is made a proper part of the transaction of moral inquiry, coercion or moral abuse becomes readily perceptible.

Social control, like environmental control, is a transactional product, an affair between knowing and doing. But since the only way to get close enough to the material of morals, purposes, to treat them experimentally is from the inside, the Self that carries the values, the character, will have to be enlisted as part of the scientific team of experimenters. We should anticipate, as immediate product, a new outbreak of character-building, an epidemic of character such as never before witnessed.

Equally important as the flowering of character is the fact that experimental social science, because of its crucially located and functioning citizen scientist, must necessarily be democratic. The social portent of this happy necessity will be explored in the second part of this book, beginning with an exploration in depth of participation. The coming chapter, however, raises the general topic of power and politics to round out the general context, relating politics to morals and tying democracy to the findings of recent research into human nature and to experimental social scientific method.

CHAPTER SEVEN

Democracy: The Taming of Power

*While [the democratic mind]
acknowledges the need for authority
in certain situations and on certain
levels of social organization, yet the
aim is still to minimize domination by
new social inventions, to replace
forms of organization based on
domination by more humanized ones,
and to bring power under the
control of the community.*

KARL MANNHEIM

THE POLITICAL PROCESS IS A SPECIALIZED FIELD OF MORAL-
ity. Within its scope lies a potential of social control. Unhappily, it is
frequently, if not commonly today, an agency of coercion instead. A
great part of the trouble can be pinpointed. The political aberration resulting in coercion can be largely attributed to the fact that power has
not been tamed, domesticated, democratized, "functionalized." Indeed, it
isn't even generally understood that there is an alternative to pushy
power, that power can be transformed, that there can be a power that is
neither spur nor carrot. As will be seen, the taming of power is a primary function and a major virtue of the democratic form of government. Functionally incorporating power within a system of social control will also be seen to relate democracy to the self-perfecting method
of experimental social science.

The aim of this chapter is to round out a schematic framework for
the foundations of utopia by sketching in the basic outline for political
reconstruction.

PUSHY POWER

There is power in a turbine, a jet, a jackhammer, a fist. The engineer
defines it as the rate at which work is done. He measures it in horse-
power or watts. There is power in a purse, a property, a pulpit, a press,
a pen. The social commentator can rarely explain what it is, though he
is equally rarely reluctant to talk about it. He measures it in more and
less.[1]

Hobbes defined power as an emanating substance, a thing possessed
by some persons, a sort of magnetic repulsion. Locke thought of it as
a relation between persons, a bond between leader and led where one
person had power *over* another. Friedrich tries to combine Locke and
Hobbes by saying that it is a relation between leader and led, but that
the leader must possess *ability*. He attempts thus to combine the consent toward which Locke's theory leads and the constraint implicit in
Hobbes' theory, and reads power as "a human relationship in which
the leader and the led are banded together for the accomplishment
of some common objectives, partly by consent, partly by constraint." [2]

More recent writers use different words but come out at about the
same place. T. V. Smith: "Power is no mysterious and elusive phantom;
it is, forthrightly speaking, *the capacity to effect results.*" [3] Harold D.
Lasswell and Abraham Kaplan: "Power is participation in the making
of decisions: G has power over H with respect to the value K if G participates in the making of decisions affecting the K-policies of H.
. . . But power in the political sense cannot be conceived as the ability
to produce intended effects in general, but only such effects as directly
involve other persons: political power is distinguished from power
over nature as power over men." [4] James K. Feely, Jr.: "Power is the
measure of the degree to which what is attained, as a result of calculated action, conforms to the initially sought desire or purpose. Power
is the measure of the accomplishment of purpose through prediction" [5] L. S. Shapley and Martin Shubik: "The power of an individual
member [of Congress] depends on the chance he has of being critical
to the success of the winning coalition." [6] Charles E. Merriam: "In
political power situations, there appears a type of force through which
masses of human beings are manipulated as if by some magnetic
attraction or aversion." [7] Max Weber: "In general, we understand by
'power' the chance of a man or of a number of men to realize their
own will in a communal action even against the resistance of others who
are participating in the action." [8] There are, of course, other views of
power, but these are by all odds representative of current interpretation.

Some of these same writers go on to describe politics in terms of
this definition of power. " 'Politics' for us means striving to share

power or striving to influence the distribution of power, either among states or among groups within the state." [9] "The political process is the shaping, distribution, and exercise of power (in a wider sense, of all the deference values, or of influence in general.)" [10] "Of course, politics is a power-phenomenon: no power, no politics; much politics, much power. We must take it or leave it at that; for politics is, willy-nilly, a pulling or a pushing around of somebody." [11] If this is what it is, no wonder "politics" is a dirty word! No wonder administrators shun "politics"!

But politics just cannot be reduced to the manipulation of some men by others, by equating it with "power"—even when manipulation is taken in the mildly coercive form of propaganda or persuasion. The misunderstanding seems, however, to lie rather in the characterization of power than the description of politics in terms of power.

Because they insist that in any manifestation of power there are two parties involved—the powerful and those over whom power is exerted—the writers whose definitions are given above *seem* to be understanding power as a relation. As a matter of fact, Hobbes' emanating substance shines through their poor disguise. If power is a relation, it is not "the *capacity* to effect results," but the effecting of results; it is not "the *ability* to produce effects," but the producing of effects—and so on down the line. The engineer has done much better with his "*rate* of doing work"!

In final analysis, these descriptions of power leave it where Locke in final analysis (relation having deferred to emanation) left it—as a push of "that which we call the will" from the mind of his poor two-part man.[12] To try to deal with existential phenomena on the basis of such an understanding is like trying to preside over a chemical laboratory in terms of acidic, basic, saline, and saccharine "forces." No wonder the profound analysis of so many generations has been so fruitless. No wonder, precarious and fortuitous balances excepted, power has never been brought under control.

So entrenched are inherited ways of thinking and perceiving that even those who fully understand that the Cartesian world has been superseded continue to speak of power in Cartesian terms. It is not at all surprising when a social scientist points out the lack of language for the new science of man and notes that those attempting to think it through tend to be thrown back on the older, inadequate terminology for lack of a better one, and then lapses himself into the old ways.[13] This is how strong the mesmeric hold of the Cartesian world view is. Indeed, it is not to be expected that the present book will evade all the pitfalls of the ancient trap.

Probably the most unyielding obstacle raised by this widely accepted, "common sense" way of thinking about power is the stubborn corollary that interprets power as something evil but essential. The anatomy of power, its composition out of simple human purposes, is obscured as a result. Power becomes something that can be handled only superficially and in its own terms, by being counterbalanced with another vaguely specified gross manifestation of power.[14] To leave power on the level of *ability* or *capacity* to produce results is to return to Newton. It is to say that only a balance of *forces* is possible, and to leave this balance fortuitous for lack of understanding of the composition of power and thus its control. It leads to such magic illusions in refinement as the tale about "countervailing" power of powerful buyers growing up as a result of (caused by) the existence of powerful sellers.[15]

TOWARD FUNCTIONAL POWER

If power is to be understood and won round to the betterment of mankind, we shall have to eschew the Aristotelian approach that treats only its superficial manifestations and gross qualitative characteristics. Instead of merely counterbalancing gross phenomena, we shall have to go below the surface of appearance. We shall have to study power as an aspect or attribute of human transactions, complete with experimental logic and with scientific handling of its anatomic human purposes. And this is not at all impossible. The power of eminent domain, for example, can unquestionably be handled with neither a push nor a pull, but rather to the complete mutual benefit and satisfaction of the parties involved. (For an illustration, please take a look at Herman Danforth's article on right-of-way acquisition, reproduced in Appendix A.)

A red-blooded investigation of power in context of transaction needs to emphasize a number of departures from tradition:

1. *Expect transactional complexity!* Power is not *simply* a relation between men, as Lasswell and Kaplan seem to believe. Especially it is not a relation between half-human beings separated from one another, in the Cartesian or Lockean way. Power is a common ordinary "organic" bond between Selves, a reciprocal co-relating, a full-dimensioned aspect of transaction. It is always more complex than the mere imposition of the "will" of one atomic individual upon another.[16]

2. *Study Anatomy!* Power is not a final residue that can be understood as given. It is a situational attribute whose anatomy includes the purposes, values, wants, aims, fancies of the people involved.[17] To

understand it in its full dimensions will mean to have investigated it through experimental variation of the elements involved in its appearance—relying heavily on the purpose-full democrat scientist or subject-matter scientist.

The following description will serve to illustrate these two points and to lead to two more important emphases:

> [Don Calò's] whole life has been dedicated to one purpose—the acquisition of power. His words must be obeyed, his enemies must be defeated, nothing within his empire must be done without his knowledge and approval. Land must not be sold, girls married, officials shifted, criminals jailed, business ventures started, without a nod from Don Calò.... To achieve this position he has to forgo many pleasures, including that of making money, and steel himself against all temptations, because the man who assumes within himself all the responsibilities of a multitude must have no weakness.
>
> He has no weapons, no organization, no visible means to enforce his will. He moves mysteriously, skillfully playing one force against another—helping the law against criminals or criminals against the law, according to his judgment, the rich against the poor or the poor against the rich. In his own way he is a moral man, because *he uses his power mostly according to an ancient sense of justice* and does not abuse it. Nobody tries to equal him.
>
> Some ... remembered and tried to apply, in American industrial slums, the real Mafia heritage—a sure *knowledge of* the secret laws of human affairs and *human nature*, and the way in which to use power and fear when the law offers the individual no guarantees.... But the new country and the new conditions were so different that the old ways quickly degenerated.[18]

3. *Look beyond coercion!* Power need not be coercive. It need not be reduced to pushy force, to might, or even to the less blatant forms of manipulation through propaganda, prestige, persuasion, and so on. True, an infinity of paltry, petty coercions literally surrounds us. They are almost habitual, reducing frequently to mere thoughtlessness: when a doctor's waiting room is packed on the principle of "first come first served" instead of being "humanized" by an appointment calendar; when a draftsman is told what to do without an attempt being made to engage his understanding by explaining why, and thus imparting meaning to the job; when an inquirer is referred to the "proper" office although the office referring him on has a "file copy" containing the requested information. Sometimes, however, power becomes functionally incorporated into a system of social control (described in the preceding chapter), thereby losing the coercive aspect by which so many people identify it. Early man looked beyond the danger and destruction of fire, learning how to control it, to make it function to his profit. Beyond coercive power is the positive potential of power under control, power that fulfills effective function in social control because

tamed within a reciprocal control system, controlling the human agent while itself under control.

4. *Ground power in knowing how!* In Don Calò's case, the power he acquired tended to be made functional by his sensitivity to, his knowledge of, human nature—by his transactional realism. There is a tendency for power to be functional where wisdom is stable. Where, as in Sicily, human nature has been held fixed over a long period of time under the shepherding, under the control of a system of folkways or moral customs, knowing how to act without doing violence to human nature becomes a badge of the ruling class. The rulers acquire what seems almost to be an instinctive feeling for the workable way. Instead of coercion, a sense of justice is felt to ensue—even, strangely, when physical force is applied to criminal offenders.

Until it is fused into a system of social control, power subverts or perverts knowledge while elbowing its way to supremacy over truth. *Knowing how* is what sublimates brute force into effective function. The crumbling wall cannot be coerced into shape by kicking the pieces together. It is the mortar of know-how that em*powers* effective reconstruction. *Knowing how* legitimizes power by permitting its assimilation within the mutuality of social control. This is the moral of Don Calò. Functional power finds its effectiveness in dependence on knowing.

MODERN DEGRADATION OF POWER

Power in the present era is patently and undeniably coercive in the main. Even the widely applauded soul-force of a non-resisting Gandhi, though perhaps pure in intent, is a form of coercion. It cynically manipulates the opposing forces through their inclination to act *like* gentlemen. In a changing world, with human nature turning somersaults yearly, if not weekly, it is not surprising that the reliability of knowings about human nature derived from custom, tradition, Teleological ethics, or common sense should be shaken.

A look at the recent history of the power called "property" will illustrate the modern degradation of power in a field of social change.

Things—properties, owned or not—are so important to people as to be properly parts of human Selves. A scholar separated from an adequate library becomes a frustrated, lost soul. So too a pianist minus piano, a gardener minus garden, a child whose dog has died, a man whose wife has strayed . . . A woman who cracks up under the strain of redecorating her home is not victimized simply by the ardors of unaccustomed decision-making, but also by the fact that such reorganization entails a reorganization of her Self.

With the human Self thus extending beyond the human skin, it is not at all surprising that a system of individual appropriation, individual ownership, should come to be thought "natural," as an institutionalizing of Self-protection, Self-defense. As a matter of fact, however, the part of a scholar called "library" may be (generally is) owned by some one else and still be his very own. The garden part of a gardener may be bought and sold by others while his Self remains intact. The fact that wives are no longer possessions makes them no less parts of men's Selves. Nevertheless, with each change in the ownership relation, the nature of the human Self changes. Human nature, both male and female, is something quite new and different when woman has a soul of her own. Relating people to property, Isak Dinesen says of the Kikuyu of her African farm,

> It is more than their land that you take away from the people, whose Native land you take. It is their past as well, their roots and their identity. If you take away the things that they have been used to see, and will be expecting to see, you may, in a way, as well take their eyes.[19]

The institutionalized allocation to individuals of things of all kinds (goods, chattels, land, money, credit) as possessions hit its jealous peak in post Civil War America, as a final embodiment of atomic individualism. The system of private ownership worked wonders in the development of the resources of a new land, and served in the creative broadening of individual Selves. At the same time, however, it served as a limit. It served to halt the growth of the Self at the rigidly set boundary of the next Self's possessions. In another culture in another age, this particular limit could have been avoided, for some, by extending possession to include other persons. As it was, there had to be an end to expansion. Obviously, the restrictions imposed by such a property system become coercive with the disappearance of the frontier and the concentration of population. They become coercive at the point where, instead of encouraging the expansion of the Self, they exact contraction.[20] (Incidentally, there may be a limit set by mental hygiene to the density at which human selves can be packed—at least this would seem to be the lesson taught by the March Hare and the Norwegian lemming, not to speak of recent systematic studies with rats.) Those who uphold the system against the erosion at its edges tend to occupy extreme positions: they are either persons who, because of particular favored circumstances, find the system still filled with possibilities for the growth of their Selves, or persons whose Selves have reached a static, premature plateau, at which level of growth they are content to rest.

Significantly, it is only at the point where property begins to become coercive, exacting contraction of Selves, that it begins to be widely recognized as a power relation. Not until degradation is underway, effectiveness is eroding, and the exercise of power is becoming so abrasive as to obtrude across customary apathy to stir common perception is special notice of it taken.

Changes away from unlimited, dogmatic private ownership are by now quite extensive. Society, through governmental action (zoning ordinances, security regulations, labor laws, etc.) has curtailed the individual prerogatives formerly linked with ownership. Significant segments have been given over to direct public ownership and operation. In important areas the prerogatives of ownership have been assumed outright by groups or eclipsed by the authority of managerial and engineering functions. This is highlighted by the displacement of the entrepreneur by the "technostructure" in America's large corporations, as John Kenneth Galbraith explains.[21] Furthermore, the character of ownership in land and personal property has been subtly changed: a new automobile is more of a badge of possession today than a house and land; urbanization and mobility have cut great inroads into the sanctity and prizing of private land ownership; and, in addition, ownership of automobile, TV, and kitchen sink has been so undercut by installment plans as to become, except for tenacious pretense, very nearly meaningless. (Incidentally, the change in the meaning of land ownership is far reaching. It has gone so far as to alter the impact of the United States Senate, and, through the one-man-one-vote decision of the Supreme Court, the effective structure of state bicameralism.)

All these changes reflect or entail changes in the nature of the human Self. They correspondingly involve adjustment of the warp and woof (nexus) of power, for the springs or atoms or quanta (we know not yet how to characterize them) of power are in the purposes and penchants of people. Powers degrade, they become coercive as times rapidly change in a fluid society. They are thereupon counterbalanced by pressures from other directions, groups, functions, or governments. But these, too, are desperate and transient, built on hope and little more, unless and until caught and tamed in expanding understanding.

THE MORAL PROCESS CALLED POLITICS

The political process is traditionally thought to begin where traditional morality leaves off, "at the point where formal programs and planned political action supersede the evolutionary process by which, in every stable society, a body of tradition and culture slowly accumulates, under the influence of which succeeding generations of men are gradually disciplined and domesticated."[22] This view is nicely consonant with the overly rational contract theory of the state and with the juxtaposition in battle formation of the Individual vs Society, referred to in earlier chapters.[23] It is also quite suited to independent, uncongested, and uncomplicated conditions of life where men are able to give vent to their expanding Selves without the need to take their fellows into account; that is, when the environmental aspect of their Selves is more largely material than human. Up until a symbolic 1911[24] such a division between politics and morality set an understandable limit to formal political activity.

In the last fifty years, however, it has become increasingly inappropriate. The rational theory of the state has been gradually diluted with emotion and character. We are now beginning to realize that there is no essential warfare between the Individual and Society, there being no separable essence in the former and no distinguishable essence in the latter. And life has become patently congested, environment ever more human. Morality cannot be understood today as *purely* non-rational or *primarily* individual. The political and the moral have merged.

So far as anyone *knows*, political problems *are* moral problems. It is, of course, true that not all moral conflicts are handled by processes we call political. Many, or most, are informally resolved. So far as anyone can see, political questions are distinguished out of the general run of moral questions only by magnitude. If, somewhere along the line there is a "leap" from the quantitative to the qualitative, so that we should be able to recognize the political as a particular kind of moral question, the point of take-off—the springboard—and the ensuing difference have not yet been convincingly identified. The political process is a non-habitual outgrowth of morality. It springs up to handle those conflicts with which, for one reason or another—too big, too serious, too new—customary morality or Teleological ethics has failed— where the slow processes are inadequate. Thus the common law, originally based on immemorial usage and universal reception, is supplemented by statutes or by judges exercising political functions in *relatively* rapid response to rapid technological change.

The political process, like morality in general, can be a method of social control. Again like morality, it is frequently coercion instead. Perhaps explicit appreciation of the political-moral merger will serve to facilitate creation of a reciprocal control system through the correlating of the rational tradition of politics with the emotional-aesthetic tradition of morality. There might be some considerable promise of integration in just such juxtaposition. Drawing the two traditions together at least brings them that much closer to analysis in terms of transaction.

Government, as the formal aspect of the political process, works only at selected points—for example, controlling the land-use in a metropolitan area by strategic location and timing of highway and sewer facilities—to marshall as much coordination as is necessary to keep an even keel. It deals only with a portion of the great mass of moral seethings and becomes at best a system of strategic control.[25] But to gain effective control it must first achieve a functional power. *The* function of government is to functionalize power. The more successfully it fulfills this role, the more democratic it becomes.

Government, or the state, is not just an instrument for achieving definite ends that cannot be effectively realized by private and group activity. Although a great many of the tasks it does perform are pre-set and standardized, government is more than a tool for accomplishing given ends—ends that have been chosen through some other process— traditional morality, for instance. It is also a method of selecting, perfecting, and creating goals. It is a process that reaches way down into the stuff of which power is composed, way down below the group (where some would have it stop) to the conflicts of value and purpose whose resolutions are moral (and political) achievements. Government (politics) has a generality of purpose found nowhere else in so broad a pattern; but this generality of purpose includes, besides the maintenance of civil defense and the preservation of law and order, the general welfare, under which falls a purpose such as no other group of today entertains—the purpose of agreement, the purpose of comprehensive and creative integration of purposes.[26]

Here upon the shoals of creativity and integration is where group approaches to an understanding of politics threaten to founder. Politics is something more than the groups involved and their interactions, particularly when "group" is defined as a collection of people interacting on the basis of a shared characteristic.[27] David B. Truman has done well to emphasize that the crucial aspect of a group is the interaction and not the shared characteristic. Nevertheless, if "shared characteristic"— presumably referring to some purpose, value, or the like—is to be taken as a defining aspect (which is to say that it is set and permanent, immune to transformation by the interacting that also defines the group), groups must remain obdurate before the broad governmental purpose of developing more adequate purposes, and inimical to the democratic bent toward re-creation. This characteristic of associational life, the inertia of institutions entrenched behind set purpose, is, indeed, one of the gravest curses of politics. The special recalcitrance that mere association in groups adds to human reluctance to look beyond and to improve upon inherited moralities and power structures, does not set final limits to politics, however. It only accentuates the unique position of politics within the nexus of human purposes as agency of overriding generality of purpose.

DEMOCRATIC CONTROL

If it would be democratic, a political system for integrating purposes must functionalize power; it must be a method of control, as outlined in previous chapters, instead of coercion. Democracy is a moral method. It is a way of handling conflicts of purpose. In abstract perfection, a situation is democratic when the purposive conflicts involved are handled in such a way that progressively richer, more satisfying resolutions are achieved, in terms of the integration, improvement, re-creation of the purposes involved. Dewey's statement of the democratic faith cannot be improved upon. He says, "Democracy is a belief in the ability of human experience to generate the aims and methods by which future experience will grow in ordered richness." [28]

For the upper level that is politics, democracy involves many things:

■ Control of the physical environment must first have been secured. It goes without saying that purposes cannot well be controlled so long as they are haphazardly blown around by the winds of their physical environment. (They must, of course, be reciprocally controlled by environment, but not unknowingly coerced.) This is why, as was previously suggested,[29] the first dawning of conscience in ancient Egypt had to await a large measure of technical achievement in environmental control.

■ Social perception—that is, perception of the purposes of other people —must be acute enough so that purposes can be imaginatively and sympathetically related to each other in the process of resolving conflicts between them.[30] This dimension of democracy has gained significance in the last one hundred years of American history. An agrarian democracy, where the Self is not greatly involved in an environment of human purposes, is simplicity itself compared with the democracy a world congested with Selves will need to develop. Social perception will involve not only vision and aesthetics but communication and, in final analysis, a method of knowing that provides progressively more reliable guidance.

■ Purposes must be released from attachment to status, hierarchically conceived. It is the situation, the problem, the conflict, the transaction that should provide the material and milieu for the rounding of purposes, not the extraneous austerity of independently assumed status. A challenge to the authority of the democratic method by a pretending authority of static status, cannot be admitted.

■ Democracy involves acceptance of the virtue of change, in the interest of continual betterment. Indeed, that is what it precisely is—a process, a method for improving unsatisfactory situations. At its most sensitive, democracy will itself be an experimental method through which men try out and test alternative ways of thinking, acting, feeling, purposing.

■ Democracy will perhaps in the future be identified, if not measured, by the extent to which individuals achieve control over their own lives. But it must be understood that such control can only be the sort of Self-control described in earlier chapters, involving:

■ The participation of others in the construction and testing of purposes.

SUMMARY

Such an understanding of democracy is not very companionable to the perennially popular, easy going, public-opinion, "get out the vote!" "everybody participate!" view of democracy.[31] Its elaboration will be the major effort of the remainder of this book. The radical aspect of this understanding is that it relates democracy specifically to current findings about "the nature of human nature" and to an improved method of knowing in the realm of political-moral events. Radical though it is, however, it is not revolutionary in the sense of forceful, wholesale over-throw of existing constitutional or legislative institutions. Democracy that is a system of reciprocal control, a functionalizing of power, will have to be a slow growth proportionate to development of improved moral knowings by subject-matter scientists and proportionate to its fruitfulness in social control. By its fruits ye shall trust it.

Between the environmental sciences and certain practical arts runs a two-way street continually streaming with two-way traffic. Sometimes predominant influences flow one way, sometimes the other. In early stages of a science the flow is heaviest from practical activity toward the science—as from the art of artillery and the constructing of steam engines toward physics. In later years the flow reverses and the science feeds back into the practical art—as chemistry now feeds the clothing industry, and biology feeds agriculture.

It is very tempting to expect a directly parallel situation for social science, relating the social sciences to practical arts, such as the art of government, the art of winning friends and influencing decisions, the art of holding meetings, the treatment of criminals, the integrating of races, the dispensing of justice. Progress in these fields will no doubt sustain intimate relations with progress in social science, but these relations will be by no means the same either in kind or in degree of intimacy as those between physics and manufacturing. The parallel breaks down because, if there is an experimental social science, it is democracy itself.

To the extent that there is a science of government, the art of government becomes a science of government. Perhaps it should be said that the science gets inserted into the art. It is as if the physicist moved his workplace into the factory and functioned within the scheme of production, though sometimes affecting a change in it.

The laboratory of social science is life, rounded not remote. It is wherever the subject-matter or citizen scientist can be found to participate in it. The social science to come will be a true leavening, a yeast working within society to bring about the taming (functionalizing) of power, converting power from coercion to creation. Obviously, not every human being-doing will forsake other pursuits for the pursuit of knowledge—even as subject-matter scientist—but the help of those who can be enlisted will be critically important.

When you come to think about it, the modern attitude toward the findings of the environmental sciences has been extraordinarily grotesque. It has complacently assumed that the scientific effort is complete —except that the end is never reached—in knowing how to control the causal linkings in environment. It has made blind commitment to the irresponsible aim of controlling events without regard to further events. In a fluid culture freed from the hegemony of folkways, it therefore gives the fruits of science over to whatever chance purpose happens to lurk behind whoever is in command of power at the moment. Even within the scientific method of his discipline, the environmental scientist has no viable technique for deciding what value judgments he ought to use when making decisions and choices.

In correcting such a situation, social science, seeking know-how in the realm of purposes, intentions, values, desires, becomes reformer, a leavening within democracy. And the reconstruction, the reformation, the control of power stands out as the democratic achievement of political organization. In turn, the environmental sciences find their range subsumed and their ways corrected within the larger scope of moral science.

As will be remembered, physical science is approached in its third and most basic frame of reference as a collective enterprise or structured system of social transactions. This is only another way of saying that the physical sciences are necessarily deeply set within the laboratory of moral science. Chemists, biologists, and physicists will sometimes even find themselves in the unaccustomed role of subject-matter scientist participating in a system of social experiment. There will be changes and resentments. More desperate or unreasoned resistance to extension of experimental social science might be expected to come from the very orderly ranks of the environmental scientists than from the less disciplined universe of other human being-doings—simply because the special group ethics developed in the environmental sciences is relatively new and, correspondingly, closer enough to the needs of the times that its obsolescence will not be so dramatically apparent as will the obsolescence of the diverse Teleological ethics informing the run of mankind. Yet there will also be an internal sort of mitigation of this resistance, coming from the deliberately progressive aspect of the scientific attitude and its insistence upon rising above personal advantage and personal fame. In the end, generalized theory and cross-fertilization between scientific disciplines should win the day.

The foundations of utopia, of a newly truth-tuned democracy pitched to the key of twentieth century scientific findings and methods and the fluid social conditions they have engendered, rests on a taming of power that in return enables gradual introduction of the politics of truth within which the merger of the social scientist and social reformer has been started. As unified theory begins to appear, bits and pieces of knowledge will begin to fit together and in terms of theory to make elegant sense.

EPILOGUE ON THE MASTER SCIENCE

As democracy develops into an experimental method for improving thought, action, feeling and purposing, coming into its proper role as the broadest, most generalized, and comprehensive inquiry (comprising even the environmental sciences as a sub-category), political science will emerge as the queen among the social sciences. The broad view of government as a moral agency of strategic control and of democracy as an aim at Self control through the taming of power implies eventual revision respecting the ranging and interrelating of the social sciences.

The view of government and democracy developed in this chapter places political science at the vortex as *the* comprehensive social science. In face of attempted relegation of political science, politics, and government to the inferior position of "applied science" with the subordinate task of applying the basic findings of the pure social sciences—namely, psychology, psychiatry, cultural anthropology, sociology—it is time to speak up from the perspective of the democratic administrator, the democratic politician, and announce that a moral science (which these "basic" disciplines have not achieved) can only be a democratic and political growth.

It is political science that is strategically situated to serve as the shepherd of political (moral) experiment and the custodian compiler of know-how. Such a moral science will deal with the ordinary and extraordinary, daily and occasional purposes of "participant" or "citizen" scientists. How the pure scientists will range themselves in respect to the theoretical undertaking can at this point be only a matter of conjecture. The likelihood is that there will be a grand reshuffling of "disciplines."

Inclusion of the concerned as "citizen" scientists will also render obsolete the typical research situation projected in the following passage:

> The social psychologist bent upon entering into housing research ... must know that he is forsaking the relative calm and peace of his academic laboratory for the strife and embroilments of the institutional battlefield. What is more, belonging to neither army, the social psychologist must be prepared to be caught in the heavy cross-fire. Little if any of his research work will be taken for what he intends it to be: scientific analyses. ... Instead, each research finding will be taken as a sign of abiding allegiance or of desertion from one army or the other.[32]

Equally exasperating difficulties, however, can surely be expected to arise.

It is to be noted, too, that the political scientist deserts the strictly outside observation post set by David Easton's defining question for political science: "How are values authoritatively allocated for a society?" in favor of a progressive effort at improving or re-creating the values themselves—in effect denying that values are self-contained nuts to be rationed among skin-contained "selves." [33]

Part II

REMAKING OF COMMUNITY

CHAPTER EIGHT

Participation

> *In all areas of life men are
> increasingly affected by policies and
> other factors over which they have
> little or no control. What is
> called for . . . is the making of a society
> in which men may acquire more
> and more competent control
> over themselves and the events which
> contribute to their shaping. We
> need democracy and
> more democracy.*
>
> FRANCIS M. MYERS

DEMOCRACY IS SAID TO BE A FORM OF SELF-GOVERNMENT. Previous chapters explained the need for an essentially democratic regime in the experimental method of social science, specifying the dependence of social science on the crucial involvement of democrat or citizen scientists in an experimental situation of Self-control. In this situation lies the germ out of which can grow a theory and practice of self-government centered in administration and attuned to the post-bomb world.

It stands to reason that a social science democratized, humanized by involving ordinary mature human being-doings in practical transactions, in "real life" situations, and experimentally changing, transforming current, living, and throbbing values, intentions, purposes is at the very heart of politics, a working part of the governmental concern—since a great many of the moral conflicts involved are necessarily at the upper level called "political." Government is becoming daily more dependent on reliable knowledge—not only in the area of environmental science, but also in the realms of organization and social action. It should be expected to accord greater and greater, deeper and deeper recognition to reliable methods of knowing—even to the extent of reshaping its organizational patterns in accommodation. Isn't this what is now happening to a limited extent in federal scientific research programs involved in the race for outer space and for supremacy in nuclear weapons? Is it not what automatic data processing is also doing in its own limited way?

There is another side to the coin, however. Political democracy, self-government, is as vital to experimental social science as knowledge is to politics. A physical science laboratory can be set up under a great variety of regimes. All it needs is non-interference and this—with temporary exceptions such as the Lysenko episode—has been granted by the great cultural dualism that separated morals and physicals, liberating the last, while keeping the first in transient chains of Teleological ethics. But a moral laboratory is society itself. Far from non-interference, it needs positive and sustaining social organization. Indeed, the larger and deeper secrets of moral and political life may well remain hidden until political democracy is comprehensively reorganized for the pursuit of truth.

The first step back toward self-government is the fundamental step forward in a new adventure in understanding. It is the awakening perception of how it is that individual Selves from out of the "teeming masses" assume a meaningful and productive role in popular politics and government, in the organizing of functional power, the taming of power under a democratic system of social control.

* * * *

To avoid misunderstanding, this is the place to pre-announce that, as will become clear in the next five chapters, the democratic participation appropriate to the politics of truth will be selective, Self-selective. Obviously, no one can be directly involved, either meaningfully or slavishly, in more than a few facets of modern life or government. Also, there must be ample room for apathy. Ralph K. Huitt has used the term "the aristocracy of the concerned" (not to be confused with minorities rule) to capture a feel for today's shifting configuration of participants, dividing up the labor of primary involvement in government according to particular interest, where the many are indifferent or unable, and decision is left to the few. As finally developed below, participation in the administrative democracy of the politics of truth will be saved from the historically associated autocratic overtones of aristocracy by sidestepping attachment to status and by approaching majority rule through the universalizing device of collective test.

PARTICIPATION IN ADMINISTRATION

Participation is frequently enough raised as the keystone of democracy. The image of the Greek city state and the New England town meeting persists despite the fact that republican institutions officially delegate the business of participation to chosen representatives. Beneath the formal legislative façade has always fermented a seething of popular participation—in the form of political party activity, organized group pressure, professional contribution, private donation of time and talent, lobbying, graft, and corruption, or just plain private pleading. It is not, then, surprising to find the demand for participation dusted off and put forth anew as we settle into a new era of administrative government.

There has been a fairly clear paralleling of the Greek device of office by lot in some of our northeastern towns where direct and unsalaried participation in administrative office is required of citizens. But this has not been a very widespread phenomenon. The Jacksonian slogan of rotation in office, on the other hand, is the closest we have come in theory on the nationwide scale to the Greek approach to direct democracy (citizen participation) in administration. The slogan, however, had little in its favor, apart from its use in partisan politics to justify the turn-over of administrative jobs to an in-coming, job-hungry party and to solidify party discipline. Its relevance to widespread participation must in fact have been slight considering the few offices and the many citizens. And it was put to naught because it denied the ever-growing complexity of administrative service: the need for experience, continuity, ability, and technical or professional education in public office. Recruitment through impartial civil service systems on the basis of merit is now considered to be a more democratic method.

More recent approaches to public participation in public administration have relied on the majority rule element of representative democracy embodied in the vote. Direct election of a multitude of local officals from coroners and justices of the peace to county clerks, recorders and district judges, however, soon led to impossibly long ballots which by their very length fostered quite the reverse of meaningful participation.

While participation through selection of personnel was being discarded as a democratic technique, the straw poll of the politician and his party was being adapted to the use of administrative organizations. With the aid of social scientists, it has grown to flourish in many fields of profound public opinion research. In the hands of a skillful administrator armed with the latest statistical methods of sampling, it can become a sort of participation by proxy. It can be used to take the pulse of the people, to test citizen reactions to administrative policies, to assess popular preferences and aversions. Thus, in a sense, without the people having to bother actively to participate, the administrator can adjust his program to their needs and wants. With a minimum of fuss he can mold his organization into a model of responsiveness, though it is very doubtful that any administrator entertains thoughts of such total use of public opinion research.

There is, however, something very undemocratic about public opinion polls; something about proxy participation rings distinctly false. It is not simply that sampling systematically selects only a few from among the total population for active "participation." After all, if a statistically perfected sampling system could achieve the same result as a compiled vote of the total population, why should the citizenry at large be bothered? There is value, too, in apathy and laziness.[1] Nor is it only that there is an element of prying and ensuing resentment inherent in the polling process. Such resentment is particularly felt in industrial situations when every-day channels of communication and complaint are displaced by research devices. Distrust of face-to-face contact between boss and employee is thereby admitted. Resentment is, however, only a symptom of something much more basic in the background. Nor is the sour ringing of opinion polls due to the fact that the information obtained may be cynically "used" and/or distorted by the opinion collectors. By now the use of polls for manufacturing consent is almost customary. The deeper discordance, the great limitation on opinion polls as substitutes for full-blown participation is that, like the vote hallowed by the practice of legislative democracy, it, far from being a process itself, is merely a record copy, a flash cross-section of human temper.

If the universe were timeless and essentially motionless, corresponding to the Cartesian description of it, public opinion research could theoretically be the end-all of participation; participation in a wider sense would not be an essential ingredient of democracy. A motion picture world, a series of stills, would be the common reality instead of the illusion we know it to be. The calculus was an ingenious and tremendously productive invention. It temporarily "solved" the problem of describing and controlling motion by treating it as a series of infinitesimal statics. But the description bequeathed us, being essentially motionless, has proven inadequate for analysis and control on the frontiers of science where process, growth, development, purpose are recognized as realities. In particular, what it thus fails to comprehend is the irreversibility and creativity so fundamentally characteristic of existence—it falters in face of the reality of time. If Cartesian description dissolves among the particles, waves and what-not of atomic physics, what hope can be held for a calculus of pleasure and pain in politics?

ROUNDED EXPERIENCE—PARGIVING AND PARTAKING

Participation, to be meaningful to the persons directly involved, and to be valuable to society, must transcend the static limitations of the vote. It must become, or become involved in, a dynamic process comprehending rounded experience. Such process is not to be achieved in terms of yesterday's "objectivity." A psychological attitude (administrative, legislative or electoral) of dispassionate "fair-mindedness," giving equal weight to the perspective of each man and doing no more—which is the most that can be said of the vote taken by itself as institutionalized "participation" in today's democracies—is a pale pretense of participation.

Its culminating fecklessness is clearly evident in the ephemeral and manipulated character of the perspectives reflected in almost any popular referendum and the downright lack of perspective engineered by the long ballot. The following newspaper account, though grossly distorting the situation it describes, beautifully testifies to the realistic disrepute of referenda: "The city council Monday night ruled out a $13,378 retainer fee for services of _____, Chicago Municipal finance consultant. _____ offered to build voter support for a referendum election on an $8,878,000 bond issue for flood controls. If the issue were to pass, _____ would claim his fee and advise on marketing the bonds, he said."

In particular, current "participation" devices do not let the public in on the formulation of problems. Problems well up from feelings, attitudes, values. Exclusion from participation in their identification, formulation, or creation is clearly undemocratic.[2] There is a sort of vicarious participation involved in the intangible, ineffable qualities which are a part of voting on the basis of personality or character rather than on issues.[3] But even this remote aspect is excluded from the process of opinion polling. To become democratic, administration must find a substitute for and a peer to the vote of representative democracy.

Genuine participation would comprise more than one-way contribution. It would be transactional. It would involve partaking as well as pargiving. In this sense the present day contributor to organized charity or the spectator-"sportsman" cannot always—perhaps not even ordinarily—be said to be participants—though, as will be shown later, there are vicarious dimensions to participation that are as genuine as any other. Mary Follett speaks of the "onlooker fallacy." "You cannot see experience without being a part of it," she says.[4] What the man in the bleachers largely or comparatively misses is the return from his doings; he only enjoys release of energy. In contrast, the player is involved in a process; his energy is being organized and reorganized as he expends it. What he does rebounds upon him and his enjoyment is enhanced by his own growth, development, progress, perfection, whether in skill or in knowing, in short, by his becoming. Participation must thus provide rounded experience or it degenerates to fad or fashion—a phenomenon clearly peripheral to democracy. Participation depends upon what Gordon W. Allport calls "ego-involvement"; it is an important element of democracy only when and as it returns a content of meaning to the individual.[5] But, more than that, democratic participation is just a trick (like propaganda) to achieve consent unless it succeeds in bringing about representation of interests that would otherwise be ignored and unless the resulting action or decision is different from what it would have been had participation not been sought. It should be obvious that of all the show put on in politics (including administration) there is very little that can be clearly called participation. At the upper levels of administration rounded experience may be fairly prevalent, but it rarely seeps "down the line" and infrequently leaks out among the public.

Furthermore, in avoiding being reduced to mere contribution, genuine participation would insist upon content deeper in time and broader in relationship than pre-set perspectives or disconnected points of view. Participation, if it is to be democratically significant in terms of self-government, must be, not an expressing of atomic selves—as in the totally futile party-line radio programs—but a relating in situation of transactional Selves. It must be a participation of interests as embodied in character.[6] This is a process in which perceptions,[7] perspectives, and points of view are evolved, made, remade. It is a process of criticism, of creation.

SEARCH FOR INSTITUTION

The institutionalization or structuring of participation must thus honor the nature of human nature—changing and transactional as it is—or it is in danger of diluting the genuine article to ineffectiveness as an aspect of democracy. Particularly dangerous is the blind faith that an institutionalized attitude, an attitude that expects to derive the "objective" truth from a sympathetic and impartial consideration of partial and divergent perspectives, can serve as sufficient structuring of participation in a democracy.[8] This would be naively to accept the limitations and false promises of status-in-equality, the limitations of accepting everyone's perspective as being as valid as everyone else's, simplistically denying the value of the individual, the rounded Self, and undermining respect for genuine functional or situational differences.[9] And in the process, building up an intolerance for objective verification. In fact, social truths—like any truths—are wrought from a participative process.

Agreement on the objective truth amid differing perspectives is achieved by a process of making and remaking perspectives in appeal to considerations apart from all the perspectives in conflict and in reliance on continuing correction from experience. The nature of an object seen in the night sky is not arbitrated by argument among those who saw saucers, those who saw cigars, and those who saw comets, but by invoking something independent of them all—what is known of the behavior of light. And it is to be noted that agreement is seldom achieved on upper hierarchical levels when it is not first achieved down below, before the process of abstraction has distilled the juice out of basic values and over-simplified the wholeness that is character. Objectivity is finally found in public test according to public rules, procedures and processes. Indeed, the objective feeling called "justice" is a function or an attribute of procedure. The great limitation on our courts of justice as instruments of justice is, correspondingly, absence of procedure encompassing the creative aspects of process.

Happily, the majority rule part, the electoral aspect, of the American governmental system does not stand alone. The vote is not all we have by way of process or participation. There is also the vast and infinitely complex operation of many, many political parties (or party parts—federal, state, county, local) and innumerable interest groups in a context of a decentralized national legislature, a decentralized national executive, decentralized state governments, frequently weak and frequently disorganized county and metropolitan governments and hundreds of thousands of local special governments, from school boards and cemetery districts to mosquito abatement districts. Unquestionably, in such a welter of jurisdictions and responsibilities there is much opportunity for participation. And instances of genuine participation (of the sort described above) do occur—for example, a voter tries to convince a school board that it has chosen the wrong site for a new school.

Part of the meaningful, though perhaps not the creative, aspect of participation is provided by interest group organization whenever it performs what David Truman considers one of its main functions: "to speed up and sharpen its members' perceptions of the consequences of actions (events) occurring or impending in the environment and related to the group's interest." [10] When this is extended to include evaluation of the group's own actions in terms of consequences (for example, the Wisconsin Committee on Forest Land Use, 1931), the group is beginning to function as an institutionalization of genuine participation. Unfortunately, this is not, in America, the common way. So long as groups remain aggregates of individuals interacting on the basis of a shared characteristic, they cannot be expected to further the achievement of genuine participation. Not only is their organization predicated upon pre-set interest, but the organization itself tends to perpetuate such interest unchanged and imperturbable, and in so doing, furthermore, incapacitates itself for appreciation of either the desirability or objectivity of terminal public test.

The activity of interest groups in the United States thus takes the pattern of bargaining usually characterized by compromise as an end product and commonly lumped in a category called, with some distaste, "power politics." This is, of course, again the ordinary method of the legislative way of life in which votes, personal favors, persuasiveness, friendliness, influence, authorities of status, the national interest, the general welfare, are "realistically" balanced against each other. The overall structure is most appropriately described as "polyarchal democracy"— minorities rule. The product is a kind of political process through which it is highly probable that any active and legitimate group can make itself effectively heard on the topic of its determined concern at some crucial stage in the process of decision.[11]

That much activity and many people are involved, much push and pull, in the struggle for group ascendancy in respect to this political matter or that, there can be no doubt. On the other hand, it is quite clear that no very significant portion of this serious activity rises above the cold bargain-compromise method to become what was described above as "genuine" participation. What participation there is arises informally—like the lady battling the school system—or takes place deep in the recesses of party conclaves or in the unheralded hush (from the public's point of view) of administrative officers. There is virtually no public, even semiformal institutionalization of "genuine" participation.

Administration is not ordinarily thought of as a participative, or even a potentially participative process. Popular stereotype pictures governmental administration as a Kafka Castle at the gates of which the little man may respectfully, or insolently—it makes no difference in the stereotype—lay his suggestion, but from whose vast and devious machinery (the paper work, red tape and insouciance in its maws) no recognizable product of the suggestion could be expected to emerge. The citizen therefore, where there is no ombudsman, voices his grievance directly to his alderman in typical bargaining fashion, to have it *forced* upon the Traffic Engineer or other "offending" party.

Indeed, the surprise would be to find that administration had developed in superb disdain of and immunity to the predominating methods enveloping it. As Robert A. Dahl remarks, "In the context of decentralized bargaining parties and a decentralized bargaining legislature, it was perhaps inevitable that despite the powerful efforts of many

Presidents and the somewhat Utopian yearnings of many administrative reformers, the vast apparatus that grew up to administer the affairs of the American welfare state is a decentralized bargaining bureaucracy." [12] The same may be said with equal relevance about local government and local administration. We find administrators and administrative agencies identifying publics relevant to them and their particular problems (somewhat as electorates are relevant to legislators) and thereupon establishing with these publics relationships patterned after (and for purposes similar to those served by) the relationships obtaining between legislators and their constituents. Not only is administration sometimes thrown into the act as balancer or reconciler of opposing interests by deliberately ambiguous legislative mandate carefully formulated to shift the burden from the legislators' backs, but it also enters the game as contender seeking support where it may from the publics (individuals or groups) with which it deals. The Corps of Engineers and the Veterans Administration afford outstanding examples. Here the ideal of public participation collapses and the practice of public relations burgeons.

BEYOND RESPONSIVENESS

For the most part, the relationships between the administrator and the public have been noted for public contribution to, rather than participation in, administration. The administrator does not depend upon his public in quite the same direct way the legislator depends on his votes. But, as far as participation is concerned, his suggestion box, in whatever disguised form it appears, generally does not significantly differ from the ballot box. The administrator is well advised to consult the man whose shoe pinches before setting about to repair the situation. All of the relevant facts are seldom in the hands of the organization's personnel. An attempt must therefore be made to tap the expertise among the citizenry—including both the special knowledge of professional and technical experts, and the unique perspective, local, occupational, or personal, of the affected common man. In a democracy responsiveness of public administration to the needs, desires, values, purposes of the citizens is rightly emphasized.

But responsiveness is wrongly taken for participation and dangerously identified as *the* mark of democracy. Unless participation can be clearly seen to be more than responsiveness, there is danger of retreat to a Platonic Republicanism or to a well meaning Mayo paternalism. This is where participation leads when it is reduced to a question of "morale." Such paternalism is exemplified in the rigid distinction the Mayo persuasion seems to see between Managers and Subordinates[13] with the former accorded the task of creating "morale" by various "scientifically" discovered devices of "participation."[14] This approach contains, in addition, an element of Machiavellianism which becomes particularly apparent in studied prescriptions for relating participation to motivation, where participation is treated as an instrument of the leadership group for attaining the goals it has set.[15] There is Machiavellianism even in the way Wilson's classic essay, of all things, reads:

> He must first make public opinion willing to listen and then see to it that it
> listens to the right things. He must stir it up to search for an opinion, and
> then manage to put the right opinion in its way.[16]

Business and industry have liberally experimented with ways to make the worker feel a real sense of participation in the enterprise he works for. Labor-management production committees, profit-sharing plans, bonus plans, worker-dividend arrangements, stock-buying programs, and general-welfare funds may be mentioned as examples. And such devices (or philosophies) as "conference training," "multiple management,"[17] "consultative supervision,"[18] and "union-management cooperation,"[19] give evidence of genuine achievement of participation—especially at the higher levels of administration.

The question remains whether any motivational devices for the work situation or even the most enlightened personnel policies can return to a man the character, the integrity denied him by the process of production. A man's job is only part of his life and his interest—certainly seldom a fulfillment. Much more is involved in the association, the inter- or transrelating of people than adapting to technical change, lessening conflict, resolving differences, creating "job satisfaction," efficiency.[20] It is for this reason that apathy to plans for total "participation" in partial problems is as often a sign of mental health as of slothful ignorance. And America has a history full of such healthy, though not always clearly understood, passive resistance: resistance to the Department of Agriculture's fomenting of local democracy through a citizen participation program emphasizing farm problems and almost no others; resistance to management's free enterprise campaign;[21] resistance to the totalcommitment hopes of union organization. . . .

Elton Mayo's paternalism is based on a gross over-simplification of the human situation. From his readings in history he has concluded that administration (as well as government) alternates between phases of "centralized" control and "normal democratic" control. Centralized control is for meeting emergencies that periodically arise; normal democratic control is for the intervening periods of peace and for the "civilized" society "based on understanding and a will to work together."[22] History may indeed display a cyclical alternation between such modes of control. But it also gives evidence of fundamental, irreversible change and development. Ignoring this, Mayo is content to settle in on a happy medieval plane of "cooperation." [23] In doing so, he puts a premium on stasis, on security, throwing out all the value in conflict and growth.[24] The difference between his paternalism and genuine participation is the difference between identifying purposes and developing purposes, between stasis and process.[25]

On the other hand, participation should not be confused with mere activity either. The child who hums loudly at the dentist's request in order to drown out the frightening buzz of the drill is taking part in an activity, but he is not participating in the sense the term is here being used. Activity of this sort, not even being a technique for tapping knowledge or purpose, is a means of engineering consent—like a football rally, indeed, like many a political rally, like stuffing letters and licking stamps in a campaign headquarters. One of the criticisms, whether justified or not, of the Department of Agriculture's "new democracy" (New Deal and after) has been that its purpose was merely to involve citizens in substantive programs in order to facilitate execution; it was not a decentralization of the decision-making process.[26] If it would be genuinely participative, such activity must be meaningfully incorporated into a process of rounded experience. Simply involving people is not enough; they must be involved through a deliberately chosen process that will contribute to their growth and to the integration and perfection of their purposes.

Many administrative devices have been invented to facilitate responsiveness, to draw on national resources of special knowledge, experience, and particularity, and to enlist a broadened taking-part in administration. The following classified list was developed by John D. Lewis:

1. Decentralized administration through citizen boards, not selected on a group-representative basis.
2. Decentralized administration through boards or committees selected from a particular occupational group.
3. Consultation of a whole occupational group through referenda for advice on or consent to administrative action.
4. Delegation to an organized interest group of initiative in setting standards or formulating policy.
5. Delegation to an organized interest group of initiative in setting standards or formulating policy, with responsibility for enforcement.
6. Representation of vocational or interest groups in administrative agencies for any of several functions including setting standards, regulation, and conciliation.

7. The use of commissions of inquiry set up *ad hoc* with expert personnel for advice on overall policy.

8. Regular administrative consultation of permanent advisory committees composed of experts or group-representatives.[27]

Other categories should perhaps be added. They run the gamut from Natural Beauty Commissions to the General Advisory Committee of the AEC.

The various devices to encourage responsiveness have various drawbacks, however. For example, delegation to an organized interest group should be balanced with the warning that democracy is not promoted by putting rabbits in charge of carrots. Advisory boards frequently degenerate to sounding boards for administrative suggestions. The degree of representativeness possible in any group organized for consultation is highly debatable. Committees are sometimes very handily "used" for avoiding responsibility, and then they sometimes veer off in unanticipated directions.[28] Administrative organization may even, in many instances, be in a more sensitive and understanding position respecting private interests (in effect more representative) than the formal advisory committee. Taken together, however, this list of devices is clear evidence of inventiveness and of administrative desire to profit by accumulation of scattered wisdom.[29]

Besides securing possibility of responsiveness, of tapping citizen expertise and purposes, these devices can help serve the further purpose of assuring accountability. Undesirable attitudes, habits and methods on the part of the personnel, or the administrator, autocratic or mechanical tendencies, may be avoided or held in check. Although other failings may develop, simply involving numbers of citizens in the doings of administration helps obviate some administrative failings. Nevertheless, accountability must remain insecure so long as it is not deliberately built into a regular and habitually accepted method. In particular it must avoid attachment to a pre-set standard and accept alliance only with a democratic method that is currently evolving standards out of give-and-take.

THE OTHER HALF OF PARTICIPATION

Finally, the administrator may reverse the flow of the special knowledge tap and attempt to direct a stream of information, education toward the "outsiders" who have become involved by the various techniques mentioned above. This maneuver sometimes is, and frequently is interpreted as, a sheer propaganda effort designed, again, for the engineering of consent as a support in the balance of bargaining groups. It can be perverted into "managing the news" or into public relations jobs for "controlling" referenda. Nevertheless, it is vitally important that government programs be explained and interpreted to those whom they affect. This applies both to regulatory and service programs. A regulatory program tends to work with a minimum of friction when there is understanding of the need it serves, the objectives it aims at and the methods it uses. The OPA in wartime rationing, for example, made a notable attempt in its use of community service panels at the local level both as organs for spreading information and as sounding boards for public complaints and suggestions.[30] The value of a service program is diminished when the potential clientele is not adequately informed of its availability and advantages. This is why each extension of social security coverage is preceded by such a barrage of information. Furthermore, the development of research activities as an essential part of many administrative organizations, with important findings coming in at an increasing rate, has made it imperative to seek new channels whereby such findings may be disseminated or directed into education. The scientific information services of the United States Department of Agriculture exemplify such efforts to disseminate information. With science since World War II increasingly requiring financing by public funds, upsetting traditional relationships between government, science and the private sector, the matter of the outward flow half of participation becomes vital.

It is not generally appreciated that the flow of information and suggestion *to* the individual or group is as important an aspect of participation as is the barrage of suggestions and information *from* the individual or group. Talking is considered to be active, and therefore participative, while listening is passive and more inert than not. This lack of understanding comes about mainly because participation is thought of as activity and action in turn is considered to be characterized by directly perceptible movement. It is another case of mind-matter dualism. But activity so interpreted soon becomes murky, and eventually nears meaninglessness.[31] Where human being-doings are concerned, there is no convenient place at which activity can be cut off and separated from inactivity—short of death. The moment neural activity and the transference of electrical impulses in the brain were discovered, feeling and thinking had to be admitted within the stretch of activity. With matter now interpreted by a simple formula, $E=mc^2$, as a form of energy, the erstwhile wall between being and doing crumbles, and doing becomes primary in terms of significance to the human situation. This has brought us back somewhere near Aristotle's "virtuous activity of the soul" to a point where "passive" listening can be participative.

The meaningful distinction within the realms of contemplation is between active thought, feeling, listening, that makes an experienced difference within a particular situation in terms of results, and passive thought, feeling, hearing, that cannot be so related. Much of what goes under such heads as reading, writing, speaking, listening, speculating, considering, deciding, etc. is activity as truly as is a wrestling match. And these activities can be participative if they are not blocked off in the isolation of indifference, in the passive resistance of misunderstanding, from systematic interrelation with other sorts of activity. The channeling of information into education is frequently the return process from public contribution, the active rounding of experience that makes a practical difference.

Both administrative dissemination of information and public contribution of specialized knowledge are essential parts of the process of participation, though neither of them is the thing in itself. Together they comprise genuine participation only when transactionally related by a deliberate or habitual method. An indiscriminately broadcast barrage of information does not necessarily pertain to anything resembling participation, though it may accidentally fall on fertile ground due simply to the dispersed spread of its impact. Psychologically it is equivalent to propaganda unless organically related, unless integrated, within a total perceptive-purposive process.

PARTICIPATION AND PUBLIC PURPOSE

The purpose of participation in government—legislative or administrative—is larger than any of the specific purposes mentioned above or than their sum. The purpose of participation is to develop common or shared purposes. The overall purpose of participation in government, of Self government, is to develop public purposes. This is not the same as to say that the overall purpose of Self government is to achieve agreement on purposes of fundamental importance. The persuasive, charismatic leader, the skillful demagogue, the battle-blessed military hero, inspire agreement on purposes, but on purposes that are antecedent in respect to any of the individuals coming to adhere to them. Such purposes are espoused after the fact. They are accepted because they appeal to some already formed element—prejudice, fear, stereotype, purpose, principle—in the make-up of the individual. To say that participation *develops* purpose is to say that it is a method through which purposes are created out of the basic raw materials of the situation rather than superimposed on them. In any case, it is not agreement that validates purposes. It is the developing of purposes that counts, holding them tentatively "true" as hypotheses in motion, in a given stage of transaction.

An administrative information program that does not relate to a process out of which purposes are developing tends in the direction of persuasiveness on the basis of ready-made principles, purposes, or what-not. All too frequently the fate of new creative organization (e.g., TVA) is to degenerate from participation to persuasion. Such a program of persuasion, far from comprehending participation, reduces to measures for avoiding conflict. It becomes a program where decisions and policies are made in ways designed to avoid the need for public justification or to dodge the possibility of intellectual attack, "public relations" replacing reasoned argument. In result, it perpetuates coercive power and rigid authority in place of functional power and social control. Instead of avoiding conflict, conduct should attempt to take into account all of the values, purposes, intents, desires involved, defining these by the conflict out of which they arise and take shape. As George Herbert Mead says, "For purposes of conduct, values define themselves definitely enough when they are brought into conflict with each other. So facts define themselves in scientific problems." [32] The business of participation is to find a way of dealing with conflict without stifling it. Only by taking the raw materials that make their presence known through conflict, and reworking them, can the public or publics *develop* purposes. And only as participation succeeds in developing public purposes can it be the keystone of Self-governing democracy.

SUMMARY

History has not bequeathed a pattern for democratic participation in government that is workable today on this newly populous planet. For the completion of a Self what is needed is what has been called "rounded experience." [33] For the community likewise, the need is an institution more encompassing than the paternalism of governmental responsiveness. What is needed is a participation that includes both contribution and growth, par-giving and par-taking, governmental responsiveness and information program, and that can be considered democratic in the face of continuing, abundant, and abounding apathy.[34] Participation, in abstract description, mounts to a goal of creating public purposes by nurturing the conflict out of which they can emerge and then extracting them through a deliberate process of full-bodied transaction.

CHAPTER NINE

In Search of a Conservative Theory

Content is a word unknown to life;
it is also a word unknown to man.

LOREN EISELEY

TWO ASPECTS, FACES, TWISTS OF LIFE DESERVE PARTICULAR attention in the course of inquiry into effective participation. They are called, in the pages that follow, the "radical bent" and "conservative drag." An attempt will be made to sort them out and to indicate how, as modes behind behavior, an understanding of them is essential to understanding and thinking about democratic participation. In particular the characteristics of "conservative drag" will be seen to determine the possibility and conditions of a democratic participation and of a correlative theoretical construction. The virtues of apathy will be reviewed in chapter 10.

BACK TO FUNDAMENTALS

No man has ever lived who did not want to turn something inside out, upside down, or round about. Whether it is rearranging furniture in the living room, or reorganizing a government bureau, someone always thinks of an improvement that will be in some sense preferable to the current condition. *Characte*ristically, people are unwilling to let things remain as they are. This is the radical bent that twists human nature from deep down in its roots.[1] It is the stirring of creativity in the individual in quest of enhanced values, renewed or improved satisfactions. It is even more. It is an eternal dissatisfaction with what is. Is it perhaps the genius of life itself? the squirming germ of evolution? the elementary particle of purpose? the characteristic human expression of the law of the living—ceaseless change?

The elements of the conservative mood, on the other hand, appear to be surface phenomena—petulance counter to the currents of change.

Appearances are deceiving, however. The elements of the conservative mood find common deep root with the radical bent, of which they are essentially an inverted version. Indeed the elements of the conservative mood may be deeper than we know. As of just yesterday we are brought up short and projected into open-ended speculation by a conceivably relevant advance in physics: physicists have begun to detect something they call "strangeness"—a reluctance to change, built into the very heart of matter. Where this discovery leads, if at all, we can scarcely guess.

The stuff of which "conservatism" is the far removed abstraction is the demand for participation. It is the claim of the other man, the man left out. It is his Self-assertion, his claim to the enhancement of values in the culmination of the transaction, the situation, at hand. A particular proposal for change (for example, a suggestion to change from hourly work to piece-work, or to reorganize a filing system) meets positive opposition, to be sure, by those who would be hurt by the change. But it also, and more immediately, encounters conservative drag, an almost automatic resistance on the part of those concerned whose decision it was not.[2] Opposition to federal aid to education comes first from those local individuals and groups who fear that future decisions will no longer be their own. This is not a struggle for "power" as usually interpreted, nor simply resistance to change *per se*. It is a direct derivative from and a simple reaction against the fact, or fancy, of a Self (or Selves) unilaterally decreeing or proposing where other Selves are involved. (NB: The large S, to repeat, is used to specify the social Self, the intimate Self extending beyond a man's skin, not at all to imply an unchangeable essence—not transcendence but scope—in the sense that a teacher's Self includes "her" class, a child's Self includes his mother, a hunter's Self includes his trophy, or an author's Self includes "his" book.) Conservative drag is a Self protection, the obverse of the radical bent, being not the divine discontent itself leading to quest for enhanced values and improved satisfactions, but rather determination not to be disqualified in the quest. One of the most clear collective manifestations of conservative drag is the way the American lower-middle and middle classes, in the aftermath of riots and campus disorders, stand up at the polls in city after city to express their sense of political neglect—in resentment of agitation to spend "their" tax dollars on others who are not expected to "make it the hard way."

It is not intended here to suggest that anyone can be interested in many things, or concerned enough in more than a very few matters to be dissatisfied about them, or even aware of them. Looking back from the larger perspective, it is clear that only a concerned few are involved in the decision on any issue, today. Looking ahead from the personal perspective of the Self, it appears that each person is as much involved in as many, if not more, things as ever, though he cannot be attentive to, aware of, or able about many of the issues that affect him. It is the quality of such involvement as there is, and the exclusion from involvement in areas of awareness and concern that are most critical to the Self.

In anticipation of succeeding chapters, it is to be noted that the threat implicit in a change, a solution to a problem, a new idea is put aside when the new comes out of close association, that is to say, when the suggester is, however momentarily, a part of the Self. Everyone has probably at some time noticed that the quality of a solution is not quite the same if the other fellow solves the problem. There is even a sort of resentment to be felt. On the other hand, a secondhand elegant solution can be eagerly embraced when it develops out of a sufficiently sensitive associational relationship, like a symphony orchestra, or an improvising jazz combo (or even sometimes out of a vicarious associational relationship),[3]—which is not to be wondered at considering the fact that human nature itself is a group product; that everything man is or does, and what he has become, is molded in human association. It cannot be denied that externally imposed or proposed change may sometimes be received without reluctance for any of a number of reasons aside from association; for example, for relief from boredom, for plain deviltry, whim or playfulness of the moment, or just for the simple sake of change. But it will be observed that in most cases of ready or eager acceptance some extension of the Self is involved—a close friendship, a religious, political or moral identification, an habitual or spiritual followership, a desire to be one of the gang, a wish to solidify a beginning acquaintance.

This basic stuff, this conservative drag is so prevalent, so pervading that it seems almost "natural." It is so basic as to be almost the condition of stability in human organization. As an insistence on working together, it points back again to the fundamental importance of the group basis of human nature, to the fact that the human being-doing exists only because of and through association, being from the very first— from prehuman days, from the day when dawn man invented the permanent family in celebration of the dawn of non-seasonal sexuality (if not before)—innately gregarious, the very creature of his fellows. Perhaps it points back to the primordial sin of deviating from clan behavior, the sin of breaking taboo without first, through organic leadership, bringing the group to grow beyond it. At any rate, conservative drag is essentially an elemental expression of the operation of the group character of human nature.

This kind of resistance to change is a dim awareness on the part of the individual that he loses his soul when someone else solves his problems for him. Each change made in a man's behalf (even if only incidentally), but not by himself, lessens his immunity to the disease of stagnation and leaves him thus much less equipped to face even the problems that are unavoidably his own. (This is recently very vividly seen in the plight of a sizable group of American black men called "unemployable" and literally down and *out*. Out of society, that is. It also provides more of the background to student protest in American universities than has yet been appreciated—even by the protesters.) His most precious stock in trade, his Self-control, that is, his part in the control of a social situation, is denied to him.[4] Instead he is invited to exercise the "virtue" of self-suppression, and he is personally (apart from the collapse of social control, which at some remove follows the shaping or shambling of contributory Self-controls) left to dread a future precarious because to him haphazard. Unfortunately, clear awareness of the potential havoc from this sort of sabotage of human souls sometimes comes only at the extreme—when the process of damnation has culminated in the climactic degradations of Nazism or some other modern tyranny (or "plebiscite democracy") established "for" the people and oversimply defining as democratic any act satisfying the needs, wants, interests of the people.

Confronted with over-much unchosen change, a natural reaction of fear and lost confidence is blindly to strike back, to bomb churches, to beat civil rights demonstrators. On the broader political level, conservative drag shows forth in such social movements as self-determination and anti-colonialism. It can even be expressed in revolution. Resentment of charity by the recipient is another of its many obvious appearances. Externally engineered change in fact imposes impotence. The gift of economic aid to less developed nations must be resented. This is why American generosity must be felt as oppression. Aquinas' metaphor or the light of the sun and the seeing of the eye[5] may be of value here. Somehow gifts, instead of sapping Self-control and shrinking souls, must convey the capacity for Self-help[6] or else they should not be tendered at all. This truth holds as well for gifts of wisdom as for gifts of goods, credit and service. Participation must somehow be evoked by the Grace of conservative attitudes.

The conservative protest is a deep down denunciation of evil. Change is wrong when it impedes the emergence or enhancement of value.[7] This is commonly recognized in simple situations involving only one person, as for example when John puts too much salt in his soup. A more subtle but directly comparable wrong is committed in more complex and social situations, however, for example, when the chef's new dish is spurned, he is warned: "Never again!" and is thenceforth handed detailed and unvariable menus from above. From then on the craftsman is producing out of his raw material changes that have little or nothing to do with creation. That the wrong in such a situation is frequently not recognized, indicates again the frailty of social perception.[8] Restricting the participation of those involved in a choice or decision is not only wrong in that the change or choice, the product, is more likely to obstruct and less likely to promote achievement—pleasure, satisfaction, development, or fulfillment. It is also wrong, and more importantly, in that the fact of being omitted from the process of choice or decision-making lessens the enhancement of value (purpose) embodied in the subsequent results.[9]

The values brought into the process of choice and those created in and shaped by the process are bound to vary with the amount and quality of the participation involved. They will be subtly shifting, changing, transmuting during the entire process. Values are not something external, beyond the skin of the chooser, something picked out of the sky. They are complex products of transaction pieced together, made, altered, transmuted, tempered, qualified, rebuilt in the transaction of choosing. The success of a choice in enhancing values thus cannot be divorced from the process through which the choice was made, and every exclusion of individuals from the process obstructs for them the emergence of value attributes, leaving them that much the poorer.

Limitation of participation bids fair to lay bare the raw nerves at the very core of character, those that hold the Self in coherence. For one thing, the circle of rounded experience described above[10] is broken apart when participation is limited. This is one of the major dislocations of the present age. Completed experiences are increasingly rare. We do many more and many more diverse and interesting things than our ancestors did, but we more and more rarely see or feel the end results of our doings. Things are really less interesting now because we can see only fragments. We are compulsively sending rockets into the void, so to speak, without any means of assessing their impact on the universe. Within the confines of Newton's relatively simple social system, the apple (or word) one tossed into the air descended on one's own head—one saw the universal pattern—and the shoemaker's shoes hurt his own feet, if not those of his testy next-door neighbor. Today we know not where our words or apples fall—the new pattern is too vast and complex to view—or whom our shoes pinch—except perhaps after extensive team research, but then only statistically, seldom with any immediacy or with a possibility of correlating original action with final reaction on a one-to-one basis. Without a grasp of the impact of action, human purpose hangs limp and unassured, unconfident and un-Self-possessed. Deprived of the return from his doings, the rounding of his experience, the modern human being-doing is thumbless among the extensive intervening middle-man mechanisms of today's technology that disrupt the completion of life's meaningful transactions. The wonder is that there is as much co-herence in character as there is.

Humanity is tolerant and malleable. Over the years men have learned to live with disjunction. They compensate by satisfying themselves with completion in family life or organized sports; or by return to religion they console themselves for social failure. Some suffer along, living half lives, denying responsibility for their actions, putting it off on the system or "the guy whose job it is," and are preserved, quite simply, by their own apathy. Fortunately there is a small point of salvation here on earth, taking advantage of the specially human device, the brain. Community need not slavishly follow the pristine pattern of physical, emotional, kinesthetic, barter-market relationships. Vicarious experiences can some-times help to some extent to span the void for the some who will expend the thought, the time, the energy, and the imagination.

For another thing, perceptions are distorted and capacity for percep-tion is diminished when participation is limited. As is now well-known, perception is a two-way, back-and-forth event, a reciprocal relationship; it is not simply a matter of the "outside" world impinging on sense re-ceptors and etching thereon true copies of "reality." Perceptions don't happen; they are *made*, composed, constructed out of the "booming, buzzing confusion," in an elaborate transaction of give and take between organism and environment. Perceptions are not pictures but signals, cues to conduct. They are tested (as was explained in a previous chap-ter)[11] by the success (value enhancement, integration) of the choice to which they, as signals, point. When change is unchosen (including those many situations when the change is chosen by someone else and the many affected are excluded from participation) the haphazard usurps the place of the verifying process in perception; without the choosing, the question of the success of the perception becomes moot. This is the stuff of which visions and fantasies are wrought. Anxiety and thumb-lessness, and at the extremes compulsive dependence (groupism) or eclectic, blustering independence may ensue. Certainly Self-assurance is sapped where the sense of the reliability of perceptions and thus choices is undermined.

In sum, coming full circle, conservative drag flies to the aid of the radical bent. It wars against the evil that would cripple character by short-circuiting experience and blighting perception. It erects a wall of Self-defense to shelter the tender stirrings of creativity, the human ex-pression of the genius of life, organizing participative battlements to

assure that humans in association will not be overwhelmed by uncoordinated change.

IN THE POLITICAL ARENA:
PROGRESS AND COMPROMISE

Resistance to change based originally in conservative drag is intensified at the political level by difficulties in communication. These, in
turn, are essentially problems of objectivity—of the objectivity that
is found in public test.[12] Operational and not ontological, objectivity is
pursued through seeking assurance that we understand each other, a
bypath unfortunately not always travelled by what passes for communication. Facts, as we now understand, are man made. Potential
facts (to speak loosely) become objective, they are validated, as they are
put through a process of social *determina*tion. Interference with this
objectivizing process—with the social determining of fact—must pro-
foundly influence human reaction to proposed changes, for the relevant
facts-in-the-making, the proposals themselves, are thereby cut short of
full fashioning. Doubt and resistance automatically arise where the objectivity of mutual understanding is blocked. Where new understandings,
explanations, formulations, are needed, common language ambiguities,
plus the ever-recurring, difficulties of talking about new things in old
ways—within the confines of an old and limiting universe of discourse,
that is—add further obstacles to objectivity. They commonly hinder
objective handling, analysis, or display of emergent ideas, proposals,
purposes. Intensified by failings in objectivity, tendencies that are conservative of the integrity of individual Selves and insistent upon abundant participation in the first instance ripen at the political level into
social attitudes and movements of boundless diversity.

Any conservatism that becomes clearly apparent in the larger social,
political arena can be said to be a growth from out of moral failure—
almost by definition. Somewhere along the line, for lack of objectivity or
for whatever reason, social, political organization has failed adequately
to recognize the group character of man, to coordinate pertinent participation; it has failed to achieve the modicum of coordination needed
for the maximizing of values, satisfactions, so they in turn may stave
off a snowballing protest. Here is the basis for the social, political conservative movements and organizings that become constructive elements
in the social system.

What may be called "arch conservatism" develops as a perversion,
a sickness from the basic conservative protest, ending up by convincing
itself (from Plato to Kirk) that there are fundamental unchangeable,
imperturbable elements, aspects, forces, or what-have-you in the make-

up of human nature, and maintaining on this account that many or most attempts at change are and can be foretold to be futile, if not iniquitous, from their inception. Such an arch conservative position, however, can alternatively spring up as a simple febrile rationalization of a position assumed in response to a practical threat or series of threats. It is interesting to note that torpor, stagnation, rest, relief, though sometimes prized as values in themselves, are secondary or derivative only and can trace their lineage by turns to the radical bent or to arch-conservatism. In some circumstances they are plain and simple expressions of the radical bent, desirable ends to be achieved by grace of change. In other circumstances they can be fully understood only as perversions, inversions, withdrawals, inordinate compensatory reactions.

In recent times the dominant conservative strain of Western culture has come to be expressed in the doctrine of inevitable or automatic social progress. This doctrine, incidentally, should not be confused with the melioristic concept of scientific progress discussed above.[13] Its anomalous culmination has been a pervasive cultural reluctance to organize control—or even to think about it—in broad sectors of political, social life. The organization it has implied and fostered has been the compromise system of resolving conflict—in turn anomalous because compromise, in which each side must sacrifice part of its interest, involves a systematic disavowal of the insistence of conservative drag on value enhancement.[14]

This "progressive" turn in the evolution of conservatism was historically linked with two very significant factors in the development of Western Europe: (1) the scientific revolution, and (2) the conditions of political stalemate from which arose the political virtue of toleration. Progressive conservatism can be said to be tinged by both.

Because it produced continual change willy-nilly, frequently so remotely related to inventions and intentions as to seem outside the scope of human control, the scientific revolution directed the organization of the basic stuff of conservatism toward veneration of automatic regulation —the unseen hand of the market in economic affairs, and later the compromise methods of legislatures in political affairs. Because science undermined the relatively stable social customs which had automatically regulated the functioning of society and because society was not prepared to substitute intentional regulation or control, the job of regulation was not performed at all. It was left to an imaginary automatic market, to chance.[15] True to the scientific spirit, the conservatism of progress declined to repudiate change. On the contrary it accepted it as entirely appropriate—the to-be-expected, and even encouraged, way of the world. The conservatism of progress remained, nevertheless, a resistance to change; not to change as such, but to human, which is to say, moral, directing of change. It became, and remains an opposition to deliberate planning and thus to effective effort at social control.

Here again the influence of Cartesian dualism can be seen and the fact of the half-way (meaning, "natural" but not social) success of the scientific method. There seems to be something in the scientific method that helps to arrest the development, within its provinces, of aberrations from out of the basic stuff of conservatism. Unfortunately there is not much that is comparable in current social methods to afford relief from the canker of conservative excesses in morals and politics.

Change is a built-in feature of scientific method. Science *is* deliberate change; within the halls of science change is accepted as a way of life. As experimental science took over from ancient science of direct appreciation, a scientific ethos[16] directly opposed to generalization from the basic stuff of conservatism took shape; an ethos that demanded creative tension between (1) devoted loyalty to scientific method and its fruits in knowing, and (2) determined effort, even joy, in finding science at fault and its knowings incomplete, wrong, or deceptive; an attitude, as one zoology teacher put it, of entertaining theories but being on guard against being entertained by them.[17] As a result of this ethos, this scientific attitude, the basic stuff of conservatism is found to be organized right into the method of experimental inquiry; the otherwise almost automatic play of conservative drag is neutralized because the demand for participation is subsumed within the social relations of science; each individual's demand for inclusion is so caught up in the network of social relations that "automatic" resistance to change has no opportunity to take shape. And it is on this basis that the scientific method has come to be felt to be authoritative.

The inner working of scientific method that helps individual scientists rise above the deep-seated resistance to new ideas in their fields of inquiry is understandable only in terms of the special social system of scientific method (the third scientific frame of reference described in chapter 5) wherein picking holes in old beliefs is systematically encouraged and change is institutionalized as a technique of observation. What happens is that, as a special collective enterprise, science provides an especially effective environment for the extension of the human Selves involved. Innovation sensitively developed within the collective enterprise is correspondingly brought also within the ambit of the extending Self. The basic stuff of conservatism, the clamor for inclusion, is thereby accommodated in a special human sort of way sometimes identified as vicarious experience.[18] Exposure to frequent change, to continual self-correction, within a reliable method or way of knowing begins to affect the very bones of participants, conditioning them to novelty through knowing, as the method gains the stature of authority.

The contrast to this of the situation in social affairs is sharp and clearly evident. In the non-"natural" area where human desires, values, purposes were more obviously and intimately involved than they were in the "natural" world, and where experimental science had got no substantial foothold, the clamor for inclusion, for participation, was historically extrapolated into a generalized resistance to change. (Incidentally, the fact that change in social affairs is irreversible, that time is here a reality which cannot be disregarded, also distinguishes moral from macroscopic physical affairs and reinforces resistance to social change.) The idea of government as an automatic balancing machine served conveniently to permit generalized conservative moral recalcitrance at the same time that it officially tolerated the headlong pace of "physical" innovation—in which field it had been undercut by scientific method.

The tolerance we pride ourselves on today can be described as a direct result of social conditions of political and religious stalemate in the struggle for ascendance in choice, though there were no doubt many other factors involved. Powerful reinforcements have since arrived from the legions of science and technology, which have so compressed the world, so bombarded the individual with so many additional matters relevant to his life that it has become impossible for him to be ardent about them all (span of control), and have at the same time so expanded the complexity of experience as to obscure the degree of involvement of human Selves in the choices of others. In America the openness and isolation of frontier life further abetted this denial of involvement. Under these combined conditions tolerance comes easy.

The spirit or virtue of tolerance that gradually unfolded neatly contributed to the organization of the conservatism of drift. Under the aegis of this spirit the method of compromise was institutionalized. Both uncontrolled change and tolerance are prerequisites to the propagation of compromise as a mode of political action. It is possible that the spirit of tolerance and the method of compromise ripened together. Perhaps the two are only distinguishable aspects of the same gross development. At any rate, it came about that adherence to a method of drift-compromise rather than to a group, an aristocracy, became the focus of American conservative tradition.

In mid-twentieth century, sticking to drift ends in distrust of deliberate planning and in opposition to its effective extension. In place of control with its promise of melioration through the agency of coordinated human intentions, Americans cling ever more to the method of compromise and drift, cherishing the idea that government is a matter of balancing out competing interests, only occasionally renewing the balance by median-struck compromises.[19]

One of the most curious aspects of this equilibrating philosophy of government is that so much—very nearly all, except in particular conflict areas for which we have inherited special sensitivity from bygone ages —of the pulling and hauling of individuals and groups in behalf of their particular interests should be so grandly dismissed as amoral. It is, of course, by definition immediately a moral matter, a moral situation being found in simplest form wherever two sets of human interests clash. That it is not so by feeling comes about from the tempering of ardor by the spirit of tolerance.

Time and again, however, the conservative clamor for participation wells up clear and refreshed from the deep springs of human being-doing. Usually called "liberalism," it unfurls the twin banners of self-government and democracy, declaring the first the second and the second the all. Now, as always, is the time for renewal of the human spirit through abundant participation. Now, as never before, is the basic understanding available so that a genuine participation can be effectively institutionalized on a conservative theoretical groundwork that permits —no encourages!—improvement. The world must now in its burgeoning ripeness be ready to replace wind-blown tumbleweed participation with a measured, growing, perfectible institution. The mid-twentieth century black American emancipation movement and the world-spread awakening and arising of the non-Caucasian races are essentially conservative in deepest impulse. They need to be reinterpreted and the radical bent aspect of their occurrence played down, given its proper perspective. Then only will it be possible to work toward guidance through formulation of a positive and useful theory grounded in conservative drag.

ADVANTAGES OF CONSERVATIVE BACKGROUND TO PARTICIPATION THEORY

Talk about and agitation in behalf of participation in governmental decisions seems at first appearance to spring from the divine discontent of the radical bent. Radical support has never been completely satisfactory, however. It tends to be too singular in purpose, too sporadic in impulse. The precise underpinnings to each cry for broadened inclusion may be impossible to uncover, and to try to search them out would certainly be a feckless occupation at best. In final analysis, however, the radical bent is probably always mixed with conservative drag in any social movement toward self-government. Thus the Jacksonian movement with its doctrine of rotation in office, while at least primarily sparked by individual and group desires for specific improvements in their lots, was nevertheless, though perhaps dumbly, a movement of soul salvation in claiming a broadened part in decision-making.

A theory of participation needs a foundation broader than the radical bent. Creativity, escape, the occurrence of novelty, these being the essence of the radical bent, mark the limit of experience,[20] the bound beyond which experience falters as guide to action.[21] By the very nature of novelty, when the emergent is encountered, precedence, if there can be said to be any at all, is unreliable; there is no pertinent standard of judgment. Correspondingly, if it would not be fantasy, participation theory grounded in the radical bent retreats at this point to the eclectic, to elaborations and justifications woven around particular plans, proposals, or packaged programs. This can be said to explain a crucial inadequacy in classic socialist theories of participation developed after-the-fact, so to speak, of economic demands for a share of the wealth of the world. G. D. H. Cole comes to mind as a good example of such elaboration.

The problem to be attacked by participation theory for today is the tragic cycle described many years ago by Charles E. Merriam:

> The wide gap between the understanding of machines and of social mechanisms is one of the greatest danger points in our civilization.... As danger comes on, the mind trained in machines but not in social mechanisms recoils in panic and turns against all forms of social change, falling back upon the traditional and unchanging as a port of security, at the very moment when it has been rendered untenable by the new forces of invention and discovery. The next step in this *non sequitur* is to employ violence to repress changes necessitated by science.

> Machine mining in coal—distress—proposed socialization [radical bent]— resentment [conservative drag] and appeal to tradition [arch conservatism] —violence and repression—this is the tragic cycle of our day in other than coal fields, over the wide range of industrial and social reorganization.[22]

The organized agencies of political and social change in the more stable democracies have been able to handle these crises—the internal ones— tolerably well, though by no means with justice all around. But the way of escape from the cycle has not so far been found.

Remedial impulses stemming from the radical bent, while they have provided phases of the cycle itself, have not pointed the direction of release from such repetitive turnings of events. They have not so far been able to break loose from or to transcend the enveloping balance of the theory of compromise conservatism which, in embracing the convenience of daily compromise, hand to mouth with daily bread, has served only to perpetuate the tragic cycle while merely mellowing conditions on its fringes. "Get out the vote!" combined with freedom of speech and political parties, has been America's standard theoretical answer, the peak of its wisdom about citizen involvement in solution of political problems.

On the other hand, participation theory grounded mainly in the basic stuff of conservatism has also tended—with the important exception of Calhoun—to be ineffectual. It has frequently seemed unrealistic, wishy-washy, ivory-towerish. Hard-headed, practical folk have read it as over-eager, over-wishful humanitarian or religious sentimentality. There has been something essentially artificial, for example, about insistence upon "one man, one vote" on the grounds of equality in the sight of God. Continuing exhortation is a sure sign of ineffectiveness.

Of course the recalcitrance of existing traditional representative institutions has held back and/or diverted the search for a meaning of participation outside of the purview of the compromise method. New patterns of association—administrative patterns—however, have now come to predominate in the counsels of government. And here is, realistically, where expanded participation, if it is to be effective, must be sought. It is true that the administrative way of life now affects a protective coloration of compromise. However, it is equally true that compromise is not a necessary theoretical base to the administrative as it has been to the legislative way of life.

As we all know from watching Congress and the President during the last few generations, the maelstrom of decision-making centers now over administrative, not legislative, halls. Both administration and legislature now make policy. But administration, in addition, is constrained to fill in the chinks of the necessarily very general policy legislatively proclaimed. It must refine and interpret legislative laws, reconcile inconsistencies, adapt policy to unanticipated contingencies. . . . Fortunately the branch of government most active and persuasive in matters of decision is also the branch most possibly amenable to reorganization on the basis of new patterns of participation. New patterns of administrative association abound and reluctance to try out even more can be overcome. There is room aplenty for patterns well grounded in conservative drag. And the new light that has been thrown out by fresh understanding of the nature of the human being-doing begins to show them in sharp relief.

SUMMARY AND POTENTIAL

This review of root attributes of the human spirit has served to point up the unreliability of the radical bent as foundation for participation theory and to emphasize the need for a firm footing in what has been called conservative drag. Down deep among the roots of human behavior a fundamental merging of radical and conservative appears to be the working reality. The restless urge to alter and improve is not simply opposed by a counter-weight of reluctance to change. Instead, the conservative tendency is identifiably part and parcel of the radical bent, a circumstance of the social or group condition of human nature. Recognition of the interdependence of radical and conservative should make it possible to begin to get around and behind compromise, affording the opportunity to arrange participation within a transactional and non-sacrificial matrix.

As an inversion of the radical bent—that is, as a rejection of attitudes or procedures that foster unilateral action (instead of transaction) excluding part of the human group from the effort of reformation, betterment, overhaul—conservative drag is potentially itself a working agency, not necessarily a dead hand of torpor and stagnation. As a soul-saving and perception-purifying protest against contraction of Self, the conservative drag is the innate beginning of a theoretical formulation, the starting point for the framework of organizational restructuring. If it does not degenerate to burning resentment, it is a demand that something be done about the structuring of society so that the value attributes of as many Selves as possible involved in any particular transaction are enhanced. Becoming involved in the process of decision, which is what conservative drag insists upon, is participation itself.

The term "conservative drag" may, in final analysis, identify the pith of what it means to say that man is a social or group animal. Conservative drag does need to be singled out, however, as the important attribute of human group nature upon which a growing and perfectible theory of participation can be founded. If properly exploited it will permit us to penetrate behind the habit-established bulwarks of "progress" conservatism to gain a foothold beneath the shifting, chance-drifted sands of compromise. Characterized not by rest but by creativity, it makes scientific emphasis on change workable in the arena of political participation. Perfectibility, as a deliberate social choice (the controlling of change), therefore, again becomes a live option, instead of remaining in the limbo of happenstance. In the place of the pseudo-participation of public opinion and the partial participation of progressive compromise is the potential of an intentional participation conservative of human Selves and productive of associated control of human fortunes.

CHAPTER TEN

Everybody Integrate!

> [Mary Follett] was one of the makers of
> life. Centuries hence, when the
> present ills of the distracted world will
> seem as strange and futile as Nero's
> massacres, [her] ideas will remain—the
> first intimations of that great science
> of human organization which
> men will build against
> ultimate disaster.
>
> LYNDALL URWICK

IT SOMETIMES HAPPENS THAT A KEY DISCOVERY, FORMULA-
tion, or perception, unlocking the door to new worlds of thought, is
worked out simultaneously but independently by separate searchers. The
coincident achievements of Darwin and Wallace, or of Newton and
Leibnitz come immediately to mind. Another such double achievement
was wrought in the social, political, moral field of conflict resolution by
Mary Follett, a political scientist in Boston, and Max Otto, a philosopher
in Wisconsin. Neither of them knew of the work of the other at the time.

Otto called the process he discovered and formulated "creative bargaining"; Follett called it "integration." Whatever it is called, and it has
no doubt been namelessly noticed or dimly recognized by many others
(as was evolution before Darwin and the New World before Columbus),
it has become in the hands of these two pioneers a basic alternative to
methods of coercion, sacrifice, or compromise and a focal point or core
concept around which may be rallied the parts of an ample theory of
participation stemming from the change-oriented conservatism of the
conservative bent (analyzed in the previous chapter), deriving creativity
out of reluctance—in a manner of speaking.

This and the succeeding chapter will take in turn the thinking of Mary

Follett and Max Otto and place them in the context so far developed. The ideas of Mary Follett must be looked at first because there are lessons to be learned and new directions to be pointed from the detail and penchants of her work, and because Otto's work has carried on to a greater generality that will be of subsequent use in pursuing the utopia of administrative democracy.

* * * *

Follett wrote two remarkable books considered important, or "significant" by many people: *The New State* (1918), and *Creative Experience* (1924). Almost every time her name occurs in the literature of political science, public administration, or business administration it is with praise or appreciation—never with deprecation, patronage, or condescension. Her ideas are unorthodox, comprehensively organized, system-seeking, and, judging from the lack of public criticism, sound. Among a small circle she has been influential, as amply attested by the volume of her papers (*Dynamic Administration*, 1941) that was compiled and published after her death by Metcalf and Urwick.[1] Since then there have been a handful of short articles and reviews about her and her thought—for the most part containing highly complimentary comments and digging out for renewed emphasis her "significant contributions."

Yet, despite this acclaim—not wide, but enthusiastic—her ideas have not grown since she died. It is odd that with all the high praise for originality and "significant contribution" no one has thought deeply enough of her contribution to develop it further in any systematic fashion.[2]

Though radical in the sense of digging down deep in order to begin reconstruction from the root of things, hers is the *essentially* conservative approach that does not stir men's minds. Perhaps this in part accounts for the abeyance of her ideas. Perhaps too, the deceptive simplicity of statement coupled with the insurgence of a daring anti-traditional—and thus unfamiliar—view of human nature is accountable for the sudden quiescence of her "significant" thought. One of her final papers, for example, summarizes her conclusions in the form of four deceptive principles:[3]

1. Coordination by direct contact of the responsible people concerned.
2. Coordination in the early stages.
3. Coordination as the reciprocal relating of all the factors in a situation.
4. Coordination as a continuing process.

Her exhortation to coordinate quickly quells to surface ripples. For these four "principles," standing by themselves, are shallow statements—

bland, bloodless, and innocuous; deceptively simple. Unless related to her basic philosophy, especially to an understanding and appreciation of her idea of "integration," they achieve very little meaning for the casual reader. They strike no fire.[4]

* * * *

It is clear from Follett's writings that she would agree with us as to the main outlines of the needs of today's world in terms of organization and theory of organization. She would also agree as to the inadequacy of Natural Law "rights"[5] and the inadequacy of "consent of the governed" as a base for democracy.[6] She would agree as to the ineptness of our prevalent dualisms and our atomic view of human nature.[7] And she would agree as to the need as well as the proper direction for a reunderstanding of the nature of power,[8] that it must involve progress beyond mere balancing.[9] She even uses the terms "purpose"[10] and "control"[11] in much the same way they are used in chapters 4 to 6, above.

Without going into the subtleties of the "new psychology" that Follett champions or into analysis of the process she calls "circular response,"[12] we can say with Harry Overstreet that "she has stated with psychological precision what most of us vaguely refer to as the process of 'give and take,'"[13] and add that in the process she has achieved a remarkable early approach to the transactional understanding of human nature. Here, for instance, are two neat statements worthy of Dewey and Bentley:

> It is not that the significance of the nut and screw is increased by their coming together, they have no significance at all unless they do come together. The fact that they have to be different to enter into any fruitful relation with each other is a matter of derivative importance—derived from the work they do.[14]

> Man ... is the interplay of many functions.[15]

CONSERVATION OF DIVERSITY

Follett's dominant interest is apparent in her definition of democracy. "The essence of democracy," she says, "is in that organizing of men which makes most sure, most perfect, the bringing forth of the common idea. Democracy has one task only—to free the creative spirit of man. ... Democracy is a method, a scientific technique of evolving the will of the people."[16] The key word of her philosophy is "creation." Not only does she define democracy in its terms, but everything else is at some point related to it. For example, "The essence of the social process," she maintains, "is the creating of ever new values." [17] For her, creating is the very substance of life itself. "Give me your difference," [18] she cries, "and together we shall create something new, we shall make life!"

Follett's insistence on the creative, unique contribution inherent in each human being (non-atomic) and her conservative interest that as little as possible of this creativity, of these social resources, be lost, leads her to call for a thorough reappraisal and reconstruction of social machinery.[19] Her greatest insight is that to bring human creativity, the value of radical tendencies, to fulfillment does not require the suppression or avoidance of conflict and the establishment of an even plane of happy cooperation.[20] It is not the conflict itself that is important to her, for warfare is nothing but destruction, but the process of conflict-plus-resolution. She shapes creative conflict into the central category for participation within the dominant forms of social organization.[21]

Follett is not content with "consent" as the substance of participation. She is eloquent on the failings of the vote as a technique of democracy.[22] The consent-of-the-governed theory of democracy, she maintains, "rests wholly on the intellectual fallacy that thought and action can be separated. [It] rests on the assumption that we think with our 'minds' and we don't." [23] In fact 'minds' that cannot be swayed by persuasion and careful reasoning are often changed upon entering on a course of action. Furthermore, consent of the governed "gives us only the benefit of the ideas of those who put forward the propositions for consent; it does not give us what the others are capable of contributing." [24]

"Participation," she says, "means playing one's part in an integrative unity." [25] The key term, "integrative unity," is something more than a merging of 'minds' and than a collation of parts. It is a process involving whole men, purposes, and a Gestaltist relating of relations between parts.[26] It is the fundamental characteristic of growth on the biological and psychological as well as on the social level.[27]

This "integration" is a way of agreeing, of progressing, of resolving differences, of handling conflicts. It is "the active principle of human intercourse scientifically lived." [28] Follett insists that "instead of condemning [conflict], we should set it to work for us." [29] She particularly wants to preserve, enjoy, and make constructive use of the diversity of which conflict is a product, and she fears that eliminating the one (which she also feels it is impossible to do) would eliminate the other. "It is possible," she contends, "to conceive conflict as not necessarily a wasteful outbreak of incompatibilities, but a *normal* process by which socially valuable differences register themselves for the enrichment of all concerned." [30] This *normal* process she calls "integration."

THE WAY OF INTEGRATION

Follett counts three main ways of dealing with conflict: domination, compromise, and integration.[31] Domination is unqualified victory of one side over the other. Compromise takes place when each side gives up or sacrifices some of what it wants. Integration takes place when a solution is found that does not involve sacrifice on either side. "When two desires have been *integrated*, that means that a solution has been found in which both desires have found a place, that neither side has had to sacrifice anything." [32]

Here is her favorite illustration of the way of integration:

> In the Harvard Library one day, in one of the smaller rooms, someone wanted the window open, I wanted it shut. We opened the window in the next room, where no one was sitting. This was not a compromise because there was no curtailing of desire; we both got what we really wanted. For I did not want a closed room, I simply did not want the north wind to blow directly on me; likewise the other occupant did not want that particular window open, he merely wanted more air in the room.[33]

Follett points out that if a compromise is engineered "the conflict will come up again and again in some other form . . . we shall [continue] to try to get the whole of our desire." [34] Eduard C. Lindeman notes the following drawbacks to the method of compromise: (1) The compromiser expects to change fronts and expects others to do the same. (2) No one expects the situation to change. (3) "Relativity in conduct with corresponding rigidity in the situation involved means that creative action is excluded." (4) Each participant always asks for more than he expects, and is prepared to take less than he deserves. This falsifies the situation at the outset. (5) The underlying situation is unexplored. Discussion centers instead around how much of this and how much of that. (6) Discussion is around demands—not around the relevant situation.[35]

When the way of integration is pursued, however, a particular conflict is settled for good. The next one is new and occurs on a higher level. Out of the original situation something new has been created.

Here at last is a context for genuine participation! While compromise may involve much activity in the form of taking part or contributing, here finally is a process characterized by rounded experience wherein social value is enhanced, and meaning, growth returned to the individual.

Follett took her idea of integration and applied it first to politics, to organization of popular government, and then to penetrating analyses of administration, particularly business administration. Her participative process led her to radical conclusions and revolutionary prescriptions for administrative organization, management, and operation. In a very general sort of summary we may say with Dwight Waldo that "the effect of the application of her ideas in administrative theory is to introduce horizontal lines and circular processes into an area previously dominated by vertical lines and linear processes." [36] This is no mean achievement.

Details of Follett's administrative theory will be incorporated into later pages of this book. First, however, the fundamental inadequacies in her basic formulations should be noted. Before proceeding, the pattern for democratic participation should be refined as much as possible.

RELAX!

Follett's emphases and enthusiasms have lent an air of unreality to her writings. In her excitement over integration she gets carried away to unseemly and exhausting excesses of participationism—participation for its own sake, it would seem. In *The New State*, for instance, everyone is politically organized into neighborhood groups, furiously participating, busily integrating. "Democracy does not exist," she announces, "unless each man is doing his part fully every minute." [37] In her later lectures on business administration she is anxious "to get what each one has to contribute" [38] ... "to draw out the capacities of all and then to fit these together." [39] Her tendency to fall into exhortation betrays a lack of balance and a lack of appreciation for the unevenness, the discontinuity in life. As Eduard Lindeman remarks in another context,

> Advocates of conference method, and those who believe in the integrative potentialities resident in human conflicts, often stray from the paths of realism by imagining that conference is a suitable and appropriate instrument for every occasion, and that integration is always possible. Such a viewpoint becomes a new form of dogmatism which again renders behavior inflexible. It is to be hoped that future inquirers will strive to free themselves from that apostolic zeal for a particular method and a special interpretation of the possibilities of unity which has at times led their predecessors to play the anomalous role of doctrinaire propagandists.[40]

Follett's neighborhood organization is the first figure in a grand design of cumulative integration of differences. She envisions a grand unifying of variety, that begins with Community Centers (where it is possible, as it is not, she says, in occupational and professional associations, to achieve face-to-face juxtaposition of differences, fundamental differences)[41] and culminates in a World State which, as a result of the unifying process, expresses the Will of humanity.

The artificiality that thus comes out of enthusiasm for committee work is readily apparent. If we take seriously Emerson's dictum that "society always consists in greater part of young and foolish persons," [42] it is difficult to see how such widespread and indiscriminate integrating unrelated to particular problems or difficulties can frequently produce more than an integration of foolishness, much less become a means of co-ordinating and translating variety and spontaneity into larger community values. There may be conflicts (arising from unimportant differences) that are too trivial, too unworthy to be dignified by integration—or the whole enterprise may prove artificial because the intent (or purpose) to integrate preceded the conflict and so, in a sense, led to a false search for and rejoicing in conflict.

Neighborhoods today, if or when they can be said to exist at all, do not rise to Follett's specifications or expectations. It is possible that they once did. Perhaps some of them, in a partial way, do now, or will again, tem-porarily—occasionally in poverty areas, particularly where racial or ethnic concern is mixed in. It can be argued that neighborhood has been a training ground for democracy. The first step in citizenship has been to organize alley-dwellers' complaints about garbage collection. Nowadays, however, many neighborhoods are showing unmistakable signs of segre-gation on the basis of income level, age group, occupation, or pre-occupation. They tend to become breeding grounds for conformity rather than for difference and integration. And where they don't, they find that the effects of proximity and locale are overawed by the physical inability of any citizen to participate in more than a few of the decisions arising from the overwhelming multiplicity of issues that affect him. The old fashioned, functioning neighborhood appears to be largely obsolete in a technologically complex society.

But the important thing about neighborhoods is that they are too un-important to sustain interest, too insignificant to be democratic.[43] In-deed, their chief virtue is that they are a-democratic, amoral. They are themselves one of the great integrations, one of the great *creative* resolutions of our times. The emergent value issuing from urbanization has been the increased possibility of living separately. One of the virtues of the institution called "city" (contrasting to town) is that it has per-mitted city man to simplify life, to find refuge, to hide from impotence behind the apathy of unconcern. The anonymity of urban life may be looked on as creative relief from a set of essentially insignificant conflicts (mostly in the manners realm of morals—sexual or theological) endemic to the small community. Urbanization thus furnishes an important il-lustration of the suggestion that the creative, integrative resolution of a conflict may be to not integrate.

GROUP FUNCTIONING

Much valuable work has been done in the study of the inner operation of groups. We are well advised that participation in groups is superior to representation as a method of overcoming resistance to change.[44] It is well established that groups can sometimes achieve better performance in problem solving than can an equivalent number of separated individuals.[45] Groups can even on occasion produce creative results beyond the capacity of the individuals composing them.[46] Furthermore, group activity is an excellent way of developing Self-reliant individuals.[47] Lindeman provides a convenient listing of what discussion can do:

(a) measure fact against fact;
(b) bring opposing attitudes and beliefs into comparison;
(c) humanize experts by exposing them to social realities;
(d) bring science and experience into relation;
(e) minimize prejudice and place a premium on intelligence;
(f) evaluate and test programs;
(g) reveal conflicting drives and motives;
(h) dissipate merely temperamental differences;
(i) lead to discrimination between facts, opinions, and prejudices;
(j) direct research toward needed knowledge;
(k) suggest avenues of fresh experimentation;
(l) re-evaluate aims, purposes, objectives;
(m) create new unities;
(n) initiate new integrations on intellectual and emotional levels.[48]

Finally, the reluctance of committees to take action until all their members agree[49] may be counted as a great and largely untapped resource of democracy.

These bright features of group experience encourage the social philosophies—among them Follett's—that insist upon the vital necessity to the individual of participation in primary group activity. And these philosophies, in turn, are valuable correctives to overemphasis on stark individualism. Groups, however, have their limitations and their vices. They sometimes succeed in pooling ignorance instead of wisdom. Highly creative ideas may be rendered mediocre through group discussion with less creative persons.[50] There are many kinds of facts that groups are ill equipped to bring into existence or scientifically to test.[51] And, even though group discussions usually lead to a higher degree of involvement, they do not as a rule lead to decisions.[52] As has been amply, perhaps overly, insisted, group membership frequently holds out the peril of seduction to irresponsibility under the protection of group values. Here also is the oppression of conformity to group standards. Particularly, an action vote in a small group, even if unanimous, is not infrequently coercive.[53] To the extent that the background of motivation provided by group decision is associational or fraternal—that is, rooted in simple fears of disapproval or in desires for prestige or status or good will extraneous to the wisdom or desirability of the decision—to that extent coercion enters the situation.[54]

"It is a fallacy to assume that individuals if left alone will form themselves naturally into democratic groups." [55] It is not enough to assemble a group and let it loose on the assumption that genuine participation will ensue. Psychologists working in the realm called "group dynamics" have effectively shown that training and leadership can significantly increase the participative activity within groups and raise the problem-solving capacity of groups. In particular, Norman Maier has found that a group's performance is directly improved when it understands the inadequacies of first ideas, the meanings of different directions, lines, or ways of thought and how they function in selecting ideas, the importance of remaining receptive to new ideas or new directions, and the falseness of the cultural habit of looking for someone to blame.[56] Such understanding can be contributed by an imported leader. Moreover, "even when the leader possesses exceptional ability in solving technical problems, he need not sacrifice this ability in order to maintain group goodwill. Rather can he learn to conduct conferences in such a manner as to stimulate thinking and thereby have his ideas rediscovered and accepted." [57] When there is an "elegant solution" to a problem [An elegant solution would be described by Follett as a once achieved integration for a problem that recurs in different but equivalent settings.] a group can be directed toward its discovery and acceptance by democratic leadership.

Democratic group conduct characterized by genuine participation is clearly something to be learned—as Robert's Rules of Order must be learned. But this is not very surprising considering that authoritarian and compromise methods are also learned modes of conduct. In passing, the group technique called "role playing" should be mentioned for its participative promise. Through role playing each member of a group is enabled to approach the problem from the points of view of the other persons involved. In a sense role playing depersonalizes purposes and makes it possible to treat values as events, as consequences within human interests.[58] Change must be at the individual's own option or it leads to frustration and resistance. The efficacy of group decision lies in the fact that in the process the individual's "own" is enlarged—through the fortunes of propinquity, sympathy, and discussion, if not through the deliberate device of role-playing—and as it is enlarged the agreed upon option becomes his. At this point lies the important distinction between democratic group functioning and the tyrannies of group pressure for conformity through extraneous status devices of approval and disapproval.

There are dangers, of course, in the internal tyrannies of groups.

Follett was very sensitive to these dangers and even went to the extent of specifying a severely limited meaning for her use of the word "group." She distinguished between the herd (gregarious instinct), the mob (abnormal suggestibility), the crowd, and the group. The difference between the last two is that "crowd action is the outcome of agreement based on concurrence of emotion rather than thought, or if on the latter, then on a concurrence produced by becoming aware of similarities, not by a slow and gradual creating of unity. . . . Suggestion is the law of the crowd, interpenetration of the group." [59] But then Follett very oddly, inconsistently, and blindly commends as illustrations of the "group principle" the U. S. Army device of holding a complete company responsible for the offense of an individual[60] and the incentive system at the Cadbury works which calculated wages on the basis of the output of the whole work room so that everyone in the group suffered from the laziness of the laggard.[61] With such devices honored, where is the integration that is not smothered by coercion? The fact remains that a group must be carefully cultured or nurtured, from without or within, if it is to be called democratic—particularly if it predates the conflict, problem, decision, or situation it is called upon to handle.

Much of the current clamor, however—the fear and trembling in the face of widespread adapting to group standards and conforming to group pressures—comes from perspectives informed by atomic individualism. The simple fact is that people *do* conform to group standards. That is, in a sense, what culture is all about. The individual finds firm anchorage for his intentions in group experience and group decision because group experience provides *more* sympathetic, *more* realistic environment for the transactional nature of man than do the separated lives—joined only by a disembodied "market" and a disintegrating family—men have been *trying* to live.

While group organization may *more* closely approximate an effective organizational expression of man's transactional nature than does the disorganization (meaning, fortuitous organization) of atomic individualism, the drawbacks of its internal coercive action are not to be denied. Follett may be right in suggesting that coercion is not a necessary or inevitable attribute of group life. If groups did not exist in their own right but were called into and out of existence like specific function committees—the prototype of which Follett sometimes seems to be thinking when she speaks of groups—they might conceivably be brought into fairly close conformity with man's transactional condition, becoming organizations of publics at particular times and in particular places around particular problems, difficulties or conflicts. But the groups we usually envisage when the term comes to mind are tenacious, lasting things—even though their membership fluctuates violently nowadays. And the whole tenor of Follett's approach is to activate groups irrespective of conflicts or the need for a group approach.

GOVERNMENT AND APATHY

Meanwhile social problems have outgrown voluntary groups. Problems do not occur only where there is disagreement or conflict between existing groups. The really big coercions are found in wide-striding events and conditions. Group action may sometimes be merely counter-coercion. Problems now usually have as their setting an environment larger and more complex than any existing group or set of groups. In result it cannot reasonably be assumed that group claims are likely to be adequately directed to the source of trouble. Surely neither groups as such nor atomic individuals can be considered to be the touchstone of social organization. Transactional man looks to government for organization appropriate to his problems.

The approach of Follett's later lectures is more realistic, less wholesale than her earlier neighborhood flights of fancy. Here she deals mainly with business administration. The mass aspects of political problems are no longer in the fore. Yet even in the course of propounding principles for administrative conduct she gives a feeling of too wholesome totalism —something slightly artificial—as if everyone should and could participate in everything that concerned him,—as if a man's function in an administrative organization were or could be every moment a burning interest to him.[62]

The fact is that an administrator need not necessarily engage in a testy process of integration as a prelude to each "order" he gives. Some matters, as has been mentioned, are too insignificant to merit the integrative attention of a multitude. The integrative process is time consuming and thus not always suitably or economically employed where the creative increment, the emergent values, could only be of trifling importance. (It must, however, be hastily admitted that, in the nature of the case, any judgment of the worth of something as yet uncreated can only be done in the dark of ignorance.) Furthermore, it is hard work: to fight or to sacrifice is the easy way.[63] And there is no possible assurance beforehand that an integration will follow upon the efforts expended. "Not all the differences . . . can be integrated." [64] There is also the deep twilight zone filled with unjelled or partial purposes where a unilateral decision sensitively delivered is embraced by "sub"ordinates or "co"ordinates as "just what I was about to say myself," thus achieving integration without integrating except in terms of belated adherence to the creative solution.

Under this heading perhaps falls the whole category of "elegant" solutions.[65]

Nor should it be forgotten that non-participation, apathy, indifference may be a value. In many cases, of course, apathy derives from a failure on the part of the individual to see that he is involved in a particular situation; it is a question of limited understanding or, in the broad sense, of limited perception. In other instances, however, apathy is the sensible approach to a situation where participation is not worth the effort.

In a sense any organization is a structuring of apathy. If a public, defined as a group of people extensively and indirectly affected by some particular condition or conditions, organizes itself through government,[66] then government, in addition to being a servant of the public interest, becomes in an important sense the organization of public apathy. At the same time, and in a similar fashion, apathy relieves the arduousness of participation within governmental structure by institutionalization in the form of established and effective procedure—eventually stabilized by habit. An accounting system, or a filing system, or an assembly line, or a garbage pick-up route, once agreed upon, permits its users to settle back a-pathetic to the values involved in its detailed operation. Apathy, when not founded in ignorance or blindness (insensitivity), becomes a limit to participation, an even plain of trust or loyalty that participation does not disturb. It becomes a block to conflict and, in terms of integration, may perhaps be said to represent a unified situation, a rest from virtuous agitation, an achieved integration lasting over time.

DISJUNCTION TO TRUTH

Participation must be related to particular problems or difficulties or situations. Participation in general gets one nowhere. Indeed, it is for the most part justly subverted by apathy. All of which is to say that there is no such thing as participation in general—just as there can be no conflict in general. What might go by that name turns out, upon examination, to be a clamor for contribution—the everyone-roll-up-your-sleeves-and-pitch-in approach. "Many people think that democracy means all taking part," Follett says. "If it means only that," she adds, "I do not believe in democracy. It is the fruitful relating, the interacting of parts, a co-functioning, that we want." [67] But her final goal is "integrative unity." Her thought is oriented not so much toward the solving of problems and the resolving of conflicts as toward ensuing unity. Her ultimate vision is totality, not process. Integration is converted into a method of piling up contributions.[68] A mystical purpose is superimposed—a hyperwholesome passion for wholeness. The purpose of integration subtly changes from creatively resolving conflicts to busily constructing unities.[69]

"The spirit craves totality. This is the motor of social progress,"[70] Follett tells us, revealing clearly and simply the assumption about human nature that coordinates and orients her thinking. While her assumption seems accurately to characterize the condition of human nature in primitive society,[71] its viability for our time is questionable. It leads her to make such assertions as: "unrelated experience means partly wasted experience,"[72] carrying on to mean that everything must be related to everything to amass the perfect whole. This is a kinesthetic, flower-in-the-crannied-wall mysticism[73] against the grain of which today's scientific findings seem to be running.[74] At least there is no compelling reason to assume that continuity is not man-made, a moral achievement rather than a natural-moral imperative. Perhaps eventual understanding of what the physicists refer to as the "strangeness"—a reluctance to change apparently exhibited by matter[75]—will throw some brighter light in this direction, as well as on the nature of conservative drag.

When it is seen that disjunction in experience is not incongruous with the nature of the universe, that discontinuity in life (punctuated by catastrophies, which over time are *normal*) may be endemic and the potential of continuity only sporadic, it will be understood that organization (in administration or elsewhere) oriented toward totality must soon suffer from the depression that generally follows inordinate enthusiasm. As of today, though our Selves are vastly extended, our experiences broadly proliferated, and our dependencies thoroughly intertwined, we remain a granular society, experiencing no need for *total* relatedness, whether organic or integrative. (This is the excuse behind excuses for federalism.) What is needed is not organization that stimulates indiscriminate contribution, but organization that *permits* and encourages integration when integration is needed, when the even keel of apathy is tilted by the radical bent, by gusty proposals to change—to install a new accounting machine, to drop an obsolete filing category, to simplify motions in the assembling of parts, to investigate corruption among garbage "pickers." Follett's administrative prescriptions, as we shall see, are promising and fruitful.[76] But their totalism, their enthusiasm must be diluted.

To gain progressive, integrative unity within the elastic boundaries of discontinuity is a splendid goal. There is, however, a greater prize than to be One to be won. I refer to the grace called "truth." Straining for an impossible totality is not the way to truth. Straining for an imaginable totality of uncertain potential is likewise a deceptive path—except as the goal is held in suspension and the way is broken with assurances. Truth finds no adequate assurance in a compilation of partial perspectives. Even integration of points of view, of purposes, is no clear warrant for truth. Many ideas, values, purposes, perspectives of a great many people may be worthless, dumb, or destructive. Agreement on values, resolution of conflicts between purposes, does not validate the values or the new purposes achieved.[77] Validity does not depend upon agreement as such. The truth is not to be found in integration itself—but in public test of the validity of purposes and values according to perfectible public rules. This aspect of participation will be discussed at greater length in the following chapters. It leads to the suggestion that consensus (agreement) is not an adequate basis for democracy, but that democracy must become a validating method.

VICARIOUS PARTICIPATION

The barrage of wholesale participation in government can be abated to a considerable extent by admission of vicarious participation as a legitimate category. Democracy does not exist if participation is restricted to a selected few—even if they are self-chosen; that is to say, even if the unchosen have selected themselves out. On the other hand, neither could it exist if there were no such thing as vicarious participation.[78] If vicarious participation were somehow ruled out (it would have to be by magic) and we yet perversely tried to sustain democracy, we should all die of exhaustion over-night.

Yet, quite without qualification Follett declares: "There is no such thing as vicarious experience." [79] "Integration," she says, "must take place on the motor level, not on the intellectual level." [80] Her position can best be understood from the illustration she offers:

> A man goes home from an international conference and wonders why he cannot carry his people with him in regard to what has there been agreed on. We assign a number of reasons for this; the real reason is that agreement has to come from and through what is going on every day in that nation. To persuade his people into verbal acceptance means only a pseudo agreement, and the underlying dissent (the dissent which is synonymous with unchanged motor sets) will only crop up again in some other form. The unadjusted *activities* in the situation will continue their conflict. Genuine integration occurs in the sphere of activities, and not of ideas or wills.[81]

She notes the hiatus between the expert with his specialized knowledge, his facts and figures, and the unbelieving citizens. She deplores the "pernicious tendency to make the opinions of the expert prevail by crowd methods [propaganda, prestige, lecture, 'public relations'], to rush the people instead of educating them," [82] and maintains that the gulf will not be bridged by scientific investigation until the expert and the citizen are considered each to have a particular kind of experience and until the experiences of the two are integrated in face to face confrontation—on the motor level.[83] "Experience meetings" is what she calls the institutionalization of her projected motor-level method.[84]

"Experience meetings" would be exemplified by integrative relations between TVA agricultural experts and participating farmer groups, or between the County Agent and local farmers. Now, suppose a group of farmers and an agricultural expert do succeed in integrating—"on the motor level"—their diverse experiences, thereby learning from each other and coming out with something better than either brought to offer. Suppose even that the results of the "experience meetings" lead them on to continuing relations and to full-blown experiments on the members' farms. First of all, how can either of the kinds of experience (expert or farmer) be communicated to the other party—even in an "experience meeting"—except as vicarious experience? Secondly, is it possible that men are so unimaginative, so unsympathetic that each farmer the world over will have to go through an identical "experience meeting," personally helping reproduce the same or equivalent results (integrations) on the motor level, rather than vicariously profit from the results wrought by others?

Follett is not alone. There has been a fairly common tendency among those who deplore the prevalent separation of thought and action to note the effect of experience—meaning motor activity—on learning, and then to talk as if thinking could not take place without an *ad*mixture of physical action.[85] This is in effect to continue to accept the mind-matter dualism, though seemingly denying it. Thus, for example, Follett deplores "a tendency to divorce for the moment thinking and doing," and seemingly corrects that fallacy by declaring: "We do not think, and do, and think again, but the thinking is bound up in the doing." [86] Notice they remain two distinct things, even though no longer far apart. The dualism is almost, but not quite conquered. It is finally eliminated only by noticing that thinking—even the most refined contemplation—*is* action.[87] When found sitting on a couch with your hands behind your head and a stupid look on your face, and asked, "What are you *doing*?" don't you automatically reply, "Thinking."?[88] Democracy is created on the motor level[89] but only as the sights of the level are raised to scan the heights of contemplation.[90] A theory that dilutes participation by disclaiming vicarious experience will not go far in providing a workable basis for democracy.

In the nature of man's transactional situation, it is impossible that he should be so lacking in imaginative sympathy, fellow feeling, understanding—even trust—that he could not sometimes project himself into the give-and-take of a proxy's participation. Admittedly this is the crux of an extremely complex political problem—substantially the problem legislative democracy has tried to solve through "representation." The past half-century has, however, witnessed a great widening of sympathy, an extraordinary, far flung extension of the bounds of moral concern. The Point Four program, and the Supreme Court school integration and right to vote decisions (being at least in part a reflection of concern the world round) are instances in evidence. One need only think of the amorphous expanse of today's involved ego, the encompassing Self,[91] to appreciate the dynamics of expanded sensitivity. But we must avoid the mistake of reducing fellow feeling to emotional exercise. And today's sympathy, American soap opera notwithstanding, *is* somewhat broader than the emotional thrill that accompanies old-fashioned communal charity. Sympathy that we call "not cheap"—on the aesthetic level perhaps—that verges into understanding, is what makes vicarious participation attainable.

Trying to understand the other fellow's purpose and thus his character—the job of social perception set by our transactional circumstance—[92] is the beginning of impartiality, the kernel of all we know of objectivity, of all that is meaningful in it. Out of the accuracy of social perception—the quality, dependent upon objectivity, of our understanding of each other—springs the possibility of vicarious experience. In proportion as social perceptions are trustworthy or reliable, vicarious experience flourishes. The attempt to understand one another, being the beginning of objectivity, is also the elementary particle, so to speak, upon which public test of validity is built. What becomes known as valid through such public processes is a distillation of experiences and becomes preeminently candidate for trust. Knowing is a kind of behavior and an ingredient in any and every happening that can be called participation. So far as the structure of happenings is studded with verified knowns, knowing as vicarious participation can temper the ferocity of total participation. Properly constructed, a theory of participation for democracy— which will then be administrative democracy—must refuse to stop with integration but rather provide further for validation of experience through participation.

"AUTHORITY" OF ORGANIZED KNOWING

In a sense vicarious participation would seem to refer to just any reverence for authority. But to accept such a position is to retreat from the characterization of participation so painfully worked out above. If the authority is one of personal status, hierarchy, or of dogmatic, absolutistic creeds, vicarious participation immediately withers to contribution.

Unless the "authority" is itself fluid, perfectible, tentative, tractable there is a travesty on genuine participation. Ideally, the "authority" that permits knowing to alleviate the burden of participation is an "authority" of method, of public validity-testing procedures, the first approximation to which has been the method that has been used with such devastating effect in the physical sciences. Further distinctions leading to discard of the term "authority" in description of social scientific method are made in chapter 15.

John M. Gaus asks,

> Are there emerging, in the "planning" activity developed in the factory or the unit of government, controls of operation based not on the ordinary type of coercive direction but upon the use of *organized knowledge*—budget estimates and analyses, personnel classifications, land-use maps—that enable us to achieve agreed solutions without the frustrations that come from "domination" or "compromise"? Is this not the central problem of government in the widest sense? Is not the alternative an endless and meaningless clash of pressure groups and personalities? Can we operate our vast institutional systems, interdependent as they are, if *more impersonal and objective methods* of facilitating agreed policies that will have broadly based support are not invented?[93]

Within a context of group specialization, where no citizen can hope to know everything, organized know*ing* [I like to change the emphasis to underscore the condition of continual change.], impersonal and objective methods are not surrogates for participation. They *are* participation or a kind of participation. If administration is to become democratic, it must rely increasingly on this kind of participation.

The "authority of the situation" and the "authority of function," found in Follett's writings[94]—in turn deriving from the Scientific Management movement—were early approaches to an "authority" or organized knowing. Although Follett does not explicitly specify them as kinds of participation—her rejection of vicarious experience ruled out such a possibility—she, nevertheless, happily conjoins them very intimately with the process of integration.

Follett never tires of going back to the beginning of situation and insisting that the first step in integration must be fact finding. Final agreement cannot be had unless it starts with joint effort at uncovering and agreeing on the facts. In a very fundamental sense facts are made rather than discovered. In addition, the activity and effort of agreeing must continue all through the process to final culmination in achieved integration complete with emerging new values. She summarizes in her now classic four principles of organization:

1. Coordination by direct contact with the responsible people concerned.

2. Coordination in the early stages.
3. Coordination as the reciprocal relating of all the factors in a situation.
4. Coordination as a continuing process.[95]

Out of these comes authority. For her, "authority flows from coordination." [96] The authority of the situation thus manifests itself through the working of these four functional principles—elsewhere described as "evoking, interacting, integrating and emerging" [97] but all comprised within the description of the process of integration in her broader use of the term.

But Follett is so concerned with the inner process of integration, with authority *in* the situation, that she pays little or no heed to the potentialities of its *product* as a kind of participation (vicarious), to the authority that comes *out* of the situation. The authority of function resulting from coordination is not extended. There is little if any systematic extrapolation beyond, into the productive organized knowings lasting through time that ensue. Follett's pattern is to proceed to the next situation in a dynamic spiralling from integration to integration without pause for condensation or contemplation.

SUMMARY

The idea of "integration," the discovery of the underlying, preexistent process to which it refers, is no less than epoch-making in its contribution to our developing understanding of participation. As one of the first to announce its discovery, Mary Follett deserves enduring fame. Hopefully, her formulations will soon sound archaic—indicating that progress has been made. As of the second half of the twentieth century, however, while they may seem a little quaint or dated in language usage and in enthusiasm, they are still well ahead of the times.

A clear and healthy understanding of the current failings and limits of compromise-bound American politics, government, and democracy is also found in Follett's writings. She has an inspiring vision of democratic accomplishment in both public and business administration. More of this will be brought into later chapters.

Meanwhile, from the recognition of the importance of integration as conservative base to participation, the next step must be to convert the brute occurrence into a process; to insinuate it into a way of life, so that, instead of being a sometime event, it becomes an ever-present option, a palliative to conservative drag; to bring it to life as an organized and practical method for democracy. After all, isn't this what legislative democracy did with the tolerance-compromise way of resolving conflict?

As was said in an earlier chapter, the purpose of participation in government, of Self government, is to develop public purposes. Integration is a process that does just that—almost. In contrast to charismatic leadership or even to compromise, integration is a way of developing purposes, creating them out of the raw materials of the situation. It is a process that involves both par-giving and par-taking—the two Janus-faces of participation. But it needs more generality before it can be said to develop *public* purposes. The State is not Committee writ large, and it is more than a summation of committees or groups.

Analysis of Follett's thought has in addition indicated a number of directions of further major concern. Apathy, repose, respite from virtuous activity or even from understanding or awareness must be built into the process of participation. Something less than totality must be made viable, special emphasis on truth being the needed corrective. If vicarious participation can in some way be admitted, the course opens out into a process of participation that ends in an "authority," so called, of organized knowing.

The next two chapters will address themselves to these problem areas.

CHAPTER ELEVEN

Creative Bargaining

> Suddenly I saw he was more real to
> himself than I am to myself, and
> that what was required of me was to
> experience this reality of his not as
> an object but as a subject
> —and more real
> than mine.
>
> DAG HAMMARSKJÖLD

MAX OTTO, CO-DISCOVERER OF "INTEGRATION," CARRIED IT
forward toward a more practical future by building around it, in workable detail, a structured moral method for the creative handling of conflict. This is a singular achievement and must have taken extraordinary
perceptive penetration and imaginative understanding.

Many other sensitive individuals have noted the occurrence of the phenomenon Mary Follett was so eloquent about, but they seem merely to
have glimpsed it in passing, apparently failing to grasp the full potential
of its impact.[1] Still others have paused to remark about its crucial importance to democracy—but have passed on without particularly elaborating on the point or contributing greatly to an understanding of it. In
this group falls Karl Mannheim, who emerged from the Black Forest of
Continental thought and from *Ideology and Utopia* to an appreciation of
British and American political institutions, eventually to proclaim: "One
who has never been trained in integrating purposes has never experienced true democratic co-operation, since the essence of democracy is the
integration of purposes and not mere compromise."[2] A few—notably
Ordway Tead, Eduard C. Lindeman, Harleigh B. Trecker, and Harry A.
Overstreet—have placed great emphasis on the idea of integration and
have applied it to their particular fields of interest. Excellent as has been
all of this work, however, we must turn to Max Otto for the first pene-

trating understanding of the structuring below the surface of factual occurrences of integration.

As would be expected, since his work was unrelated to Follett's, Max Otto developed his own terminology. At first known simply as "right by agreement," the method, as he worked with it, later came to be specified more clearly as "creative bargaining." The correspondence between "creative bargaining" and "integration"— that is to say, between the two conceptual handlings of the basic phenomena they both refer to—is no less than amazing, considering the separation of their independent formulations. The point at which they mainly diverge is the point of generalization. By theoretical clarification of creative bargaining as an adjudicating method, Otto has succeeded in adding cubits to its depth, extending thus its significance and importance for all human endeavor.[3]

In the previous chapter it was explained that there is a greater prize to be won than totality, than comprehensive integration. That prize is a progressively achieved approach to truth. In integrative behavior lies the kernel of a moral science. The structuring of creative bargaining as proposed by Otto gives a solid beginning framework. This will be developed in the present chapter. The succeeding chapter will go into the refinements, elaborated by Horace Fries, out of which the beginnings of a self-perfecting democratic social science can develop.

THE COMPLEXITY OF CONFLICT

Follett's favorite illustration of integration, quoted above on p. 180, points to what could become a serious misunderstanding and misapplication of the way of integration or creative bargaining. It will be remembered that she and her protagonist in the Harvard library resolved their conflict by opening a window in an adjacent room. Satisfaction was achieved with the feeling that, in Follett's words, "We both got what we really wanted." Here is the danger. A denouement climaxed by a happy 'that's what we "really" wanted all along,' tends to be an emotional, a "heady" falling together (collusion), stopping short with unity as a cloture to thought. Such an attitude may blithely skip from happy resolution to happy resolution, content with its prize of fine feelings— without pausing to notice and analyze how it came about, without generalizing as to how a similar "it" could come about another time, without thinking about the happening in order to perfect it as a method.

Yet this is the stuff from which a science can be extracted.

Though all due respect must be accorded Follett as eyewitness, participant observer, her description is nevertheless almost certainly faulty —and if she could be confronted on the point, she would surely agree.

The original conflicting purposes in her illustration were: (1) open *this* particular window and cool off, and (2) close *this* particular window and leave things the way they are. (And this vastly over-simplifies the situation, leaving out such values as: "I was here first." "Drafts don't give colds." "Why don't you move to the next room." "She's got all the light." Etc.—among which probably were crucial factors in the bargaining process.)[4] In fact, neither of them got what they orginally wanted. The creative process they were involved in resolved the situation, not by finding a solution to the problem presented, but by reformulating the problem, changing the purposes and then satisfying the new sets of purposes. Thus the "really" in Follett's loose description of the process, instead of referring to pre-existent wants, describes the growth, the creation, the jelling of new purposes. In fact, the original purposes lapsed and disappeared; they were eclipsed by the shining promise of a more inclusive good.

Specific conflicts are very rarely simple affairs. They are complex collisions of patterns of interests, desires, values, purposes, or what not. When, through creative bargaining, a new pattern of interests is found, it must be acceptable to both parties and deemed preferable by each to their old interests—*given the fact of conflict*. Creative bargaining does not find a solution to satisfy the old opposing patterns of interest. Rather it finds a new common pattern which is more satisfactory to both parties than the old interests-*in-conflict*. In any deadlock of opposing interest patterns, the deadlock itself, as part of the total situation, becomes a discordant part of each interest pattern. A creative resolution of the deadlock consists in reorganizing the patterns and changing the interests—the values, if you will—and thus finding a mutually acceptable pattern that is more satisfactory in its situation than the old ones were in theirs. Superficially, this kind of resolution might appear to be a method of sacrifice by all. Actually, in the re-creation of interests, the old is willingly discarded in favor of a more inclusive good; it is simply surpassed, lost and forgotten.[5]

Otto has described creative bargaining as containing the following distinguishable processes:

(1) getting a sharply defined perception of the essential aspects of the conflict,
(2) developing a disturbing concern for the satisfaction of interests opposed to each other,
(3) hitting upon new possible aims in which conflicting ones can be absorbed to the larger advantage of all that is at stake,
(4) embodying the new aims in a practical program.[6]

In thinking about creative bargaining, it is sometimes convenient to take these distinguishing markers as successive steps of the method. As the method unfolds in a live conflict situation, however, they over-lap, both in time and dependency.

SHARPENED PERCEPTION

Will Rogers once explained that the reason the Indians never got lost in the woods was that besides looking forward to see where they were going they looked back over their shoulders to see where they had been, to gain the perspective that would be needed for the return trip. Will Rogers never disagreed with a man face to face, he said, without first going around behind him to look over his shoulder and see how the situation appeared from that point of view. Fortunately Will Rogers is not the only one to behave this way. He is more typical than eccentric.

Gordon W. Allport, for one, agrees. He has concluded that with growth from infancy to maturity "there comes a diminution in preponderance and intensity of personal inclinations, and a growth and extension of other-regarding sentiments." And he adds: "In proportion as an individual is democratically socialized he finds it intolerable to seek happiness at the expense of others." [7]

Moreover, there is a slow trend in this direction. As Otto says, "Seen in historical perspective the centuries bear witness to the increasing capacity and readiness of human beings to put themselves in the position of others." [8] The last few centuries have seen such a vast extension of the individual Self beyond the limits of the skin that this capacity and readiness to look over the other man's shoulder, this basic sympathy, is quite simply a natural development—which is to say that it goes *pari passu* with the development of human nature. As a matter of fact, social perception in itself involves sympathy.[9] It can now be described as a generalized purpose. The attempt to see the other man's point of view is not only a natural development and the center of moral evolution, it is also the center of creative bargaining and the beginning of objectivity.

Creative bargaining, in locating at the focus of conflict, enjoys the advantage of the arena. As Follett says, "One of the greatest values of controversy is its revealing nature. The real issues at stake come into the open and have the possibility of being reconciled." [10] The beginning of creative bargaining is the intensifying, the sharpening of conflict by pointing up the purposes and their relations with the circumstances in conjunction with which they have arisen, so that all may clearly see the whole of the relevant field. This involves not only acumen in social perception,[11] in identifying the purposes of other Selves, but also honesty in revelation of purpose.

In passing, it should be noted that such an honesty need not be brought to the bargaining conference. It can develop out of the bargaining context. Here may lie one of the chief functions of a professional mediator—using the technique of "role playing" perhaps. There is an enormous contrast here, of course, with the compromise encounter where every effort is made—and expected—on all sides to conceal primary aims and limitations and fundamental facts while advancing inordinate claims over which to haggle in horse-trader style. It may be that honesty in revelation of purpose is natural in the same sense as is the sympathetic look over the shoulder of fellowman, being the other side of the coin, so to speak, in the attempt to understand the enlarged Self. It is certainly a *sine qua non* of scientific method.

Many purposes, aims or values are held in only vaguely specified form as we hold an insight or a hunch before we achieve a formula or a phrase or an art form to express it. The revelation of purposes depends upon a resolute Self-in-situation, character-in-context, or purpose-in-position analysis on the part of the purposer. As with most of us who are largely inarticulate, there is common call for help. The revelation and the perception of purposes are thus, as would be expected, coordinate activities.

Creative bargaining entails elimination of the belief that facts can be objective in a "natural" or absolute realm apart from people and their purposes. This belief permits each side to a controversy to cling to its viewpoint by blessing it with an honorific "objectivity" while disparaging the opponents for letting their values figure in the judging of their facts. As Otto once said in a radio lecture, "Facts are where you stop seeking (going back) and begin explaining (going fore, building)." Data may be described in terms of stream of consciousness. Fact is something more. It is the giving of meaning to data by identification, organization, selection; purpose goes into the basket, not with, but as a part of, each fact, each plum collected. Quite literally facts are made, not found. They become objective as they are subjected to social *determination*,[12] subjected to public test.[13] Thus the facts presented at a bargaining table become objective, for the purposes of the conflict, though not necessarily for other purposes, as they are multilaterally agreed upon. When they become objective they also become effective for resolving conflict.

It will be noted that the objectivizing of facts cannot be accomplished without an accompanying, coordinate objectivizing of purposes.

As our minds become more deeply aware of their own subjectivism, we find a zest in objective method that is not otherwise there. We see vividly, as normally we should not, the enormous mischief and casual cruelty of our prejudices. And the destruction of a prejudice, though painful at first, because of its connection with our self-respect, gives an immense relief and a fine

pride when it is successfully done. There is a radical enlargement of the
range of attention. As the current categories dissolve, a hard, simple version
of the world breaks up. The scene turns vivid and full. There follows an
emotional incentive to hearty appreciation of scientific method, which otherwise it is not easy to arouse, and is impossible to sustain.[14]

Men acquire a new respect for facts as they expend effort in bringing
them into existence.[15] Through the public process of objectifying, facts
become trustworthy.

A DISTURBING CONCERN

Raising a trustworthy set of facts is only part of the battle for the
creative resolution of conflicts. Even objective facts and clearly articu-
lated purposes or aims may not be enough—though they sometimes are,
in simple situations.

There are dimensions of purpose that can perhaps never be fully
verbalized. And even more ineffable are the ethical-aesthetic qualities indicating satisfactoriness of purposes, and of consequences or projected
consequences of purposes. Creative bargaining, therefore, must be
marked by transformation of the basic sympathy necessary for social
perception into a "disturbing concern" in behalf of both sets of conflicting purpose patterns. Only in this way can the conflict be internalized
so that it can be grappled with as a within-character conflict of purposes
staged in the intimate arena of the individual personality.[16] As someone said, "What we need is more clear thinking straight from the
heart."

Poetically enough, these anonymous words, and indeed also the sense
they carry, hark back to the Egyptian dawn of conscience when the discrimination between right and wrong was sensed as a function of human
intelligence and ascribed to the heart—as moral distinctions still are—
since the heart was, in those times, considered to be the seat of intelligence.[17] Now that intelligence has migrated to the cold dome of the
skull, leaving conscience to the cozy comfort of the heart, we have lost a
valuable association. There is need to reconcile the two again in popular
understanding. "Having a heart" is linked with "keeping a cool head,"
and "losing your head" correlates with a "hardened heart." Perhaps best
would be to lodge them both in the blood where they might freely circulate, intermingle, fraternize.

One of the most important constituent supports to creative bargaining
as a workable method is the vitality of the intra-character process of
integration by which personal problems, within-character personality
conflicts, are frequently handled—the way they are handled whenever

they are well handled, in fact. Allport describes the difference between this inner process and the Freudian conception of it as follows:

> According to psychoanalytic conceptions the defeated impulse is thought to be repressed, and to continue to plague the individual from the limbo of the unconscious. I am suggesting that under certain circumstances—especially when the comprehensive propriate motive holds sway—the incompatible impulses are not normally repressed; they simply evaporate. Freud himself made a similar observation, though he did not follow through its theoretical implications. In a too seldom quoted passage he writes that he has become "mindful of the distinction between the mere repression and the true disappearance of an old desire or impulse." [18]

It might be said in this context that when conflicting impulses or parts of them are repressed a compromise is struck. When intra-character conflicts of impulses follow the non-Freudian course, the process is one of integration. Here in the fertile ground where integration has been tested and proved as a daily, an hourly event, is solid support for creative bargaining. When a conflict is internalized or subjectivized through creative bargaining, it falls into an arena not unaccustomed to the task of creative resolution. It is not without significance that the method of creative bargaining, reliant as it is upon internalization of conflict, was not identified or specified until after the dramatic enlargement of the Self in recent history. The Self of the creative bargainer must be large enough so that he can take interests to heart which are at odds with his own.[19] "One is always justified," as Jean Rostand says, "in hating the adversary—as one sees him." [20] But one is no longer justified in seeing him from the small-self perspective.

Without a basic sympathy for fellow beings, which is itself a general purpose, it is impossible to gain an accurate social perception—because the accuracy of any perception, its success as a signal, depends on the purposes that are a part of it. For the same reason, without a disturbing concern for opposing aims, without taking them to heart, again a general purpose, the purpose of satisfying those aims, it is impossible effectively to perceive conditions or consequences that would satisfactorily take them into consideration.

The intention (purpose) to bargain creatively does not derive from exhortation any more than do other purposes. Sometimes it arrives as the possibility and promise of creative bargaining is known, understood, or imagined. More often it develops as an aspect of the sharpening of the conflict—a derivative of concern over deadlock. It can be expected to develop at a more rapid rate as the need for a non-destructive method grows and as the process of creative bargaining itself is perfected—somewhat the way intent to measure time has developed as industrial and

scientific need for more efficient methods has grown and as each refinement in time measuring devices has made possible yet further refinements.

CREATION OF PURPOSE

The creative aspect of creative bargaining would seem quite mysterious
were it not for the fact that creation is an everyday human happening.
We do not well understand creation and cannot command its occurrence.
But it is such a familiar part of life that it is mostly taken for granted
unremarked. Only when it comes in large doses, as welling from the
creative genius of a Beethoven or an Einstein, are we set back on our
heels to marvel and to puzzle. Dewey says that "activity is creative in so
far as it moves to its own enrichment as activity, that is, bringing
along with itself a release of further activities." Under this understanding
creativity becomes "a normal accompaniment of all successfully coordinated action." [21]

Creative actions or events cannot be reversed or repeated. Take as
example the growth of a chicken from an egg. Perhaps in final analysis
all events are of this sort. Even the freezing and thawing of water—the
standard example of a repetitive and reversible operation—is repeatable
only when considered macroscopically; that is, in terms of probability.
Perhaps the term "creation" is really nothing more than a dramatization
of the reality of time. A creation is, as we say, something new under
the sun.

The possibility of repetition, not precise repetition but equivalent
repetition—that is, repetition sufficiently reproductive of value to satisfy
the practical purpose at hand (within the human tolerance to variety that
"makes no difference")—is one of the most important attributes of the
universe. It pertains particularly to the physical phenomena peripheral
to the valuing, purposing nucleus we call the "individual." But it is also
present in social and even personal realms, notably where statistical
treatment of subject matter is productive. In the arena of morals, where
purposes clash, however, the incidence of even equivalent repetition is
very low indeed; intentions are (to repeat an earlier assertion) the
cohesions of time, and as such are, of all things, most characteristically
fraught with "creation."

P. W. Bridgman has observed that "the notion of error is not applicable to events of stark simplicity," to "the unrepeatable unpredictable
elementary processes of the quantum domain." [22] Since there is no way
of checking the observation of an elementary happening, (that is, one
sustaining very little involvement with other occurrences, one that is
discrete, discontinuous) the idea of possible error is inapplicable, the

question of mistaken perception is meaningless. And correspondingly meaningless becomes the idea of a dualism between perceiver and perceived; the two are not even separately distinguishable.

On the scale of ordinary life floating above the quantum domain, we encounter countless situations punctuated by occurrences of extreme simplicity. Flash insights or ideas, momentary tropisms, orientations or directionings, flickerings of feeling or emotion may spark and subside with such minimum of involvement that to speak of error in respect to them is meaningless. They are the limiting events we may call "purely subjective," not forgetting that even so they remain as genuinely and stubbornly real as any purely physical events. We can all probably remember having experienced a stroke of brilliant insight that escaped while yet aborning. A moment later it proved too elusive to recapture. It could not be exactly repeated in the fine flush of its original rapture, what was reconstructed in the attempt being tinged with a flat, disappointing tone. An insight attains the level of possible error when it obtains enough relationships, enough involvement to have an influence lasting through time. An insight is not creative until it is objectified, in a sense publicized, until it is possible to distinguish it from its perceiver.

Will Durant suggests that if we could look out from inside the atom we might find something very much like purpose among the electrons.[23] Imagine what a difference that would make in our perspective and in our perception of quantum events. In such an imaginary situation we would find the problem of error transposed. Systematic involvings would be added. The continuities, the relatings of "on purpose" would put the lie to stark simplicity. Purposes, desires, values, intentions, aims are continuities. They are reluctances to change, defiances of the ravages of time. On the macroscopic human scene, the realms of *mere* contemplation, of ranging *pure* ideas (if indeed there can be said to be such things), do not accede to the category of error. The common occurrence, however, is for flickering feelings, directionings, ideas to be born in and from a sea of seething purposes, and, if not born attached to, then immediately to be snatched up in the continuity of purpose—thereby accruing involvement that not only permits their retention in memory but also permits them to "make a difference" in the world and thus at once to be creative and to be susceptible to the tests of society.

Purposes, in a sense, are on a par with perceptions. We ordinarily think of perceptions as being verifiable or subject to error, we off-hand assume that there are no perceptions to which the concept of error does not apply. It comes as a surprise to find that there are instances where it makes no sense to raise the question of mistake. Equally common and deep in our ways of thought is the notion that the category of error is extraneous to human purposes—except in the sense that we may have mistakenly "perceived," "identified," or "interpreted" an autochthonous purpose. We readily assume that purposes spring full clad and finished from some inner, private, "subjective" realm of our being. We are so used to considering them in terms of good or bad that the suggestion that they may be in error arrives, if not as a shock, as a curious incongruity, a confusion of categories. Nevertheless, the fact remains that we can err in purpose as we do in perception.

We often speak as though we perceived our own purposes. This is a loose and unfortunate use of language. We perceive and we purpose. Of course the two actions are interrelated, interdependent; but we no more simply or directly perceive our purposes than we simply or directly purpose our perceptions. With the dichotomy between in here inside my skin and out there in the "objective" world now discredited, and with perceptions now understood to function as signals for action rather than as reflections of "reality," error becomes, not lack of correspondence with the "objective" world, but unreliability in affording cues for ongoing activity.

Using this same transactional point of view but turning attention now to purposes, it is possible to begin thinking of them too as correct or mistaken. If a perception, which is inextricably intertwined with and fundamentally dependent upon purposes, attitudes, assumptions, falls into error, is not the guilt shared by its accomplices? Take for example the common occurrence of hunter shooting hunter mistaken for a deer. If the marksman errs in perception by seeing as deer what in truth is man, is not the purpose that cradled the vision also in error? It is of course possible to assign the error to overzealousness, to the intensity or the intemperance of the purpose. However, these are not things separate and apart, but rather characteristics of a particular purpose or set of purposes. Particular purposes rarely come in the simplified abstract form of "to-kill-a-deer." Instead they appear in some such shape as "everyone else in my party has got his deer wouldn't I look silly if I let one get away may have only one chance must shoot it before someone else does wife's already mad because I went off without her would never be able to get away again." The abstract expression of a purpose— to-kill-a-deer—is a short-hand notation for convenience in thinking about and referring to what would take pages to explain if it were to be identified in all its dimensions. Indeed, in many cases there are ineffable dimensions to purpose that would have to be "explained," if at all, through the medium of art. Whether it is that behind the fatal shot is one highly complex purpose with subtle nuances or that purposes relevant to any action come in bristling bundles, overzealousness or intemperance remains a characteristic of a purpose somewhere along the line and the purpose that pulled the trigger remains clearly in error.

The network of purposes that constitutes character is what, through the continuity we call "intention," gives structure to reality. Insofar as men avoid falling into error they perceive reality or portions thereof. Correspondingly, to the degree that purposes rise above error men can be said to purpose reality or portions thereof. Which is precisely to say that reality is not found but made, not uncovered but created.

As in the perfecting of perceptions and the eliminating of illusions, so for the perfecting of purpose, doubts arising from conflict or incongruity are the harbingers of perfection, the occasion for reconsideration, for reevaluation and for the elimination of error. The habit, when dealing with perception, of correcting for error by comparing what is seen with a supposed independent existence "out there," while not a complete approach, is frequently sufficient to the macroscopic matter in question. Such an approach, however, has little warrant when dealing with purposes. The purposive error of the hunter is not exposed through review of the dead man "out there" with a bullet in his body, but through the doubts arising from the disruption of other purposes (for example, to be good to others.) Error in purpose is found and corrected, not by comparison with a perfect or a "natural" purpose but through conflict with other purposes.[24]

The moment of conflict, the dawning of a suspicion of inadequacy somewhere along the line, is likely to be marked by a sense of detachment and objectivity. It is frequently described as characterized by a pause for "perception" of purposes. One has a feeling of "standing outside" and "looking at" his purposes. In fact, it has little to do with perceiving, except in the metaphorical sense of "seeing" a purpose "in a new light." This sense of observing purposes, when it is not merely revelling in them, is in reality the beginning of a process of alteration; the objectivity correctly sensed is a recognition of the beginning of the process of comparison, criticism, deliberation that makes purposes "public." Thus we blame the hunter of the above fable for being "uncritical."

The function of critical intelligence, of criticism, is to strip off error. As purposes arrive or arrive in part at the level of articulation, they become susceptible to all the tricks and wiles of intelligence. When a moral situation—a conflict between purposes—arises, one of the first products is the generation, somewhere within the nexus of writhing purposes, of another purpose—the intention of reestablishing a unified situation, of removing the block manifest in conflict and thereby facilitating the resumption of directed activity. With this intention as backdrop, intelligence can swing into action its complement of tools (ideas) to chip away, hammer and chisel, the rough edges of the inessential, the misplaced, the obstructive, the misguided, the erroneous. The activity of criticism is a clearing of the way for the intuition, the creation of a more satisfactory purpose or aim than those blocked in conflict. Indeed, at its highest levels criticism becomes indistinct from creation. As Norbert Wiener remarks, "After all, what Michelangelo does is purely critical, namely, to remove from his statue the unnecessary marble that hides it. Thus, at the level of the highest creation, this highest creation is nothing but the highest criticism." [25]

"Criticism," says Charles Frankel, "though it has an indelible trace of what is subjective and a-rational, is a public and rational affair. The native bent of the individual spirit, the brute preferences and aversions, are not the pre-established desiderata of criticism, but the problems with which it begins. Criticism, indeed, is precisely the process by which what is private and solitary is chastened and socialized by being made to move out in a public world." [26] The idea of value is said not to arise until some critical comparison is made between wants, interests, purposes that press for recognition, that is, until evaluation takes place. By means of critical comparison, interests are necessarily expelled from any private, cloistered, 'inner' status to become objective and public.[27] There is, however, another aspect to evaluation. It is not simply that an object of direct enjoyment evolves into a "value" when it is evaluated in competition with some other object. It is not simply that some objects are selected through criticism to become enstated as "values" while others are rejected. Choice is not always, perhaps not even usually, between given alternatives. As criticism strips off superfluous accretions and erroneous aspects, it leaves gaps, faults, crevasses, even vacuums it would almost seem, in the erstwhile unbroken terrain of simple enjoyment. Choice may then attach value to the emergent or the unheralded created to fill the breach, or to an alternative so transformed as to be new, recreated. It is interesting to note, in this context, that Webster derives "create" from a latin word meaning "to select." Value is not just found or attached to something in the course of criticism; it is also made. A thing is not a value until a purpose has been attached. And a newly created purpose may have been called forth in the process.

Weiner's remark points up the fact that there are non-rational, at least non-articulate, aspects to criticism at the point where it shades into creation. Indeed, unthinking, nonintelligent appraisal may be said to attend all criticism and choice. It may well be that the wants of a mature person have all in some inarticulate way been compared with and preferred to other wants before being evaluated at the more verbal level by criticism. The process of perception itself is a critical and evaluational transaction in the sense that it is selective and is oriented by relation to purposes. An object of direct enjoyment has from the beginning been "criticized" by simply being perceived.

Creation, for all the abetting it receives from the public activities of thinking criticism and conscious evaluation, begins as a sub-articulate, an aesthetic phenomenon. Max Wertheimer illustrates this point to perfection in his analysis of the process of Einstein's productive thinking.[28] Einstein arrived at his special theory of relativity by the non-symbolic route of inspiration, intuition; the onerous task of forging the mathematical language by means of which it could be made public came only later, as a second phase.

Creative bargaining establishes a setting friendly to the intuition, the creation of new and improved purposes. The sharpening of the conflict between opposed intentions, being essentially a vigorous form of criticism, blazes the way by exposing the erroneous and the superfluous. Internalization of the conflict brings the important aspects of the total situation into the crucible of character from the turbulent boilings of which the inspiration of new purposes may erupt. Creative bargaining creates values by engineering critical comparison of proposed enjoyments— mine and yours-taken-as-mine. New approaches, newly created aims inspired to point a satisfactory road out of conflict come, as does any artistic achievement, "as 'a happy accident' to him or her who has formed the habit of expecting them to occur, who recognizes the promise they hold out when they do occur, and who knows how to put their potentialities to good use." [29]

PRACTICAL PROGRAM

In a creative bargaining situation, as in any situation, brilliant intuition of a liberating purpose does not complete its creation. A creation is not finished until it is put forth in a form that permits its retention in memory and secures its objectivization.[30] When we say, in respect to a moral situation, that mere good intentions are not enough to justify or to exonerate, as the case may be, we generally refer to the intentions of unsocialized morality described above.[31] No matter how pure our purposes in respect to an absolute or outmoded ethic, we continually find them unreliable, "not enough," in the fluid conditions of twentieth century social life. In decrying "mere good intentions" we may also be attempting to distinguish epiphenomenal, largely verbal, Sunday intentions from those that involve considered character commitment, emotional and intellectual. The chief objection to "mere good intentions," however, (and which may be taken as a rephrasing of the two objections just mentioned), is their involvement with an immorality of ignorance. "He acted from the purest of motives," it is said. "Too bad he didn't know...." There is always some taint (though perhaps very remote at times) to purpose that runs amok through avoidable ignorance. (This is, incidentally, the immorality we feel when power is used coercively in a situation where control could have been had.) A pursuit of ends that has no working concern for means is blind.

Thus it is with the emergent purposes from a creative bargaining situation; the bright new purpose, the good intention is nothing until it is embedded in a program, a plan that can be tested for workability. The relation of purpose to program in creative bargaining runs a parallel course to the historical relation of fact and theory in experimental science. The following passage from James Conant illustrates the structure of creative bargaining working within the sweep of experimental science. (It also anticipates the substance of the coming chapter.)

> We can put it down as one of the principles learned from the history of science that a theory is only overthrown by a better theory, never merely by contradictory facts. Attempts are first made to reconcile the contradictory facts to the existing conceptual scheme by some modification of the concept. Only the combination of a new concept with facts contradictory to the old ideas finally brings about a scientific revolution. And when once this has taken place, then in a few short years discovery follows upon discovery and the branch of science in question progresses by leaps and bounds.[32]

After a promising purpose is worked out to the surface of objectivity for participant acceptance, after it is fully created, that is, it must be organized into a plan of actions whereby it can be carried out. Only when newly created aims have been thus put to work in action and have proven preferable by their fruits in satisfaction to the consequences to which old aims would have led, has a particular instance of creative bargaining reached its terminus.

CREATIVE BARGAINING AS POLITICAL PARTICIPATION

Some change or other is behind every instance of conflict. It may be a simple physical change that affects two parties differently, such as a change in the weather. Or it may be a change in aim, purpose, intention on the part of one party that affects another. Change of all sorts is taking place at such an increasing rate since the beginning of the scientific revolution that would-be reformers should be cautioned to sweep easy. There is so much change taking place apart from social control that our greatest need is not more sweeping change but more directing of already plentiful change into socially productive channels.[33]

Creative bargaining as outlined above is a preeminently conservative way of dealing with change. A built-in feature of the process is the way in which what has been called conservative drag, the almost automatic resistance to change inspired by someone else, is accommodated. Creative bargaining itself is a deliberate process of interest changing, purpose changing, value changing. But there is nothing sweeping about it. It takes a situation unsettled because of change or unilaterally proposed change and substitutes for haphazard indirection (haphazard, for the reason, if for none other, that opposing intentions are unaccounted for) a deliberately unified, and thus, in terms of the situation, a directioned change or proposal for change. Integrative behavior means exposure to change, but to change that undermines the reluctance of conservative drag because value enhancement has been socialized, so to speak, within the limits of the particular situation.

Without acceding to the conservative demand for participation, creative bargaining could never happen. Indeed, nowhere, it might be said, is participation achieved more fully or in greater perfection. Creative bargaining *is* participation. Not only is joint effort required in the sharpening of the conflict, the criticism, comparison, and search for a way out, but each participant must have developed a personal concern for both sets of opposing interests or purposes. Unless they are prepared by having internalized the conflict, they will not be ready to see, much less accept, the integrated aim intuited out of the situation. This is the converse of the obvious observation that a newly created aim is not truly integrative until it appeals to all parties to the controversy. The new aim may, in fact, be a genuine joint product of group thinking.[34]

Participation, it was said above, involves take as well as give. Having given of his energy, thought, imagination, ingenuity, and creativity, the creative bargainer receives not only the gift of greater understanding and appreciation but a personality, a character larger and deeper for the integrated purpose it has embraced. By participating in decision he is able to grasp it with a full understanding and *allegiance*. Allegiance is an attribute of purpose, describing it as fully blown, matured—not fleeting as a vain imagining, but cohesive—a sinew of time. The allegiance is essential and must be emphasized for without it it is impossible either to bring the new aims to public test or to embody them in a workable program. The whole enterprise will come to nought if the new intention is not given a fair shake by all concerned, for plans are quite literally carried out *in* people's lives. The test of participation is not the quantity of contribution or the amount of physical activity but the fullness of understanding, the firmness of allegiance and the willingness to pursue a plan to the terminus of objective test. A true participant undergoes change;

his personality, character is enriched in the process of participating.

As a participative, evaluating process, creative bargaining is a way of deliberately building larger, more inclusive Selves. It is thus in the highest sense an educational process. But on account of its public character it is also a political process. As Karl Mannheim has suggested, integrative behavior is rooted in a certain kind of personality structure—democratic personality.[35] This in turn, however, is not a simple matter of heredity, luck, or individual achievement. It is rather the human product of accumulated transaction, the product of society. Patterns of personality integration are forged in and passed on by society. They are political achievements. For where else does "society" in turn get the patterns but from the actual working out of individual and group needs and satisfactions in particular situations?

As human Selves get larger and larger in a fluid society, the working out of conflicts by methods of domination becomes less and less tolerable—and likewise methods of sacrifice and compromise become (for parallel reasons) less and less viable. For one thing, the authoritarian finds that as he is dominating others he is increasingly dominating parts of himSelf—for the simple reason that his extended Self includes those "others" he dominates; the right hand binds the left. For another, he finds that problems are too large for him, ramifications too widespreading. His knowings are not acute enough. And even the help of a great hierarchical organization may not avail. For under fluid social conditions (that is, under conditions no longer structured in detail by folkways) detailed knowings can neither be reliably derived from folkways nor effectively abstracted apart from transactional situations. It will become increasingly impossible to blink the transactional character of man. In contrast to methods of domination, the method of creative bargaining will find itself ever more readily accepted as days of social fluidity flow by, for it deliberately honors man's transactional nature and carefully accommodates the processes of knowing and perception attuned to it. Creative bargaining systematically avoids involving the Self in schizophrenic flagellation of its "other" part.

The classification of creative bargaining as "politics" will seem incongruous to many. Yet politics is precisely what creative bargaining is or can be. It is both a moral and a political process.[36]

The word "politics" imparts to many Americans, if not to most, a connotation of something distasteful, suspect, shady, somehow bad.[37] It has come to mean horse-trading, the habit, mentality, and expectation of compromise.[38] The chief fault it points to may be identified as "partisanship," the fault of agitating in respect to a particular problem considerations, insistences, that are unrelated to or irrelevant to that problem, bringing to bear upon it as material with which to bargain extraneous factors from remote and alien situations. "Politics" has taken on the flavor of the governmental process of the times. The fact is that people, from the vantage of their private lives, recognize the moral inadequacy of the compromise method that has been sanctified as the way of politics. Mannheim has warned that "the more often we accept compromise as a satisfactory substitute for real and progressive integration, the more likely creative tolerance is to degenerate into a policy of neutrality with gradual elimination of discussion of fundamentals." The eventual product is "a type of emasculated mentality . . . that cares neither for principles nor a deeper understanding of life, but only for working compromises." [39]

But the popular distaste for "politics" shows a dim public awareness of these evils and limitations in compromise and a beginning readiness to reject compromise as the be-all of politics. The corollary observation is that the public is implicitly prepared for new, creative, more satisfying patterns of politics. If the semantic block to "politics" is too great, we may call the more satisfying patterns "government," instead. At least creative bargaining can come to be understood as a pattern of Self government.

SUMMARY

Placed within the context and terminology of earlier chapters, creative bargaining will be seen to be a formalization of the basic social transaction with which this book started, shaped in the sweep of its grand design so as to give proper play to what is being found as to the changing nature of the human being-doing.

Again the persistent matter of perception preempts front stage; the first of the processes Max Otto distinguishes in creative bargaining places initial emphasis exactly at the point of perception. From what we now know of the transactional condition of mankind, and the function of perceptions as signals, it seems simple good sense to approach knowing in a therapeutic setting, by the road of sharpened perceptions.

The aim at refining perception—essentially a search for truth—shades by fine gradation into Otto's second process, that of becoming concerned to satisfy the opposed interests as well as the initially intimate ones.

> In proportion as we love truth more and victory less, we shall become anxious to know what it is which leads our opponents to think as they do. We shall begin to suspect that the pertinacity of belief exhibited by them must result from the perception of something we have not perceived. And we shall aim to supplement the portion of truth we have found with the portion found by them.[40]

As the saying goes, "seeing is believing." Men do not readily disregard what they can perceive.

The real key to creative bargaining, and the focus of Mary Follett's integration as well, is the creative process—number three of Otto's formulation. Creation is an everyday event and creativity is a very human characteristic—part and parcel of the radical bent. The steady state or continual creation theory of astronomy presently on the wane was contrived appropriately enough in this, the century of creativity. If men can continuously create *ex nihilo*, why not also energy or matter? Why not let the rest of the universe in on the act? A theory that postulates an inconceivable creation field to explain the expanding universe as a matter of continual creation of atoms, instead of a big bang from out of a nucleus of unimaginable density, has enough affinity for the human condition to support a mass movement of neo-Ptolemaic anthropomorphism. The creative aspect will be the bright human spark of allegiance, attention, enthusiasm, and expectation—compelling because intriguing—in the moral pattern of creative bargaining.

The universe changes with each creation. It is never quite the same after a novel occurrence as it was the moment before. Following a creative perception, the world never again looks quite the way it used to. This helps to explain, for instance, why it is impossible to recapture the vividness of childhood impressions in after years. Some beautiful words by Boris Pasternak have captured the culminating creative moment of integration in creative bargaining.

> All of a sudden in the course of the melody an answer or an objection to it bursts in in another voice . . . in another and simpler conversational tone, an unexpected dispute, a discord that is instantly settled, and a note of a shattering naturalness is introduced into the work, the sort of naturalness that decides everything.[41]

The other half of creativity in the creative bargaining setting, fitting as complement to the intuition of a new possibility, is the creation of a purpose to accompany, confirm, and sustain the vision. Further reinforcement of purpose by successful action is important to regularizing, perpetuating, entrenching the stability of new perception. A mere flash-in-the-pan novelty, a stark simplicity, is seldom securely created. The fourth process (Otto's) is essential to stabilization. Creation can be lost; it can dissipate among the random discontinuities of the universe. Apparently creations, discoveries, emergents are not all alike. While some are born full feathered, dauntless shapers of the cosmos, others, and by far the most, need to be cherished with nest and nurture.

A practical program (Otto's fourth process) must be devised as an extension of—really an intimate part of—the created resolution of a conflict—or else all but the most stalwart participants will defect or fall by the wayside. New purposes have this in common with unaccustomed perceptions or mere information: without the reinforcement of successful action they tend to be end-played by habitual assumptions.[42] The creation way out of conflict that emerges from the creative bargaining situation must include, besides an idea, an intention to put that idea to work. The intention to try out an agreed-to course of action involves determination to adhere through time; it involves a reluctant-to-change reinforcement of conservative drag, precisely at the highly unexpected moment of supreme radical success. Deriving creativity out of reluctance in first instance, creative bargaining immediately brackets the radical again in a new conservatism.

While people feel the inadequacy of compromise and sense its invidious tendencies, they also equate it with politics and accordingly indiscriminately damn politics in general for the faults of its currently popular and dominant method—compromise. Creative bargaining, if it is to be recognized as a political process, must offer itself as an alternative to compromise, and, since it must avoid the invidious connotations that politics has accrued from its long association with compromise, it must first appear in non-political, if not anti-political, semblance.

To be fully accepted as political process, creative bargaining will have to work its way into habitual acceptance in non-political—perhaps in reformist—guise, becoming at least as habitual a way of handling conflict as compromise now is. When that utopian time will arrive is, of course, an open question. The non-political stance of public administration—sometimes even assumed by top administrators, though they know very well their actions are political in the broader sense—being to a great extent an attempt to dissociate from the compromise way of life that is partisan politics, gives clear evidence of a "natural" setting for the first investiture of creative bargaining as political process.

Creative bargaining is a moral process of inestimable worth. Providing as it does the major viable alternative to compromise, it holds out promise of great achievement in politics. It will be the task of later chapters to search out the elements of political structuring that can be supported on the continuities of this sensitively participative, reluctance-replete mode of human conduct.

CHAPTER TWELVE

*Scientific Mediation**

> *There remains, so it seems to me, one constant motive operating in the direction of integration and normality, and that is the desire for truth.*
>
> ROGER E. MONEY-KYRLE

> *The total and complete answer may never come. But with each generation the riddle moves to a higher and more sophisticated level and the game grows more rewarding and more delightful.*
>
> ISAAC ASIMOV

THE TRANSITION FROM CREATIVE BARGAINING AS A METHOD of handling specific conflicts to creative bargaining as a deliberate, accepted, and acknowledged political (administrative) process will not be achieved simply by the proliferation of individual instances of successful integrative conflict resolution. There must be a further generality in the process, something more than is to be got just by extending or compounding activity; and there must be an institutionalization appropriate to the process and marking deliberate adherence to the method through organization of human effort.

Horace S. Fries provided the lead for such a transition toward generality and institution. At his hands, creative bargaining has been

---

*This chapter makes free use of Fries' thought without attempting a full presentation or exposition of his complex and germinal philosophy. See Appendix B: Bibliography of the writings of Horace S. Fries.

transformed into a scientific approach to moral, political problems. His insights and careful logical analyses point the way for conversion of individual instances of integration into material for scientific generalization and thence into the possibility of vicarious participation through verifiable knowings. In the process the elements of political structuring begin to become apparent.

UNION OF KNOWLEDGE AND POWER

Creative bargaining in every instance advances at least one step beyond rank pluralism,[1] beyond parochial group moralities. It is particularly a way for merging or dispelling group differences.

Group divisions within society, within politics, are among the most basic and stubborn realities. Growing in great part out of the break-up of experience described above,[2] they are so pervasive as to culminate not only in the foreshortening of purpose and the compartmentalization of moral life, but in perceptual barriers to inter-group communication and mutual understanding. A farmer, a banker, a house builder, a recreation director, and a surveyor, looking at the same forty-acre tract of land, for example, *see* it in five different ways, as five different things. The moral and the political merge and problems become governmental concerns when conflicts are so intensified by diversity of ways of seeing things that they are no longer informally resolved. Thus it is that, in a scientific-technological society with its many divisions and perspectives, more and more matters are brought up to the level of governmental attention, with resulting swelling of administrative cadre and activity. The process of creative bargaining is a counter motion, counter to the perpetuation of division and to the proliferation of government. It serves, in each instance, to bring divergent perspectives together where it finds them—most simply and frequently on the non-political level but also (perhaps relying on more deliberate effort) on the political level.

It must be granted that a certain amount of pluralism may be inherent in the nature of things. Certainly the tolerance of social life for variety, where specific situations and definite problems are involved, suggests that pluralism *per se* is not an evil genius that must be vanquished. Certainly it would be unwise to fall back into a Follett-like totalism. There may be call for some integration of purposes in respect to land use, for example, but there can surely be little need to synthesize a common *view* that will be equally valid for bankers, builders, farmers, surveyors, and wild life fanciers whenever they behold a likely forty-acre tract. Integration of purposes may not, probably does not, necessarily depend upon achievement of identical ways of looking at things in general. Creative bargaining, however, reaches down below the group to the conflicts of value and purpose in their intimate setting within character. And, because it thus deals with purposes at their roots, where they are still tender, it can serve to socialize morality—to merge group moralities when and where needed.

Social control is built upon human moral knowings.[3] Government that approaches perfection—democracy, for our day—as a system of strategic control (not coercion) through the functionalizing of power[4] derives its effectiveness and authority from the organized moral (or should we say, political?) knowings of the citizens with whom it deals.

C. Wright Mills struck close to the heart of the problem of establishing strategic control when he deplored the separation that exists today between men of power and men of knowledge, between political leaders and knowledgeable publics. He contrasted this current separation with circumstances prevailing when the American republic was brand new, when the men of affairs were also the men of culture. And when, as was sometimes the case, they were less than cultured themselves, they at least belonged to the social circles where culture and knowledge abounded. There was an effective "classic public"[5] that held knowledge and power, in effective touch with each other, and that made many of the decisions that were made. This sort of effective public that holds both know-how and leadership no longer exists.

It is possible that the knowings of the "classic public," presided over by a still fresh and effective Natural Law formulation of common-sense moral discoveries, served to some extent to functionalize power in those rude times. This at least should be the moral of the tale.[6] It is not enough, however, that men of power be cultured or group-related with men of knowledge; there must be a relevance, an intimate cross-relating, between knowledge and power. If the "classic public" did succeed in functionalizing power, George Washington and his America might well be said to have benefited, in terms of more sensitive social control, from his readings in Locke. But what, in a culture of multiple cleavages, is the modern President to read? He might do better than Eisenhower did with cowboy and detective stories,[7] but it will not be easy to find something directly relevant to the functionalizing of twentieth-century power. I would suggest his reading Gordon W. Allport and Max Otto, but even this would afford only a beginning, an introduction to the directly relevant knowings needed.

The outstanding reason men of knowledge are hired men, "consultants" as we sometimes grandly call them, instead of the peers of the men of power is to be found in the character of their knowledge. A subsidiary reason will be found in the drag of the forms of social organization inherited from the Age of Reason but still dominant and abounding. Whereas the moral knowings embodied in Natural Law have by now slipped out from under us,[8] a new pattern of moral knowing has not yet formed. When it does, it will be recognized by its good works. Men of power, after due lag, will welcome its promise and effectiveness in functionalizing power, and will not forever falter before the problem of reorganizing institutions to ensure its effectiveness.

It was Horace Fries who provided the insights needed at this juncture. Fries converted creative bargaining into a laboratory for the moral science—the new pattern of moral knowing—that, upon the break away from Teleological ethics, must develop in order to functionalize power under the fluid conditions of the twentieth century. In so doing, he pointed the way for the transition—via vicarious experience—from grass roots creative bargaining to creative bargaining as a full blown and acknowledged political process.

MORAL SCIENCE: MARRIAGE OF ARTISAN AND THINKER

Fries adds a fifth process, or logical factor, to the procedure of creative bargaining:

> (5) formulating the ideas employed throughout the procedure in a way which will provide for the identification of their deficiencies as they are employed.[9]

He contends that "the unique nature of each specific conflict does not preclude the possibility of discovering and testing principles and techniques which can help us in the resolution of other similar conflicts." [10] We can get beyond specific instances of creative bargaining, provided that we can create abstract instruments suitable to the occasion.

All ideas are tools.[11] Some are sharp with the bright edge of definition, others dull and rusty. Some are up to date, others as obsolete as the Roman chariot. Without question, obsolete conceptual tools should be discarded, and obsolescent ones should be repaired, replaced or displaced. Ways are needed for determining when concepts need to be sharpened, improved, or redesigned. There must be ways of testing concepts to see how well they serve their functions and how they can be improved to serve them better. Only when concepts are so constructed that they can be logically connected with the actions of men, as the sharp (or dull) edge of an ax is connected by a (logical) handle with the aims and arms of a man, can they be tested.

A set of experimental concepts is a kit of tools for working in realities. It may be profitably likened to a map, for its function is not to picture "reality" but to guide the course of inquiry through the transformable realities that constitute the subject matter under investigation, and the test of its merit is its success in serving this guiding function.

The key to the success of a set of experimental concepts in its role of scientific control lies in the care with which it has been drawn; whether on the one hand it is so vague, or so disconnected, or so discontinuous with the rest of life that an experimental demonstration of its inadequacy ends the matter once and for all, without further implication, or whether on the other hand it is so finely pointed and precisely related to other scientific concepts that it has value even if it leads the investigation into a dead-end or an ambush. In the latter case, for example, association with related concepts may result in indications that lead to its revision (correction for error), or in implications that point to hitherto unanticipated inadequacies in the related concepts. The function of logic in this connection is to link hypotheses with the map of high-level abstractions in such a way that the map is perfected as a result of the adventures, the fortunes, good and ill, of the hypotheses and these are brought out of chaos into some degree of order.[12] Thus, for example, description of heat as a mode of motion rather than as a kind of fluid or as a chemical element has permitted a vastly extended and improved interconnecting of the world of crafts with the world of thoughts. It has also permitted unexpected connections with other phenomena similarly described—light, sound, friction, chemical reactions, atomic structure. The value of the kinetic theory of heat as a scientific control concept is in the quantity, quality, fertility, and assurance of these relationships. With tightly drawn strings of implication throughout an extensive system of interconnection, any disturbance of the course of hypothetical conjecture within the system will ring back repercussions and point to a need for theoretical adjustment.

It must be forcefully emphasized, in passing, that the concept of "power" has not yet been related to other high-level abstractions in any way that could possibly be compared to the way heat is.

In the more advanced sciences the job of shaping conceptual tools has tended to become specialized. The applied scientist concerns himself principally with achieving increasingly sensitive control over environment, while the pure scientist concentrates on improving the concepts of control as such.[13] It is probably not at all necessary for an incipient moral science to ape this division of labor, but the new science will have to perform both pure and applied functions eventually, if it is to attain full stature as a modern experimental science.

It was Fries' contention that if procedure number five were deliberately added to the process of creative bargaining, a moral science could ultimately be brought into being. He hoped to do in moral realms what Galileo did in the study of mechanics, what Black did in the study of heat: to arrange a marriage "between the artisan interest in concrete tools of control and the theoretical interest in logical demonstration." [14] The change would be from the use of concepts that are *mere* generalities —ideas held firm in splendid indifference to changes in their context, as are Teleological ethics; ideas which were once bright tools but have long since lost their original luster of social usefulness, acquiring instead new roles as dark tools of obscurantism for whatever dilatory or obstructive purpose; ideas so vaguely or transcendentally defined as to be logically independent of any specific happening and therefore superbly immune to the criticism of daily events—to the use of concepts which are operationally defined and perfectible in context. John Dewey describes such operational ideas as temporary escapes:

> When the flight lands upon what for the purpose of inquiry is an idea, it at once becomes the point of departure for instigating and directing new observations serving to bring to light facts the use of which will develop further use and which thereby develop awareness of the problem to be dealt with, and consequently serve to indicate an improved mode of solution; which in turn instigates and directs new observation of the existential material, and so on and on till both problem and solution take on a determinate form.[15]

A sportsman uses tools, two of them generally speaking, with which to control the course of his canoe. One of them—a paddle—he holds in his hands; the other—know-how, including habit—he carries in his head, nerves, muscles, bones. The paddle directly controls the canoe, but it in turn is controlled by the sportsman's knowings and his "feel" for the situation. As long as canoeing is mere play he gets along with a few general rules and some simple instructions as to how best to handle the paddle. Most of the paddling is in the "feel"; it can even become an art. But should canoeing become a serious business or even a serious, highly competitive sport with prizes to be won, or should unfamiliar currents and undercurrents complicate the course, "feel" would give way to more rational efforts[16] and in the extreme instance a scientific approach should be welcomed as supplement to playful trial and error. Instead of trying out new ideas haphazardly as they happened to occur, the scientific attempt would be made to order them systematically so as to put them reciprocally under the control of the instrument directly controlling the canoe.

Prescientific days would have seen know-how *limited* by the tools of direct control and new ideas bleakly affirmed or denied—and nothing more. The new era would see attempts at deliberate and systematic ordering of a set of abstract concepts "in such a way as to indicate operations of concrete control, the failure or success of which [in turn would] tend to be reflected throughout the set of concepts" [17] to indicate, not simply the success or failure of a concept, but possible directions in which the set of concepts might be improved.

Even a wrong idea, an idea that fails, can be highly productive if related, by a system of implication, as one of a set of abstract concepts. A very simple illustration of this use of implication is seen in the field operation of an army mortar squad. When the first shell falls short, instead of raising the trajectory and firing for the target, the squad deliberately attempts to overshoot the mark so as to "bracket in" accurately on the third try.[18] An experiment that fails—witness the Michelson-Morley experiment—is frequently more revealing, more productive than one that succeeds,[19] because of the wide spread of implication through a tightly drawn theoretical framework. Operational concepts—that is, concepts which direct (control) specific operations with a paddle—would thus in their turn be redirected (controlled) by the fortunes of the instrument of direct control.[20] The canoeist learns to control his paddle so that he can give a powerful stroke, a shaded twist, and many other sensitive directionings. A similar order of delicate nuance is implied in scientific control of conceptual tools. Thus in scientific endeavor any tool, whether paddle or idea, is both an instrument of control and an instrument controlled.

When a science gets underway no tools are sacrosanct. The fanciful science growing out of canoeing would be expected to dig deep into the secrets of fluid flow, perhaps seeking relevance in molecular action, ionization, and even thermodynamics. In so doing it would not hesitate, even in the face of cultural traditions or established "rules of the game," to suggest redesign of the paddle. The aim of the abstract or pure aspect of science being the improvement of the abstract tools of control, or, stated another way, "knowing for its own sake," science does not gracefully submit to limitation of its horizons. There is no limiting where it may lead. Paddle gives way to propeller and birchbark to aluminum.

PURPOSE IN SCIENCE

Tools embody purposes. When they have been around for a long time, additional purposes attach to them. Once created, a tool may be turned to completely unanticipated ends—such is the ingenuity of men. Scientific impatience with limitations (a highly developed manifestation of the radical bent) which does not respect established reverence for existing artifacts impinges willy nilly on the realms of morals. A two-bladed paddle, kayak style, while leaving untouched the overall purpose of winning a canoe race, would scramble individual purposes of contestants and transform the sport, heart and soul. Some individuals, unable to adjust, would be disadvantaged; others would be favored who had been all thumbs with the earlier tool. Perfection of the propeller would quite similarly transform purposes in the area of commerce. Because perfection of tools complicates them or their use, it brings into being a host of purposes of specialism and expertise. Any trapper could learn to navigate a canoe for transportation of his furs. But with the development of commercial shipping his boat is restricted to the back woods frontier while navigation specialists take over the trade routes.

Unfortunately, while constantly meddling with purposes, science has never deliberately or systematically brought them within the purview of its self-perfecting system of reciprocal control. Purposes alone it does not attempt to rescue from the precarious condition of haphazard occurrence. Yet purposes are just as natural as trees or rivers, atoms or electric sparks—as the pleasure paddler soon observes when pursuit of his purposes interferes with those of a fisherman. The crew in a racing shell would have little need to treat their purposes scientifically: all their purposes are subordinated to an antecedently espoused goal. Yet even within such a stern framework subordinate conflicts can and do arise, and moral science might play a minor role. But change the scene to a merchant ship with a mutinying crew and there will soon be reason to regret, from one side or the other, that a moral science dealing with conflicting purposes had never been perfected, that moral (political) coercion had never been displaced by moral (political) control.

The test of a tool—manipulative or conceptual—is in the control accomplished through its use. But this leads back again to purposes. And the test of a tool can (though less generally) be described as "an operational correspondence between the aim anticipated and the end achieved by the use of the tool" [21] As Follett says, "every activity carries within it its own tests." [22] An ax is tested as it serves the purpose of felling an enemy or a tree. The "mapping" function of a scientific concept is tested as it serves the purpose of improving operational concepts. A set of scientific concepts is tested as it serves the purpose of mapping a course through which the conduct of inquiry may be guided.[23]

PURPOSES AS TOOLS IN SCIENCE

The next step, the step of moral science, is to see what can be done about purposes. In our time it is notoriously purposes that are out of joint —not atoms or genes or bombs.

Like so many of the things men make, like ideas and axes, purposes too are tools. They can be employed to yield scientific control of behavior or conduct.[24] And their test will, correspondingly, be in the control achieved—the operational correspondence between anticipation and achievement. Thus purpose, too, is ultimately judged in terms of purpose.

Perhaps this is the place to begin distinguishing three overlapping aspects of purpose. First there is purpose as the *stuff* with which each of us, but especially the leader, the administrator, works—purpose as the material of an experimental situation, the material the scientist investigates by means of careful and methodical insertion of change and over the changes of which he aims to gain sensitive control through the establishment of casual relations. Second there is purpose as a *tool*, a determinant, a causal factor, a director of behavior. Third there is purpose as *end* to be gained, however tentatively it is held. These aspects can be called respectively "interests," "intentions," and "aims." In physical science control of change in concrete materials (physical transformations) is through the use of technical instruments (tools) under the directioning of aims which are very largely haphazard, except for the abstract aim of the "pure" scientist: to improve control concepts. In moral science control of change in material interests (purposive transformations) is through intention (tools) under the directioning of abstract aims (ends) which are (including the abstract aim of improving control concepts) in turn controlled by the experimental situation.

It will have been noticed that earlier chapters employed such terms as purpose, intention, aim, desire, value, and goal indiscriminately and interchangeably. This is because concepts in this area have not yet been operationally distinguished. They will not be until a moral science is well under way. And by then these particular terms may be quite obsolete; the things or aspects to be distinguished may require entirely new namings. As John Dewey says,

> Matters that are distinctively human and moral ... will continue to be matter of customs and conflict of customs until inquiry has found a method of abstraction which, because of its degree of remoteness from established customs, will bring them into a light in which their nature will be indefinitely more clearly seen than is now the case.[25]

At any rate, the namings here selected to characterize the tripartite nature of purpose (as seen from a primitive perspective) should perhaps not be considered more than a particular convenience in statement.

It seems desirable, however, to make these preliminary distinctions in order to avoid the appearance of mysticism.[26] For, strictly speaking, purpose is a behavior; it is a kind of activity.[27] While we usually think of behavior as including only instinctive, habitual, random, and purposive physical *movements*, it does also include the activities of thinking and purposing wherein motion is not directly perceptible. To say then that "purposes" can be used as tools for the scientific control of behavior is to say that they can be the instruments not only of instinct control and habit control but also of thought control and purpose control. The resulting semantic haze is somewhat lifted when the above distinctions are honored and the material is called "interests" and the tools labeled either "intentions" or, if more abstract and conceptual, "aims."

However it comes about (and perhaps someday we will understand), human beings guide themselves by means of values—of chosen or inherited goals.[28] For example again: the crew of a racing boat. And mature human Selves are constantly in the process of intentionally reshaping even the stubborn culturally inherited aims that control or coerce their behavior.[29] This is preeminently the basis of the circular process to be called Self-control.

SCIENTIFIC MEDIATION: USE OF IDEALS FOR SOCIAL CONTROL

Since long before the dawn of conscience administrators have made use of human aims (goals, ideals) in order to control or coerce human conduct. They have most frequently used them to gain hidden or half-hidden ends of their own or of the state. By now there exists a rich heritage of time-honored devices for manipulation of aims, beliefs, and choices—running all the way from the superstitions cultivated by the Egyptian priesthood and the oracles "consulted" by Greek and Macedonian politicians to the economic incentives of modern industry and the mass brain washings attempted by local newspaper editors. "Like the pre-scientific mechanic [the practical administrator] has tried to transform concrete realities (human behavior) for practical purposes by appeal to beliefs and aims. Many times he employed deceit. But seldom if ever did he try to get control by letting the subject know (or believe in the case of deceit) that the subject was being kept in the dark." [30] The seeking of control through manipulation of aims from the outside, that is, in avoidance of genuine participation, is properly termed Machiavellian—whether inspired by *The Prince*, by Goebbels, by Dale Carnegie, or by any current manual of advertising practice.

Control, as explained above,[31] tends to degenerate into coercion in proportion as it is separated from knowing.[32] Furthermore, in times of extreme social fluidity the knowings must be organized in a self-correcting system if the separation from control is to be overcome. Under conditions of extreme social fluidity knowings derived from common sense or Teleological ethics cannot keep pace with the changing circumstances to which they relate. In place of Machiavellian manipulation Fries, accordingly, seeks to instate what he calls "scientific mediation" [33] —which is, concisely, creative bargaining mediated by a self-correcting method.[34] Aims, instead of being simply tools for controlling conduct, become, at his insistence, scientific controls that are themselves controlled. The system as a whole is characterized as self-corrective.

The sharpening of the conflict in step one of creative bargaining serves, in Fries' analysis, to reduce discontinuous abstract moral rights and duties, which can only be fought over, to a set of operational concepts that can be embodied in plans for action.[35] In the scheme of "scientific mediation," the plan emerging from a creative bargaining situation becomes a scientific hypothesis. It logically relates the abstract tools (aims and concepts) of the theoretical approach to the concrete tools (intentions) of the engineering approach in an experiment which inquires into the nature of its subject matter by observing the effect of deliberately inserting change—described above as "on purpose [intentional] change of purpose" [36]—to uncover the causal relations upon which purposes (or interests) depend.[37]

The plan is the thing that gathers up the consciences of those involved in conflict into a system of reciprocal control that can provide steadily more reliable knowings. Such knowings will perhaps depend most dramatically upon the sharpness of the technological-level tools of direct control—the intentions which draw character into coherence and link cause and effect.[38] But they will depend equally upon the sharpness with which the operational abstract instruments of control are defined. "The mediating plan, which formerly was a practical instrument for the resolution of conflicting interests, becomes in experimental inquiry an instrument for testing and improving the underlying abstract ideas." [39] In one direction the intention-embodying plan seeks practical control of human conduct—and, of course, environmental conduct as well since, as a transactional truism, control of human conduct cannot be attained without control of environmental conduct. In the other direction it seeks, through conceptual organization and reorganization, to learn what purposes and character are and how they can be created. Each instance of intentional change (the basis of experimentalism) yields information about the adequacy of purposes and the causal relations in the background of human interests. In oversimplified form, the question is asked, "How good is this intention?" And the answer develops: "Well, I won't try that again!" or "Yes, it was well worth the trouble. I hope I can remember it another time," or "Something here needs to be smoothed out. When that becomes clear I'll know what I'm really after." In the end, through perfection of plans (hypotheses) controlled and corrected from "above" and from "below," a noncoercive control of human conduct (purposive) may be achieved for cultures in flux: contact will have been established with a self-perfecting way of knowing.[40]

Fries insists that the method of scientific mediation must automatically avoid the manipulation, the cynical "control" of others, that we associate with Machiavelli. As he says,

> Used in social experimental inquiry, control concepts cannot logically be intended to promote the frustration of human interests. The aim of experimental inquiry ... is the improvement of conceptual controls. The concepts are to be tested in actual situations which call for a transformation of human relations. The concrete transformation plan must, therefore, be treated as a hypothesis designed to test the concepts used in drawing up the plan. The concrete plan must work as well as possible or else it will not serve to test the concepts it is designed to test. To be successful as a test, it must first be successful as a plan. . . . The successful working of the plan entails a minimum of frustration to the interests which are operating in the execution of the plan, and a maximum satisfaction of this interest pattern. . . . To plan an unsatisfactory plan (by no means a difficult job) is to plan to wreck the hypothesis. . . . If [instruments] are employed to improve the instruments of human control they cannot be deliberately employed for ill.[42]

But we can go further and point out that, when generalized as a political process, control of conduct based upon scientific mediation must be specifically democratic.[43] Not only does it "include an ethical concern for the progressive enrichment of the life of human desire," [44] as does creative bargaining; it also fosters and incorporates, as a crucial methodological technique of the scientific quest after knowings, the participation of ordinary human being-doings.

The third scientist[45] is the key and logically the only indispensable character in the whole drama. It is his intentions that are the immediate, the "concrete," tools of social control (control of human conduct)—paddles of the ship of state, so to speak. They are also the instruments of the scientific transformations of purpose that lead to improved knowings about the causal relations behind human interests. And, furthermore, they are the causal factors that, having developed through the conflict situation, bring plans (hypotheses) to test and control the abstract tools (concepts, aims) that in turn control them and human behavior.

> But in the social field the concrete material consists of individuals able to know and to choose. If they are to be controlled scientifically, it must be by their participation in a common aim or plan. The general aim in an experimental democracy would be the aim at less costly or more satisfying resolutions of conflicts of interests. As the self-corrective procedure moved along, the specific plans or hypotheses would be improved; and with their improvement would come greater scientific control. In the development of the nature

sciences control (like numerical precision) was and is a product of the method, not primarily an antecedent condition.[46]

The democratic significance of the reciprocal control system of a moral science is that it resolves into a congeries of contributory Self-controls of Selves related in transactional situations. A moral science must be democratic because control, to be achieved at all in an experimental setting, must be Self-control of participating subject-matter scientists.[47]

VICARIOUS PARTICIPATION

When a plan is wrought by methods of sacrifice, domination, or compromise, either some of the people directly involved give up participating entirely or all give it up in part. In contrast, a creative bargaining plan and its refinement in scientific mediation is the very embodiment of give and take (contribution and growth) participation by all. In addition, scientific mediation pushes beyond the resolving of specific conflicts; it seeks the greater prize of improved knowings. In so doing it puts the vicarious (which Follett it will be remembered, imperiously discarded) squarely in the foreground and presents the supreme opportunity to mitigate intemperate—and physically impossible—wholesale participation.

From a transactional point of view, from the perspective of situation taken complete, involvement of the greatest possible number of human *organisms*, or atomic individuals, is not necessarily a productive, or even an operational ideal. What is important is that all relevant interests participate and face the vicissitudes of change.

Of course, interests apart from organisms are no more credible than organisms apart from environments. But they can be factored out for analysis and experiment in inquiry just as colors, sounds, or atoms can. Character (or Self) may be viewed as carrier of interests, and interests in turn can be considered transactional aspects of dynamic organism-environment. The basic effort of scientific mediation is to integrate the relevant participating interests of Selves-in-situation into plans to be tested by the quality of the reality they create.

The visiting farmer, who is able to learn from the evidence of a TVA experimental farm, has staged his own integrations, via the vicarious medium of test "demonstrations," without himself directly participating in the original conflict situation out of which the solution or plan first emerged. Discovering, learning, knowing how events, whether physical or moral, whether colors, sounds, interests, or purposes, do come about gives a start on selecting, arranging, and combining the factors and conditions, the means, to make them happen again.[48] Secondhand integrations, otherwise known as "elegant solutions," may be enthusiastically welcomed when they have evolved out of associational relationships with which the "outsider" is sensitively and trustingly enough involved, when they have evolved within the outer reaches of the "outsider's" extending Self (which for some purposes and in some instances may be said to stretch to the limit of his imagination), when, particularly, they have been experimentally arrived at, and when they are verifiable and repeatable. Knowing can thus be a viable substitute for "in-person" participation. Each "elegant solution" wholeheartedly embraced is a back-stage integration. Both the par-giving and the par-taking are present—the first in the equivalent interests brought for bargaining by someone else, the second in the growth achieved through learning. The result is an open route of vicarious participation through knowing. The need for bodily involvement is immediately cut, and a peculiarly human efficiency is brought to bear to permit replacement of old coercions of custom and Teleological ethics by new institutions of democratic control.[49] (Herman Danforth's article, included as Appendix A, illustrates the promising potential of this approach.)

The possibility of vicarious participation can be said to reside in the accepted, or felt, justice of scientific Self-control. It will depend on the success of moral science in achieving satisfactions in terms of the quality of the reality created. As science develops reliable information about the nature of human purpose (interest) from experiments in Self-control, tolerable methods for social control of human conduct will emerge, and self-government will become Self-government as new basic moral ideas are vicariously accepted in popular understanding in the fullness of their implications. Participation is restricted to majority rule of "public opinion" so long as, and to the extent that, the full flowering of Selves is restrained.

Prominent among the components involved in the completing of the Self are—to refer to earlier themes—tolerable achievement of rounded experience (perhaps vicariously) and increasing sharpness of social perception. These in turn grow with the success of moral science. As was pointed out in the discussion of conservative drag,[50] the threat to a Self that is implicit in a change or a proposal tends to be dispelled when the novelty originates from a locus that is in some way included within the extending Self, when somehow in transaction the other fellow has crawled within the skin of the otherwise threatened Self. Where there is sensitive association, resentment dissolves in the joy of common achievement. Experimental science provides a special milieu—the scientific way of life that sticks firmly to its procedures and findings while resolutely trying to find them at fault—which contains an inner working, an institutionalization of change, that helps extend the scientist-Selves party to the collective enterprise so as to obviate resistance to innovation. The extending Self, the citizen scientist informed by direct "in person" involvement in the transactions and the collective enterprise of social science and by direct experience in changing purposes, will be eminently equipped to credit—that is to say, vicariously to participate in—the scientific achievement of "other" Selves.

"AUTHORITY" OF ORGANIZED KNOWING

In place of the authority of majority rule, of mass "participation," of the calculus of pleasure and pain, which under legislative democracy tends to be a collection of uncoordinated opinion, scientific mediation offers an "authority" of organized knowing[51] that is not a substitute for but an outgrowth of "genuine" participation and that is supremely suited to the democratization of administration. The emphasis must be continuously placed on the participle. It is organized know*ing*, not a *body* of knowledge that is authoritatively respectable. Such an "authority," even with its vicarious aspects, will remain democratic as long as the method is honored and embodied in institutions, since its knowings, to continue to grow and surpass themselves, must be constantly refreshed from the work and inspiration of subject-matter or citizen scientists.

Millenniums of ethical development (progress) unfolded before compromise was institutionalized—fashioned into governmental forms and procedures—in such a way and to such an extent that compromises engineered within government could be accepted and endorsed by constituencies back home. There is no reason why an "authority" of knowing based in scientific mediation might not, perhaps after a like interval of revolutions and world wars, acquire equivalent loyalty.[52]

By using the conflicts of aims and interests that occur throughout life as opportunities to test and improve moral concepts, it is possible to create progressively more reliable principles and techniques for guiding the resolution of succeeding conflicts in widening areas of application.[53] As participation within the plans and the cooperative planning venture becomes more widespread and more thorough, the authority of the self-corrective procedure will become less and less an external restraint and more and more an organic, intrinsic part of the individuals involved.[54] Fries envisages a progressive reformulation that eventually attains "trans-cultural" stature:

> As the concepts of social control become progressively tested by the improvement of concrete normative transformations, social truth becomes "transcultural" with reference to any single culture; although the specific concrete

norms which are transformable by such concepts remain capable of multi-
plication. The "trans-cultural" status of such conceptual truth is analogous,
and logically related, to the "trans-cultural" truth of the scientific concepts
we have today. It simply means that the concepts can be employed for a
specific transformation in whatever culture is concerned to make such a
transformation. It does not mean that the concepts or their dependable traits
exist outside all cultures, any more than a fountain pen exists as a fountain
pen outside all cultures.[55]

It means merely that they transcend particular assortments of Teleological ethics—particular customs and folkways. It means also that they will
supersede them in the end.

By taking the raw materials, the perceptions and purposes, that make
their presence known in conflict and reworking them so as to transform
them into more satisfactory form while at the same time learning what
they are and how they can be created and controlled, we are in the act
of inserting in the place of haphazard change the chosen and controlled
change behind a verifying process.[56] For times of cultural fluidity,
providing for orderly change is moral science's answer to apostles who
would return to the various absolute ethics of the past.

Moral science, moreover, accommodates the objections of conservative
drag;[57] it reshapes the interests of the participant by incorporating his
interests within itself. It grows directly out of extensive participation.
Furthermore, it is presided over by the characteristic conservatism of
science, which derives from an objectivity insisting that we be quite sure
we understand one another and are able to check up on one another.[58]
This objective criterion for truth is perhaps the crucial element that
tends to immunize the scientific method against aberrations arising out of
the basic stuff of conservatism.[59] The accommodation of conservative
drag through effective participation plus the conservatism of objectivity
will play no small part in assuring acceptance of the kinetic authority
of moral science as the proper substitute for the rigid authorities of
yesteryear.

SCIENTIFIC MEDIATION AS POLITICAL PROCESS

Combining vicarious participation (which makes use of a verifying
process undermining conservative drag) with extensive direct participation will permit gradual conversion of the creative way of developing
more and more satisfactory private purposes—creative bargaining—
into processes for creating public purposes and the publics to accompany
them.[60] There is a generality—indeed, a universality—about scientific
mediation that promises to extend it beyond discrete instances of creative
bargaining to recognition as political process.

Extension of scientific mediation into politics will have to take place mostly within the reaches of administration. Any very extensive adaptability of the other branches of government to scientific mediation does not appear to be likely. The legislative is too fondly wedded to compromise as a way of life and too vulnerable to the temptation to admit irrelevancies into the making of decisions. That is to say, it is prone to let decisions be influenced by matters unconnected with the problems to be solved. Votes can be gathered from confusion or from contrived bargain—from mere appearance. The judiciary also is too solidly established in its own way of life, the adversary system; it expects to find truth in the balancing—the juxtaposition—of opposing falsehoods (to word it cynically). A creative bargain is seldom achieved unless it begins down where the basic values are and has some assurance that precedent can be recreated in the process.

Just as the essentially legislative system of compromise carries over into administration, the essentially administrative procedures of scientific mediation will increasingly carry over into legislative usage—most probably in the background areas of commission, committee, conference, and party operation. Similarly, judicial recognition—perhaps very extensive and perhaps in some respects leading the way—will find appropriate place for scientific mediation, possibly through extending the "friend of the court" idea, especially in dealing with extremely technical matters, arbitration tribunals, divorce courts. . . .

Nevertheless, it will be by way of administration that the resurgence of democracy through renewed participative Self-government will take place. Fries puts it very concisely:

> Participation lies at the heart of a genuine ethical democracy. The exclusive identification of American democracy with majority rule and mere political forms of representation constitutes the most dangerous fifth column which infests our country. For "representation" and "majority rule" without genuine participation in the decisions which shape their destiny is already an extraneous control of the people. This extraneous control is as arbitrary as dictatorship. The only difference is that within the latter the arbitrary decisions are voluntarily reached by the dictator whereas in non-participating "representative" governments the "decisions"—if such they may be called—are reached by the involuntary, accidental outcome of the conflict of desires. Given the best will in the world on the part of the legislative and executive personnel to consult, and to abide by the interests of their constituents, the fact remains that the transcription of these interests and desires into needs harmonious with themselves and with the complex conditions of our economic order is a complicated scientific undertaking which requires new and complex administrative agencies. Hence in our traditional democracies we are too likely to witness the interference in the achievement of democratic objectives by part of the very democratic forms, the legislative branch, which were originally designed to assure their realization.[61]

The foremost task of administration will be to replace the fortuitous drift of legislative decision unstructured by coordinated intentions with an administrative substitute—a way of *controlling* change, a way based on deliberate (no longer accidental) and know*ing* agreement; that is, on testable and perfectible plans.

The coincidence between scientific and democratic processes[62] focuses in administrative organization and activity, to manifest itself in the dual (direct and vicarious) aspects of participation. If agreement is not first achieved down below, before the process of abstraction distills the juice out of the basic values involved and oversimplifies the wholeness that is character, it will not come about at the higher hierarchical level. The knowings and verifications necessary for vicarious participation will not emerge. A democratic-scientific administration will be so organized that, as worthwhile conflicts arise, it can serve as a laboratory of scientific mediation for directly participating material scientists. In its activities it will continuously apply and test the findings, the knowings, of the laboratory through efforts at strategic control of human behavior, relying on the vicarious participation (the knowings) of its publics.[63] Thus the mediator, the professional administrator, becomes both an experimental scientist concerned to find better principles and hypotheses and an expert social technician making particular applications of the findings of science.[64]

Participation may be the *sine qua non* of democracy. But democracy does not flourish until government begins successfully to perform its chief function—that of functionalizing power.[65] As administrators learn how to act without doing violence to human nature (rapidly changing as it is) and as they learn to accept the deep significance of recent discoveries in the psychology of perception and to join in the search for a more adequate definition of reality, they will be able to remodel the organic bonds of power, reciprocally relating individuals in situational context so that power may be divested of coercive attributes and a feeling of justice may abound.

The first thing a social plan bumps into is human resistance,[66] conservative drag. Successful undermining of conservative drag is then the first test, the first validating, of the power arising from a situation; it is the first indication that power has become functionally incorporated into a system of social control. As power is functionalized in the reciprocal control system of scientific mediation, or as the functional character of power is revealed in actions taken in accordance with vicarious participation, conservative drag is overcome; it resolves into a feeling of justice. Functional power is found in *knowing how* to achieve results— whether in performance or in moral agreement. Detailed specification of its nature, of the conditions of its occurrence, of the causal, intentional dimensions behind its appearance, is an immediate task for the experimental science that investigates the purposes and relations that constitute its anatomy.

In the early years of the industrial era, power found its justification, to a much greater extent than ever before, in the institution of property ownership.[67] And, without much question, the actions of business groups based on these moralities many times flowered in results that were graced by the feeling of justice. It was possible for the control achieved over the lives and affairs of men to be noncoercive so long as the dominant property concept related realistically to the transactional nature of expanding Selves.[68] However, if such actions were in fact felt to be just, it was a happy accident of local isolation. The unseen hand of a self-regulating system represents in fact an explicit avoidance of control; it represents a deliberate refusal to recognize the causal role of human intentions in moral affairs. Thus, as the happy historical coincidence of leave-alone philosophy with relatively discrete or independent Selves was being destroyed by the continued expansion and complication of the human Self under swiftly changing technological conditions, increasing concentration of financial "control" beneath the shadow of the unseen hand turned out to be coercive and culminated in spasms of injustice. Political organization has since been left with the tremendous task of gathering in the reins of human intention, the reins of social control relinquished by the unseen hand. The choice is more and more clearly seen to be between private regimentation and public control.[69]

The reconstruction of systems and devices to regulate human behavior in terms of intentional social control, rather than old-time political chance-compromise based on "purely" economic leave-alone "control," is *the* great task of administrative government today.

Lest social control be confused with or identified with total planning—planning without interstices or respite—for which there is as yet neither a need nor a clear indication of possibility, considering the apparent tolerances of reality for disjunction and creation, the controls sought must be clearly specified as strategic controls. While the scientific mediator and his participating subject-matter scientists may be led, in their pursuit of knowing, to invesigate many remote corners of morality, of conflicting human interests, they are only seeking resolutions of conflicts that have been sufficiently insistent, urgent, widespread, or significant to call for formal coordination at the level of government. The strategic moral-political controls of government will be set up at critical intersections as traffic signals to direct and facilitate the circulation of human conduct and social change in the quest for richer satisfactions.[70]

SUMMARY

Creative bargaining becomes scientific mediation when the ideas involved are so formulated that putting them to use will put them to test. Creative bargaining is thereby converted into a scientific dicipline, a social method that can be characterized as self-corrective. The bargaining situation becomes a scientific laboratory. The magic of prediction, involved in much current social science, gives way to the miracle of control, as reciprocal relationships of interdependence are established between concrete materials and conceptual tools. The *creative* solution to a bargaining situation becomes, through the mediation of moral science, the *elegant* solution of objective, verifiable knowings.

Scientific mediation is well rooted in conservative drag, but it is creative. It is supported by the self-corrective inner working, characteristic of experimental science, that helps individuals rise above the deep-seated resistance to new outside ideas. The result is a verifying process that makes a live option out of a vicarious way of participating that is democratic without being frenetic. The need for mass involvement is obviated by the trustworthiness of generalizations from particulars publicly tested. Scientific mediation provides the generality that is necessary before a participation in government that involves par-giving as well as par-taking—otherwise known as Self-government—can, by using purposes as scientific tools, develop deliberate public purposes out of the arsenal of integrations. Such generality is also needed before this process can be *recognized* as a political process.

Looking backward, we can see that the elusive nature of the human being-doing is the vital part of the process. It is the extending Self, encompassing other human beings and sensitively describable only by way of transactional statement, that is behind the potentiality for scientific handling of social conflict—of morals and politics, that is. Because of the outreaching and enveloping trait of the human Self, it is possible not only for citizens as third scientists to work out creative solutions to moral impasses (internalizing conflicts as in step 2 of creative bargaining) but also for others to participate vicariously via authoritative knowings embodied in elegant solutions. Progressive destruction of barriers to intergroup and interpersonal communication is bound to follow from gradual accumulation of achievement in scientific mediation. It will lead to a progressively more reliable incidence of social perception (perception of the purposes of others). In return, the Self is made *whole*some with the "rounding" of experience.

In common with the other disciplines of experimental science, scientific mediation rejects the middle hypothesis which would straddle the fence when there is evidence for both of two contrary hypotheses. Beyond compromise, it seeks the deliberate creation of public purpose. It takes the scientific leap, the jump from fact-finding to fact-changing and sets deliberate change firmly on the conservative base of integration.

Control, as an aspect of the knowing transaction,[71] becomes, through the service of the reciprocal controls of the social scientific method, a noncoercive product of intention—an effective way of dealing with change through working in intentions. No longer aloof, science, in its aspect as collective enterprise (under its third hat)[72] becomes directly and actively involved in the live, uncloistered world of jostling moralities. Scientific mediation works from the "inside"—that is, inside the bodies and souls of the subject-matter scientists—on the details of the nature of human purposes. But then it submits its production—the purpose-replete plan carefully and hypothetically formulated—to the rigor of objectivity, the public test of communication without ambiguity. Here at last is a viable technique for deciding what value judgments ought to be made—a technique that will have as great a value within the laboratories of the physical sciences as, extended through vicarious experience, it will have in the world at large.

The control of purposes through the creating and testing of practical but scientifically formulated plans thus becomes the basis for deliberate directing of human destiny. A way (not entirely new to this coercive world) of functionalizing power is provided, to substitute for the wanton ways of the unseen hand. The search may now begin for appropriate devices for institutionalizing it in government, with the primary expectation that democratic administrative organization and procedures will develop the strategic controls appropriate to an era of fluid change. When adequately expressed in governmental structures and practices, scientific mediation will be seen to be a powerful political way of life, truly participative and fully democratic—an effective surrogate for obsolescent ways of compromise.

* * * *

After a brief interlude—a speculative chapter on art and its potential roles in democratic society—the chief remaining task of this book will be to take this so-far-developed scientific and participative way of building human purposes into a functional power that can control without coercion, and fit it into the framework of the advanced, though defective, democratic institutions of today, aiming to begin to bring it to life as an organized and practical method for democracy.

CHAPTER THIRTEEN

Purpose in a Pot

> .. song, which while it makes known
> the evil, announces also the awakening
> of salvation, knowledge-aware,
> knowledge-fraught, knowledge-
> persuading, the provenance of
> every true song.
>
> HERMANN BROCH

SO MUCH EMPHASIS HAS BEEN PLACED, IN THE LAST SOME pages, on the importance of knowing to control that an antidote is long overdue. This chapter is in the nature of an interlude of ventured suggestions, though it has also a direction of its own. It also follows in part a lead from Horace Fries.

"Feel" cannot be dismissed off-hand without doing violence to the understanding or analysis of any particular situation. "The growth of understanding," as Fries points out, "reduces superstition; it does not reduce the mysterious, ineffable qualities of existence." [1] The organic, mutual interdependence between knowing and feeling has been sufficiently stressed in previous chapters. Further comment is, however, due on the role of the ineffable aspects of experience and on methods of their organization. Ideally and in fact, both scientific and artistic activities, both the knowings of the paddler and his feel for the paddle, are involved in virtually all human situations, from gigantic government administration to simple grocery purchase. Indeed, the two are not always distinctly separable activities.

ART, PURPOSE, AND PERCEPTION

The purposes of people, like the wetness of water, emerge from sustained transaction.[2] Purposes do not belong only to *us*—except contingently as "us" refers to enlarged and extending Selves. They are rather products of existential situations.

As cultural realities, purposes are sometimes very largely "feel," not always readily communicable by inherited words and symbols.[3] For this reason, artistic activity—whether by professional artist or by the artist in Everyman—has important functions. Straining at the edges of communication to devise new ways to say what the present "language" of art does not countenance, the artist continually promotes the identification and perception of purposes. As Roger Fry once said, "A feeling of purpose comes to us from contemplation of a beautiful pot." [4]

The artist in each man, like the moralist, is concerned with moral truths.[5] The historical concurrence of new directions in art with forward steps in moral progress is not merely a matter of curious accident. It is not pure coincidence that the times of Ikhnaton, Praxiteles, and Lorenzo the Magnificent witnessed both desperate searches for new meanings and brilliant exfoliations of art—contrasted to the art of celebration of the Ancient Kingdom, the Byzantine Icon, and the Cathedral at Chartres. The sudden burst of novel artistic expression that coincided with the world's first experiment in monotheism during the brief reign of Ikhnaton is one of the most dramatic cases in point. James H. Breasted even goes so far as to draw particular connections, feeling that the beginning of portraiture in Egyptian art signified a new interest in the interpretation of human character.[6]

There is ample reason to expect continued connection between art and morality. Each generation remakes what it widely considers moral. It feels the moral in its inheritance but makes it anew for itself. It may well be argued that even evolution itself can be converted to the employ of art as a device for projecting the advance of morality. As Albert E. Wiggam suggested, art may furnish the principles of natural selection for the one animal that has risen above the tooth-and-claw level of survival of the fittest. Art sets up new ideals and, since men marry the women of their dreams, "it is highly probable that the very face and form of civilized man has changed under its influence." [7] Is this why there are more women than men? So that purpose may have a slight edge of influence over evolution? It is not so certain that art will, as Wiggam also suggests, "lead men by its gentle selective processes and all its creative ideals toward a wiser, saner, healthier and more beautiful human race" [8]—at least not in a straight, unswerving course. Art, having first presided over the extraction of purpose from nothingness, may become the medium whereby purpose (ideals) is diffused, and in the end may be the instrumentality for putting purpose to effect in evolution. The process will not however, be simple and automatic. Something will have to be done to see that right, good and worthy purposes are at hand and ascendent. It is the job of science, capitalizing on the claims of conservative drag, to socialize, to humanize the creative twists of the radical bent. For a prosaic example, the purposes most obviously in need of attention with reference to evolution are those expressed in the social aspects of modern medicine which perpetuate the unfit for procreation, as well as in the population policies of church and state that tolerate reproduction of the congenitally unfit.

Each human perception perforce relates "fact" and "value." Acts of perceiving are creative factors in the shaping of a developing situation. This is the import of today's revised understanding of the mechanics of perception, the understanding that no longer credits an arbitrary separation between environment and organism, between "out there" and "in here." [9] In Fries' words, the "epistemological function of perception is to guide action in securing its purposes." [10] Perceptions in this sense are signals or "prognostic directives," as contrasted with disclosures. But by relating "fact" and "value" at the elementary level, perception performs an aesthetic function in the creating and developing of purpose. Whenever a new perception marks delivery from perceptual illusion, error, or inadequacy, it also announces or heralds the overcoming of confusion, error, or inadequacy in purpose. Time and again paintings that at first appear ugly, unreal, and immoral lose the immorality as their beauty and reality become perceptible. Manet's *Olympia* is a classic case in point.

Joseph Conrad places the focus of the artist's function—with specific reference to the creator in prose—precisely at the point of perception.

> My task which I am trying to achieve is, by the power of the written word to make you hear, to make you feel—it is, before all, to make you *see*.

> The task approached in tenderness and faith is to hold up unquestioningly, without choice and without fear, the rescued fragment before all eyes in the light of a sincere mood. It is to show its vibration, its colour, its form; and through its movement, its form, and its colour, reveal the substance of its truth—disclose its inspiring secret: the stress and passion within the core of each convincing moment.[11]

John Ruskin once said that "there are one thousand who talk to one who can think and one hundred who think to one who can see." This ratio would seem to describe as well the talents of mankind: one thousand words per thought; one hundred thoughts per fresh perception. Art activity has perhaps always been, to a certain extent, a matter for specialization, because people differ in talent and temperament. When there are new sights, new relations, new purposes to be seen, however, specialists in perception are at a premium—more so, at least, than when art serves only the function of direct satisfaction or of celebration.

The excessive specialization that flowers in "art for art's sake" movements would seem, at least in large part, to be a response to intensified need, to special social need for new purposes, or to a special need for perceiving and communicating purposes that are emerging at a newly rapid rate. With an unfortunate turn of human perversity (due in root instance to the Self-protective automatic mechanism of conservative drag) there is a constant tendency for society to retaliate against the specialist in perception with scorn and segregation. And the artist, unable to articulate even to himself, so ineffable his inspiration, at times is constrained to play along. Rather than play the fool, however, he withdraws to the esoteric, thereafter sometimes pursuing his muse with undeflected determination, but sometimes also, in alienation, elaborating the esoteric into isolated private preciosity.

If only he can be kept out in the open, the artist can have timely impact through his important function of helping to change perception with changing times—helping individuals, groups, and societies to break loose from stereotype.[12] It is through acting—that is, through skills—that illusions are dispelled and perceptions are brought in line with more adequate understanding of reality.[13] The artist with his special skills breaks set patterns of mind so that the eye is free to observe. By making individual responses perceptible, he reveals emerging purposes and displays new facets of human nature and human problems.[14]

The artist works in the ineffable realms of experience where meaning is in direct and primary contact with "fact" and "value." By his skills, particularly his skill in organizing the material of his medium, he brings new insights to the surface of perception.

The artist's effectiveness, his success in putting his mark on society, is due to the kinship in artistry of every man; it may well be because "we are all more sensitive to relations aesthetically than we are in our everday jobs," as Mary Follett says.[15]

Only as aesthetic communication is eventually won can logical analysis be brought to consolidate and preserve the victory.[16] One of the uses of art is to communicate the new meanings which have not been and perhaps cannot be put into words, but which must be communicated if people are going to be able to get along together in a society, if they are going to have a tolerable understanding of or sympathy with each other,[17] if—in terms of the second step of Max Otto's creative bargaining—they are going to be able to raise a "disturbing concern" for each other's values or purposes.[18] Hence, art can be described also as an essential agent of objectivity, particularly so far as ideals or intentions cannot be put into precise words. It can be crucial to objectivizing* experience—particularly to the extent that Follett is right in her assertion that "the very essence of experience evaporates in analysis." [19] Einstein is said to have replied to a questioner: "I cannot give an answer to your question but I can play it on the violin."

Before knowing, reasoning, thinking are unduly subordinated, it should be remembered that art even at its most ineffable, at least the art of modern man, is never entirely independent of knowing. The masterful skill which forms the ground base for any art today is not a thing apart; it demands both heart and head. Surely it can be said that physics since the days of Galileo has done as much for music as music since the days of Monteverdi has done for physics.

One wonders if art, in the evolution of the species, may not have sprung from the death of vigilance. Relieved of the need for constant alertness, the need to catch the slightest secret sounds of preservation, the twitching antelope-ears of anxiety have atrophied. Has not their instinctive alertness and sensitivity resolved into diversity, elaboration, and educable sensibility—into artistic capacities? Decreased biological capacity for vigilance can be observed in captive animals as well as in domesticated man. It is what makes survival under the confined conditions of civilization possible; the race would otherwise have gone stir-crazy long since, as caged animals sometimes do. Vigilance has been sublimated, so to speak, into exalted playfulness, into creativity. [20]

The signal functions of animal perception appear to include "purposes" that are largely instinctive, simple fight-or-flight matters for the most part. From this animal inheritance man has derived the great bulk of the sights he sees—those that seem to thrust themselves on him—perhaps via embryonic and infantile rerun of the development of the race. In addition, as an elaboration from the demise of vigilance, what have come to be called human purposes begin to emerge as distinguishable aspects of life. These complex phenomena are products of refinement and leisure (released time), of release from need for constant alertness, permitting free elaboration, the playfulness of trial-and-error, and the development, transformation and sharpening of skills. Purposes come to life only after the world has been brightened with color, music, form, and grace of movement—for art precedes appreciation. People see what they are prepared to see, either through the evolution of the species or through the special device of artist-derived (whether the artist is a specialist or not), art-purveyed purposes.

---

*Objectivizing: making sure we understand each other without ambiguity.

FREEDOM THROUGH SKILL

The special role that art plays as (at least metaphorical) heir to vigilance seems to grow, and to grow in importance, as the centuries and
ages pass. From very small beginnings in an edge of creativity and an
elaborating of purpose, art has become freedom's champion. From the
dying gasp of vigilance, it received as inheritance the office of standard
bearer for the banner of freedom, the charge of carrying freedom forth
in the daily struggle of the expanding spirit. Since then it has witnessed and abetted such an unfurling of freedom, augmented star by
star, that its primitive precursor is all but lost in metamorphosis.

Probably the most significant connotation of the term freedom for
today is skill. In a sense, skill has been essential to the most primitive
freedom from the very first—essential to the biological freedom for
survival and then to the freedom from fear, which is the forerunner to
the subsiding of vigilance. It was the skills behind alertness that eventually won riddance from the need for complete preoccupation with
vigilance and afforded the opportunity for the elaboration of creative
activities—for further flexibility and increasing adaptability. Eternal
vigilance is the price of freedom, but when the skills behind vigilance
have more than paid the price, the difference may be claimed in extensions and refinements of freedom, permitting increasing freedom with
increasing adaptability and creativity. In man, the "adaptation" of earlier
and more general evolutionary processes has passed into habit and skill,
and in these latter are sunk the deep roots of the elaborate freedoms of
democratic society.

Nowhere does skill find more comfortable nurture than at the hands
of artistic endeavor, whether homespun or refined. Indeed, the two
terms "art" and "skill" are frequently used interchangeably; at least
occupations employing special skills are often called "arts" in disregard
of the degree of creativity involved. While on the one hand skill is
almost a *sine qua non* of art, on the other hand art is the excuse for
efforts of the finest and most refined skill. It is because of this special
place of skill in art that art becomes an agent of freedom, for when art
accomplishes release from the old by displacing it with original creation,
the release is achieved through the mediation of skill.

He who has the skill is the one who is free—in a way different from
him who is freed by the novelty of a perception received from a creative
artist. There is a feeling of freedom in being able to walk up stairs on
your hands, to drive a car at breakneck speed over stone and broken
glass, to chair an expeditious public hearing, to project a mood at will by
grimace and gesture, to hammer a straight nail, to put thoughts into

words, to perform a Paganini caprice, or to amass the money to buy the skills of others. In this sense of the term, freedom is not a riddance as was the freedom from fear or freedom from foreign domination; it is positive and forward-looking. There is a positive aspect to the skill connotation of freedom that reaches far beyond the freedom of good-riddance. Man makes his freedoms by probing into the unknown with the spearhead of sharpened skills. Although in retrospect every skill can be considered a freedom from the limitations imposed on the unskilled, in fact it is a positive achievement because the "limit" is generally not conceived before the flight of aspiration that immediately precedes creation. Can the caveman bemoan the limitation of his lack of literacy?

Any process that effectively accommodates conservative drag, as does creative bargaining or scientific mediation, displays the consummate skill of preserving each man from the achievements of the others. This may be counted the great freedom arranged by the skill of genuine participation: preserving to each the enhancement of freedom, including especially his own opportunity for growth through his own exercise of skill. It is possible, however, for one man's skill to complement another man's freedom—just as one man may grow from another man's participation —vicariously. When this happens it is art that has officiated. In Horace Kallen's words,

> Art is a new use of nature, or of other art, which liberates the spirit, if for an instant only, from the coercions and constraints which beset it. Whatever other relations a thing may have, we are disposed to attribute beauty to it if it consummates this liberation, and we tend to realize its beauty as *a relation* between ourselves and the liberating power. Let the power be pattern and good order, let it be disorder and confusion; if it be liberating, we call it beautiful. Esthetic experience is experience of such power. During it we are freed, and in the degree that we are freed we feel sure and safe and at ease.[21]

By helping in its special way to bring about change, art becomes a solvent for conservative drag, providing relief through the immediacy of aesthetic involvement.

There are dangers, too, in freedom vicariously received. They attend particularly the freedom in the skill of amassing money. When so widely separated as to be dissociated from the skills of earning, the "freedom" bought in the hire of the skills of others or in the purchase of their production can easily become a mockery. The sudden non-skill-related affluence of America's adolescent class may just possibly (if there are not compensating skills at work) pose a real cultural threat of undermining the skill-foundations of freedom.

T. V. Smith has properly emphasized the importance of middle-class skills to the development of American democracy.[22] Historically they are, to all appearances, the basis of liberty, in the sense of freedom from outside domination. The compulsory public school system can be read as a response to the need of the industrial revolution for skilled employees. President Johnson's poverty program, the junior college movement, the head-start program, the black man's finally effective insistence on equal education and the right to vote—all these found significant impetus not only in humanitarian ideals of equality and opportunity but also, and probably more effectively, in changing industrial needs for skill—needs for new skills tied with a sudden gap in the market for "hired hands" with no skill at all.

A positive freedom on the political level, however, cannot be sustained by a mesh of discrete and unconnected individual skills, important though they are. An all-star football "team" would be mighty pathetic without a chance for workout and coordination before game time— despite acclaimed individual abilities. Imagine a chorus of prima donnas! The many long ages extending between the skills of vigilance that won biological-level freedom from fear and the skills of social perception (perception of the purposes of others) that will yet win freedom from the goodwill coercions of the other man's radical bent have not been completely spanned. The last few generations may be the longest. Again, all the resources of artistic sensitivity must be brought to bear, and they are only too meager. As William James has said,

> Only in some pitiful dreamer, some philosopher, poet, or romancer, or when the common practical man becomes a lover, does the hard externality give way, and a gleam of insight into . . . the vast world of inner life beyond us, so different from that of outer seeming, illuminate our mind. Then the whole scheme of our customary values gets confounded, then our self is riven and its narrow interests fly to pieces, then a new centre and a new perspective must be found.[23]

Coordination, socialization of the skills of social perception in social habits or machinery, will demand sharpened skills in communication as a part of a renewed institution of free speech.[24] It is doubtful that new modes of association, accommodations of conservative drag, requiring improved social perception will gain firm foundation without the heightened appreciation that can come only from art.

> And the true realism were that of the poets, to climb up after [a man] like a squirrel, and catch some glimpse of the heaven for which he lives. And the true realism, always and everywhere, is that of the poets: to find out where joy resides and give it a voice far beyond singing.[25]

A democratic society of Self-control will come to life as horizons are expanded, as other Selves are fully accepted, and as an associated freedom is made perceptible.

With all our machines, each one a distillate of skills, a potential building block of freedom, we may, through proper management, be closer to utopia than we suspect. With increasing skill in making clocks comes increasing freedom, provided we do not let ourselves be enslaved by clocks. There is also freedom-fraught skill in knowledge, in knowing-how, just as there is knowing involved in every skill. This back-and-forth between thought and artifact is not confined to formal fields of experimental science. There is something basically human about it—as if in distilling a skill, making an instrument, machine, object, artifact, man the transactor, the human being-doing, were laying out a portion of his brain on the table and fashioning these things of it; in fact, Self-extending his mind, his thinking apparatus, creating new mind-cells on the far side, the outside of his skin. Among the arts, this phenomenon is most clearly seen in the growth of the architect in dialogue with materials and machines. But it is apparently continually at work in all fields—city planner and bulldozer, sculptor and blowtorch, musician and electronic tape. Perhaps one of the most striking is the thirteenth and fourteenth century transaction between musician and the gradually perfecting organ keyboard. Technically the new keyboard permitted a new freedom in experimentation with sound combinations and undoubtedly had a great deal to do with the creation of modern harmony. The instruments that mediate scientific experiment—the microscopes, accelerometers, atomic piles, psychiatric couches—are at one and the same time skill-distillates and objects to be skillfully handled: there is skill in controlling the instruments of control; there is freedom in the knowings-how of scientific inquiry. In fact, here is the locus of the greatest possible concentrate of freedom potential: the knowings-how of (democratic) moral science where the Self grows, expanding toward increased enrichment in Self-liberating transactions of reciprocal control.

THE SERVICE OF ART TO SCIENCE

The service of art to science cuts deeper than we shall ever know. This follows inevitably from the nature of the case, the communications of art being outstandingly ineffable. If one can get a feeling of purpose from contemplating a beautiful pot, how intimate and enduring must be the impinging of art on all social activities! Science, in one of its aspects, is a collective enterprise, a structured system of social transactions. Depending as it does on the most sensitive and refined of human capabilities—perception, thought, skill—science may be the most in debt of all human enterprises to the services of art.

Compared with experimental science, Greek science was more a matter of aesthetic appreciation, but less a matter of art. Modern science is so much more complex than the ancient science, which consisted of direct perception followed by construction of verbal facsimiles, that art must impinge upon it from many more directions. Since the time when purposeful change was first injected into the scientific method, so many dimensions have been added to scientific activity—experiments, technical instruments, above all, purposes—that increased involvement of artistic activity has been inevitable, and so, correspondingly, has the dependence of science on art. The simple situation is that, as mankind approaches more and more refined frontiers in inquiry, more and more sensitivity is needed, involving progressive technological development in precision instrumentation, but also progressive refinement of human sensibility (perhaps heightened capacity for suffering as was suggested above) [26] and thus the utmost in artistic effort.

Very little attention has been paid to this important area of relationship. But it will become increasingly important, particularly in moral or political science. What follows here can only be considered a beginning exposition of the vital relevancies of art activities (of the perceptive layman as well as of the specialist, the "artist") to science.

IN THE BEGINNING—THE HITCH

It almost goes without saying that artistic sensitivity may be necessary to perceive the hitch, difficulty, contradiction, conflict that is the very beginning of any scientific inquiry. By no means are all conflicts apparent—even to the people involved. This is most particularly true of social conflicts and of the subtle contradictions encountered in the more highly refined sciences.

The role of art in raising purposes to the level of perception or articulation has already been mentioned. Frequently, purposes first become perceptible in conflict. At other times the reverse is the case; sometimes conflict cannot be located or defined until participating purposes are uncovered and named.

STRUCTURING PROBLEMS

Even where the fact of conflict—of a hitch in the ongoing activity of a developing problematic situation—is commonly felt and there is no doubt of its reality, the task of formulating the hitch or difficulty into a problem remains. The way the problem is formulated is crucial because, unless the problem is properly put together out of a problematic situation, solving it will not resolve the original difficulty. Van Meter Ames gives art a very central role in this regard:

Awareness of the solution in a problematic situation, and of the problem in the solution, is aesthetic experience. . . . A work of art induces aesthetic experience by representing a problematic situation. . . . Art is essentially a harmony in discord, a unity in variety, a reciprocal relation of means and ends. . . . Aesthetic experience is contemplation of values in a problematic situation, and there are no values to be contemplated where there is no problem.[27]

To the extent that a situation is unprecedented, so that already made formulas are not applicable, the service of the artist or the artist-in-everyman is needed.

Ideas function as tools, as instruments, in arranging, organizing, orchestrating the elements or contents, the material of problems. When an unprecedented problem arises, customary conceptual tools are no longer entirely appropriate: they need to be adapted to the new material. Sometimes entirely new tools must be fashioned. Sometimes the old tools can be newly felt out, rebalanced, retooled. At other times intuition of a new feel for the use or handling of conceptual tools is sufficient adaptation to permit resumption of work in the new material—much as when a young woodsman intuits a new feel for the use of an ax after encountering knotty log-problems for the first time.

Here is where the artist comes in—at the point of raising a new feel for conceptual tools. He brings "a non-conceptual sensitivity to materials . . . which dissolves the rigid boundaries of traditional concepts without breach of continuity of their meaning and precipitates them again in the form of new crystals to be employed for the new problems." [28]

This problem forming function of art is only possible because thinking and feeling are *not* separate activities. It is the compenetration of feeling and thinking, the basic unity in human nature, that permits the highest scientific achievements of thought. As Horace Fries explains:

Since feeling and thought are not separate activities or faculties, art . . . serves to promote (incidentally to its deliberate and direct aesthetic function) the *relevant* conceptualization of problems. It does this through its office of enabling the *formulations* of problems to take better account of *novel* difficulties. It formulates, aesthetically or non-conceptually, felt meanings for communication and use, so that concepts can work more sensitively and more adequately in the novel materials at hand. The non-conceptual meanings it formulates are the material by means of which the intuitive act bridges the gap between the old concepts and the new, the latter serving for the formulation of new problems.[29]

Without dependable feelings—feelings that can be relied upon in organizing inquiry—it is impossible to have dependable (abstract) instruments of control. It is because men are not vegetables, because they are the most sensitive and suffering of the beasts, that they are able to think. Artistic activity is the important intermediary mechanism that holds up the lamp to illuminate the patterns of intercourse between the feel and the thought. In moral science the dependability of perception of purposes (our own as well as other people's) is particularly critical. The surer our perceptions of purposes, the more sensitive the social control possible through refinement of intention.[30] Again, it is not only the raising of purposes from the level of the ineffable to the level of articulation—through the art articulation of perceptual cues (and the aesthetic process, called "value judgment," of weighing, adjusting, and integrating)—that is important, but the organizing function of art in inquiry.

The relevance of art to science, particularly its relevance in the formulation of problems, is found, not in the water color ash cans of the artist, the tunes of the composer, the arguments of the poet, but rather in the forms—especially the new forms—that the artist, the composer, and the poet evolve and elaborate. Peter Drucker observes that "the more 'scientific' the biologist has become [that is, the more he has progressed beyond Cartesian ways], the more he has tended to talk in terms such as 'immunity' and 'metabolism,' 'ecology' and 'syndrome,' 'homeostasis' and 'pattern'—each of them essentially an aesthetic term describing not so much a property of matter or quantity as of a harmonious order." [31] This he can say despite the fact that harmony and other moral-aesthetic terms were ostentatiously discarded when science was "devalorized" and have been honestly resisted as influence, direct or analogical, by many conscientious scientists ever since.[32] Indications are that moral science will begin with terms that are essentially aesthetic (like chains of command, organization charts, land use maps, spans of control, group dynamics—even general systems, field theories, and parallelograms of force) and proceed to refine them—those that prove not to have been false starts—after the fashion of the organic chemist with his benzene rings. Their refinement for problematic situations through intuition of a new feel is an aesthetic job, the artist's stock in trade.

No one knows the degree of transference from the forms and unities of the established arts to theory and practice in problem solving. It may be extensive. A poem is said to begin by giving structure to an experience and to end by giving experience to a structure.[33] An obvious intermediary to such achievement is the characteristic internal conflict, the dialectic form of a poem so well exemplified in the sonnet: "one thing against another across a silence." From the *meaningful* (non-conceptual) shaping of a poem's "technical performance" [34] can come experience that will give the necessary *feel* for mundane problems. The relevance of such non-conceptual structuring of experience to the formulation of problems out of dumb sensing of discord is not difficult to appreciate. Art (of which the established arts are only the most conspicuous and durable display) shepherds, shapes, and organizes the dependable feelings that are the initial criteria of the relevance of concepts to problematic situations.

VISTAS OF EXPECTATION

The physical sciences have organized their conceptual frameworks in residual reliance on self-evidence. Always, at furthest remove, at the bottom of analysis, resides the unproved, the axiomatic. The recent history of science has, furthermore, witnessed use of more and more unproved concepts as tools for improving mathematical construction.[35] The repeal (for some purposes) of Euclid's fifth axiom, and its replacement by parallel lines converging at infinity is a case in point.

The value of and final evidence for such concepts lies in their usefulness for improving conceptual tools of control and thereby securing improved control of practical transformations. But their initial warrant is self-evidence, "a perception of the relations between the unproved concept or axiom and its materials and aims." [36] As Einstein describes it, "To him who is a discoverer in [theoretical physics] the products of his imagination appear so necessary and natural that he regards them, and would like to have them regarded by others, not as creations of thought but as given realities." [37] Although, on the one hand, there is danger in the use of self-evidence when it is taken as a final limit to inquiry, on the other hand, the liberating effect and potential of new self-evidence (which is not evident to eyes cast down in homage to cultural traditions) is increasingly apparent.

Clearly, the artist in man must play a crucial role in the organization of the relation-sensitive perceptions that mount to self-evidence. No doubt self-evidence, particularly new self-evidence, will have cultural variations relating to variations in perception. Was there, for example, a significant relationship between the meaning of time carried in Jewish tradition, particularly in the Old Testament, and Einstein's disquiet over the self-evidence of simultaneity? It used to be thought that fundamental postulates in physics were logically derived from elementary experiences by a process of abstraction. With the advent of the general theory of relativity, however, has come the recognition that, while experience may be suggestive, basic concepts are invented rather than deduced. The feeling that a postulate or concept is "so necessary and natural," as Einstein put it—the feeling of profundity, "that we are making new, more extensive, contact with reality" [38]—is the expression of the artist behind and within the scientist selecting, creating, "zeroing in" on an axiom with commitment, courage, and conviction. Such self-evidence only comes to the sensitive few. According to Michael Polanyi,

> we should acknowledge our capacity for recognizing scientific value by our sense of harmony—by our emotional response to the intellectual beauty of science. And since no part of science can be said to be beautiful unless it is also believed to be true, we must claim for this emotional response also that it makes contact with reality. A discovery is beautiful if it reveals a new vision of reality.[39]

It should be apparent that the converse relation also pertains. Can it not be said that the new vistas opened by artists (specialists) provide the release that allows new philosophical bases of self-evidence?

> Our vision of reality to which our sense of scientific beauty responds must suggest to us the kind of questions that it should be reasonable and interesting to explore. They should recommend the kind of conceptions and empirical relations that are intrinsically plausible and which should therefore be upheld —even when some evidence seems to contradict them; and tell us also, on the other hand what empirical connections to reject as specious, even though there is evidence for them, and even though we may as yet be unable to account for this evidence on any other assumptions.[40]

Polanyi draws an interesting parallel between the scientist's artistic progression and that of the artist.

> Intellectual passions do not merely affirm the existence of harmonies which foreshadow an indeterminate range of future discoveries, but also evoke intimations of specific discoveries and sustain their persistent pursuit through years of labor. The appreciation of scientific value merges here into the capacity for discovering it; even as the artist's sensibility merges into his creative powers.[41]

Is there not more than a suggestive parallel here? Is this not a locus of promising transfer as from left hand practice to right hand performance, or from skillful joints to appreciative ears, or from muscular coordination to wide angle vision? (Refer to page 51, above.)

It is repetitions, forms, patterns that affect a man as a whole, direct the movement of his joints and mix his viscera with his thoughts. Out of these there is a category called "invariance" that takes particular prominence. Very generally described, invariance refers to the man-made (in the sense of being a product of transaction and not of the "out-there") coherence or reality of things. It is the trick, that man presumably shares with other animals, of being able to extract or sublimate something constant, unchanging, invariant out of the never-identically-repeated impinging of sensory data on neural receptors. Perhaps this is merely to say again that man is transactional, that invariance is the direct product of the transaction called perception. However it is, man and nature together do make structure, and the happening is awesome and spiritual; it is the making of reality. It is how we directly see a boat as a boat whether it is under foot or a mere speck on the horizon. Apparently a perception is a transaction that organizes, forms, patterns invariant characteristics. These are said to be "perceived," and they are called "reality."

When a man enters a new area of experience, as he does every time a new instrument extends his perceptual sensitivities—X-rays, radar screens, electro-magnetic amplifiers—he is, like the babe in the woods, left without bearings. He encounters chaos. His perceptual processes are not prepared biologically and experientially to organize the invariant characteristics that will put meaning into what he "sees."

Patterns can be taught, transmitted from person to person. But their first working out to the light as invariance is a creative job—creative perception.

Since the making of invariance is a formidable task, whatever aid can be extended is gratefully received. The fact that so many creative scientists are accomplished in one or more of the fine arts suggests a fairly obvious source for intuition and transference. A pianist will explain that the kinesthetic patterns he feels out on the keyboard can help him in hearing the structure, the beauty of a piece of music. All the perceptual sensitivities and offices of art can be made use of. Orderly repetition of pattern in any medium is an aesthetic activity (perhaps it should be said the other way round: aesthetics is largely based on invariance) and transfer from one medium or activity to another seems to be a regular and constant occurrence. Think of the impact of Jackson Pollock on the art of City Planning. From the third frame of reference of science—science as a collective enterprise—comes the persistent suspicion that the regularities of science are an outgrowth of transaction involving human being-doings, that regularities are as much man-made as man-found—through selection of procedures, of ways of observing and experimenting—and that man's aesthetic sensibilities have inevitable impact though perhaps exceedingly subtle and recondite.

In physics invariance has become a formal concept. Symmetry, not mere repetition, but orderly repetition, repetition in respect to some principle, is emphasized as one of its fundamental aspects, and leads into mathematical formulation. Thus the invariance in a snowflake (and its beauty) is defined by repetition of a figure at intervals of 60 degrees around an axis, and invariance of a circle through any degree of rotation develops the formula of $X^2+Y^2=a^2$. From this point on, complex mathematical elaboration ensues, taking advantage in the process—while avoiding the mathematician's trap laid for unwary scientists in mathematics for mathematics' sake—of the special beauties the mathematician feels in his refined formulations. Matters of aesthetics are indeed relevant to science. The aesthetic category of invariance, in particular, participates in the advance of thought.

Consideration of invariance points on toward discussion of the logical category of simplicity in science and the idea of elegance in aesthetics. This has been deferred, however, to later pages. The important point here is simply that aesthetics can be seen at work in science, guiding thought, leading to fruitful results. It is of further profound interest that reliance on aesthetic considerations is accounted to be on the increase in recent research.[42]

In moral science, aesthetics may be even more relevant to self-evidence than it is in physical science. Indications are, however, that the concepts behind social control will not be mathematical, except to a very limited extent. As Horace Fries suggests, the concepts that are basic to social science may even turn out to be essentially aesthetic themselves. Because they are working in purposes, they can at least be expected to subsume the reality of time. The abstract tools for dealing with intention may then quite possibly appear in terms of expectation instead of existence. And in this case vision (and kinesthesia) [43] must make room for hearing in the organizing of self-evidence. Of all the arts, music deals most obviously in "vistas" of time, though it is by no means alone among the arts in concern with intention and expectation; there is an element of self-evidence, self-expectance in all creative work.

Expectation is the underside of intention. Men would never have developed the biological characteristic of *intending* to remake segments of the world, of experience, if they had not *expected*—thousands of theologians and mechanists to the contrary notwithstanding—that their intentional actions would make significant differences.[44] When it is not mere fatalism, expectation further involves perception of the purposes and intentions of others. Some such category as self-expectance, in which is incorporated the reality of time, the dimensions of irreversibility, would provide for moral science the equivalent of self-evidence for physical science.

But expectation is the chief foil against which the composer of music pits his compositions, his structurings of time, tone, and timbre; it is the human medium in which he works. Indeed, much of the meaning of music is to be found in its maneuverings with expectation.[45] Grieg's description of Liszt's first reading of his (Grieg's) piano concerto affords a very direct illustration:

"Towards the end of the finale the second theme is repeated ... in a grand fortissimo. In the preceding bars, where the first note of the theme's first triplets, G sharp, changes to G in the orchestra, while the piano in a tremendous scale figure traverses all its range of the keys, he stopped suddenly, rose to his full height, left the piano and paced with stalwart, theatrical step and arm uplifted through the great hall of the monastery while he fairly bellowed the theme. At the G I have spoken of, he stretched out his arm commandingly like an emperor and shouted, 'G, G, not G sharp! Famos! das ist so echt schwedisches Banko!' and then, as if in parenthesis, almost pianissimo, 'Der Smetana hat mir neulich etwas davon geschickt.' Then he went back to the piano, repeated the whole strophe, and finished off. At the end he said with a singularly cordial accent as he handed me the book, 'Fahren Sie fort, ich sage Ihnen, Sie haben das Zeug dazu, und—lassen Sie sich nicht abschrecken!'" [46]

Against a background of stylized experience, of familiar artificially or aesthetically organized patterns or structures, the composer constructs new compositions involving reorganization of the expectations built on past experience with the style.

Some of the maneuverings of music with expectation are in a sense repetitive. Interest in rehearing music, aside from interest based on celebration or rejoicing (familiar forms revisited), is sustained by lapse of memory.[47] As memory abstracts, it subordinates and/or discards detail. Interest in rehearing a familiar work then derives from the surprise afforded as expectation is jolted and subsequently recreated. Error in memory may be considered a quality of abstraction; the two are dual workings of memory. Inherited groupings or purpose are artificial in the same sense that styles of art are, though the latter are simpler, purer, and more nearly encompassable. Both are man made. From the repetitive correction of error of expectation within the contained quarters of art forms there are relevancies and parallels that will apply to the perfecting of prognostic reliability in the realms of purpose.

But others of the maneuverings of music with expectation are creative. These are the new hearings that break with the forms of musical tradition (and expectation) and break out new paths, new "vistas" of style. An art is creative when it changes the world as men see it. In the revelatory role of change in perspective through art, there is a direct parallel with the validating role of controlled change through experimental science. One of the nodes or key points of creation is just here. Music, perhaps more obviously and directly than the other arts, plays around with change—differences, rubatos, appoggiaturas, free cadenzas, ad libitums (any child at a piano with "chopsticks"). Even when securely within a style, the muse of music keeps pushing out the walls, or attempting to steal base. The other arts do the same, but never so notably in time.

It is important to recognize that not only the composer but also the performer, and even the listener can be creative in musical expectation. The creative, participative listener is involved in a conversation with the composer so that it isn't always "Well! I didn't expect that!" but sometimes, "Why don't you do this next!" and then, when he doesn't, "Well, I guess you were right" or, stubbornly, "It would have worked better my way." In other words, the listener can lead ahead out of the backlogged experience of style just as well as the composer can. His role is not simply a passive one of surprise and shock or delight.

The sense of physical pain in destruction of an expectation engineered by a composer [A wrong chord from faulty performance, while not composer-engineered, gives the most vivid illustration.] can be qualitatively comparable with and relevant to the physical or moral pain in expectation dashed by a turn of social fortunes. When creative maneuverings and expectations are involved, perception and purpose merge for the moment. There is in each instance, through shaping in perception, an awakening to dimensions (meanings) of time in intention.

If self-expectation is understood as perception of the relations between the unproved axiom and the interests, intentions, and aims—in short, the purposes—upon which it bears, the organization of such time-laden, relation-sensitive perceptions would seem to attend upon the opening of vistas of expectation by the creative artist, most especially by the creative musician.

JUXTAPOSITION OF THE WORLD OF COMMON SENSE AND THE WORLD OF COMMON SOUNDS

Music has long held a special place in the heart of science. With unusual regularity, the most abstract of the scientists, the theoretical physicists, have been highly musical. Heisenberg, Helmholtz, Born, Teller: pianists; Einstein: violinist. And Planck invented a new musical instrument, and Galileo wrote music for the lute. History shows some very suggestive correspondences between the development of music and the development of experimental science, though it should be admitted at the outset that the effects of music on science must be exceedingly subtle. It is interesting, for instance, to note in dim history that Pythagorean experiments relating musical intervals to arithmetical ratios of lengths of string at uniform tension were among the few instances of scientific experimentation by the ancients and possibly among the very first in the annals of early civilization. It would seem fairly clear that the Pythagorean discovery of the mathematically simple regularity of beautiful musical intervals had something to do with the growth of the Pythagorean conviction that number was the reality of everything—

perhaps also with the subsequent resurrection of mathematics in the Renaissance in readiness for the scientific revolution. In other words, there appears to have been a sort of translation of human satisfaction from the forefront of musical taste into scientific curiosity or inquiry. In what now seems to have been a simplistic spirit of overenthusiasm, the Pythagoreans, in their astronomical studies, went on to suppose that the whole heavens was a musical scale, combining music and astronomy in an elaborate "harmony of the spheres." As it developed, the Pythagorean tradition of "harmonics" became an elaborate and self-propelled discipline. Its major and continuing inspiration was found apart from musical impulse in a mathematically viewed general interest in the nature of the universe.[48] Practically, Greek music was a product of ear and voice; theoretically it was analyzed in terms of stretched strings.

Did Greek aesthetic development, particularly musical development, in some mute way presage Pythagoras' great original idea of geometrical demonstration, the idea that a particular fact is explained when shown to be deducible from a more general principle?[49] The Greeks learned in music, and in architecture as well, of the dependence of beauty on proportion. They discovered that the qualitative elements of the world could sometimes be described by mathematical relations. But what is most interesting, and in the end perhaps most significant, is that the art that determined the acoustic facts and structural proportions preceded their understanding by science and their subsequent elaboration. The aesthetic must have had a role in intellectual awakening and research.

Exactly what role the growth of sensibility and discrimination played in the historical development of theoretical speculation would be extremely difficult, if not impossible, to establish. Resumption of scientific thinking after a pause during the early Middle Ages is marked by the recovery, in the twelfth century from recovered Greek texts, of the Pythagorean insistence on the importance of generality; that is, the notion of general principle as referent, as explanation, and as source by deduction and correlation of rational knowledge. From then on (though also before then, to some extent) there was continued low-key influence from the changes taking place in musical environment. (Rapid strides in the other arts could be alternatively cited.)

The idea of an experimentally grounded and mathematically formulated science of nature was worked out in the thirteenth and fourteenth centuries. It came to fruition at the end of the sixteenth century with Galileo. Meanwhile decided changes were taking place in music, changes so profound that it can be argued that a new art, the likes of which the world had never heard before, was just then beginning.

There seems now to be some question that medieval European music followed in direct linear descent from Greek music. Nothing remains of Greek practical music, though classical Greek musical theory had profound and pervasive influence. Perhaps there was a hiatus. More likely a number of influences were at work, including eruptions of local creativity. Very recent scholarship indicates precocious indigenous growth of a harmonic music based on the interval of the third in Ireland—well before anything comparable developed on the continent.[50]

Greek music seems not to have been an independent art, but rather—except as it accompanied dance—almost exclusively a secondary device for heightening the effect and beauty of poetry. It was seldom independent of verse. Its rhythms were subordinated to, and made to correspond with that of verse—so much so that it probably gave no separate or distinctive musical sense. And there was no harmony in our sense whatsoever. Medieval Church music until about the twelfth century was virtually restricted to plainsong, characterized by non-recurrent configurations of movement. Except for the earlier start in Ireland, it was in the twelfth and thirteenth centuries, in the descant or measured music of the time, that rhythm was finally firmly enough established to permit different voices to sing different melodies simultaneously to produce harmony in contrasted rhythms. The new art of polyphony that grew in the thirteenth and fourteenth centuries and became fully mature in the fifteenth century had to adopt rhythmic modes, drawing from the sense of bodily movement in dance rhythm, to provide a structure sufficiently powerful to hold the parts together.[51] With the liberating aid of improved rhythmic strengths, a new coordination of voices occurred, leading to new concords of separate voices, new organization of harmony (beginning first as cadences) in the later fifteenth century, and eventually to modern sense of key.

Harmony began developing on the continent in the thirteenth and fourteenth centuries. The Ionian mode (virtually the modern major scale), which had not been employed in plainsong but was popular in secular music and found there from the eleventh century, lent itself particularly as a vehicle for the awakening harmonic feeling. It had been rejected by the medieval Church as *modus lascivus* and was not officially recognized by the Church until the sixteenth century.[52] The major and minor scales came to be used almost exclusively from 1600 to 1900. Meanwhile, the developing harmony finally arrived at tonality describable in terms of modern key in the supreme sixteenth century art of Palestrina and his contemporaries. The life span of Monteverdi, the great pioneer of modern harmony, coincided almost exactly with that of Galileo.[53]

To days, moons, seasons, heart beats, and a hundred other recurrences of things, the musician's aborning art added new sorts of rhythms of human aspiration. To what effect? Merely to hold a burgeoning art form together? To bring artistic order out of a threatening chaos of dithyrambic ornamentation? Or also, perhaps, in some respect to stimulate, awaken, channel, deflect, or orient sixteenth and seventeenth century theory of periodicity—Kepler's planets, Galileo's pendulums, Newton's sound waves, Huygens' light waves, Mersenne's vibrating violin strings? To pave the way for the physicist's invariance? From what stock of sensibility did Galileo draw the germ of his great seminal concept of acceleration? Is Kepler's system of celestial harmonies merely mystical speculation and entirely devoid of other justification—even in initial impulse? Remember that Ptolemy, also a great astronomer, was the man who set the musical scale in order in the second century A. D. As W. C. Dampier suggests, "The regularities of science may be put into it by our procedure of observation or experiment." [54] Indeed, they may be put there by our perceptions and the social organizing of our perceptual capacities, by contagion from aesthetic forms of harmony and rhythm. "Apart from recurrence, knowledge would be impossible; for nothing could be referred to our past experiences. Also, apart from some regularity of recurrence, measurement would be impossible. In our experience, as we gain the idea of exactness, recurrence is fundamental." [55]

The revolution in science was preceded and accompanied by an equally fundamental revolution in hearing. It is undoubtedly highly significant that experimental science and harmonic music, as we know it, grew up together in the same culture, and that neither of them developed at any other time in any other culture.[56] The medieval parallelisms of fourths and fifths of the twelfth century were already a world apart from the musical experience of the ancients who, as far as can be determined, conceived of concord in choral singing as consisting only of voices in unison or doubling at the octave. The modal harmonies of the fifteenth century, culminating in the sixteenth century golden age of polyphony, and the dramatic opening out of the possibilities of modern harmony at the end of the sixteenth century, is an even more exciting exfoliation of the human spirit. It is hard to imagine that in the beginning of the fifteenth century the major third could have been considered harsh to the ear.[57]

It is doubtful that a modern ear tuned to its own times in European musical heritage could regain an understanding or appreciation of the spirit and temper of the classical Greek musician. We know from direct experience how inaccessible are the meanings of oriental and contemporary primitive music. Indeed, much of the study of the music of primitive cultures has been given over to anthropological and ethnological sciences in the Anglo-Saxon countries. It is felt that their electronic devices and new analytical techniques may be able to penetrate to a better understanding of unaccustomed primitive sounds than can the ear of the trained musician or musicologist caught in his own traditions. The revolution in rhythm since ancient Greece and the revolution in harmony since the Middle Ages have been complete. The classic Greek rhythms that were attached to verse, built around the poetic flow of musically chaotic minute undulations, have been lost. If reconstructable, they would surely seem unnatural to modern ears. Conversely, the tonal harmony of the modern key system has attained the status of the natural. Giraldus Cambrensis (Welsh ecclesiastic, geographer, historian c. 1146- c. 1223) gives a vivid glimpse of the magic hold of early Welsh harmonizing:

> In their musical concerts they do not sing in unison like the inhabitants of other countries, but in many different parts; so that in a company of singers, which one very frequently meets in Wales, you will hear as many different parts and voices as there are performers, who all at length unite, with organic melody, in one consonance and the soft sweetness of B flat ... The practice is now so firmly rooted in them, that it is unusual to hear a simple and single melody well sung; and, what is still more wonderful, the children, even from their infancy sing in the same manner.[58]

Once learned, the patterns of harmony are almost impossible to shake off. As D. F. Tovey has said, "The effort of thinking away our harmonic preconceptions is probably the most violent piece of mental gymnastics in all artistic experience." [59] While the scientific revolution of Galileo's time gave us "common sense," the musical revolution that immediately preceded it and then joined with it gave us equivalent, if not more rigid, "common sounds."

A part of the history of musical development can be described in the language of physics and acoustics by reference to waves, frequencies, amplitudes, beats, maskings. And perhaps in some respects this is an essential part of the twentieth century understanding of and education in music. The gradual historical procession from unison to octave to parallel fifth to major triad to key tonality to ... was, however, entirely the work of art, a development of purely artistic achievement. Music may be unique in the steadfastness of its independence from science, its entirely autochthonous development. Perspective in painting, in contrast, sustained quite the opposite relation—one of direct dependence on physics. Before it entered into painting, perspective was understood by science, and before that it was explicitly recognized in experience. Technical inventions have, of course, been very important to musical development. For example, the development in the thirteenth and fourteenth centuries of an organ keyboard that lay comfortably under the hand must have been critical to the opening of the ear to new harmonic possibilities because it so facilitated playing around with tone combinations—a somewhat cumbersome pastime when separate singers or separate instruments must be mustered into service. The Irish harp of thirty strings, which was probably perfected by the tenth century, must have similarly aided development of the early Celtic system of harmony. The tape recorder may be performing an analogous service today. Nevertheless, it must be insisted that the language of music has been wholly art-created; the acoustical facts were uncovered and arranged in pattern by art by ear before scientific understanding—what there is of it— was won. And the art has pushed ahead to such complexity as to remain still well in the forefront, far ahead of the laboratory understandings of acoustics that would pretend to adequate explanation of musical experience—so subtle the patterns of song, intensely stirring or no.

The correspondence in point of time between the break-up of the world of "common sense" and the break-up of the world of "common sounds" is even more interesting than their parallel inceptions—because possibly still observable and at least more accessible to searching inquiry. The "mental gymnastics" of thinking away harmonic preconceptions has been practiced for quite some time now by a courageous minority— not in an attempt to reconstruct the hearing of the ancients, but in an attempt to carry musical creation, musical development, onward and upward from the plateau of exhausted potentiality on which the harmony of key tonality was felt to have spent itself.

The artist takes part in a process of crystallizing forms out of the first premonitions of a style—a process of style creation. When a style reaches its completion, the artist loses interest in it because the possibilities of participating in a live process have come to an end, because potential for deriving new expectancies has been exhausted. Composers were straining at the limits of harmony toward the end of the nineteenth century. Arnold Schoenberg is credited with announcing the end of harmonic development and with opening up a vista of new sounds in a land of music devoid of key feelings.[60] The resulting chaos of style is not unlike that following for a short period the opening out of the possibilities of modern harmony at the end of the sixteenth century. In addition, an explosion of rhythmic experimentation and a deliberate extending of rhythmic irregularity punctuated the end of harmonic development.

Thus it is that the recent breakup of the comfortable Cartesian universe was accompanied by creation of a new man-made world of sound, a new world of hearing. Regularity gave way to irregular meter while stable harmonies gave way to kaleidoscopic change or to complete lack of harmony as the difference between dissonance and harmony reduced to a matter of individual definition by the individual composer. Is the fact that substitutes for the worlds of "common sense" and "common sounds" have not penetrated far into the fibre of the population explained by a lingering chaos of style?

Meanwhile the mathematicians, artists in their own rite, had been playing around with their own harmonies. Before Einstein needed a non-Euclidian geometry, Riemann, Lobachevski, and others had been working out alternate elaborations of mathematical patterns, "pure abstractions," for their own intellectual-aesthetic reasons. As Poincaré describes it, mathematical creation is a product of "long, unconscious prior work" which in turn "is only fruitful, if it is on the one hand preceded and on the other hand followed by a period of conscious work." [61] It follows a course closely parallel to that of the other arts. Its product is again a basically aesthetic order—form and pattern. Besides music and mathematics, all of the other arts too are involved, in their own ways, in creating and manipulating patterns.

If the regularities, the patterns of science are put there by human agent (as used to be said) or through transaction (as should be said), the question should be, not whether, but how and how much the other pattern-making or aesthetic engagements of men—found most polished in art activities, and extracted and refined in the finer arts—impinge on inquiry and its productions.

Social manners and customs (including scientific method) and their changes are patterned phenomena. The social fabric is held together by patterns of behavior and it adapts and advances through their favorable modification. Good and evil end up being defined in their terms. Environmental science has found in mathematics a powerful instrument for the advancement of inquiry. Though less directly and less apparently, the other arts, among them music, are also powerful instrumentalities. Social science, on the other hand, has yet to make a primary, lasting and self-conscious alliance with a particular artistic formulator.

And the irregularity of modern art? Assuming it to be genuine and not just new, unaccustomed, ungrasped pattern, does the irregularity of the new music relate to the irregularity of the atom? For example, must it have run ahead and cleared the way to permit man to perceive, through the mesh of man-made instruments, the uncertainty of "elementary" particles—or to conceive the concept of complementarity? Is there a bond or a kinship concealed in the similarity between the way the new music rests on the basis of "common sounds" and the way the new physics rests on "common sense," the new in each case being a generalized expression of which the "common" is a limiting case?

But is it not likely that the finer arts will more aptly serve the social than the environmental realm with both irregularity and pattern? Music, which so quickly passes in refinement (rhythms, harmonies) beyond the gross patterns of Cartesian "common sense" even while remaining in the old camp of "common sounds," may perform a function beyond certainty and beyond sanity when it escapes the limitations of pattern. Do the irregularities of new art—currently culminating in the aleatoric or "random" music of, for example, Pierre Boulez's Third Piano Sonata —point beyond crude causality, beyond recurrence, beyond pattern, auguring a new "mathematics" for the master science, a "mathematics" attuned to the uncertainty of the human soul, the peculiar self-determinacy of purpose? Is there a place here for "categories" (if such they can be called) of creativity for a social science of purposes? Having established rapport in kinship of irregularity, may the triumph of the art over chaos bring form within the reach of purpose—man-made regularities for the science of moral life?

ART AND THE CONCORD OF CHARACTER

Many, many concords are struck below the formal level of language. And many of these are artistic or aesthetic achievements. Indeed, Dewey defines art as "the name given to all the agencies by which . . . the union of ideas and knowledge with the non-rational factors in the human make-up . . . is effected." [62] Men like to fancy that, for failure of their brains to interrelate more than a handful of items at a time, their total beings can somehow—not apart from consciousness, but at least beyond it—amalgamate a great complex of stimuli, needs, social demands, physical limitations, memories, fears, probabilities, etc., their intensities and importances, and from that amalgam project a purpose, a course of action. Such a happening is especially an art event—and a character event.

In the creative bargaining situation, the internalizing of a conflict, bringing both of opposed sets of interests into intimate juxtaposition within the crucible of character, is clearly an art activity.

Since the experimental material of the moral scientist is himSelf (human character), he would rightly expect to get help from the artist, both in understanding and in achieving basic concord of character out of the disparity of conflicting cultural fact-values—especially from those artists whose central concern is also with character. Don't Joseph Conrad's *Under Western Eyes* and *The Secret Agent* tell us more than the Kremlinologists about the world of conspiracy and even communism?

"If," as John Galsworthy says, "a novelist has any use in the world apart from affording entertainment, it is through the revealing power of his created characters. . . . By the creation of character he contributes to the organic growth of human ethics." [63] Lionel Trilling believes that

> for our time the most effective agent of the moral imagination has been the novel of the last 200 years. . . . Its greatness and its practical usefulness lay in its unremitting work of involving the reader himself in the moral life, inviting him to put his own motives under examination, suggesting that reality is not as his conventional education has led him to see it. It taught us, as no other genre ever did, the extent of human variety and the value of this variety. It was the literary form to which the emotions of understanding and forgiveness were indigenous, as if by the definition of the form itself.[64]

Clearly there is much to be learned from the novelist that is immediately pertinent, first to the perception of character, of purpose, and then to the improving of character, the integrating of purposes. A Personnel Director, it follows, should be required to read novels on company time.

It is interesting to note the historical proximity and parallel between modern democracy and the art of the novel, and to speculate on their possibile interrelatedness. Has the novel been instrumental in the development of democracy? The realistic novel, as a form of art, undoubtedly enlarged the social aspirations of the nineteenth century. Truly, in contributing to the ideal ends that imagination discerns, art helps to unify the Self.

In order to function successfully as instruments of integration, as integration-promoting tools (either within character or in an interpersonal or intragroup setting), concepts or ideas must be supported by perceptual sensitivity to the dynamics of all the factors involved in a transaction.[65] Here art can be directly involved. Experiments demonstrating the integrative value of drawing activities were discussed in chapter 3. By these artistic activities, kinesthetic-tactual responses were integrated with visual responses. But such integrations have further carryover, helping to coordinate conceptualizing and generalizing functions. It appears to be the pattern-forming part of art that leads the way. Learning to draw—or simply practicing drawing—teaches one to see patterns and to make patterns in an abstracted and therefore simplified circumstance. In the elaboration, extrapolation, application of pattern in differing circumstances is the seed of integration.

Art activities, which inherently relate fact and value through perceptual experience, provide a first approach, and all too frequently an only approach, to the integration of purposes, the integration that creates character and involves a degree of total satisfaction instead of a fractional satisfaction of mutually isolated or compartmentalized interests—"personal," "material," "aesthetic," "economic," "religious," etc.[66] As art activity carries over into conceptualization, it can become more and more directly relevant to integration of these same fractionated aspects of experience when they turn up on the social level as ingredients of serious cultural cleavage.

This matter of forming patterns is perfectly fundamental. Pattern forming activities can be traced back to the deep, unknown process of forming conditioned reflexes—a supplement to the slow natural-selection process of creating variation in inherited patterns of response—permitting the individual to associate a patterned response with repeated experiences. (Pattern forming goes back even further, to the basic repetition, rhythm, harmony of the cell as it makes a copy of itself—to the patterns and symmetries of RNA). As H. J. Muller explains it, "This faculty of modifying actions in accordance with experience must depend upon the ability to make and to retain neuronic connections between different patterns of neuronic activity that given experiences have aroused in conjunction with one another." [67] Notice that this could almost be a description of the creative integration process in creative bargaining.

This way of patterning, of associating, grows by degrees into learning from experience and is finally called intelligence. Throughout is the pervasive primacy of form and its variation and recreation. Perhaps what can properly be called art does not come on the scene very early in the life of the species, but aesthetic sensitivity surely does. It is born of form and cannot have waited long in gestation.

The aesthetic category is a doing, not merely an appreciating. If anything, appreciation follows creation. The tune is loved only after it has been given form by its creator—and then generally only after a certain amount of repetition impels its acceptance into aesthetic grace. This is partly why so much emphasis has been placed in recent years on learning by doing. More properly, aesthetics should be understood as a normal manifestation of the give-and-take of transaction. The transactional understanding should be especially kept in mind when pondering over precedence between appreciation and creation within the agonizing soul of the composer at work.

Art is not, in the beginning, self-conscious. It starts very far back indeed—with the most perishable and forgotten artifact, with the remotest gesture of dance or defiance or sociality. It is the beginning of *making* sense out of the world. The making of pattern is all-important.[68] Mankind grows out of pattern to new pattern, the artist in him presiding.

The awesome influence of art through pattern can hardly be exaggerated. In the end each man has his personal style—characteristic patterns which he as artist (though sometimes also as drifter) has made. As a group, the young bucks of every society in every generation have their special, though more generalized, styles. And so on, throughout the artistic webs of human behavior: pattern presides from mathematics to mischief-making—and expectations follow.

One of the most direct, but seldom stressed, benefits of pattern (and thus, at one remove, of art) is its service to memory. An aesthetic pleasure is derived by many people from roping off in memory special fields of collected fact. When a pattern is made, its components are so arranged in special relation to each other that their order and invariance become reliable. This forming and reforming, creating and recreating, of invariance becomes a special human pleasure in itself.

The human brain seems to be a particularly sensitive pattern making, receiving, and using instrument. The heavy incidence of RNA (ribonucleic acid) in the cells of the brain suggests the possibility of an ultimate chemical explanation of this pattern penchant inasmuch as the RNA molecule has an extraordinary pattern-forming capacity. Experiments involving the transfer of learning between organisms by direct physical transfer of "educated" RNA are even more suggestive.[69]

Once a pattern is perceived, or even dumbly sensed, the effort of remembering one of its component elements is eased. This is why recall is aided by writing out a new acquaintance's name or by deliberate art-use of patterning mnemonic devices. Art performs a recreative function in memory.

Poincaré finds just such a thought-facilitating function in the aesthetic patterns behind mathematics:

> A mathematical demonstration is not a simple juxtaposition of syllogisms, it is syllogisms *placed in a certain order*, and the order in which these elements are placed is much more important than the elements themselves. If I have the feeling, the intuition, so to speak, of this order, I need no longer fear lest I forget one of the elements, for each of them will take its allotted place in the array, and that without any effort of memory on my part.[70]

Ordered arrangements of mental data occur in infinite variety, rising to consciousness in different degrees and frequently remaining semi-conscious or rising not at all—for example, the proportionate organization of frequencies plus overtones in a tonic chord. Mathematics, the art of numbers, probably the most conscious and rational of the arts, is also the most powerful instrument for analyzing pattern relationships and making deliberate use of patterns. Interestingly enough, mathematics had its beginning in patterned dots and dwelt in the pattern land of dots for millennia before growing on to refinements of abstraction.[71]

It is in the art of writing, however, that the mnemonic utility of arranging elements of things and thoughts in art-allocated or patterned spaces is most clearly seen. From its pictographic beginnings to the present, writing has extended memory in an *artificial* fashion, just as ballad, legend, epic, and bard—the art of the story teller and myth-maker—had done in earlier times. But this service of scribe and bard to memory is a mere extrapolation of the way-back, unconscious aesthetic ordering in the patterns that make up words—vowels and diphthongs, and pitches and meters, timbers, etc. If there was once an extensive conscious sensitivity to these communications patterns as patterns—as there appears to have been in the ages of aural poetry (with, for example, the Greek dactylic hexameter)—it must have been lost in later centuries of refinement, as was the taste of the ancient Greek musical genius.

These remarks about form and memory point back to the earlier discussion of expectation. Without the background of pattern and its stabilization of memory, neither self-evidence nor self-expectation can make a start. Should it not be said that the self-evident, the self-expectant, the axiomatic, stem from inarticulate, unspoken pattern?

The patterns that aesthetics makes out of all its arts and wiles are what permit men to think. It is because men are sensitive in so many directions that they, and not vegetables, have inherited the earth. The patterns that art makes in its media, by arranging allotted places for elemental data, make things memorable. Most men are equipped to work with only a few ideas at a time. But the tremendous background of unseen order (pattern) that they have received in the growing-up process of acculturation, in the course of becoming human, contributes a framework that holds the data from a great backlog of experience in a state of readiness for instant recall. It enables men to keep readily on tap the extraordinary range of recollection needed for productive thinking.

It directly follows that the new patterns devised by art add to the stock of awarenesses underlying productive thinking, and that these new patterns permit still other new combinations to develop and emerge on the conscious level of creation. We have already seen that the aesthetic category of invariance becomes, on a formal plane, a productive instrument for theoretical work in physics. Progress per se may consist of a process of renewal—a refreshening dip of thought into meandering streams of unconscious or semiconscious new art-provenient patterns. With memory refreshed from the new storehouse provided by new pattern, new combinations and permutations become possible due not only to the stimulus of new pattern as something to emulate but also to sudden liberation from the rigidity of established order.

Here is a point of contact between aesthetics and the creative aspect of creative bargaining and scientific mediation. The creation that takes ideas or feelings or facets, sorted and stored by pattern, and combines them—whether under inspiration of pattern or not—into previously unexpected pattern (in the form of idea, feel, direction, purpose, or the like) is staging an elemental creative bargaining integration, a resolving, a concording of character at, above, below, or beyond the threshold of consciousness, as the case may be.

UNIFICATION

While the work of the artist is notable for the novelty it presents, for its success in breaking new ground, in making two distinctions grow where there were none before, it is also to be remarked for its efforts in the direction of harmony, for the new patterns of unity it creates out of what was plurality or aesthetic contrast.[72]

The scientific mediator is involved in just such an artistic work of unification, striving to bring integration out of conflict. He finds that creative bargaining comes to a halt before an unbridged barrier of divergent vision, and that the limit of scientific mediation is where vicarious participation breaks before unrepentant divergence of group perspectives. Even self-evidence and self-expectance vary in relation to cultural variations or divergences in perception. This breaking point is therefore clearly a problem point at which special effort must be applied. The fact that, among the community of physical scientists, divergence of vision in respect to matters scientific does not establish a final limit suggests that in political, social, moral realms the focus of the problem of intransigent perceptual divergence is not in the area of the theoretical or technical scientist but in that of his subject matter. It is in his material. One wonders if there will be a significant change when the material or subject-matter scientist, the Third scientist, begins to function Self-consciously in the strife of scientific mediation.

The unification of diverging views will need all the help it can get from all the arts there are. Nowadays it needs more help than ever before. As long as everyone was doing much the same thing everyone else was doing, they all tended to see things in much the same way. Specialization of function has significantly undermined this age-old way of deriving common seeing from common doing. A special premium is therefore set upon effective communication. If communication is not to rest at cross purposes, much effort must necessarily be directed toward sharpening all around sensitivity to common and conflicting aims, purposes, intentions operating in the everyday world.

It is possible that national art movements, instead of leading the way, merely follow trends otherwise established. They are, however, generally believed to have some effect, indirect and intangible, in promoting national or social unity. And there must be something to this if, as is said, ugliness creates bitterness and if, as evidence seems to indicate, attitudes toward, for example, land ownership, gregariousness, or public recreation are products, in part, of the space in which people grow up.[73] From Plato to Stalin and after, the persuasion has held that state regulation of artistic expression could help hold people together and set the tone of society. The arts may not have precise correspondences with, or particular relevancies to, individual social events. It is probable, for example, that meanings in music do not relate to particular emotions, and that all Plato's profundity on the social impact of diverse musical modes was simple foolishness. But the condition of the arts can be a cushion to the rough riding of society. The teachings of art, its general influences, can project a basis, a resource for common seeing in a world without common doing, unifying the divergence of group perception. It can extend an inclination toward sensitivity to ends and intentions, purposes and aims. Here function most clearly the mass arts—television, movies, advertisement, house design.

SIMPLICITY

Artistic sensitivity may be seen to play a coordinating role for speculative thinking analogous to its role in social unification. Important in this connection is the criterion of "simplicity" honored by the physical scientists.

"Nature is pleased with simplicity, and affects not the pomp of superfluous causes," says Newton. Part of the aim of theoretical science (which, it will be remembered, strives to improve the abstract tools of control) is to simplify or unify the working set of abstract concepts so that they will be more serviceable, more universally applicable, more precisely interrelated in systems of implication. The glory of a theoretical scientist is to combine two (or more) logically independent or contradictory sets of conceptual tools into a simpler or more unified set.[74] For example, quantum theory is simpler than Newtonian mechanics because it subsumes the latter and in addition a further enormous complexity of phenomena. Simplicity is often illustrated by reference to the triumph of Copernican astronomy over that of Ptolemy. This provides a particularly clear example because it can be written out in numbers. Copernicus succeeded in reducing the number of unrelated epicycles needed to describe the heavens to 17, whereas Ptolemy had used 83. Obviously this reduction simplified the prediction of heavenly movements. Perhaps a better illustration is furnished by Kepler's achievement in converting planetary orbits from circles with epicycles into ellipses. Simplicity is not so much a matter of quantity as of the way in which experience is explained or described. Partly it is eliminating the unnecessary. The ether may be dispensed with because it is simpler to let light waves pass through empty space. The Principle of Causality is unnecessary because it is simpler to represent the experience of cause and effect as a result of statistical laws.[75]

There is also a Pythagorean mysticism behind the expectation that it will continue to be possible, as it has been so far, to write the fundamental equations of physics in simple mathematical forms—even in the absence of a convincing argument or of a hope of empirical verification that this must be so. Simplicity, as a formal characteristic of scientific theories, is remarkably lacking in fine definition. It is difficult, for example, to make sure of a difference between simplicity and "saving a theory." Would not the idea of adding epicycles to the supposed circular orbits of planets have appeared as a great simplicity when it was first propounded?

Lack of clarity in definition of simplicity indicates that there is a heavy component of aesthetic experience mixed into it. At the time of its enunciation, a new simplicity is based on an aesthetic sense of fitness, neatness, however much it may subsequently be shown to provide scientific convenience. Simplicity frequently, perhaps generally, begins in aesthetic feeling, only later being transformed into articulate insight.[76] Perhaps, indeed, it is but a special case of the ordinary struggle to raise an original idea from the aesthetic depths of the ineffable. At any rate, here is artistic activity working to converge diverging perspectives.

Murky though simplicity is as a metaphysical postulate, its importance is firmly established in the fervency with which it has been avowed by so many eminent scientists—Einstein, Kepler, Planck. . . . Presumably it will turn up some day in social science too, acknowledged and explicit, drawing ideas together, unifying theories with the aid of artistic sensitivity.[77]

THE TEST OF QUALITY

The effectiveness of science depends on art. In the physical sciences, reliance on art at the end of the process of experimentation is minimal, restricted usually to dissemination of information, directing results of research into education. Quality may be, nevertheless, very important. The form and the spirit of the form in which information is presented can make considerable difference. A recent example is "the new math," which is essentially a new development in the art of teaching. Great things are expected of "the new math" because it is a new way of organizing mathematical patterns for dissemination, a simplifying of forms.

It is important not only as expediter of learning and communication but as clarifier, simplifier of the educational foundation from which new generations of thinkers can step forth to new forms, new patterns, new thoughts.

Social science is different, at least in emphasis. It too must stress quality, the art in purveying news and in imparting an educational basis for expedited thinking, inventing, creating. But in social science there is a Third scientist (chapter 6) who must work with exceeding sensitivity within the experimental situation. The stirring of emotion, perception, and appreciation is not enough. Art activity must also function in the leavening of vicarious participation.

It is well known that the performance, the skill of the left hand improves by vicarious participation (on a subrational level) in the active practice of the right hand. Similarly, muscular activity with a football is vicariously improved by drawing activity in a darkened room,[78] and the musical appreciation of the performing artist is enhanced by the kinesthetics in his skill. What seems thus to be transferred from place to place within the semi-confined bounds of a Self is a pattern—of muscular to visual, or of kinesthetic to aural, activity. Bringing two parts of the Self together into coordination by a common pattern may be the very essence of integration.

The integration of scientific mediation must aim beyond mere putting together of elements within character so that they will be mutually compatible and supporting; it must take a broad interest in pattern, form, art as storehouse of useful molds for such character integration. The ways in which thoughts are tied together, the forms and relationships between them, of which logic is only a special category, establish the possibility and ease of generating new thought, of breaking old habits and liberating new skills.

On the inter-personal level, the possibility of vicarious participation depends very crucially on the reliability of social perceptions. The artist's service in sharpening the latter will directly advance and benefit the cause of the former. Indeed, an artist is continually engaged in vicariously "as if"ing experiences.[79]

The artist's work in formulating the problem has a pervasive influence in seeing and communicating the solution to the problem. Refinement precedes communication, and this refinement takes place all the way up the line. In the end, the elegant solution stands alone. A part of its elegance is its intrinsic persuasiveness, placed there in no small part through aesthetic mediation. Broad sympathy, art engineered, together with art sharpened social perception prepares the soil for transplant of elegant solutions; and this is the very process of vicarious participation.

Art can be the extrapolating medium by which the sensitive associational relationship—typical, for example, of a troupe of actors or a team of baseball players who are sufficiently attuned to each other, through the fellow-feeling characteristic of man's group nature, eagerly to embrace second-hand elegant solutions—is passed on into the wider public.[80]

In social and political spheres, the delicate matter of bringing to test ideas, theories, and hypothetical solutions to problems is more complex than in physical science. No doubt there are aesthetic dimensions to the construction of almost any experiment, in making both apparatus and formulas. Testing a social hypothesis, however, involves numbers of people, directly or indirectly, in common endeavor. Correspondingly, the apparatus of experiment is composed of the interhuman structures—social, political, and moral—of the material (subject matter, citizen) scientists, and the formulas are found in the citizen scientists' purposes, aims, and intentions. Aesthetics is more thoroughly, more pervasively involved in social experiment than in physical because it cross-connects the individuals, the materials, or the bearers of the materials of experiment, as living aspects of design, while it also cross-connects the formulas.

By its performance in unifying ideas and knowings with the non-rational, subarticulate factors in human makeup, art can lead toward increasingly satisfactory choice.[81] A feeling of certainty, security, or reliability derives directly from the organizing of perception.[82] The further de facto reliability of social perceptions adds to the feeling of certainty that comes from aesthetic organization, the basis of trust building up to the possibility of vicarious participation. Making social perception reliable makes vicarious participation viable. Objectivity, being found in the two-way attempt of men to understand one another,[83] has very clearly an ultimate reliance on the reliability of social perception. It is in its decoration or celebration aspect that art adds timelessness to intention—art's time-binding performance—(for example again, Chartres, the Byzantine icon, the art of the Egyptian Ancient Kingdom) so that purposes may be grasped for social test.

In both the physical and social sciences, the test of validity is built upon objectivity—upon the objectivity that grows from the effort at mutual understanding. This objectivity, since it requires both clarity of expression in communication and sensitive, discriminating reception, must rely heavily on all the arts and aesthetics that can be involved. But in social science, objectivity and all the arts and aesthetics involved are doubly involved. Not only do they serve in collective test and dissemination of results, but they must serve as part of the apparatus joining the subject-matter scientist with his purposes. They are tools for defining and creating purpose.

In objectivizing purpose, intention, aim (that is, in achieving mutual understanding clear of ambiguity, as a part of social experiment,) art deals with quality, with value. In dealing with qualitative discriminations of meanings, purposes, intents, values, art objectivizes them. In the end, social science is tested by the quality of the satisfactions it achieves, the reality it creates.

Horace Fries insists further that criteria for gauging the satisfactoriness of satisfactions can be shaped out of aesthetic sensibilities. Objective qualitative differences can be made into dependable criteria for testing the satisfactoriness of plans, and thus the purposes behind them. "For on the practical side the history of wisdom is the history of relative failures and successes in formulating more adequate purposes; and on the theoretical side the concrete criteria employed in the laboratory today are themselves reshaped realities, the product of scientific discoveries." [84]

As the cultural cleavages between guiding ideas and emotions, minds and matters, beings and doings, seeings and makings are bridged with the aid of the unifying engineering efforts of art, the enhancement of value, the "becoming" through propriate striving, the perfecting of purposes, will be characterized by higher and higher levels of achieved satisfaction. The *felt* justice of successful integrations will record the progressive enrichment of life. In Fries' words, "As the artist works aesthetic contrasts (conflicts) into new patterns of harmony, so the art of life does and can work ethical conflicts into progressively deeper patterns of satisfaction." [85]

SUMMARY

Not much ground will be gained as the administrator day-dreams in a hall stocked with purpose-full pots. The service of art is more subtle than that. Nevertheless, the services of the artist and the participation of his purposes are clearly crucial to the growth of scientific-democratic organization. There can be no question but that aesthetic sensibilities, sensitivities and sensations are among the most persuasive agents that urge to great achievements.

Art——through persuading populations to new perceptions, thus helping them rise out of the sloth of inadequate purposes; through its special role as freedom's champion, nurturing the skills behind positive freedom and pointing toward associated skills of social perception accommodating to conservative drag; through heightening sensitivity to the hitches that precede problems and helping to structure attackable problems via non-conceptual formulation of experience; through painting vistas of expectation—the equivalent for the moral sciences of the self-evidence art helps establish in the physical sciences; through pattern-forming and other tender influence in gentling concord of character out of discord of cultural conflict; through coordination or unification by way of merging diverging views in the social arena or, on the theoretical plane, by way of aesthetic fitness as proclaimed in the category of "simplicity"; through the leavening of vicarious experience, the transplanting of elegant solutions, and the setting of criteria for testing satisfactions——by all these dodges, maneuvers, and emanations, art contributes to the growth of social science.

Above all it contributes by objectivizing purpose through sensitizing social perception, laying the groundwork for creative bargaining. An insight is not creative until it is objectified and made distinguishable from its perceiver. Only then is new reality created, made, formed, patterned, and the regularities of moral science, indeed, *purposefully* put there by human transaction.

Creativity is one of the things men, in contrast with other animals, are best at. It is one of the specialties of the species. A good bit of it is mixed up in what has been called the radical bent. And a good bit is involved in artistic activity and aesthetic appreciation.

A search for the elements of creativity leads to a penetrating look among the chinks of the structure of Self-correction. Drawing a deep breath *ex nihilo*, creativity steels itself for the boot-strap self-levitation needed to break out of the circle of reflex action and reaction to win new ways of Self-correction leading to the reciprocal system of deliberate experimentation. Through the creative arts and skills of criticism—chipping off the superfluous—Self-correction converts the circle of simple reflex into the progressive spiral of Self-control.

Moral science will involve an intimate merging of scientific procedure and artistic activity—a merging even more close, intricate, and pervasive than obtains in the present condition of the physical sciences. If man is as biologically social as has been said, the greatest depth of enjoyment will be found in ethical integrations between Selves, in creatively struck bargains. And the supreme artistic function will be the formulating and communicating of such creations. In pots there is purpose; in song the awakening of salvation is announced. The ultimate significance of songs and pots is beyond imagination. Buttoned down to the mundane art of government, and hooked up to a breadth of vision characteristic of great scientific innovators,[86] they will provide the medium that can lift democratic-scientific organization into the realms of utopia.

CHAPTER FOURTEEN

Beginnings: Administrative Democracy

> *The notion that it is possible to get*
> *bodies of men to act in accord with*
> *finer moral sentiments while the general*
> *scheme of social organization remains*
> *the same is not only futile, it is a mark of*
> *the subtlest form of conceit,*
> *moral egotism.*
>
> JOHN DEWEY

> *Men talk much of matter and energy, of*
> *the struggle for existence that molds the*
> *shape of life. These things exist, it is*
> *true; but more delicate, elusive, quicker*
> *than the fins in water, is that mysterious*
> *principle known as "organization,"*
> *which leaves all other mysteries*
> *concerned with life stale and*
> *insignificant by comparison.*
>
> LOREN EISELEY

IT IS PRECISELY THE CONTENTION OF THIS BOOK THAT A detailed structure of administrative democracy cannot be laid out in the infancy of moral understanding. On the other hand, current institutions are inadequate. They do not bear out the claim that government is effectively democratic today. Specifically democratic forms of administrative government will grow gradually from the ground of transacting Selves, conflicting purposes, and functionalized power.

This chapter will begin drawing the material so far presented into a focus on administrative government to give some indication how it all points toward administrative democracy. It will stress the need to bring the complexity of administration down to understandable proportions, the importance to administration of dealing with morals directly through character, the place of participation through conflict, and the democratic urgency of perpetual revolution.

Previous chapters of this book have developed a language that uses old words with new or unaccustomed meanings. The coming chapters on administrative democracy will try to be consistent in continuing with this special language—transaction, social perception, Self, Teleological ethics, character, control, citizen scientist, functional power, participation, radical bent, conservative drag, integration, creative bargaining, scientific mediation, simplicity—but without further explication.

SIMPLICITY

A great weariness will surely overtake and envelop all but the most stubbornly steadfast unless some sort of simplicity in governmental administration is achieved. Perhaps it already has. How many administrators have tired before the prospects of yet another staff conference? How many have retreated before the certain knowledge that the public cannot be educated to an understanding of what their agency does, did, can do, or should do? How many have been numbed by the obtuse, repetitive, and circular conduct of interagency coordination? How many have become resigned to the defeating voltage-drop down the line of much resistance into the field as high-powered ideas eke forth with little effect? The second Hoover Commission reported a truly dismal and discouraging situation in the administrative branch of the Federal government. It pictured "a sprawling and voracious bureaucracy, of monumental waste, excesses and extravagancies, of red tape, confusion, and disheartening frustrations, of loose management, regulatory irresponsibilities, and colossal largesse to special segments of the public, of enormous incompetence in foreign economic operations, and of huge appropriations frequently spent for purposes never intended by The Congress." [1]

Public administration is not complex and bewildering only in structure and function, in size and multiplicity of forms, and in diversity of activities and approaches. It is also complex in theory—which is a more serious matter. It may alternatively be contended that there is no theory or no respectable or agreed upon theory in public administration at all. But this is only to say that there are many bits and pieces in a chaos of theoretical scraps.

Simplicity in organization and operation can happen only eclectically or haphazardly unless coherence in thought can be brought about, unless great segments of complex phenomena can be unified in the simplicity of theoretical formulation. The disconnected and dithyrambic state of current team research dramatizes this unfortunate state of affairs in public administration. It should be clearly apparent that a search for theoretical simplicity, akin to that continually pursued by theoretical physicists, is desperately necessary. Yet it is doubtful that many administrators are looking far beyond their practical problems.

Ordway Tead has called for a return to personal leadership as a way to escape many of the frustrations in administration. "Reliance upon procedures and precedents, and ... distrust of the exercise of personal power of true leadership caliber," he describes as the essence of "bureaucracy." [2] We may take the cue from this and maintain with some insistence that refreshing simplicity will not come to public administration until "bureaucratic" or mechanical thinking respecting all aspects of organization is put aside, until character has become an accepted part of administration. Then only can bureaucracy become democracy.

The move from mechanics or "bureaucracy" to character is a move to put morality back as a conscious concern of administration. The laboratory of moral science must be set up in Administration Hall. If administration is deliberately organized to harbor experimental search for moral truth, not only should democracy ensue but it should start to triumph in beginning simplicities.

CHARACTER IN ADMINISTRATION

Administration is truly a natural phenomenon, a culmination of the descent of man. The administrative way of life, like the family way, is a mode of organization for a particular stage in the development of human nature and social cultural complexity, and correspondingly for a particular range of problems. As such, the high point of its concern lies above decision making. It is found in deciding conjoined with purposing, decision making in dependence upon purpose making. So far as administration is deliberately organized to exclude character—the conceiving, nurturing, and metamorphosing of purpose—it must be foredoomed to failure. Principles, procedures, and precedents that dehumanize administration by squeezing the very human blood of morality out of it in the quest for coherence or simplicity, either in operation or understanding, cannot be expected to attain their goal.

Administrative organization must be tempered by a substantial respect for the dynamics of human nature—for human purposings in transaction. John M. Gaus once noted a "healthy scepticism as to whether the principles of organization and procedure, of classification, for example, as embraced in one decade are really supportable principles for another."[3] Such skepticism is justified not simply by the fact that each decade sees new problems to which it must tailor its organization and procedure, but also by the fact that each decade, if it does not actually see deeper, fancies that it has, at least in some respects, an improved understanding of human nature. The lack of general agreement on fundamental principles of administration, together with the fact that not one principle has ever been experimentally validated, would seem to indicate that the cock has not yet crowed the dawning of an administrative science. Luther Gulick's statement of the characteristics of an ideal administrative structure, for example, has had a long life of practical usefulness—particularly in formal reports on administrative management by private consultants and by Presidential committees and commissions. But it is far from generally accepted and is certainly not scientifically validated.

In the clear light of hindsight, Elton Mayo's discoveries in the Hawthorne Plant of Western Electric[4] must be reckoned among the most extraordinary of modern times. Their extraordinary aspect was not in themselves, in what they revealed, but in their reception—that they were so widely acclaimed as revelations. Did not every poet, every novelist, every worker, even the researchers themselves know, in whatever inarticulate way, that a man does better the things he believes to be important? Did they not already know that people, no matter how we squeeze them into test tubes or devitalize them in assembly lines, never shed their aspirations, and that these aspirations inevitably condition performance? At least they must have known that their own aspirations affected what they themselves did. What was amazing was that so much formal thinking had somehow become so twisted as to deny what should have been patently obvious. Professional thinkers had apparently been so engrossed in "rationalization" of administration that character, purpose had been squeezed out—if not out of the work world, at least out of their view of it—presumably to be left home with the family.[5]

Naturally any administrative organization is "artificial" in the sense that it is a man-made arrangement, a tool wrought by artful men. It need not, however, be "artificial" in the sense of being false, unnatural, inhospitable to human nature. There is nothing unnatural about people working in association to solve social problems. Indeed, men would not be human without their transactions.[6]

The essentially artificial aspect of today's administrative society—an aspect which contrasts it with hunting, pastoral, agricultural, or handicraft societies—is its vast collection of artifacts—man-made tools and things: agricultural implements, manufacturing machines, communication systems, transportation vehicles, electronic equipment, scientific instruments, structures of all sorts. All these things are important to us as human being-doings; they are part of our very existence. Every use of a telephone, a bridge, a match, an automobile, a thermometer, or an insecticide to resolve a difficulty involves the control of judgment and intention by some distillate of science. By now the artifacts produced by science have remolded the forms within which human thought and action occur. They are the objective delimitation and structural reinforcement within which intelligence must behave. In less swiftly changing societies artifacts become integral parts of human nature, incorporated within the expanding Self. In scientific society, however, they multiply too rapidly to be assimilated apace (commercial fertilizers and insecticides are current examples) and, partly for this reason, contribute inordinately to the cleavages, conflicts, and problems of the era. This is why they are felt to be "artificial" in the second sense of the word, inimical to human nature.

Even so, the artifacts of scientific society, except for occasional inspired creations *ex nihilo*, are responses to felt problems and as such are not necessarily unnatural. The unnatural aspect that shows up in the administrative organization of an artifact-ridden society appears in a romantic yearning for the deceptive (deceptive for the twentieth century, that is) simplicity of uncomplicated bygone ages. To this is added the unnatural denial of human complicity, denying that artifacts, together with the knowings that call them into being, become, through transaction, a part of men's Selves, a part of human nature.

This denial is, unfortunately, only the base stratum exhibit of the Great Cleavage (between being and doing, knowing and feeling, soul and body, morality and science, etc.) that besets Western culture. In government its classic expression raised a partition between politics and administration, between policy and performance. The two were thought to be clearly distinguishable. In time this classic expression had to be abandoned because facts just would not have it so. The merging in experience of policy with performance could not be denied. So tough and enduring is this basic cleavage, however, that the classic expression in government has been rapidly replaced by the more subtle positivist separation within administration between minds and morals, between fact-finding and value-judgment.[7] The situation is therefore considerably worse. Instead of a partition between politics and administration that was so unreal that it was consistently violated in practice—even while boldly protested in voice and print—a within-organization separation is erected that is adamantly persistent, readily accepted because based in the personality split of "common sense" inherited from Descartes. Until character wins out over this tendency of administrative organization to fall back into formalities based in the past, it will not come into its own.

CONTROLLED CONFLICT AS ADMINISTRATIVE CATEGORY

Administrative organizations are sometimes defined as "systems of cooperative behavior." [8] How idyllic if it were all that simple! The fact is that such oversimplification is bought at the price of considerable distortion. It assumes an overriding pre-set organizational purpose and an unnatural inter-human agreeableness, thus catering to the convenience of lazy thinking, but also to the disservice of rigorous statement and sensitive discrimination. Broader behavioral description avoids such distortions. In fact administrative organization is broader than cooperation. It is human. Administrative organizations are "simply" systems of human behavior.[9]

Certainly business administration can, as a rule, be said to be oriented by the overriding set purpose of profit. And perhaps some preliminary distinctions can be identified in public administration following Philip Selznick's observation that the problems and interests which impel to organization are quite different from those which occur in running an organization. There is a singleness of purpose involved in the organizing of an organization that very quickly breaks down into, or is augmented into, a seething of differences. Organizations that remain circumscribed by given purpose could be termed "proprietary," [10] and those concerned with the creation or the development of purpose could be called "governmental." Even within "proprietary" organization, however, there are subordinate systems—informal organizations, workways, folkways—concerned with the development, creation, and working-out of vast complexes of human purposes. In the words of Philip Selznick, "The actual procedures of every organization tend to be molded by action toward those goals which provide operationally relevant solutions for daily problems of the organization as such." [11] And even "proprietary" private enterprise is permeated with broader public concern. Man is a political (in the broadest sense) animal. In an age of such ramifying interdependence, compartmentalization of groups or purposes cannot remain watertight. Indeed, we should all be busy poking holes in any water-proofing venture. Peter Drucker concludes that "it has become possible if not commonplace to assert the principle that the business enterprise must be so managed as to make the public good become the private good of the enterprise." [12] This points directly back to the overall governmental purpose of creating purpose[13]—which is put in effect through thorough procedures of genuine participation. And it shows a beginning of a recognition of administration, public or private, as an institutionalization of participation, a convergence of democracy.

Administration is not merely cooperation. It is also antagonism, conflict, and the many other things that go to make up a social organism. Even the simplest "single purpose" line organization is shot through with seethings of conflicting purposes—not on the lofty level of social idealism, but rather on the working level of usable ideas which constitute the underpinning of reliable abstraction. Conflict is an administrative reality. In sensitive administrative organization, advantage is taken of it. Adequately controlled to maximize positive and creative, and to minimize negative and wasteful results, and to sharpen the issues, bringing out the right controversy, it can become a valuable category of administrative transactions.[14]

The organizational challenge is somehow to assure adequacy of control. Staged control—prearranged, influence disposed, goal-oriented—must be eschewed for all the reasons abundantly evoked in previous chapters. The "control" of conflict within administration must begin to take on the meaning of "control" in inquiry, in the sense of directing trial procedures.[15] This will involve two critical factors: (1) The centrality of intelligence, knowing, understanding must be accepted. A man is controlled by what he knows. He is coerced (or limited) by what is outside his understanding. Any administrator will appreciate this distinction. The control of conflict will accordingly need to engage the knowing of the purpose-holders involved. (2) Genuine, democratic participation must be incorporated—the sort of participation needed for a social science. All the interests, ideas, purposes constituent to a situation must be identified and tapped. They must be allowed to contribute their full potential to the burgeoning situation. In many administrative offices this will entail some regularized opening-out to include parts of the public as participants—perhaps through special section offices. The public good is not a technical recommendation; it comes from deliberate incorporation of relevant positions-to-become-purposes in administrative processes. In addition, the basic pattern of creative bargaining must be supplemented with the elegant, vicarious aspects of scientific mediation (involving study of goals from the inside of the goal-holder) in order to arrive at an administrative democracy oriented toward the public good. The democracy of administration is clearly *not* in face-to-face confrontation *per se*. It is clearly not just more, more, more communication. It will increasingly be found in vicarious experience, in selectively communicable knowing-how, the special wisdom of administrative organization as it mediates between lathe and shoe-wearer, between giver and receiver. This is how to get from the impracticability of extensive direct participation to administrative democracy.

PERPETUAL REVOLUTION

Institutions function in important part as agencies of moral stability and readjustment. This is true of such diverse particulars—gathered under the broad meaning of "institution"—as the family, the Presidency, the language, the price system, the public schools, divorce, private property, Sears, morality, horse racing, a County Board.

Institutions, administrative or otherwise, are parts of social habit, of customary ways. When habits, or accepted ways of doing things, are institutionalized, bulkheads are built behind which apathy may, at least temporarily, rest reassured.[16] Institutions are, in a sense, erected to afford relief from participation. They are themselves the elegant arrangements solving previously encountered patterns of problems of social relationship. When they are further reinforced by the structurings of Teleological ethics, they eventually become abstracted from the very natural and relative scene of human transaction. Healthy apathy then disperses into reaction and revolution.

Moral stability, at least for our time, is attainable only through adjustment. Even when apathy has temporarily captured the public outside the formal bounds of an agency, within its portals the divine discontent of the radical bent continues to rear its disquieting head; or else technological innovation, detailed specialization of function and knowing, or increasing physical mobility disturb the even plane of stability.

Besides incorporating standardized ways of doing, administration must institutionalize ways of making purposes and decisions—a creative process of reorganizing habit or skill. Efficiency in beating a well-blazed path is admirable in itself. But it is only the stability half, the rote, of administration. It is love of ease morally masquerading as love of perfection. In administration it has unfortunately been treated as an ideal, somewhat of a final goal—this usually in the companionable atmosphere of stark policy-performance separation, which separation never in *fact* existed, in pure form. The veneration of social habit as institutionalized in administration, however, has never been wholehearted on the part of the "outside" public. Healthy distrust of one-sided administrative emphasis on habitual performance, efficiency, stability has been responsible in large part for the bitter connotations of the epithet, "bureaucracy." The antidote is to institutionalize within administration moral procedures for reorganizing institutionalized habit.

Routines, workways, standardized operational procedures (stability) may be considered organizational equivalents of the habits of individuals, though it would be dangerous to carry the analogy to the extreme of personifying organization. Administration has no organism; it relies rather on organization of the habits of individuals. However, social habits as expressed in administrative organization and procedure, perhaps because they are made up from the habits of ordinary human being-doings, provide the same sort of basis for self-reorganization as do the habits of individuals. Following John Dewey's special meaning, the word "habit" is used here

> to express that kind of human activity which is influenced by prior activity and in that sense acquired; which contains within itself a certain ordering or systematization of minor elements of action; which is projective, dynamic in quality, ready for overt manifestation; and which is operative in some subdued subordinate form even when not obviously dominating activity.... The essence of habit is an acquired predisposition to *ways* or modes of response, not to particular acts except as, under special conditions, these express a way of behaving. Habit means special sensitiveness or accessibility to certain classes of stimuli, standing predilections and aversions, rather than bare recurrence of specific acts.[17]

Thus understood, habits—individual or institutional—are initially positive agencies of sharpened perception, generalized skills, freedom fraught. And a multiplicity of them extends the field of observation. They themselves, being the carriers of purpose, the embodiment of intentions, are the means to and, when in conflict, the occasion for moral readjustment. No "balance" or dialectic between stability and readjustment need be imagined or ideally engineered. Rather should such over-abstraction be studiously avoided and a caution against compartmentalization of social habit within administration be raised to an administrative prescription. Moral readjustment and accompanying institutional reorganization must emerge from conflict of social (and individual) habits. Nothing could be more lethal than to push to its logical extreme F. W. Taylor's suggestion that "the work of each man in the management should be confined to the performance of a single leading function," without honoring Taylor's qualification, "if practicable." [18]

Ideally, a process of moral readjustment should be incorporated within administration as social habit at least on par with the already institutionalized social habits which are workways, efficiencies, routines, procedures, stabilities. Torpor and stagnation are diseases, insanities of social organization, a legacy of arch conservatism,[19] for the most part. The controlled conflict to be organized into administration must be expected to arrange perpetual revolution—based in conservative drag—analogous to the continuing bloodless revolution achieved by a democratic electoral system.

Administration has already become the central, pervasive mode for social organization of twentieth century Selves. As it succeeds in institutionalizing participation into habits of creative bargaining and scientific mediation (as outlined in chapters 11 and 12), it gropes toward effectiveness that is true governance and not mere stability.

SUMMARY CONVERGENCE

Administrative organization is an "organic," whole-human patterning of technological civilization. It has necessarily become extremely complex in expanding to cope with the endlessly complex and ramifying artifacts recently spawned by human ingenuity. Correspondingly, the discoveries necessary to provide simplicity for administration—not merely the simplicity of efficiency in work but the sort of simplicity that the physicist seeks in his continual improvement of scientific theory—have not yet been made.

There is so far no substitute for the eclectic collection of pragmatic maxims—pyramids of authority, auxiliary staffs, classifications of function, leadership of generalists. It is not to be expected that a sudden complete liberation will befall. Simplicity will be more likely to arrive in a progressive manner of successive approximations, though perhaps it will be punctuated by a sequence of brilliant flashes of intuition along the way.

Basic to any really impressive theoretical advance in public administration will be a breakthrough in the understanding of human character, an opening through moral science into an understanding of the beings and doings of purpose. And this breakthrough will not make much headway apart from a well laid out social laboratory somewhere in the halls of the predominant school of human organization—administration.

Fortunately, though not by pure coincidence, the possibility and promise of moral science and the possibility and promise of democratic administration converge, as it presently appears, arriving at a point of mutual support and dependence. The product is organization around inquiry, the politics of truth.

Each of the major topics of this chapter—character in administration, controlled conflict, perpetual revolution—demonstrates the drawing together of the science of morals and the art of administration. The purposes that build up to character and form the basis of moral science also comprise the basis of the administrative, the governmental, activity that can rise above the fact-finding vs value judgment dichotomy. Working with character is the seminal activity in construction and reconstruction of functional power. Out of controlled conflict, as organized in scientific mediation, moral science would hope to extract ever deeper understanding of the nature and mechanics of the social world. As an administrative category, conflict is a creative path to the common good. Perpetual revolution in social science is experimental try-out of newly devised or created solutions to moral (conflict) problems. In democratic administration it is the means to progressive resolution of practical problems, leading to social control and functional power. Both the moral science and the administrative art converge on an institutionalization of participation that is at once par-giving and par-taking, that generates both wisdom and public purposes through the nurturing of conflict.

Practical counsel will advocate any reorganization in administration that permits and promotes integration of purposes. It will, further, try to encourage administration to take the progressive pattern of creative bargaining and, in the process, license the interest in progressive approach to richer knowledge that is the pattern of scientific mediation. Since this participation of "rounded experience," [20] open-ended out of conflict toward improved knowings and functional power, does not come about through exhortation alone, the most important first step toward participation will be so to arrange functions and relationships that habits may rub elbows and strike sparks of creative conflict. This may be taken as the substance of remarks sometimes made to the effect that an organization must be first centralized before it can be decentralized.[21] An idea of the informality (in comparison with the regular run of governmental organization today) that may be expected is suggested by the example of creative bargaining excerpted below in Appendix A.

Eventually the separation between knowledge and know-how, between seeker and leader, accepted in current belief and organization,[22] will be junked and replaced by a new understanding (perhaps a merging) of functions, involving a reconstitution of the organizational relation between leader and scientist.[23] Eventually the not-to-be-hurried search for eternal truth will here and there merge with the process of making decisions that cannot wait until the last fact is in. This will be at the moment in utopia when moral science gains a firm grasp on time through advanced knowings about intentions.

In the meantime, long before a point of utopia is reached, the advancement of moral knowings may begin to bear fruit in moral terms of socialized control and in political terms of functionalized power. These are the more proximate goals of more-or-less upon which practical administration (and practical science) must set its sights.

The creative bargaining pattern of participation sounds at first, perhaps, too complex—as if, compared with compromise, it were too cumbersome, too unspontaneous to steady a democratic machinery. Then it is remembered that Roberts' Rules of Order are no more spontaneous or self-generating. They too must be learned and practiced. They too can be forgot, as was revealed in Italy in the aftermath of Fascism. Public administration is democratic when its processes reach down into the stuff of which power is composed, down into the conflicts of value and purpose, and when it handles the conflicts in such a way that progressively richer, more satisfying resolutions are achieved.

CHAPTER FIFTEEN

Responsibility

> *What the world needs is a spiritual dynamic in sufficient quantity to effect an harmonious relationship between the Democratic Process and Specialism.*
>
> EDUARD C. LINDEMAN

DEMOCRACY, WHEN IT COULD NO LONGER BE DIRECT, COMpletely participative, became representative and responsible. Responsibility was understood as a tactic by which government was kept moral, kept from straying too far from the sense of the public good. As administration becomes the governmental way of life, it must take its share of responsibility proportionate to its inflated importance in the counsels, decisions, workings, producings, regulatings of government. Administrative democracy cannot consist exclusively of direct participation. There is also apathy, vicarious participation, routine. . . .

The moment when government is more than direct participation; the moment it is no longer coterminous with the body politic, all members rubbing elbows in associated effort; the moment specialization of function begins to separate the agents of government from the population—at that moment special ties are needed to bind the governor to the public good. Theoretically, under legislative democracy the responsibility of administration has been a servant-of-the-public arrangement, the typical master-servant relationship complete with coercions, systems of economic reward and deprivation, incentive plans and so on.

As the master, the public, succumbing to the spirit of democracy and the division of labor (symbolically in 1911), is drawn into the working group—working in part at perfecting purposes—as participant and vicarious participant in administrative democracy, a new understanding of responsibility must come about.

This new sort of responsibility comes, by the end of this chapter, to be labeled "intentional," "mature," and even "homonomous"—the latter for lack of a proper dictionary word to describe a condition beyond both the heteronomy of constraining external authority and the autonomy of private, independent conscience. It is a responsibility appropriate to transactional men organized for governance through creative bargaining arrangements of scientific mediation. This chapter also begins specifying a lasting and vital function for legislative bodies to perform in utopia, in the democracy that admits there is an administrative role in policy formulation.

RESPONSIBILITY AND CONTROL

As environmental events have been brought within the province of human control they have, one by one, been accepted as human responsibilities. The progression has moved fitfully forward from control of floods in early Egyptian times to control of tuberculosis and polio in very recent days. There have always been instances of backsliding: people still build houses, even shopping centers, in locations that are sure to be inundated by storms of "maximum reasonable regional expectancy." But the responsibility remains—an outgrowth of the know-how of once-achieved control. The ability to control is the basis of responsibility. Misfortunes stemming from environmental events cease to be the doings of demons, acts of God, or just plain "tough luck." Men are able to dispense with nature gods upon accepting responsibility for environmental conduct.

The Egyptian dawn of conscience[1] may be regarded as marking an equivalent accepting of responsibility for human events. It was the dawn of a social responsibility of a distinctively moral variety, as distinguished from religious varieties. It was only a beginning, however; in fact, such a rudimentary beginning that we are still in the cock's crowing. Momentarily, before being dimmed by sacerdotalism, it was at least a vision of human control of human conduct.

There is another variety of responsibility. Before control was compulsion. Before men learn to control environment it compels them; before they learn to control themselves they compel themselves (by collective sanctions)[2] or each other (by war). In primitive (perhaps, pre-primitive) society, what seems to us a monolithic responsibility is ascribed for a multitude of different kinds of events—among them accidents and involuntary acts. Groups, children, insane persons, and even animals and the dead are frequently held to be "responsible." The sacred presides over human and environmental conduct alike. The distinction between purposive and random behavior is not used in discriminating "that which is hated." [3] No allowance is made for lack of intent, for negligence, or for imprudence in connection with offense. Collective sanctions and regularized punishment develop as mystical procedures of collective expiation, becoming institutions of collective responsibility whose objective is to ward off otherwise disastrous consequences of a crime, to "control" the wrath of the gods. The important thing in such society is not that the perpetrator be punished but that the sacrilege, the impurity, be expunged or averted. As long as men thought they could control nature by "controlling" or propitiating the nature gods, or otherwise persuading them to their wishes, human responsibility to do so was accepted. Current moral parallels in religion (for example, prayers for peace) are too obvious to be missed. Release from this primitive responsibility of bondage to the sacred authority of group superstitions comes only with the growth of more discriminating perception, first of environmental behavior and relationships, and later, as conscience dawns (and who knows when that cock will crow?), of human purposes in human-environmental conduct.

The same growth out of primitive responsibility can be seen in the moral development of children—apparently an instance in social realms of ontogeny repeating phylogeny. Jean Piaget describes the growth of the child as a progression from "objective and communicable" responsibility to "subjective and individual" responsibility, from a morality of constraint, of unilateral respect for parental authority to a morality of cooperation "which puts the primary emphasis on autonomy of conscience, on intentionality, and consequently on subjective responsibility." [4] Gordon W. Allport gives a similar description of growth to maturity during which "emphasis shifts from tribalism to individuality, from opportunistic to oriented becoming." [5] "Conscience somehow shifts its center from ad hoc habits of obedience to the proprium," [6] from a sense of compulsion to a sense of obligation, from must to ought. He suggests

> that the must-consciousness precedes the ought-consciousness, but that in the course of transformation three important changes occur. (1) External sanctions give way to internal—a change adequately accounted for by the processes of indentification and introspection familiar in Freudian and behavioral theory. (2) Experiences of prohibition, fear, and "must" give way to experiences of preference, self-respect, and "ought." This shift becomes possible in proportion as the self-image and value-systems of the individual develop. (3) Specific habits of obedience give way to generic self-guidance, that is to say, to broad schemata of values that confer direction upon conduct. [7]

Society still abounds in traces of primitive responsibility. Many there are who simply never have grown up. Perhaps we all, respecting some matters, fail in some measure to mature.[8] Certainly the tenacious hold-over of primitive communal responsibility, represented, for example, by the doctrine of original sin—a sort of inferiority complex (leading to no telling what needs for attention and domination) brutally imposed upon children in their formative years—in some of its more literal forms, contributes a by no means negligible drag. And the spiritualiza-tion of ethics which has been our wont—Teleological ethics, the product —weakens the inclination toward assumption of a responsibility of maturity.

Doctrines of determinism have also in their own way interfered. The inevitability announced as the condition of the universe by nineteenth century science seriously undercut the responsibility of maturity by denying the efficacy of human agency. The return of cause from physical science—it having originally been spun out of human intention and oversimply imputed into nature[9]—in the form of social determinism and social Darwinism, cuts two ways: toward exoneration of criminal or antisocial conduct as beyond the control of the individual, the fault of inevitable sequences bequeathed to him by society, and toward a return to propitiation, to religion, the attempt to control or to accommodate to and thereby control the ultimate Author of destiny. External authority relieves men of their guilt, so it appears in the years of dawning con-science, as supernatural religion relieves the world of mystery—by setting a premature end to probing, nagging thought. A responsibility of maturity is lost when guilt is nullified or absolved in ceremonial celebration evading the painful process of reforming character, the bone-stretching process of growth to Self-control.

Piaget's formulation of the two moralities should be qualified in one important respect. We cannot draw the conclusion that because primitive morality is "objective" in his terms the dawning responsibility is not objective in our terms;[10] we cannot rest content to call the new responsi-bility "subjective and individual" as if it were "inner," atomic, and inac-cessible. Walter Lippmann's vivid description brings out the proper focus:

> As our minds become more deeply aware of their own subjectivism, we find a zest in objective method that is not otherwise there. We see vividly, as normally we should not, the enormous mischief and casual cruelty of our prejudices. And the destruction of a prejudice, though painful at first, because of its connection with our self-respect, gives an immense relief and fine pride when it is successfully done. There is a radical enlargement of the range of attention. As the current categories dissolve, a hard, simple version of the world breaks up. The scene turns vivid and full. There follows an emotional incentive to hearty appreciation of scientific method, which otherwise it is not easy to arouse, and is impossible to sustain.[11]

Piaget explains the qualitative transformation of responsibility as a product of "the social differentiation and 'organic' solidarity [meaning "mutual respect and cooperation"] peculiar to civilized communities." [12] But this "mutual respect" depends, at the very least, on adequacy of social perceptions—dawning perception of the purposes of other human being-doings—and in it, therefore, are the seeds of the only objectivity we know. In utopia, responsibility *is* Self-control—referring, of course, to the elaboration of Self and control that has been given in earlier chapters, complete with all the overtones of objectivity that have been so lengthily insisted upon.

With the expansion of the Self, the socialization of morality, and the establishment of social control, it is possible to visualize an institution of responsibility that is like neither the sacred institution of primitive heteronomous responsibility, nor yet the dithyrambic responsibility of uncoordinated atomic and autonomous consciences.

AUTHORITY

Perhaps it is because we know authority so well, having grown up with it, that we are so reluctant to discard it as an organizing concept. The word should be restricted to historical and anthropological uses, but somehow it has been thought fit to be extended out of all bounds of common sense. In primitive life authority and responsibility are co-ordinate concepts. The connection between the two is well noted; it helps explain the cohesion of groups and the actions of men. But then as new patterns of responsibility develop, the completely unnecessary attempt is made to "save" the concept of "authority" in Ptolemaic epicycle-on-epicycle fashion—apparently in order to maintain the symmetry of parallel concepts. So entrenched was the old way that it is impossible to imagine the one concept without the other, and we end up talking superfluously about the "authority" of the situation, or the "authority" of organized knowledge as we did in chapter 9 following out Mary Follett's way of thought. "Authority" is comparable to the luminiferous ether that was discarded by physics, and to the will that was discarded by psychology. Once we quit using it as a theoretical crutch we will find that our thoughts, hypotheses, and explanations can proceed apace, more simply and without loss.

Obviously this is not to say that "authority" can be dropped out of historical description or explanation. The idea has had its impact—just as the luminiferous ether, the philosopher's stone, and the Northwest Passage had their practical effects. Having a more direct importance to social relations than these latter, the idea of authority has been built more firmly into social, political institutions. But taking an old concept and rarifying its abstraction so as to permit it to subsume a host of previously unencompassed and qualitatively alien situations is frequently a feckless maneuver. Or it is a dangerous practice that threatens to project obsolete attitudes and characteristics from old social arrangements into the innocence of fresh possibilities. That is what makes the discarding of "authority" more than a matter of taste or of fine intellectual preference in definition.

Authority is a term properly extraneous to democracy. It is contaminated through long and close association with status,[13] stigmatized as characteristically the command of a superior. A Protestant religious reaction may still be heard on the radio pulpit of the air decrying in horrified revulsion the idea of replacing the authority of the Living Father with the cold reptilian authority of a process (evolution). It is hard not to share the feeling, albeit from an opposing perspective, that a concept so anthropocentric and status-ridden should be left secure in its obsolescence.

The responsibility of maturity should have as little as possible to do with the contagions of an authority of sacred figments or an authority of status, parental or kingly.[14] Institutionalization of responsibility in modern democracy, especially in democratic administration, must guard against the moral regression of intellectual and institutional traps that catch transactional being-doings in billiard-ball (interactional) relationships. The persistence of authority with its old overtones in government, business, education, and religion can only perpetuate intolerance and unwillingness to seek and abide by public verification, presenting a coercive affront to conservatism where the satisfactions of control could be substituted.

We should be able to say that the old prescription about allocating authority so as to be commensurate with responsibility is an archaic holdover. We cannot, however, because much organization and many people have failed to grow out of primitive responsibility past autonomous conscience to an understanding of mature responsibility. The most persuasive reason for dropping the word "authority"—particularly in connection with responsibility—is that, increasingly, live situations fraught with responsibility are found to contain no authority at all, or insufficient authority to justify the responsibility.[15] In other cases administrators formally endowed with authority do not use it, knowing that each authoritative exercise tends to stunt the growth of subordinates, to impair their adaptability, to destroy their responsible behavior, and to weaken the organization. This argument points directly toward the art of leadership which is considered in chapter 17. Under conditions of the modern administrative state, the control which the administrator is responsible to achieve is not had through obeisance to authority (he is not responsible to "control" the authority; that is, to propitiate it by "responsible" acts) but increasingly through knowing-how, the touchstone of control. The Nirvana of social control through Self-control is apparently a long way off. Strictly speaking, the "authority" of method, and responsibility to a method of knowing, can occur only to the extent that the individual is part of a self-controlling (self-correcting) method and only to the extent that he has a part in controlling, creatively extending, the method.

CONSTITUTIONAL RESPONSIBILITIES

Even before the Great Seal went out of Court and the British monarch's major officials were brought within review of the courts, eventually to be made answerable to Parliament, administrative responsibility had accrued a system of multiple roots. The administrative officers were, of course, responsible to the authority, the will of the monarch, but also to a sense of the developing national interest (sovereignty) and to professional guild standards.[16] By then the business of government had become so centralized and complex that a feudal system of responsibility to heteronomous authorities of status, much less a simple hierarchical responsibility to the king, could no longer suffice. It is easy to imagine a similar situation in pre-feudal Egypt, as well as at many other times in the history of the world.

Continued and accelerated growth in complexity has brought twentieth century America to the point where even the triple responsibility constitutionally ordained has become a largely ineffective fiction. Neither the legislature nor the President, as the formal channel of responsibility to the electorate, can exercise enough detailed supervision over administration to insure against "arbitrary" administrative decision, or to give direction in concrete detail to the many specific policies established and enforced by administrative agencies. This situation has goaded Senator Mondale into remarking: "There's little difference between passing a law and writing a letter. It's purely advisory these days." John M. Gaus says that "while in theory it may be held that popular election of a chief executive makes the administration responsible to the people directly, and indirectly also that responsibility is enforced through the action of the legislature in law-making and other forms of control, actually the immediate master is a party or a factional machine." [17] The further unsolved problem of ensuring party responsibility thereupon complicates the administrative pattern. Because party is to such a considerable extent unseen, so little objectivized compared with formal government, it can also be said to interfere with actual achievement of responsibility by obscuring the mechanics of responsibility.

The third constitutional responsibility of administration—to the courts —is also irregular, fitful. It is, furthermore, after the fact, and almost entirely negative. The tension that develops is anything but creative. As administration in the maturing industrial society pushes at the frontiers of government, it moves "away from the simple lay conceptions of good and bad that have spooked through the annals of due process of law." [18] In times of rapidly expanding governmental activity, rapidly changing techniques and technologies, it is not surprising that administrators should find it difficult to foretell where the judiciary will draw the fine line that separates "reasonable" from "unreasonable," "substantial" from "insubstantial." The net effect of judicial review and overview of administrative action has been, as Fritz Morstein-Marx suggests, to weaken responsibility.[19] Administrators hesitate to take a stand, to assume responsibility for a decision, unless they feel reasonably sure they will not be overruled by court action.

Moreover, judicial review has produced some clearly undesirable by-products.

> The uncertainties of the situation have burdened American public administration with an understandable fear of the judiciary which is by no means identical with genuine deference to the law. They have engendered a spirit of compromise with those financially able to carry their resistance to the highest forum—compromise that cuts deeply into fundamental precepts such as equality before the law and universality of law enforcement. They have also measurably dissociated managerial responsibility and legal responsibility, two areas which can be separated only to the detriment of both. Moreover, reliance on the General Counsel's Office has tended to give the lawyer's mind a hierarchical prestige that carries weight even outside the legal sphere. . . . Administrative responsibility requires the formative influence and immediate presence of legal principle. The trend, at present inevitable, of shifting issues of law from the level of administrative operation to the General Counsel's Office, is not a wholesome development.[20]

Ineffectual, confusing, and even evil though these constitutional responsibilities may be in some respects, they need to be supplemented rather than shelved. They are, all three, heteronomous, subjections to external constraint. They are arrangements of allegiance to external authorities. As such they stand forth in coercive outrage to conservative drag, in rebuff to the demand of those involved for an effective share in final determination, for genuine participation. What is particularly missing is a responsibility distinctively appropriate to the mature Self of our transactional situation.

PROFESSIONALISM

It has been suggested, with considerable merit, that the appropriate, and perhaps the most effective administrative responsibility for our day of increasing specialization is found in a growing sense of professionalism on the part of the administrators themselves.[21] Unfortunately, there are a number of serious drawbacks to professionalism as carrier of administrative responsibility:

(1) In the first place, professionalism is usually just as heteronomous and constraining, from the viewpoint of the individual practitioner, as the constitutional responsibilities discussed above.

(2) A profession develops out of an attempt to set a group apart. As York Willbern says, "The thing that makes a profession is that it is something different, that it is based on a special lore which must in some measure be esoteric and not available to any Tom, Dick, or Harry. The status or social esteem which professionalization brings depends on difference, on separation." [22]

(3) Having gained status, professionalism attempts to set up its own authority to impose on the outside world—though almost always with benevolent intent. The hegemony of legal prestige described in the above quotation from Fritz Morstein-Marx is a good illustration.

(4) In its inception one of its chief inspirations is a kind of closed shop urge—protection of the public, yes, but primarily self-protection from "unfair" competition.

(5) There is something clearly incongruous about a responsibility of public servants that is anchored in the standards of a special group which may well be competing for its own welfare with portions of the public or, conversely, collaborating with other special groups because of affinity of professional ties.[23] The profession always protests that its standards are meant to protect the public, but it is not clear that this is always in fact the case. Public servants, whether they have a profession or not, are expected to protect the public.

(6) A further complication is the inevitable conflict of authority that arises when a multiplicity of responsibilities to different professions is permitted to develop.

(7) While establishing responsibility to profession may bring responsibility closer to the private conscience of the professional elite, it presupposes hierarchy for the rest of the administrative personnel. Below the highway engineer on the ladder are droves of draftsmen, mechanics, road crews, clerks, secretaries, receptionists.

On the bright side of the professional ledger are promises of growth beyond either the heteronomy of constraint or the autonomy of atomic conscience.

It may be that professionalization of the generalist—through such organizations as the International City Managers' Association—will lead toward a less constraining responsibility than that provided by the ordinary specialist professions, and at the same time toward a responsibility less purely relative than the conscience of the disassociated civil servant.[24] It was hoped until recently that the American Institute of Planners (the professional association of the newest of the professions) might follow the managers' lead, but the Institute seems, with freshly established membership qualification examinations, to be turning toward definition—and thus inevitably toward delimitation—of subject-matter, even though planners strive for a comprehensive overview.

PROFESSIONAL PROMISE

While civil service is not by any means a profession in itself, it does exhibit the beginnings at least of professional-like attitudes which may develop into supports for non-relativist and non-constraining responsibility:

■ One such beginning is the *dedication to the public interest* which the public administrator tends to develop as an adjunct of function. This dedication is every bit as real as that of the legislator's, although the administrator's interpretation of the public interest is quite likely to differ from the legislator's. Not infrequently, it is broader in vision and more long run in anticipation—especially where the legislator serves a limited electorate as in many cities organized under the ward system, and where the administrator is not irresistibly tempted by the narrowness of a group, or of a specialist profession to which he owes allegiance. The fact that the administrator constantly confronts the public on specific and vital problems *in the work situation* tends to give him a deeper appreciation of the public interest. In any case, some such autonomous conscience is all that is left when constitutional responsibilities are ineffective.

In a sense the administrator also shares in the responsibility to the public that is generally thought of as exclusively legislative. Administrators are imbued with the public interest in part because they cannot avoid sharing in the general cultural attitude institutionally expressed by the polling booth. The idea and impact of legislative responsibility are more pervasive and permeate deeper into human character than the mechanics of the ballot box alone would indicate.

Historically, administrators have participated in the process of constitutionalizing or democratizing the monarchical form of government. In Sweden, for example, they assumed the responsibility of leading the effort to restrict the king's power. One suspects that administrators had more part in the process in England than they are generally given credit for. True, in other cultures and other times they have not been so virtuous, but once a responsibility is established, felt and intended, it can be powerfully stubborn and effective. Dennis O'Harrow follows a long line of respectable tradition when he says that, because the Radical Right is *dishonestly* seeking to overthrow the public official, it is the public official's duty as public official to fight Radical Right extremism whenever and wherever it shows up. "Only in this way," O'Harrow says, "can he truly represent the great majority of citizens." [25] The special responsibility of administrative officials is especially important in the local government of large American cities where the administrative official is sometimes the only counterbalance there is to policy making by a handful of businessmen with exclusively business orientation or to special pressures from special groups—neighborhoods, unions, veterans' organizations, real estate developers, conservationists. The influence of expertise in this aspect of administrative responsibility is evident.

This administrative dedication to the public interest sometimes serves as an insulation against partisan pressures exerted on administration through the legislature. On the other hand, such dedication may be colored by a perspective conditioned by service in a special field, with a particular program or under a limiting set of administrative methods—for it is very likely to reflect the administrator's private interpretation of the public interest, autonomous and relative. This has been one of the criticisms of the New York Port Authority—and indeed in general of state highway departments—that the politics of specialists has been responsive to automobile drivers and bond markets, that is, to a limited segment of the public rather than to the general public interest or the Public Good. The U. S. Forest Service provides an interesting example of an organization that has done so well in orienting recruits that its Rangers apparently consider their contrived conformity merely as doing what is "right." Yet, the goals and directions of a special service organization, while they may be salubrious for now, do not necessarily provide an anchor for responsibility equivalent to the public interest broadly conceived.[26] As Milton J. Esman says, "Until career administrators have enlarged their areas of interest and identification and developed a keener sensitivity to shifting values in the community, they cannot be a creative or integrating force in administration." [27]

For, truly, the public interest is not a thing but a developing. When the responsibility of public administration gets beyond the point of identifying the public interest (at which point legislative responsibility has tended to rest) to a concern for the growth and development of public interest or intending, then new creative forces will abound.

▲ Another such promising beginning toward a new responsibility is the administrator's *refusal to take a stand on issues of partisan politics*. This neutrality is appropriately described as "the reverse side of his dedication to the public interest." [28] It is forced on him to a certain extent by civil service regulations, but it is also frequently a responsible attempt to avoid commitment on the level of compromise, refusing to compromise particular matters in face of demands that are unrelated—except "politically"—to them, declining to treat his recommendations as logs to be rolled in political popularity contests. This, the first step beyond compromise, may be the hardest. It is a beginning awareness that the real responsibility is to achieve control, not to settle for compromise.

◆ There is promise also in the fact that public administration, instead of simply sitting back and balancing the pressures on it, thereby to gauge the public interest, is increasingly taking on itself the responsibility of *identifying relevant publics and stimulating their organization and participation* in the process of policy formulation. The problem of formulating policy out of the clash and reconciliation of group interests has been "woven into the fabric of administration because of the inadequacy of traditional [constitutional] forms of securing administrative responsibility." [29] The administrative wont of seeing to it that affected interests are organized is a way of insuring that administrators may be able to resist coercion or contraint. However, its important promise is that it indicates reluctance to take things as given. It is a beginning assumption of responsibility to promote participation in the growth and development of the public interest through the sharpening of conflicts—hopefully along the lines of creative bargaining and scientific mediation. That it can, if mishandled or misdirected, miscarry and lead to corruption, is evidenced by the murderous competition among inner city groups for coercive power to dictate the distribution of poverty funds under the early programs of the Office of Economic Opportunity.

★ The administrator's practice of stimulating the organization of relevant publics shows further promise in that it is also a measure of *professional commitment to fact, expertise, rationality, skill, learning.* Only the man who is expert and current in technical developments can poignantly feel the direct responsibility to institute possible controls opened out by technical advancements. Following some current thinking, his responsibility ceases upon proposing innovation and improvement and informing elected representatives of possible consequences. More is needed, however. The elected representative must be brought vicariously to an appreciation of the possibility of control and its corresponding responsibility. This responsibility to urge use of possible controls is an extension of a feeling that first rose in the Renaissance when the ideal of progress was born. Skilled artisans then began to feel a new duty to objectify their skills and knowings and to pass them on for the benefit of coming generations. (In this may be the very essence of professionalism.) One of the great virtues of the professions, as T. V. Smith points out, is their way of socializing, among their initiates, the creative quest, opening all doors for inquiry, holding all knowledge in common. In areas where there are primary social dimensions to administrative activity—for example in agricultural, housing, and welfare fields—this involves an opening out to draw the human subject-matter into the creative quest. It is through organization of relevant publics that new social facts are uncovered and potentialities of social control are created. This skill gives the administrator the freedom to be responsible. One can only "acquire a proper respect for facts [by] bringing facts into existence through one's own efforts. What is important is the reality embodied in the fact-finding process itself. The . . . administrator who knows what facts are because he has brought a few into existence through actual effort can be trusted to keep his feelings in check." [30] In such trustworthiness *par excellence* resides responsibility. As Luther Gulick suggests, responsibility of administrators with respect to professional and technical standards—to knowing-how—may even have a higher priority than the responsibility of popularly elected representatives in event of direct conflict between the two.[31]

ANCHOR IN METHOD

It should be clear that moral (or political) separation between citizens and public administrators is now rapidly becoming meaningless, if not dangerous. There is a sense in which governmental administrative offices should be kept open-ended, so that the public or segments of the public may, from time to time, wander into a functional, formally arranged niche in the organization. I like the way Lane Lancaster relates the two:

> A realistic view of the administrative machinery of a state reveals not an official group on the one side and an obedient public on the other, but a situation in which the community in its helplessness turns to those with competence and confirms, by making them officials, a social responsibility which is not in fact increased by the conferring of an official status.[32]

There is a point at which general social responsibility of people as citizens or as humans—the responsibility that Socrates heroically faced and for which the Contract Theorists worked so hard to devise a plausible excuse: sometimes called "political obligation"—should merge with administrative responsibility.

This point can be located where both authority and relativity are displaced by a perfectible method as the anchor of responsibility. Here is the focus—scientific method—toward which the promises of professionalism in public administration can be pointed.[33]

On the political level, mature responsibility of intentionality—taking up, in reverse order, the administrative promises suggested above— implies at least the following:

★ The administrator's respect for specialized knowledge in his own field and the fields of his associated publics can progress from obeisance to the authority of organized knowledge to *responsibility to a method of organized knowing.* Then only can responsibility be fully understood "as being cumulative, widely shared, and rarely concentrated and ultimate."[34] Preparation in the background will have included learning to develop a disturbing concern for the opposition (creative bargaining process no. 2),[35] learning to respect an antagonist while inspiring his respect. (This is the basic process of growth found in family relationships as the child matures from the stage of restraint to that of conscience.) Appreciation of the hard and unique facts in any situation and of how they are brought into being thus grows from "authority of the situation" to responsibility to a perfecting method.

The basic responsibility is concerned with the controls painfully and joyously wrenched from the reluctant mysteries of the universe. It takes anchor in a self-perfecting method of inquiry—a method which aspires to extend and improve the reach of control.

Beginnings of readiness to anchor responsibility in inquiry are seen in the "authoritative" status freely granted to inquiry boards and study commissions—sometimes irrespective of the incompetence and ignorance of the appointees. This is perhaps an outgrowth of the "authority" of the job or function. Present day reverence for the computer is another illustration of deep seated respect for inquiry. Unfortunately, the method in these cases often consists only of an uncritical pooling of brains (or ignorance) or of memory systems—as if the pooling itself were viable method. The frequently unnoticed fact is that a committee is one of the best ways of avoiding or concealing responsibility all around—though a clear understanding of this can also be the motive behind the "madness" of creating it in the first place.

◆ The administrator's concern to stimulate organization of relevant publics can develop into *techniques for securing genuine participation.* Such participation is also required for the achievement of a viable moral science—through scientific mediation—that can be accorded the governorship of conscience. The balancing of pressures and groups and interests has been a standard legislative activity within the compromise rubric of legislative democracy. Administration first shares in this balance-compromise way of life, but then begins to reach beyond to a creative handling of conflict, including the organizing of relevant publics into effective participation and the relating of responsibility to perfecting method. Just as administrators now share devotion to the public interest because imbued with ballot-box responsibility, so legislators can grow to share in a distinctively administrative institution of intentional responsibility. Increasingly, elected representatives will have had administrative experience in private life and in that way will have acquired a direct acquaintance with the new responsibility. The legislature of the future, as one of its important functions, should be expected to take a more direct, effective, and jealous role in insisting upon the expertise in every relevant point of view, and in demanding an integrated product of the participation of such expertise.

▲ Reluctance to become engaged in the compromise tactics of partisan politics (administrative neutrality) can lead to *an understanding of the value of creative bargaining.* Particularly can it be made into a resource for avoiding premature commitment. In this respect, two factors are of crucial importance: (a) So far as the particular matter permits of delay—and there is almost always much more tolerance here than we like to believe—all salient facts should be in before disposition of the matter is sought. (b) Every attempt should be made to have a matter agitated to resolution at as local or low a level as possible—meaning, as low a level as is consistent with need for comprehensiveness. Appeal of most controversies to higher "authorities" should not be permitted as a matter of course. The farther away from the actualities of the situation (realizing, again, that comprehensiveness is an important actuality) that a decision takes place, the greater are the complications to creative achievement and the greater the temptation to compromise.[36]

▓ Administrative concern to insure the public interest can deepen from responsibility to a purely private and individual, autonomous conception of public interest to responsibility that has as its goal the ever renewed *making and remaking of the public interest,* transforming it into public intending.

In the intimate arena of transaction, mature responsibility demands a positive response (something more than a rebound result of uninfluenced cause or a reflex reaction to external stimulus) that integrates all the elements of the stimulating situation. Responsible choice is choice that leads to provision within the situation of enhanced value.[37] When the individual no longer senses (perceives) the possibility of enhanced values emerging from the solution of problems (through the internalizing process whereby issues posed by groups are seen and grappled with as personal issues), he feels that responsibility is being taken away from him. Here is the germ of powerlessness, thumblessness. In organizational terms, the result is turnover, narrowing of outlook, lowered efficiency, loss of interest . . . Under such conditions, reorganization is obviously imperative—so that responsibility can be reinstated. The responsibility of Self control is intentional; its product, integrity of character.[38]

In the political arena, mature or intentional responsibility insists that men not rest content to conform with an autonomous "public interest" based upon individual consciences, but that they proceed beyond to a more comprehensive and forward moving approach that draws atomic consciences together in creative bargains. Responsible choice is choice that leads to the transformation of public interest into public intending; it leads from the identification of interests to the creation of improved intentions; it moves from consent philosophy that is content to identify what there is of "public opinion" as a basis for action to social control that works with public intending (not found but made) as the foundation of the future.[39] When progress in the direction of character growth, of broadening intention, breaks down and its antithesis—the irresponsibility of leaving things (things natural, things moral, things political) to chance—is allowed to take over, a collapse in moral fiber takes place. Here is the kernel of coercion, restraint, coercive power. The responsibility of social control is intentional; its product, democracy through functional power.

The relationship between responsibility and power is readily apparent after all that has been said on both scores.[40] In an era of flux, of rapid technological change, coercive power tends to abound when the atmosphere is one of authority and heteronomous responsibility. A balancing and compromising power structure (likewise coercive, in its own way) seems to prevail in the neighborhood of autonomous responsibility and atomic consciences. Functional power, the product of social control, finds a fitting climate in mature, intentional, homonomous responsibility.

In a fluid society of continental and global proportions, power is functional when it has been worked out as a product of know*ing* control, grounded in largely vicarious participation.[41] Power, reduced to its elements, is human wants, needs, desires, values, purposes. When men know how to make fine adjustments in and among these anatomical elements or constituents of power, and how to set up a system of continuous readjustment, appropriate to the rapidity of change, power can be made functional even in a fluid society. When the constituents of power are fragmented and uncontrolled—that is, when intentions are not on-purpose, when purposes are not deliberately chosen, when choice is unintended—then anxiety, facelessness, and escape are to be expected. Then power coerces because its incidence cannot be anticipated; it cannot be controlled. Occasional fortuitous agglomeration of the base elements of power can lead to a deceptive appearance of functional achievement and effective control, but subsequent falling apart is hovering to cry the lie. Functional power seems to flicker among fragmented desires and purposes, gaining at best precarious and passing glory.

Politics deals not merely with power—the product, the symptom—but also and intimately with the ingredients. Its success and its enduring function is to marshal them or, as is necessary today, to create them anew in such form that a functional power is produced, friendly, forward-looking, and functioning as an effective instrumentality of progressively specified goals. Acceptance of responsibility *for* human conduct is at its highest when it is found that human conduct can be intentionally controlled. But then it is discovered that the conduct controlled includes the controlling intentions, that the moral control needed and attainable can only be a reciprocal system of Self-control, and that the anchor for responsibility—that *to* which responsibility is felt—is a self-perfecting moral method. At this point, intentional responsibility takes the final step beyond control. It accepts the professional commitment of the dedicated scientist, the compulsion of the artist, the responsibility of self-perfection, of opening new doors to the control of nature, environmental and human, of creating better things and people.

CONSTRAINT IN UTOPIA

Does this then leave no room in the modern world of administrative democracy for the use of force, for compulsion, coercion, constraint? "Punishment," Piaget rightly remarks, "renders autonomy of conscience impossible. . . . Social constraint—and by this we mean any social relation into which there enters an element of authority and which is not, like cooperation, the result of an interchange between equal individuals—has on the individual results that are analogous to those exercised by adult constraint on the mind of the child." [42] But constraint in an adult world need not therefore be entirely eschewed. A political ideal of pure non-compulsion (like a world without conflict), whether it be Heaven, Nirvana, Aristotle's "bliss," or Engels' withered-away state, is delusory.

On the other hand, the sentiments of Walter Lippmann expressed in the following passage need not be capitulated to either:

> Coercion is the surd in almost all social theory, except the Machiavellian. The temptation to ignore it, because it is absurd, inexpressible, and unmanageable, becomes overwhelming in any man who is trying to rationalize human life.[43]

The place for constraint in utopia is where men fail or refuse to be responsible, where they fail or refuse to mature[44]—and no exposition is needed to demonstrate the high incidence of this occurrence. Maturity and responsibility are coordinate concepts. Men mature by accepting responsibility for their own destiny and that of coming generations, and they learn to accept responsibility in the process of maturation. The maturity coordinate with intentional responsibility is, it should go without saying, a maturity of Self-control, which in turn is a product of social transaction. As heteronomous responsibility gives way to autonomous responsibility, loyalty gives way to honesty as spearhead of the virtues, as *the* modern virtue, that without which neither the complex financial system nor the legislative democracy (particularly, the electoral system) of today could function, that but for which science would have remained among the confusions of a game of wits. Adding continuity—the lasting quality of intention—to honesty, the new mature responsibility builds the superlative virtue of integrity.

It is most probable that the ultimate "constraint" employed under integrity in utopia will be a sort unfamiliar to the twentieth century, as peculiar to intentional responsibility as compulsions and constraints have been to loyalty and truth. Meanwhile the old ways will be used. "We play at paste until qualified for pearl." Yet somehow the paste-play is an apprenticeship, a qualifying procedure. This is the age old, circular, self-levitation process of all growth, all education, all progress. It is man standing on his own shoulders to reach the stars, the process whereby tools are used to make better tools, thoughts to make better thoughts. In a sense, through constraint men learn to be free. All that is needed is the step beyond the compulsions and the oughts (described above, p. 285), though these will be used in the process. Beyond the heteronomy of external authority and the autonomy of atomic consciences lies the homonomy of perfectible method.

Homonomous responsibility in developing its own appropriate sanctions would seem to be devising a middle way between the external compulsions of the one and the internal compulsions of the other. In fact it will be amalgamating the two and urging the new implications on to a new and true conscience (the promise of ancient Egypt) that is objective, public, perfectible. The immediate hurdle will be the presently entrenched subjectivity of atomic conscience, through the centuries deeply dug into our Cartesian world. Refusal to abide by the objectivity of being sure we understand one another is the sin against the Holy Ghost that opens the way to legitimate constraint or compulsion in utopia.[45] (No doubt the old external and internal compulsions will have their uses in the process of education.) It also points at the importance of free speech (to be considered in the coming chapter) to the investiture of intentional responsibility.

As a practical matter in a particular situation, atomic conscience may be *felt* to be unconscionably coercive and external authority may be *felt* to be the very incarnation of independence. It is out of the justices of the *felt* situation that both the freedoms and the coercions of Self-control take their legitimacy as the world matures toward a responsibility to homonomous self-perfecting method. The proper apportioning of compulsion (punishment) remains a delicate matter of judicious determination. It should also be pointed out that coercion of those unwilling, unable, or unprepared to assume mature responsibility through participation—direct or vicarious—is not external in the sense that coercion by authority is in a fluid society. It is rather organic and objective in that the method to which responsibility is attached encourages responsible attack, responsible conflict, responsible criticism, responsible "bubble-pricking" in attempt to improve the method itself. Coercion is thus under the aegis of an automatically and deliberately tolerant method instead of a rigid authority.

In any case, there will be the coercion of events, of fortuitous occurrence, when men do not assume the responsibility for the human conduct that is within their province to control—just as there are the coercions of flood and smog when responsibility for control of environmental conduct is forsaken. If there is an effective spur to the invention of appropriate constraint for education to homonomous responsibility, these coercions of events falling on the heads of the multitude will provide them. Two underlying intellectual irresponsibilities deserve to be mentioned in this connection because they will have to be cleared away before extensive headway will be made. They are subcategories of the irresponsibility of leaving things to chance. One is exemplified by the divisions in society that encourage science to continue a blind commitment to the lonely aim of controlling physical happenings without regard to further considerations—in effect a half-abdication of control. The other is exemplified by the primitiveness, the eclecticism of modern social research that continues to pile up "findings" without an all-out effort at simplicity —in effect a half-surrender to ignorance because patterns of simplicity are crucial to extension of memory systems. In a sense the paramount challenge is to raise the effectiveness of over-all responsibility until it is commensurate with the product and promise of controls available in physical science.

The responsibility built into legislative democracy and its administration relates to a mixture of atomic conscience, authority, and method. Responsibility is usually conceived in modern society as a moral imperative of conscience. And this spills over into government—wherefrom derive our multitudinous interpretations of the "public interest." As it is institutionalized, however, as it is formally expressed in governmental organization, responsibility is of the external, authoritative, predemocratic variety described above. This is perhaps most of all evident in the hierarchical, chain-of-command arrangements of administrative organization. An interesting though unproductive conflict has resulted, described as a conflict between maturity and organization:

> Mature adults are expected to be active rather than passive, to be relatively independent, to have deepening interests, and to have an awareness of and control over themselves. In an organization, however, individuals have little control over their workaday world; they are expected to have short-time perspective; to be passive, dependent and subordinate; to perfect and value skin-surface, shallow abilities; and to produce under conditions leading to psychological failure.[46]

Would that this conflict could ripen to produce the intentional maturity *we* speak of!

The method of legislative democracy, open to change though it is, is also very largely an external imperative. Constitutionalism is, as Friedrich says, "a body of rules insuring fair play, thus rendering the government 'responsible.' "[47] But the result has been an *authoritative* method for two reasons in particular: (1) The rules have been opportunistic rather than creative, based in Teleology rather than intentions. (2) An aspect of the rules has been to establish, through regularized techniques, majority "opinion"[48] as an additional moral imperative to which responsibility must defer. Sporadically ineffective though this may have been, it smears the stigma of *status* equality and thus of external authority on the method that sustains it. Thus does the taint of status-equality, that from its vantage in Teleological ethics infects society and belies the autonomy of conscience, become intensified in the institutional expression of the times.

As administrative democracy becomes established in the method of scientific mediation, the legislative function will become more and more that of guardian of the mature responsibility of homonomy. This phenomenon can already be seen in embryo when a city council invokes its concurrent majority predilection and, rather than make a policy decision unpopular with a vocal minority, returns the matter (a new housing code, for example) to the administrative department with the remark that the stamp of legislative approval will be withheld until disagreement is resolved.[49] As the legislature itself learns responsibility to scientific mediation, it can begin to distinguish those groups and individuals whose obstructionism stems from unregenerate autonomous conscience or heteronomous authority, who refuse to participate, to play the game, seeking instead to erect a bulwark in legislative recalcitrance. Then the final decision on allocation of constraint becomes a legislative function.

Naturally the imperative of responsibility falls with a different incidence on different participants. Each individual will have a slightly different interpretation of his responsibility, varying with the uniqueness of his experiences, exposures, perceptions (especially social perceptions) —varying, in short, with his individual expertise. It is only natural that specialists with peculiar backgrounds in subject-matter education and training should feel peculiarly and poignantly the responsible claims of bodies of organized knowledge and methods of organized knowing. Because of the wide variety in our specializing culture, responsibility *must* be both widely shared and rarely concentrated in individual persons. Its concentration in knowing-how is already well under way. This is the trend in all technologies, in all specialties.

As part of the coordination of the broad responsibility to democratic method that is made up of the many-faced perspectives of transacting Selves, the pure scientist perceives and assumes a specialized responsibility stemming from the methodological demands of what has been referred to as "simplicity." [50] In the realms of science, reponsibility insists that choice or decision, to be responsible, must lead to consequences that improve scientific conceptual tools.[51] The supreme challenge is to create and then continually to improve an organized way of knowing in the realm of morals. In this is found the ultimate meaning of specializing in generalism.

SUMMARY

This chapter has devoted itself to two tasks: to developing an understanding of the kind of responsibility that will be needed in administrative democracy to displace the responsibility of representative government, and to showing that this kind of responsibility already has had a start in the world and has the promise of a comfortable berth in public administration.

Responsibility should not be an extra something, a refinement added to compensate for the discrepancies in a system of discontinuous natural rights. The contract philosophers, having dissolved the organic bonds that held men together in society and having set men loose as independent, atomic agents, devised a consent-contract to draw them back together again.[52] Responsibility was thrust at the free to curb excesses of liberality, to counterbalance, to limit the separateness implicit in individualist freedom, the Natural Right.

The new responsibility, instead of being an after-the-accident rescue squad, an independently posited theoretical after-thought, hastily thrown together to keep the social fabric from falling apart, will be an integral aspect of every-day human transactions. Taking its start in the basic responsibility to make use of controls that man has won over nature (environmental or human), the new responsibility skirts the dictates of heteronomous authority and of autonomous atomic conscience, and becomes an homonomous and intentional responsibility, an acceptance of mature responsibility for the control of human conduct. Recognizing that conduct and control are intertwined, reciprocally related, it throws its anchor into the deeps of Self-control, the self-perfecting method of moral science, accepting the additional scientific responsibility of extending the reaches of control. Men are responsible to make use of the control they have captured out of the mysterious universe, but they are also responsible to seek out new control, to attach their responsibility to the ascendant star of democratic method.

The public service has a long way to go before arriving at a stable intentional responsibility worthy and supportive of administrative democracy. A noteworthy distance down the road has already been covered, however. Especially bright is the promise that professional commitment may grow to responsibility within and to a method of organized knowing, the promise that the practice of identifying and stimulating relevant publics may grow into effective techniques for gaining genuine participation, the promise that avoidance of partisan politics may presage understanding of creative bargaining, and the promise that dedication to the public interest may lead to deliberate remaking of public interest, eventually enstating in its place systems of public intending.

Instead of a separation between citizen and governor—really a product of faulty institutions of participation—with the citizen admitting a "political obligation" to the State for whatever clever reason dreamed up by Contract Theorists and with the governmental personnel serving at the sufferance of the citizen under a basically hired hand responsibility, instead of this there will be one responsibility common to citizen and administrator alike and focusing on scientific method. The merging of master and servant will take place when the implications of existing administrative practices—particularly professional practices and attitudes—are understood and when organization is opened out to welcome the citizen scientist as equal partner in search of control. Then only will it be meaningful to speak of the state as having withered away.

Meanwhile, the people's representatives will begin to be infected by the responsibility of maturity and will begin to perfect a special function for themselves in insisting upon expertise in governmental performance and upon complete all around participation. They will increasingly demand integrated products from administration and will push unresolved problems back into the cauldrons of administrative conflict for renewed efforts at creative bargaining. In insisting on maturity and abundant participation (direct and vicarious) they can be expected to assume the role of superintendent of the constraint to be applied against the unregenerate who worship the false gods of heteronomous authority and autonomous conscience.

As the new responsibility takes hold and the old servant-of-the-people attitude is displaced by participation and partnership, a new job opening (at least new in formal recognition) appears in public administration, as if by magic. There will be no vacancy announcement, however, because the job has been unobtrusively filled and functioning all along. It is the job of leadership. This will be one of the main topics of chapter 17.

First, however, there is the relentless responsibility of remaining understandable, the responsibility of being objective—which is the sine qua non of experimental science, the grand device that permits associated effort in the extension of control, which indeed permits the scientific method itself. This critical instrumentality—the institution of freedom of speech—will be introduced to its active and germinal role in administrative democracy in the coming chapter.

CHAPTER SIXTEEN

Freedom of Speech: Fulcrum of Control

> *It takes two to*
> *speak the truth.*
>
> THOREAU

AN HOMONOMOUS RESPONSIBILITY MUST JEALOUSLY CULTI-
vate freedom of speech—for what is a creative method of agreement
without effective communication? Freedom of speech is not a Right. It is
rather a rule-of-the-road, essential to unobstructed circulation along the
course that leads to creation of rights by agreement. Difficulties in
communication at the political level essentially resolve into problems in
objectivity. Freedom of speech is an insistence on the objectivity that is
pursued through seeking assurance of mutual understanding in the belief
that truth is to be found in public test.

In a universe of autonomous consciences, the institution of free speech
may serve to circulate from human atom to human atom some replication
of sense impression, some private call of conscience, some autonomously
wrought opinion. The new institution assumes a positive role of encouraging the working out of the objective truth, not free and clean of
human experience, but growing out of transaction. Its major connotation
will be skill.

Truth is indeed man made. But it is not made, as popular notion has it,
by listening tolerantly to all points of view and somehow putting them
together—the method of imaginative sympathy. "There are two sides to
every question," we are always piously reminded. And indeed there
are an infinite number *if* we are collecting mere opinion or *if* the legitimacy of a position is to be determined only by reference to autonomous
consciences. Then truly has every man "a right to his own opinion" no
matter how benighted. This, however, is to treat freedom, not only as a
release from authority, but as a release also from homonomous responsibility. It is to erect a right to be ignorant. Logically, a freedom that is

"little more than an honorific name for what someone wants to do ... is ... irrelevant to man's efforts to solve his own problems." [1] If it is instrumental in the making of truth, it is so by accident alone. On the other hand, a freedom that is effective in ferreting out the truth, solving human problems, resolving human conflicts will be one that embraces homonomous responsibility, in living and dependent alliance with validity.

FAULTS OF TRADITIONAL DEFENSE

Part of the inadequacy of our present institution of freedom of speech is attributable to its traditional defense. Actually, the institution, as sometimes happens with institutions, is better than its defense. The rationale still current has been inherited, with little change, from the pens of reasonable men—men who overemphasized the autonomy of reason and imagined for it a purity it has never in fact approached. Particular failings in theory derived from Locke and Milton.

Milton, in proclaiming the strength of truth, in assuring her ultimate victory over falsehood "in a free and open encounter," assumed a sort of human tropism toward truth. This was a highly suspect assumption at best, especially as relating to the abstract level of verbal behavior, the level of discussion, argument, and oratory. Far from eventuating in the victory of truth, the market place theory of free speech has midwifed at the birth of a social system that pits one alleged truth against another and takes bits of each by a method of selection known as "compromise." In politics, the pattern is carried through with government taking the unenviable role of arbiter-balancer between giant interest groups. In justice, the pattern is traced out in elaborate rules of formal combat or debate known as the "adversary system." It hasn't been until very recently that the courts have begun to distinguish between "truth" by intellectual combat—that is, trial—and truth by inquiry. [2] As Eduard C. Lindeman suggests (using discussion to mean "inquiry"):

> Discussion [that is, inquiry] as a social device rooted in educational theory and democratic philosophy is likely to become incorporated within the texture of various administrative techniques. Governmental bodies for the most part continue to utilize the method of debate and have not yet begun experiments with true discussion. [3]

The fact is that neither compromise nor the adversary system sustains a necessary relationship with truth. It is mainly the market-place theory that has led men so long to believe that they do. It is not even generally appreciated, within the confines of the market theory mentality, that truth is involved where compromise is reached. "Only" values, interests, desires are recognized as parties to balance, and they are thought to be aside from truth.

Traceable back at least to Locke, but prominent throughout the subsequent history of the institution of freedom of speech, is the integumental theory of truth that postulates an external truth knocking on the dry skin of the human organism.[4] This representative theory of perception interprets thoughts and ideas as representations of external truth, like images left on photographic films. There being no theoretically built-in arbiter to choose between images received by different people and differing in detail—sometimes in exceedingly gross detail—from each other, it is assumed that, at least in political realms, a compilation gives closest approximation to the truth. Thus Public Opinion is postulated and an amorphous jelly-like monster is born, a Newtonian "power"—force at a distance.

Far from ending in wisdom, the integumental theory of truth and its attendant public opinion approach to politics[5]—ultimately expressed in the freedom-of-speech device of the secret ballot, the referendum and a host of informal pressures to coerce the representative into nose-counting instead of exercising mature responsibility (or even his own atomic conscience)—have produced a statistical mish-mash amalgam of wisdom with ignorance. Freedom of speech, in this view, favors truth by removing obstacles, permitting percepts to fall in uninhibited barrages on the receptor outposts of the discrete individual, then to be sifted and winnowed (under supervision of his autonomous conscience) for nuggets of truth, with sovereign public opinion miasmically arising as a confused compilation of the separate siftings. The basic fault here is that, as we now know, the truth is not a sunbeam from the outer world. Freedom of speech must be justified on other grounds than the mere removal of obstruction to the free penetration of ideas—though this will, no doubt, remain an essential aspect of the freedom yet to come.

To a very great extent the inherited tradition of freedom of speech has also been molded to conform with the eighteenth century idea of reason as something over and above sect and party—an independent agency with its own organizing influence in society—and has been designed to facilitate and liberate the reason so postulated. Traditional freedom of speech is all very well, but it is not sufficient to the transactional situation of twentieth century Selves. Freedom must become something more than a liberation of disembodied reason. The truths that it would promote are not supra-integumental, external realities.

As we now understand them, the processes of perception are quite other than what Locke supposed them to be—they even leave a small corner for the category of self-evidence[6] that he had discarded. Perceptions are signals for successful action, each with a full complement of "subjective" attributes contributed from the proprium of the transactional Self. The truths that we know are correspondingly products of the give and take of transactions. They may be described as achievements of successful action, achievements that must be ever checked and revised for improved satisfaction—just as perceptions are ever corrected and sharpened to provide better, more sensitive signals.

Faced with the same divergent images that confronted the representative theory of perception, the new view no longer assumes that the truth impinges from without, that there is one true shadow out of the many images, or even between them. Instead, it assumes that a new basis is needed. Representative perception is discarded and effort is turned toward making the truth—the truth that, as we now know, cannot be found. Emphasis is placed on organizing a social process (scientific mediation) for making truth out of "subjective" and "environmental" factors in transaction. Emphasis turns from tapping opinion to making agreement.

Because the Self necessarily involves and includes other persons, the process of checking and revising is a social affair. It is through the objectivity of being sure that we understand each other that the truth is created. This is especially the case where truths of purpose are involved, where the accuracy of social perception (perceiving the purposes of others) depends in first instance on sensitive *and* aesthetic means of communication, on mutual disclosure. The truth is something that must be worked at. Except to the few, the sensitive to discord, the artists, it is not self-evident when first encountered (conservative drag) or necessarily on repeated encounter. Truth is a two-way process. It must be worked out through successful use—through control—in directing practical transformations.

Yes, of course, open encounter is fundamental, essential. But an institution of free speech that merely liberates talk to glut the market place of ideas sustains the most meagre relation to the quest for truth. It is not sufficient to assume that unhampered talk will somehow, through sifting and winnowing by separate minds, produce the truth. If this assumption is given free rein in practice, what in effect results is a non-social inhuman process: what passes for social truth is sifted out by the fingers of an unseen hand and winnowed by a wind bellowed from imaginary lungs. This is to leave the truth to the uncoordinated happening of fortuitous coincidence.

It is not sufficient to leave the test of truth, the determination of the success or correctness of a perception, to a utilitarian computation of probabilities, to a compilation of separate "opinions." This is to impute an atomic character to the individual, to deny the transactional condition of human existence. The truth is not supra-integumental, it is trans-integumental, a two-way event, back-and-forth across the twilight zone of "sensory reception." The institution of free speech must be expanded so that validity, instead of being supplemental to open encounter, is an organic part of it. Freedom of speech must mean that it is possible for a man to apply and test the ideas he has acquired.[7] Free speech must be deliberately, intimately, and dependently allied with objective social processes of experimentation, with the truth-making process of Self-control.

In order to relate freedom of speech to truth it has in the past been deemed necessary to balance license with duty. Strictly speaking, the freedom of speech of yesteryear was an impossible ideal. Driven to its extreme it implied that everyone had a "right" to be heard by everyone else. In an absolute sense, a man's freedom of speech—of this classic variety—is abridged to the extent that other men neglect or refuse to listen.[8] After all, it takes two to make a speech. A man alone in the woods exhibits the first signs of insanity when he insists upon exercising this freedom in the face of a non-existing audience. Listening (part of the "subjective" contribution to perception) is the converse of speaking, and the latter is not free in an absolute sense unless the former is bound. Wherefore appeal is traditionally taken to autonomous responsibility and a balance is struck between John's "right" to talk and his "duty" to listen, between freedom from external authority and a separate conscientious responsibility. The balance is necessarily tenuous because of the social uncertainty respecting the dictates of autonomous conscience. It will accordingly continue to swing from one extreme of contrived or coincident conformity or non-conformity to another so long as freedom and conscience are independently postulated. Meanwhile, freedom becomes burdensome. It is felt as a dead weight of conscience since it must be kept in line by an extraneous effort of a separate responsibility. When society begins to adjust to the new freedom of speech, there will be no balancing. Responsibility will be found to be a built-in feature of freedom.

The courts have attempted to stabilize autonomous responsibility in respect to libel, slander, public tranquillity ("clear and present danger"), honest advertising of food and drugs. Perhaps in the near future, restraint will be placed on "hidden persuaders" as well. There remain, however, other and possibly more venal abuses that go unchecked and perhaps cannot be squarely met in terms of the classical theory of free speech. Perhaps, strictly speaking, they are not even abuses under that theory.

The most prevalent current abuse is the insult to inquiry and intellect when a man or a group succeeds in monopolizing the air with sound or sight waves signifying nothing, belaboring the insignificant, monotonizing and stereotyping a point of view (whether valid or not), or stimulating irrelevant, superfluous emotions. Here are the modern sins of which so many of the barons of the fourth estate and the advertisers of "salesmanship" persuasion are guilty. (It is very questionable that advertising can be related very directly to free speech, except in its adverse impact. Advertising is perhaps most appropriately and simply described as an attempt to manufacture wants or "opinions.") For lack of self-restraint on the part of some, others raise a new "right"—to not-listen[9] —which readily becomes a defense in depth of ignorance. A few there are who protest against the immorality of both ignorance and abuse of the free flowing air, as sins against the Holy Ghost. But their protest is, of course, ineffectual so long as freedom of speech retains its pristine character amenable only to an endless, synthesis-less dialectic with autonomous responsibility of atomic conscience.

Someday criteria will be agreed to that will establish inquiry, truth, discussion as the ground for publication or speech. Speech will be dedicated to truth. To try to cash in on it, to make money from this most distinctively human of all activities will be considered reprehensible —as cashing in on individual conscience is now deemed reprehensible. Making money from words will be understood as ulterior motivation. This not as a separate responsibility of free man, but as an inherent part of the new freedom of speech. Speech free of ulterior motive, free of economic consideration, free to light the way in inquiry.

It is hard to see how any of the more glaring instances of word mongering can be dispelled without a radical overhaul of social habits. So long as newspapers are profit-making ventures (either through direct sale or through building circulation the better to sell advertising space) the significant will play second fiddle to the sensational, alternative suggestions will be called "challenges," and a program with one critic, "controversial." So long as professors must publish for professional advancement they will publish—whether they have anything to say or not, whether they or others have already said the same thing a dozen times before or not. So long as words are honorably committed to the service of sales, bound to a product that must be pushed instead of being freed for a truth that must be made, advertising will insinuate its ballyhoo between communication and inquiry. Such built-in biases will not be corrected under the auspices of classical freedom of speech, though important beginnings may be made. There is the French example of publishing newspapers under public auspices. Or there could be a halfway arrangement with headlines alone separated from ulterior motives, assigned to writers paid by the public and devoted to the public interest.[10] Comparable partial public controls of "public relations" could, no doubt, also be devised. But finding suitable criteria will be a slow process. It will take time to convert to a truth-grounded freedom of speech.

FREE SPEECH AS VALIDATING TOOL

Improvement over free speech as classically defended will be a product of reeducation through which an homonomous responsibility becomes a built-in feature of the new freedom. It is not inconceivable that, as a moral science develops, men, recognizing the taint attaching to purpose that runs amok through avoidable ignorance, will admit shame at stupidity and will correspondingly, as is the case in the present-day scientific community, expect to rein in when confronted with the proofs of scientific experiment;[11] that is to say, in conformance with an homonomous responsibility.

When the institution of free speech is informed by an improved understanding of the nature of perception (social perception, in particular), by a realistic interpretation of man's transactional situation, and when it becomes allied with a feeling of homonomous responsibility, it will become an habitual instrument of deliberate validation (contrasted with accidental verification), a stable fulcrum of control. It is by taking leverage off rounded communication devoted to the pursuit of truth that the world is pried loose from obsolescent patterns of behavior and moved into new orbits of democratic achievement.

The renewed institution will be characterized by increasing emphasis on cultivating the ability to listen—the major channel of social perception. Milton to the contrary notwithstanding, there is nothing automatic about truth. It has to be worked at from both ends, from the end of inspiration, self-evidence, creativity, and criticism, and from the end of social test. Freedom of speech that would be an agent of truth must be a lubricant of the genuine participation described in earlier chapters. As has been said, the truths we know are products of the give and take of transaction. A corresponding par-giving and par-taking, responsiveness plus information program, talking and listening will be encouraged by freedom of speech as agent of social, moral, political truth.

The fundamental human value in give-and-take communication seems to have been unambiguously confirmed by one of Alex Bavelas' classic demonstrations. The demonstration set-up involved two pairs of subjects communicating by telephone, one of each pair trying to direct his partner (whom he could watch) in laying out a particular pattern of twelve dominoes. The difference between the two situations was that one telephone permitted back and forth conversation whereas the other did not. The discovery that the conversational system was uniformly successful, while the one way, I-talk-you-listen system rarely ended with a completed domino pattern, indicates about as clearly as possible that the second way has extemely limited value in satisfying complex needs for mutual understanding.[12]

Obviously there is very little free speaking that involves active listening among all the gabble that daily passes through the conspicuous media of communication. It is absolutely impossible to be anything but passive before television—short of shutting it off. Because it is so clearly an I-talk-you-listen arrangement, broadcasting cannot help being a bit contemptuous of the public (that is, when it is talking directly to its audience, not so much when it is transmitting a lecture room event or the like.) Public service programs and attempts at education are particularly patronizing. Even the Press is read in almost pure passivity. Very little, if any, of the material in our newspapers is written so that a reader can actively listen to it. He cannot engage it in probing conversation as he can a good book. The emphasis is almost entirely on imparting "information," the cynical hope of "news" monopoly apparently being to gain a voice in every copy that is read, thereby concentrating "opinion" in the pile of each atomic winnowing. Meanwhile, the public is beguiled by the promise that truth will emerge from the mutual canceling of assorted distortions coming from opposing interests. The two-newspaper town where there is genuine competition gives this the lie, as the conscientious dual subscriber finds himself confronted with what, for all he can tell, are merely opposing falsehoods.

There is continual complaint that mass public audiences are not motivated to be informed or educated. And in fact they are not. Partly this is because all ideas are potential threats (conservative drag) unless tamed in transaction. But it is also doubtless partly because what passes for communication avoids genuine participation and does not offer a respectable substitute of vicarious experience either.

In promoting "genuine" participation, the new freedom of speech will avoid affront to conservative drag.[13] It will be a conservative institution, a positive freedom for the conservation of what is found to be good that is created, and a freedom for finding good or bad what has been created, as well as a freedom for pricking holes in what is currently believed to be good, so that the better may be created. The elemental emphasis will be not so much on relief from externally imposed restrictions as on the opportunity of individuals to become "characters," or Selves. As Max Otto says,

> when morality becomes acclimated to the full rigors of daily life, goodness takes on a new character and the relation between the good man and natural laws is made intimate and inevitable. Character is no longer blind loyalty to an abstract principle or to a set of fixed rules. It is devotion, in concrete and intelligent form, to the human venture projected on this planet.[14]

Indeed, speech is precisely what permits men to be human. The value of a genuine freedom of speech is that by its grace men may become increasingly human. Freedom of speech must become a social process and it must come to involve active listening in which social perceptions are ever tested and perfected by reference to social experiment or experience.

There is a curious ambivalance in the American attitude toward government that expects government courteously to answer questions put to it but not to volunteer information without request. This is part of the old suspicion of government, the conviction that minimum government is best. It is a fear that government will move into the business of subtly manipulating public opinion—tampering with popular sovereignty. The myth has it that wisdom, sometimes called "consent," comes *from* the people in the form of public opinion. Governmental intervention must correspondingly be looked on with misgivings.

Some things are permissible—like Department of Agriculture Bulletins—because of their usefulness (though history is sure to show a record of mistrust when the series of agricultural bulletins first began), perhaps mostly because they can be argued to be strictly factual, scientific and, therefore, no threat to eminently moral public opinion. But other things, like hiring a public relations man to "sell" approval of a school bond issue to the voters, are suspiciously questioned or denounced. And the concern usually is quite legitimate. The current temptation is to sell a bond issue or any other governmental communication to the public just as a package of cigarettes is sold—with resort to just any advertising technique appealing to just any irrelevant or extraneous consideration.[15]

Nevertheless, the trail has been blazed. Scientific and technical information programs are beginning to break through the jungle of opposition to governmental talk, opening the way into the clearing of public education. And popular acceptance of communication from government can be said to be gradually developing in response to a genuine need that free speech be a two-way process. It is easy to imagine final acceptance to be won after a period of divide and conquer, as gigantic federal research and information programs persist and spread, starting first with "purely" scientific and technological matters, and then proceeding along lines of least resistance through Indian affairs, old age programs, unemployment problems, poverty programs. . . . One of these days an urban counterpart to the County Agent may appear on the scene —when the social sciences become as scientifically respectable as soils management and animal husbandry.

Some government information programs are no better than quiet versions of the sensationalism of the fourth estate, others are clearly overzealous. Though today doubtfully trustworthy in many instances, they must be developed into reliable media for transmitting vicarious participation. They must be made to bring round the "other half" of free speech, in the process of validation.

The distinction between propaganda and advertising on the one hand and communication on the other will gradually clarify as a clean break is made with the holdovers of the Public Opinion persuasion. Public opinion (assuming for the moment that it is not entirely imaginary) *finds* wisdom—if it is lucky. Validation *makes* wisdom, scorning the gratuity of chance. This latter is the course the new freedom of speech will be expected to encourage. Democracy needs institutions that can provide a more solid foundation than propaganda and advertising, that can produce a social wisdom more reliable than summaries of public opinion. Indeed, the instruments are already at hand in administrative organization. Mainly what is needed is an opening up of new institutional habits of free speech.

A number of starts have already been made. In Boulder, Colorado, for example, after a referendum was defeated by a narrow margin a survey was conducted, not to discover how to sell the defeated program to the public but to uncover the misconceptions (if any) and the points of misinformation (if any) that had contributed to the defeat. The city's information program was restructured to reflect the survey findings and the referendum was rerun with success.[16] The Boulder procedure contrasts starkly with the Machiavellian mentality that tries to pass school bond issue referendums by scheduling them off season and unconnected with other votes or issues so as to minimize the adverse vote of those too complacent to make the special effort to vote in a special election. There remain, nevertheless, dangers of misuse of the Boulder method. Here is another important locus of concern that merits legislative surveillance —from a point above the level of special purpose districts. It should be added that ultimately this method also depends upon understanding, acceptance and genuine participation by those brought into the survey procedure, for a sophisticated public may refuse to cooperate if it feels it is being "used"; it may convert survey work into self-defeating prophecy.[17]

City planners have recognized that it is usually futile to ask for a popular expression of preference and choice between community designs. It is clear that most people can not even be said to have preferences, in any meaningful sense. Preferences can be made more meaningful if, before they are solicited, an intensive educational campaign is organized in a deliberate effort at full-fledged, two-way freedom of speech aimed at explaining the meanings and potentialities of the various community design possibilities. New York's Regional Plan Association has attempted to attack this problem by educating a sample population and then treating it with opinion surveys.[18] This and other similar efforts apparently try very carefully to avoid use of attitude surveys for the cynical purpose of gauging majority attitude so that a plan or program can be subtly devised to appeal to popular prejudices or predilections. The enlightened objective is to work with rather than to circumvent uninformed or unprocessed reaction. In the long run, it is well understood, no other way is genuinely effective.

There will clearly be need for much more of this kind of citizen-government dialogue as the world progresses. Here is the beginning of the union of truth with freedom of speech in inquiry. Here is a beginning merger of citizen and administrator in a joint inquiry-enterprise of free speech, sharpening and testing social perceptions in social experiment aimed at improved social control.

PRIVACY AND THE GENESIS OF TRUTH

A difficult aspect of free speech not appreciated by the press is the press's own insistence on absolute freedom, not freedom to print what is news, but freedom to hear what and probe where it wishes. This was perhaps never part of the bargain of classical persuasion in free speech. It certainly should not be part of the revived institution. Privacy must be considered an essential aspect of free speech. As a matter of fact, when everything becomes public, it is probably the end of democracy.

When all discussion must be made available for publicity, a dangerous tyranny is raised, the tyranny of interference with thought. Whether the business at hand is public or private, lack of privacy can sometimes completely stifle free speech and suppress the truth. It is partly that the tendency to make news out of government deliberation over public questions, quite apart from the intrinsic merit of the matter, smothers spontaneity and candor. Privacy for group deliberation is akin to quiet for individual thinking; it is sometimes needed to bring out the truth.

Freedom-of-the-press insistence that reporters be admitted to any conference or discussion of public officials or representatives returns to and relies upon the obsolete atomic-individual theory of human nature, the theory that people think in their heads and then subsequently speak. In a real group discussion there can be joint thinking—not merely the collecting or pooling of the products of separately thinking brains, but literally a process of thinking between minds. The talking is part of the thinking. For a reporter to listen in is as much an invasion of intimate processes as is the tapping of an individual's brain waves while he is occupied in private cogitation. In many situations, license of the press, by interfering with the group skill of discussion, interferes with freedom of speech, with freedom of thought, with the nerve impulses of creativity. Any truly deliberating body needs privacy for its freedom to think. The Founding Fathers at the second Constitutional Convention understood this well. Potential publicity interferes with the skill of group thinking just as noise mars the skill of the musician or defeats the skill of the solitary thinker.

Another part of the need for privacy is found in the frequent impossibility of completeness. If it is impossible to tell the whole truth, it is sometimes best not to speak at all because a half truth may be worse than a simple falsehood for carrying with it a deceptive ring of the truth. The more complex the world becomes and the more divided the people by specialization, the more difficult it becomes adequately to communicate without evoking false expectations. The fault is not simply in inadequacy of or distortion by the means of mass communication; it is in natural human limitations of time, scope and attention. A vivid example of this particular need for privacy can be seen in the more or less secret agreement that grew up between the Atomic Energy Commission, the Food and Drug Administration, and the State Department after World War II. Together, these agencies set a maximum permissible level for radioactivity in canned tuna, in order to assure its safety for human consumption. Publicity of such an agreement could obviously have been disastrous to the tuna industry—because complete communication was impossible. As far as the uninformable public was concerned, dramatic news of any radioactivity at all in canned tuna would have simply removed the item from the shopping list. The industry would have collapsed over night.

The new freedom of speech, in demanding freedom from publicity until ideas can be put in comprehensible form, is insisting on homonomous responsibility, building responsibility into the institution of free speech. In the social laboratory as in the physical laboratory, even the most brilliant, famous, respected and influential individuals must be allowed the anonymity of freedom to hazard foolish suggestions. A great amount of the creativity in any situation consists in the effort of criticism,[19] chipping off the superfluous, whether in chips of stone as under the hammer of Michelangelo, or in chips of thought, discarded ideas, hypotheses, inclinations, false starts, forebodings, partial formulations, suppositions. . . . Most men are content to sweep out their discarded thoughts and outgrown hypotheses together with the scraps of statuary, and consign them to oblivion.

Occasionally the scraps of a great man are collected—as those of Keats—the chips are sorted, classified, analyzed in hope that something will be learned. No doubt if the scraps from a Michelangelo statue were to be uncovered, a research team would put them together in order to measure the incidence of the blows that struck them off. But it is not the chip, the dross, that concerns the later generations (aside from collection for collection's sake or for a touch of a hero's glory), it is the hope of unveiling the process, discovering how the statue (a work of art) or the idea (a work of thought) was made, laying bare the skill of Self-criticism behind achievement.

When, however, the privacy of the social laboratory is violated by the presence of a group of half-understanding outsiders or by a publicity-intent press, the scraps of group thinking are not left lying where they fall to be swept under the rug when no one is looking. A reporter or a group of outsiders, picking up the uncooled scraps, all too often cannot help but wreak havoc. Not having a feel for the process, the outsider catches a passing chip of thought as it flies out of discussion and empedestals it in his private gallery. The reporter, impelled by faulty purpose—so intent on findings news that he makes it, as the over-intent hunter makes a deer out of a child on a sled—misinterprets the give-and-take of transaction, the cross fire of Self-criticism in conference as controversy between atomic individuals. Or he publicizes transitional arguments of important people, immortalizing in print the scraps thrown off in groping for a better world of fuller truth. In "reviewing the high-lights" of conference, he adds to the collection of the National Gallery of discarded thought, the news gallery crammed with the shucks of creative work. Where there is a vested interest in news, the bias in behalf of its being interesting, arresting, startling, "significant," newsworthy over-rides moderate presentation of happening in context. The significance of a statement or action should be allowed to take its own dimension, to establish its own decibel level, out of what it means in the process and to the process of which it is a part—instead of being disconnected and rewritten in terms of an extraneous process of "news" dissemination.

Neither the outsiders, nor the press—nor frequently the participants, for that matter—appreciate the intimate nature of conference. Without assurance of freedom to speak freely, free of fear of these abuses of privacy, conference fails. Truth is repressed because its making is interfered with. An important part of a truth is in its making. This, the old freedom of speech has not appreciated. Instead of being content to make the truth, it has thought to find it ready-made in a happening. The old free speech protected the soap box—a half-process, talk without return— in the mistaken view that process was not crucial to truth, at least to social truth. The conference table was left unprotected, open and exposed to the depredation of unthinking interference.

As the press matures it will abandon its outside-of-society stance. It will begin treating criticism as process. Instead of salvaging and immortalizing the chips struck off in the conflict of creative criticism, the press will devote its energies to clarification of the process. Reconstruction of live creative bargaining occurrences would be invaluable. Let the press lay bare the skill of Self-criticism behind creatively struck bargains, the skill of the scientific mediator! What greater service could it give to democracy? Skills can be learned. As has been said and as will be explained in greater detail in subsequent pages, skill is an exceedingly important connotation of freedom. In clarifying democratic process and bringing its skills to the surface where they can be seen, emulated, and improved, an uncommon liberation unfurls: freedom *by* the press. Such positive efforts, more than anything, will assure freedom *of* the press in the new world of free speech.

The press, as it matures, will further seek to become a part of the process of verification. Moral ideas are made worthy, they are validated by public test. The press will reach the point of understanding that hypotheses that don't turn out are not mistakes and that the value to truth of their publicity is to make news of them only so far as serves the purpose of avoiding fruitless experimental repetition. And then it will see the challenge of helping to put ideas into testable form, making them somewhat more than comprehensible. This will be a far remove from reporting for sensation or idle curiosity. The true vocation of the press is to bring all the artistry at its command to the fight for objectivity as a working member of the truth squad. True positive freedom of the press will be found in the skills of artistry behind objectivity.

Where there is secrecy there is, indeed, genuine danger of deals, collusion, subversion. Pending utopia, vigilance must be maintained. As the world works around to ways of scientific mediation, however, the dangers will diminish. There will be less and less beguilement away from the public interest as it is fully appreciated that experimental inquiry and understanding must be democratic if they are to function in the field of social, moral, political life.[20] But the situation should eventually simplify so that this particular trust will not be necessary. As abuses of the press are corrected, legitimate excuse for secrecy will go begging and a distinction between secrecy and privacy in public affairs will become clearly apparent. It may be as simple as recognition that all that is needed of privacy is lack of publicity. When privacy is treated with mature responsibility (built in to free speech) secrecy is unneeded. Instances of secrecy can then be dealt with as what they are—instances of immaturity. Here is another point of special concern to the future legislative branch in its watch-dog capacity.

SPECIALIZATION AND FREE SPEECH

Over the years the representative organs of democracy have come to be less and less involved in situations of free speech. This change has accompanied the population shift from farm to city and may explain why rural legislatures—county boards—sometimes seem more virtuous than their urban counterparts. When, for example, an urban alderman is confronted with a proposal (growing out of technical studies of the administrative branch) to handle the problem of periodic flooding by zoning flood areas against construction of buildings, he will be contacted (mostly by telephone) by property owners who think they are affected but who understand neither the problem nor the proposed solution, by a few world savers of "property is sacred" persuasion, and perhaps by members of a community betterment group that has decided to put pressure behind this point. And of course he may read the comments of the local kept press. But out of all this there is not likely to be one instance of free speech. The alderman may make a record or a mental note of the opinions and arguments thrust at him (coming out with a very distorted picture, since those indirectly benefitting rarely take the trouble to comment, even if, which is unlikely, they know the name of their alderman) but he is not apt to affront his communicants with any show of free speech more disturbing than non-committal sympathy. In contrast, a rural supervisor from a far township unspoiled by urban encroachment finds himself in a much freer and more satisfying situation. He is more likely to be able to engage in chat with his constituents, exchanging both talk and listening. If he is socially adroit he can avoid the occurrence of conclusions before the problem has been outlined and the proposed solution laid out, and then can enjoy sharing an adventure in free speech oriented toward legislative decision-making.

The above contrast, while it admittedly exaggerates rural virtues, nevertheless illustrates a difference that is no less real for being less absolute and less constant, a difference that is also waning at such a rate that it will be a matter of history in a few decades. The factors favoring the freedom of the rural supervisor in speech with his constituents are many. Among them are the fact that his electors are fewer, the fact that his governmental business is less complex, and the fact that he, accordingly, has proportionately more time to devote to each governmental problem. But most important is the matter of perception. The rural legislator is not separated from his voters, as is the city alderman, by a barrier of divergent group perception. He typically (perhaps no longer usually) was born, raised, educated, married in the township where he continues to reside, and the tempo of his life has conformed to the common rural pattern, being natural in terms of climate and growth. Since he therefore sees things the way his neighbors do, the ardors of listening are eased, freedom of speech is not defiled by the mouthing of words that fail to carry their intended meanings, perception of purposes is classic in its comparative precision. His power tends correspondingly to be more functional because it can be applied, Don Calò-like,[21] in a context of reliable patterns of transaction.

The specialization characteristic of urban life leaves the urban politician in a functional power vacuum for the most part. Multiplicity of perspective raises a multitude of barriers to communication, fetters on the freedom of speech. In addition, specialization and division of labor can be accounted a major reason why the general public lacks desire for information (or education) about government or public problems, why it refuses to listen to all the clamor for its attention. Lost in separated corners of occupation and preoccupation, time and energy sapped in specialized activity and association, the divided general public exists in name alone and specialized groups restrict receptivity to information that is closely confined to specialty and day-by-day needs. The people are too busy to be interested, and too busy to listen—unless channels for effective participation are clearly apparent.

The newly arrived divergence of group vision is one of the great obstacles to freedom of speech. There can be little question that overcoming it is too great a job to be accomplished through the method of imaginative sympathy, through the siftings and winnowings of individual legislators. In contrast, the administrative method of creative bargaining, extended into scientific mediation, becomes itself an institution of free speech in its deliberate efforts to overcome the perceptual cleavages (the obstacles to listening) set by specialization of function. To an increasing extent the institution of freedom of speech will be expected to facilitate the vicarious participation that must fill the gap left by the erstwhile ideal rural chat.

STATUS

The listening part—and also to a lesser degree the talking part—of freedom of speech is very commonly debilitated by a relationship called status. Status differences within organizations act as barriers to effective intra-organizational communication, and class status in general tends to set up almost insuperable obstacles to inter-class communication.[22] How hard it is to get beyond the predominance of the atomic individual is shown by one of the results of Alex Bavelas' experiment with the telephones and dominoes. (See pp. 312–13, above.) An almost instinctive allocation of responsibility on an atomic individual basis interferes with search for fault in the set-up of the communication system. Bavelas found that no one blamed the system when things went wrong; they blamed the other man instead. It is not easy to repair the system when the initial impluse is to blame its operators. But even more fundamental than interference with system improvement is the apparent fact that status puts blocks in the way of communication between individuals. A man, will not communicate with complete honesty with someone who, he thinks, thinks more or less of him than he does of himself.

Status is a curious phenomenon for an age of autonomous conscience. It can variously be described as a holdover from or a throwback to parental authority or authority of bygone ages, or as a superimposed authoritative ranking of individual consciences. Status is primarily a by-product of education in responsibility that attaches authority to persons, posing the question: Responsibility to whom? Even the supposed independence of adult conscience generally fails to dispel the ghostly shadows of superiority cultivated by parents and religions.[23] In any case, status serves to preestablish the worth of opinions by reference to an individual's rank—preset on some alien basis—rather than to what is said, to a body of accumulated knowledge, or to a procedure for social testing. (A "status" that reflects and labels bodies of knowledge—for example, "counselor," "doctor," "professor"—or testing procedures is not status at all as the term is here used. It more properly deserves a distinctive label: stature.) [24] A similar personal and atomic rank-oriented distortion, though with a different directioning, is shaped by the status-equality of Natural Rights vintage where the tendency is toward a jealous, my-opinion-is-as-good-as-yours, pre-standardized leveling of the worth of opinions irrespective of wisdom or experience.[25]

It does not grant a man freedom of speech simply to let him talk when, for extraneous reasons of rank, no one listens. Research indicates that administration indeed suffers a high incidence of speech thus stifled.[26] Unless status is eliminated or out-maneuvered, only the most shining truths emerge through its filter from the lower ranks, and many untested falsehoods sift down as gospel from above.[27] The tone of the all-important man-boss relationship within organization is still pre-set by inherited expectations. Holdover attitudes still give the boss an aura of authority. There is an over-sensitivity to his likes and dislikes, to his anticipated actions and reactions. The upward flow of free speech, as a result, tends to convert from communication to news, restricted, at that, to news the boss is thought to want to hear or to carefully edited bad news. In his turn the boss is tempted to assume what has been called "executive stance," intensifying the communication problem and postponing the day of his transformation from salesman to leader.

Much of the secrecy so universally deplored as a restriction on freedom of speech is an everyday reaction against threats to status, a misguided attempt to shore up the respectability of an atomic self. "Face-saving," it is generally called, and it may well vie with the security measures of national governments as the leading direct suppressor of truth. Freedom, as at present in fact attained, may fairly be described as a self-respect.[28] It will not, however, become a Self-respect except through the elimination of inherited traditions of status. Human nature, for all the strictures laid against it, need not be interpreted in terms of the pecking order of hens.

SKILL

The important connotation of freedom for today, as was said in chapter 13, is skill, not release. This is because the present is an age of creation, an age of making; the age of discovery has passed. Though in a sense discoveries too are made, they are not marked by the same direct dependence on skill that characterizes creations, makings, artifacts; discoveries involve a greater amount of chance. The new worlds of Columbus and Einstein are differentiated by skill. So likewise are the perceptive worlds of John Locke and Adelbert Ames, Jr. The one is found, the other made.

Paganini was freed by the skills of the violin maker—notably Guarnerius. The development of harmony was freed by the skill of the thirteenth and fourteenth century keyboard craftsmen. Similarly in science the skills of instrument makers—clocks, balances, ballbearings, rockets—have freed theory to make new laws. Machines of all kinds are skill distillates, freeing men to do what they can not do in awkwardness. Words, symbols, and formulas, likewise, are skill distillates, freeing men to speak—as Einstein was freed by the refined language of Riemannian geometry. Skills are very importantly the intermediaries through which the truth does make men free. The skills of which instruments, machines, words are concentrates, are achievements of intelligence, breakthroughs of truth. They are knowings-how as well as manual or lingual dexterities.

The traditional negative freedom of speech that went with the representative theory of perception was entirely appropriate to a world that merely sifted through perceptions to find or discover the truth. A world that is busy making truth, making perceptions, demands a positive freedom of speech and the engagement of skill. The old freedom of speech aimed to give ideas a fair chance via competition in the marketplace. The new freedom of speech of scientific mediation aims to see that ideas are given adequate test via skills in the social laboratory.

In addition to removing obstructions to the free flow of ideas, freedom of speech in utopia will take concern for what was described in chapter 3 as the "subjective contribution" to perception, the reaching-out (intention) of the human organism through the twilight zone of sensory perception, the reaching out that rounds the circle of transaction. Skill is involved, as it is in the freedom to read. As an abundance of books does not guarantee a freedom to read, so an abundance of talk does not guarantee free speech. (Actually, overabundance is becoming calamitous in both cases.) For freedom to read, ability to read—a skill—is also necessary. But this skill involves much more than a capacity for absorbing information—programmed or not. Genuine reading skill achieves a discussion with the author—a curious arrangement of give and take with one of the parties present only in proxy. Similarly the skills of the subjective contribution to perception are more than hearing, seeing touching, smelling. They are listening, looking, feeling *out*, sniffing *out*.

Man does not fully perceive a dark corner of the universe until he has felt it out, until he has probed it with his most sensitive instruments and shone the light of his seeing eye into its outermost or innermost recalcitrant recess—until his skills and skill-distillates (tools) have engaged the object of inquiry in a soul-searching dialogue, a freedom fraught transaction. As one of Shaw's characters says in *Misalliance*, "Freedom, my good girl, means being able to count on how other people behave." The dark corners of the universe that are social are at once more recalcitrant and more accessible than are those out among the stars. They are more recalcitrant because they cannot be penetrated from outside by strictly physical means; they are more accessible because they can be opened from within. The fact that people are not predictable is what makes free speech so important, the veritable key to democracy, the fulcrum of control. The remarkable thing about people is that they talk. And when they don't, they have other skillful ways of bringing forth to the light of other eyes the deep meanings and intentions in their hidden recesses.

In the contemporary setting, freedom of speech is not one skill but many. It is the skill of listening that reaches out in discussion. It is the skill in bringing out intimate meanings and insights. A man's insights are freed only as he has the skill to put them in communicable form, to objectify them. Freedom of speech is a social, a political institution concerned with objectivity, with the skill of assuring mutual understanding.

Individual skills in expression and perception are important, but the political institution has to be more than an accumulation of individual skills. It must cover the full field of moral conflict. Free speech is a social skill. Instead of talk that aims to coerce or convince others with one's beliefs, emphasis will fall on such skilled talk as will help the other man grow, develop his own beliefs, perspectives, and intentions, winning for him freedom from coercions of the radical bent, preserving each man from the achievements of the others. Instead of hearing to register information or to size up or pigeon-hole the speaker, emphasis will fall on skilled listening that leads to understanding, using, testing and developing what is heard, each man preserving for himSelf the enhancement of freedom, the opportunity for growth through the exercise of his own skill. Similarly in reading, the real skill is not in assimilating information or in evaluating the author but in Self-liberation. It isn't what you read *in* a book but what you *make out* of it that counts.

If the freedom of speech institution of utopia does not come entirely clear short of the point of utopia, it should be no surprise. No one has succeeded in making its counterpart in legislative democracy entirely simple either—witness the controversies about it and the lack of agreement as to proper balance with responsibility. No doubt this is because speech itself is still somewhat mysterious.

Representative government has supplemented the constitutional guarantees of free speech, free press, and free assembly with rules of legislative procedure. There is the practical fact that where a group of people are trying to get something done there must be relief from irresponsible or unproductive or excessive talk. Complex rules of parliamentary procedure have accordingly developed over the generations to provide a responsible framework for free speech in a basically compromise-oriented setting.

Recognizing that truth does not just happen—it doesn't strike from above—and that validation of purposes does not arrive through compromise, the free speech concerned with truth in the setting of present day advanced understanding of human nature will, over the generations, develop an administrative procedure (analagous to Senate and House rules) in a setting of scientific mediation.

SUMMARY ON CONTROL

Free speech in traditional defense was a liberation from the tyranny of those who would impose opinion on their fellow men. Based on atomic individuals and on the representative theory of perception, it sought to find truth in unprocessed happenings, accepting the accumulation of unintended sensory repection as the final criterion of truth.

The new free speech places new emphasis on the process of validating, the process of making the truth. This leads to special concern with listening, with privacy, with vicarious experience as antidote to specialization, with the conversion of status to stature, and with the practice and perfecting of skills. The new freedom of speech is more complex than the old because perception is finally understood to be more complex than the photographic process. In addition to release from outside dictates, free speech is an organizing effort, an objectifying process, an intentional reaching out for the truth that is to be created. In its skill connotation, the new free speech is a negative freedom from limits placed on the unskilled, the inarticulate, on those who do not know how to objectify their purposes, desires, interests, . . . But it is also a positive freedom because those limits on the unskilled first appear and are first conceived only with the aspiration that precedes creation of new skill. It is positive in the forward thrust of burgeoning achievement. Under the aegis of homonomous responsibility, "freedom from . . ." merges with structured freedom in the skill of the consciously transacting Self. The skills in making truth are the critical skills behind freedom of speech.

On the personal, most private level, that man is freest who has developed the basic skill of Self control (the essence in some respect of what is called "responsibility") that permits (frees) him to stop and reflect (listen), to attempt to allow conflicting facts to speak to him.[29] This is the skill at the base of creative bargaining. Add to this skill of listening, the skill of talking, objectivizing,[30] the skill of making intentions, and the skill of social perception. In association these mount to a skill in making social purposes. The skills of genuine participation are necessary to win freedom from the benevolent coercions of the other man's radical bent. Add to them, as they are socialized in social habits or machinery, sharpened skills in communication (including art efforts) that lead to agreement, and the institution of free speech becomes effective in extending beyond Self control to social control. The old free speech was an individual matter, a profit to a ready-made self. The new has an added aspect; it is a process of creating a Self. A democratic society of Self control comes about when other Selves are freely accepted. The skills of free speech permit making an associated freedom perceptible.

The new alliance of free speech with validity carries beyond the market place, beyond the haunts of the huckster and the hawker, where ideas are allowed to sort themselves out by appeal to whatever device is persuasive at the moment, to the laboratory of social, political, moral affairs called democracy, where the speech skills of the leader and inquirer replace those of the salesman. While advertising may be said to liberate tooth paste and soap flakes, free speech liberates truth. Homonomous responsibility becomes a built-in part of free speech when it is fully understood, as an operating principle, that the institution of free speech must aim at liberating a process rather than a product.

Classic free speech meant no shackles, no chains—but also no links. Men were not tied together as we now know they must be. Talk was something that shuttled back and forth between transmitters and receptors, but the human transaction of agreeing was not provided an explicit berth. Individual sifting and winnowing there was, and the chance of concurrence among separate conclusions—but no collective test. Just as under the theory of free will a man cannot count on any significant continuity for his decisions, his actions or their consequences,[31] so under classic theory of free speech he cannot count on significant continuity for social or political decisions, actions, or consequences. Correspondingly, he cannot count on an end to the long human history of coercion, sacrifice, and compromise that has accompanied discontinuity. He cannot expect to see the development of an effective system of social control.

Representative democracy took the classic institution of free speech and, in attempting to make it workable, adjusted it to the facts of human association, to the group character of human being-doings, by molding it into habitual legislative patterns—generally known as Robert's Rules of Order. Administrative democracy of scientific mediation must be stabilized by analogous habitual administrative patterns of the new institution of free speech. As Jean Piaget says, "The essence of experimental behavior—whether scientific, technical, or moral—consists, not in a common belief, but in rules of mutual control. Everyone is free to bring in innovations, but only in so far as he succeeds in making himself understood by others and in understanding them."[32] The new free speech is an alliance of open encounter with objectivity, with validity. As such it establishes the basic charter for the politics of truth.

The institution of free speech becomes a fulcrum upon which to rest the levers of social control when the change is made from market place truth-finding to social laboratory truth-making. Without leverage from effective moral truth, from an objectifying and validating free speaking procedure, it will be impossible to pry mankind loose from obsolescent ways of doing, from Teleological ethics, to develop an effective method of social control and a functionalizing of power.

Freedom will not be exportable except as it is worked out in terms of skills—technical, social, political. The skills of free speech will have to be better tuned to the modern world than last century's soap-box free speech that grew a special parochial effectiveness in a corner of the world informed by a special, a Cartesian, dualism.

The world of politics is like the social arrangement of a symphony orchestra. In the transaction of an orchestral performance the conductor's control stems from his and the orchestra members' freedoms-in-terms of skill. Without precision skills all around, the many individual intentions cannot be coordinated. Without the Self control of intentions and the highly skilled art of the conductor (the craftsman in intentions) in "orchestrating" intentions, the performance falls apart, for the cohesions of time—which are intentions—are of the essence of music, as they are also, in a broader, less restricted and condensed, less formal way, of morality and politics.

Time was recently filled with the culturally conditioned intention-structure of a full work week plus home chores. Increasingly now men are freed from this kind of time-binding. And in the absence of skills upon which to build time-binding intentions they find the "free" time of leisure a new variety of slavery, an onerous slavery to time unbound and unmeasured, hanging loose and heavy on their minds and hands.

In these days of relativity, there is a constant reminder that what from one perspective is a stable fulcrum, from another is a movable object. So with freedom and control, the invert view proclaims freedom the product of control. The greatest potential for freedom is in the knowings-how, the controls of democratic moral science. From them extend freedom in the form of opportunity to make decisions, choices, intentions (for example, birth control), as freedom from disease extends out of the knowings-how of medicine and the control of bacteria. The greatest freedom is in knowing-how to make better intentions.

Free speech is just such a social skill (knowing-how) in making public purposes. More freedom, especially the freedom of speech, lubricant of truth, means better control. Out of the skills of communication comes the truth of how in association to build Self controls into social controls.

This book has taken the broad view of government as moral agency of strategic control and of democracy as an aim at Self control through the taming of power (chapter 7). Functional power, power free of coercion, derives, as has been said, from the skills of knowing-how—whether how to build a dam or how to build agreement of any other sort. The skills of free speech are fraught with power and they occupy a special central position in social organization that permits them to promote the functionalizing of power. Increased capacity for freedom (skill, a know*ing*-how) leads to increased capacity for functional power, a decrease in the drive for coercion. The public criticism inherent in free speech is creative;[33] and the freer the speech the greater the creativity, provided the speech passes beyond the market place to a place of homonomous responsibility. Through the creativity of the responsible criticism that the skills of the new free speech will foster, will come the effective approach to the taming of power and the opportunity of strategic social control.

CHAPTER SEVENTEEN

Control Through Planning

The plan's the thing
Wherein we'll catch the conscience of the king.

BUTTRESSED WITH HOMONOMOUS RESPONSIBILITY AND abetted by a new institution of free speech, administration must still be organized into effective human relationships and workways, hoping to hold utopia down to earth. Tremendous variety will necessarily prevail— probably greater variety than currently prevails among the forms of representative and parliamentary government—because administration that is democratic, fully participative, making room for scientific mediation, will give maximum play to individual character and creativity. There are broadly valid generalizations that can be drawn. They center around the problem of leadership—for which, it will be remembered, legislative democracy failed to provide adequate theoretical berth.[1]

The generalized aim of government is social control—practically meaning strategic control. The administrative leader in promoting this aim puts special emphasis on, and accepts special responsibility for, the all important function of planning, taking the lead in functionalizing power through the knowings-how of scientific mediation. The many themes of previous chapters[2] gather together in support of mature, personal, non-autocratic leadership that stresses administration as the vital aspect of modern government, that personifies and embodies the return of responsibility to the governmental process, and that, in contrast to work group foremanship, opens leadership out into effective relationship with the citizenry.

PLANNING: UNION OF POLICY AND PERFORMANCE

It is no longer necessary to argue the impossibility of separating policy and administration. That argument has apparently been settled for all time. If anything, one has now to argue that there are also significant differences. As a matter of fact, so far as there was argument in behalf of such separation, it was largely fanciful, "theoretical" we would say, using the disparaging meaning of the term. The fault was not in organization. Administrative organization had, almost certainly, always concerned itself in the development of policy. The error was rather in thinking based in either faulty observation of what transpires within the offices of administration, or on frail hopes of governmental simplicity through hewing to the line of an imaginary division of labor.

The basic error behind this classic separation has not, however, been removed. Mere insistence that administration shares in the making of policy has not sufficed. The error is now perpetrated anew in the belief that, within administration, policy can be divorced from performance.[3] It does not necessarily follow that, because these two can sometimes be distinguished for conceptual handling, they can always be separated in administrative organization. The image of a prophetic expert making social blueprint policies to be turned over to someone down the line for execution cannot be accepted as the model for administrative organization.

In the darker depths lies the yet alive, perverse root of the whole matter —the subtler separation of fact and value.[4] Particularly in the writings of Herbert A. Simon and the positivist school of thought are we seeing a divorce between scientific method and policy making, between finding facts and deciding on values. Enough has been said on this topic in earlier chapters; the failings in this way of thinking should not need to be further pursued at this point.

Within administration, the dichotomies of politics and execution, policy and performance, value and fact are integrated in a function properly called "planning." The division between legislative and administrative operation will be increasingly that of legislative policy veto on one side and administrative planning on the other.[5]

This should not, however, be taken to mean that all aspects of politics are appropriately admitted into administration. "Politics" is very commonly used in a pejorative sense to refer to situations where "deals" are engineered, where concealed or ulterior motives are jockeyed into position, where partisanship, bargaining, and compromise—everyday accretions to the representative system—are the normal modes of procedure. It will usually be found that a decision is called "political" in this sense when it has been determined by a factor unrelated to the problem or situation at hand—as when campaign support means a patronage job, or a vote for my bill means a vote for yours, or competition for tax base establishes industrial plant locations, or decision not to provide jobs for destitute high school youths is based on philosophic opposition to federal aid. Looking from the perspective of the ideal in administrative democracy, this kind of politics can be defined as the art of taking advantage of the infirmities of social institutions. Demagoguery, for example, takes advantage of the weakness of free speech by dramatizing a deceptive half-truth when the whole truth is too dull to command an audience or is too complex to be communicated to a mass audience. A feeling for the nice distinction between politics and "politics" has become a part of the art of administrative leadership.[6]

Indeed, the attempt to avoid just these aspects of politics is what has led to the unnatural location of local planning and many other autonomous administrative agencies out in left field, so to speak. By creation of a semi-independent planning commission, planning is frequently freed from narrowing aspects of politics—but at cost to the adequacy of administrative organization of purpose.[7] It is, however, difficult to say that planning should be brought in from "left field" before administration is strong enough to pursue purpose without deflection by partisanship.[8]

The difference between policy and planning is the difference between action and transaction—if indeed policy is more active than a mere statement of principle. If it is not, it must of course be implemented, as it customarily is, by a separate process of execution.

Planning becomes an administrative instead of a legislative function very simply because administration is not burdened by a limiting institution of freedom of speech. It is not necessarily bound to a voting system organized to collate truths autonomously culled from the market place of open encounter. It is able, instead, to engage the newer freedom of speech that grants equal prominence to listening and talking in an homonomous quest for validity. In short, it is in a position to educate publics to improved programs [The public listens.] and to perfect programs as their effects become visible. [The government listens.] This contrasts with the usual process of legislation where policy tends to be, if not after-the-fact and sold to the legislature by interest groups, at most a struck bargain "balancing" the wares they offer.

Except for sporadic charismatic leadership, the representative system seems to be for the most part limited to followership, trailing the electorate. In contrast, the potential in administrative planning, due to its devotion to the new free speech, is a conservative leadership of programs on trial.

Administrative planning does not imply, as does the old free speech theory and the legislative system organized under continual pressure to reflect home constituency climate, that the masses (public opinion) must be convinced before a change can be made. It must be admitted that representative bodies can and do sometimes rise to statesman-like performance. The legislative penchant, however, is to invite the neighbors in whether or not they have a viewpoint or a relevant background of information. From the view of administrative democracy this appears to be a display of invidious "politics"—either bringing in the irrelevant or playing on the infirmities of society. Administrative democracy accepts the value in the selective apathy of differing publics. Because it seeks to rely on objectively validated truth instead of opinion, it will expect and institute change in an experimental setting. If the plan is properly and experimentally drawn under the aegis of genuine participation in scientific mediation, it will carry its own persuasiveness through many twists of vicarious participation, so that extraneous tricks of sales or "politics" will not be needed. Vicarious participation should be planned into the plan.

Planning is not foresight,[9] and no extension or elaboration of computer analysis will ever make it so. The job of the planner is to make the good possible.[10] It is a process of facilitating wiser policies. There is more to planning than expert and "objective" analysis of the needs and desires of the people, followed by construction of programs for their gratification. Any such system would be scarcely distinguishable from benevolent despotism. Planning deals, not with predictions, but with intentions and the tapping of relevant knowing. Whether it is city planning, regional planning, national planning, social planning, or a more restricted planning effort to do with, for example, crime, curriculum, site, health, house, highway, or budget, when it is not arbitrarily reduced to a rote of analysis and gratification, planning is an endeavor to integrate purposes so that the good can be made possible. What is a land use map but a map of purposes, an intention chart? What is a zoning map but a control-of-purpose map? A comprehensive development plan is nothing less than a packaging of community purposes. (If it is anything less, it is nothing.) A budget is a master plan, a deliberate organizing of purposes —if it doesn't just happen. In passing, the direct aesthetic components in the maps and packages just mentioned are worth noting for the hint they give of possible eventual replacement of mathematical with aesthetic models in planning.

A plan once set upon represents intention. It is a true *re* presentation —presenting representative government at its best—in which purposes, instead of merely being reflected, pass through process, are objectified, validated, recreated, and put forth in new social form of politically created public intent. The intention represented in plan is in turn the prime tool of purposive transformation[11]—a strategic part of social control. John M. Gaus once asked,

> Are there emerging, in the "planning" activity developed in the factory or the unit of government, controls of operation based not on the ordinary type of coercive direction but upon the use of organized knowledge—budget estimates and analyses, personnel classifications, land-use maps—that enable us to achieve agreed solutions without the frustrations that come from "domination" or "compromise"? [12]

The answer is "Yes." The product of planning activities is just such an instrument of fluid control. The plan becomes the essential instrument in the amalgamation, the creation of what is good out of abounding situations of moral conflict. It is an essentially creative instrument, and from it can derive renewed institutions, institutions with renewed intention.[13]

The planner—that is, the person (any person) trying to forward planning transactions—must always bear in mind that those people who are indirectly and undramatically involved will remain apathetic until the relation of the plan to their Selves has become perceptible to them. And even then they will not be drawn into the processes of direct participation either if they find the plan to be working to their larger satisfaction or if they find their conservative drag to have been undermined or obviated through vicarious participation. The planner is therefore responsible to "represent" them through his devotion to the general interest,[14] and must not treat too weightily the militant few who have failed to mature[15] and who remain obtuse to opportunities of genuine participation. One of a number of efforts at such re-presentation was the Twin Cities Metropolitan Planning Commission use of some four hundred citizens and officials in intensive inquiry, first displaying alternatives and implications to them and then soliciting evaluation. But again it is the planner's homonomous responsibility that carries off such procedure and permits it to sustain a quality of representation.

The plan is the thing to catch up the consciences of those involved into an homonomous responsibility—in self-improving method—to test the creative possibilities it outlines—eventually to culminate in right by agreement, the creative bargain. If the plan is to work, it must contain an inner plan to involve the people affected in retraining and to accustom them to the idea of endless retraining. New wisdom, know-how, skill inevitably disturb old habits. A true plan must contain within it the seeds, the potential of its own demise. City planners have, for example, learned that renewal projects cannot be completely pre-planned. Many of the problems involved do not come to light until specific proposals are advanced.[16] Administrative planning is a transaction that preserves and promotes what has long been considered a basic characteristic of democracy, and science)—continuous peaceful and controlled change.[17]

PERPETUAL REORGANIZATION

Administrative reorganization, like revolution, is usually subverted in the end as things now go. Change decreed from above, stemming from turnover of appointed "political" chiefs, tends to sustain the character of a coup. In many instances even the usefulness of time and motion studies has hit premature limits for being involved in display of manipulation from outside the bounds of organization. Instead of coming from above by fiat, cost control, for example, should be shared between a centralized agency and line divisions. A central office for organization and reorganization planning may be a very useful device for focusing attention on a vital continuing responsibility, but, unless the responsibility is permitted to become participative, homonomous, very little but friction will come of it.

Institutional conservatism is a sort of occupational hazard to administrative personnel.[18] In addition to personal habits brought from home to the administrative scene, the institutional habits found in workways, red tape, routine, efficiency, stability, and informal organization[19] can be counted among the embodiments of conservative drag that must be taken into account in any attempts at reorganization.[20] Habits are seldom abolished or redirected by directive from authority, or even from autonomous conscience. They are rather displaced by the intentional development of substitute and compensatory habits through a participative process. Eduard C. Lindeman says that "in a Democratic state the law must be continuously revised in the light of experience. The only sure method of diminishing corruption in a Democracy is to modify the rules, just as this is the only process by which sports and games are freed from cheating." [21] It is through planning transactions that participation becomes a way of changing rules to be effective against corruption, "bureaucratic" tendencies, and institutional habits.

Alex Bavelas' demonstrations indicate heavy involvement of personality in reluctance to change. Using the dominoe-telephone set-up described above[22] and permitting an incomplete back-and-forth communication, the man giving instructions being permitted to answer questions but only with a "yes" or a "no," Bavelas found that the blame for difficulties was laid on the other man, not on the system. This reveals a contemporary cultural, if not a basic human, bias: it is easier to blame the other man than to doubt the system. This would seem to indicate that, at least for now, the effective approach to reformation of system is through character, through personality—probably most appropriately with reliance on personal leadership.

Reorganization must be built into administration as intimately as revolution has been built into legislative democracy—not by an expert from out of town in the case of administration any more than by infiltration of foreign agents in the case of legislative democracy. The imperative behind the building-in of reorganization lies in the fact that administrative reorganization today is no longer a mere intramural affair, but also an integral part, and ideally a leading part, of the adjustment of society as it develops solutions to its problems and conflicts. As Lyndall Urwick says,

> this job . . . of studying management . . . is the key to the evolution of an adaptive society. We can't rely any longer on having lots of time for people to accustom themselves to new conditions gradually and slowly. We get more technical changes in one generation today than happened in a couple of centuries two or three hundred years ago. And technical change postulates social and organizational change.[23]

The world now welcomes change though there remains, as one of the stubborn drags on deliberately systematic and continuing reorganization, the reluctance of the conservatism of progress[24] which, suspicious of the intentionality of planning, champions change only so long as it is chance arrived.

The comparative effectiveness so often noted as characteristic of newly created administrative organizations is not due so much to the special morale *per se* attaching to novel situations as to the fact that organization has not yet fallen into established patterns of function reinforced by habitual institutional workways. It is still "fumbling"—meaning that each individual's larger Self (rather than only that portion of him that accrues to a particular function) is still engaged in active concern. This virtue of newly created organization may be regularized by the pattern for perpetual reorganization that is already at hand in scientific mediation. It can even become habitual itself. Particular institutional arrangements embodying the pattern can be expected to grow out of today's elementary planning efforts. Experience already indicates two such potential-laden arrangements: (1) continuous and determined effort to keep personnel moving from position to position within the organization,[25] (2) avoidance of over specialization, by placing the generalist function as low in the hierarchy as possible.[26]

LEADERSHIP WITHOUT AUTHORITY

When planning is brought in from left field, it is found to be the central concern of leadership. If there is any one function in administration more vitally involved than any other in perpetual reorganization, it is leadership. A leader's skill in handling change is the cardinal measure of his performance.

Countless studies of leadership have been made in attempts to define what this elusive thing is. They range from historical reconstructions (attributing, for example, Ikhnaton's greatness to epilepsy for which there is osteological evidence) to biography, novels, and the latest "scientific" (based on questionnaires and statistical analyses of frequency curves) or observational exercises of the sociologists. Any number of lists of leadership qualities have been proposed. Esteem for the usual processes of social perception has fallen so low that psychological tests based on the mounting empirical evidence have been devised and even applied in screening applicants for positions of industrial leadership.

Codification of leadership traits is now understood to be largely a waste of time.[27] Leadership varies from situation to situation, from time to time. The transaction, not the human organism, is the defining context.[28] And it is to be doubted that any purely empiricist (non-normative-non-experimental) approach will carry very far. At any rate, study of what a leader is or has been will never provide the final answer to what he should be. Leadership is always a moral adventure. And its salient phase lies in directing the way out of social conflict.

It is particularly to be noted that the great bulk of mounded information about leaders and leadership derives from gross observations of operations and procedures which are characterized by sacrifice, coercion, or compromise under the auspices of authority or autonomous conscience. And the qualities counted and honored tend, correspondingly, to be the virtues of the atomic individual.

Indecisiveness is very probably the most noticed failing of traditional democratic regimes. And it is not minimized by the correlative failings of the decisiveness of authoritarian regimes. It is a sort of Achilles heel, the product of incomplete ablution in the brine of leadership. Displace authority with a freely speaking but unlistened-to assemblage devoted to a freedom of speech that finds truth in tabulation of autonomous opinions, and the growth of leadership is automatically and institutionally discouraged—except, that is, for the leadership of demagoguery and charisma in their many subtle forms. This has been the fate of leadership in legislative assemblies. Accordingly, as social problems become complex and the need for leadership becomes imperative, the United States turns to the President and the administrative branch for leadership while Britain looks to the Prime Minister and his Cabinet and France raises a Man on Horseback. When leadership occurs in American cities, it appears in the form of a strong mayor, a city manager, or the head of an administrative department.

For the most part, the leadership of executive or administrative officers has tended to be a leadership of authority, or, more properly speaking, a leadership that pretends to authoritative auspices not always credited by autonomous consciences occupying the lower levels of hierarchy. Remove the authority, as is done with increasing frequency by the turn of events, and what is left is a nominal leadership of pathetic individuals shoring up their positions with pose—with "executive stance" [29]—and carrying it off with varying degrees of bravura. The extent to which status is thought to be the *sine qua non* of administrative leadership is almost measurable in the readiness with which neophytes assume an "executive stance." The extent to which it is in fact fictitious is discernible in the felt falseness of the stance itself. Other dimensions of stature (especially those attaching to expertise and professionalism—the "powerful" secretary of the boss or "the genius" of advertising and television), however, are genuine enough in deferences accorded. The extent to which status and stance are encumbrances upon human achievement will never be measured. The toll of their quiet tyranny is in the untold losses of stifled speech. There is a silent circular process from ignorance to stance to intensified ignorance.

Both the leadership that pays homage to "authority" of function and the leadership that defers to "authority" of the situation are to be preferred to that customarily venerating personal status. In any case, the qualities of a good leader will depend on the transactional situation in which he is involved. If it is a situation of conflict, they will be those that lead to successful resolution. The good leader, like the good man is the one who knows the appropriate means to his good ends and the appropriate means for determining upon his good ends. Function and situation are "authoritative" in only a restricted sense. They are purveyors of opportunities and limitations which it is incumbent upon the leader to make the most of. But they are also fractional, function cross-secting the Self, and situation looping off minute segments of time and history. They comprise only aspects of the leader's larger homonomous responsibility—responsible leadership without authority.

The task of directing the way out of social conflict in allegiance to homonomous responsibility, places a high premium on the talents of the leader. He must first insist upon the new freedom for speech that places truth in context of process. From being a master at know-how he must grow to fit the demanding and Self-expanding vocation of master at know-*ing*, with all that entails in terms of the new free speech. Ultimately he must structure direct participation into collective free speech habits counterpart to legislative rules of debate; he must stabilize procedures of mutual Self control in pursuit of truth, complete with terminus in collective test.

In addition, he must be on the lookout for ways to give responsibility —not just tasks—to others, ways to share responsibility without authority; for it is the nature of homonomous responsibility that it must be collectively nurtured within process.

Ordway Tead's definition of leadership as "the activity of influencing people to cooperate toward some goal which they come to find desirable" [30] is excellent, provided it is not assumed that cooperation excludes conflict, or that the goal was there before the activity was undertaken. Organization is not, as it is frequently described, an arrangement for accomplishing a purpose, except in the very general sense that the purpose of the Post Office, for example, is to transmit the mails. If the leader succeeds in bringing people together to resolve conflicts through the method of scientific mediation, he is the prime mover in the search for improved moral knowings, and new purposes are the product.

It is hard to overemphasize the importance of leadership in creating purpose. He who succeeds in opening new vistas, new perceptions in art, science, philosophy, or administration (politics) is a leader, irrespective of his position in hierarchy. The leader with vision is always the condition of survival, as he was way back when the skills of primitive vigilance preserved the fit. New perception works two ways, in immediate solution of problems, and in bringing new insight into one's Self, leading to new dimensions of Self-expectation[31] and, in turn, to growth in leadership.[32]

But, in final analysis, the political leader's objective is to develop power—functional power.[33] This power, in turn, is made up of the wants, interests, purposes of individuals and is achieved through the knowings of Self-control.[34] It must be clearly distinguished from the push-pull power of Lockean vintage as being the product of what we have called "genuine" participation—the power that springs from the consolidation of intentions into a social plan (for example, a budget or a development plan) and from the correlative rejuvenation of organization.

An extremely important function of leadership is to resist the temptation to final statement. There is seldom, if ever, a place where experience, whether individual or institutional, rounds out with a full stop. Final statement may be a particular vice of the mentality of authority, but it is also an indication of ineptitude. As Follett says of the production manager, the chief test is whether his policy is a contributable one.[35] Beyond the immediate present lies an immense future that should be approached with contributable statements, statements composed of ideas that are so couched as to be perfectible. Thus, while final statement in itself limits the productivity of the larger present by blocking freedom of speech, failure to produce perfectible ideas shackles the future by rendering impossible the development of a moral science.[36] The leader has an homonomous responsibility to eschew vague or untestable generality and to put handles on his statements so they may be grasped by others for social test.

In addition, the leader will find that his (functional) power grows in proportion as he is able to direct dissidents, not into cooperation, but into active and productive criticism, while at the same time preventing a communication barrier from being erected between the majority and the minority. As Lindeman suggests on the basis of his work with group processes, "the minority ought expressly to be used in scrutinizing every step of the experiment, setting forth criteria, testing, criticizing. And when this happens the minority gradually disappears. After a time the group finds itself capable of arriving at the experimental stage without ever having to take a vote." [37] Each such happening is an illustration of the true creativity of criticism.[38]

LEADERSHIP OF CHARACTER

After shepherding the planning process down the way of scientific mediation, the leader-executive will, until the point of utopia is reached, find himself faced with choices that cannot await the outcome of participative methods. If he is responsible he will have held out as long as possible against the temptation to make a simple choice between existing imperfect options, preferring to give full play to the possibility of creating a better way out. However, the press of the world will still be on him. Nevertheless, the fact that decisions must be made when and as necessary, irrespective of the degree of completeness of plans, need not be taken as evidence of inherent difference between "practical" and scientific approaches, between men of power and men of knowledge.[39] Decisions of leadership in supplement to or in lieu of plans are in the nature of extemporizations filling in for the immaturity of moral science.

To the extent, however, that planning is given precedence in organizational honors and organization is seen as a device for purpose-making before it is a machine for decision-making, the executive has behind him a reserve from which to draw in facing any of his decisions.[40] Purposes are prior to decisions. Unless purposes are reliable decisions are not. Out of the understanding and the feeling he has gotten from his own direct, purposeful and responsible participation in the planning process the executive derives a background sensitivity to situation, to function, and, especially, to intention (step one of creative bargaining)[41] that promotes the success of decisions forced on him before the planning process has approached comprehensiveness. Internalization of these sensitivities into value orientations of the proprium (step two of creative bargaining)[42] provides the administrator with schemata within which specific decisions can be made with relative ease and assurance.[43]

Assurance derives from the fact of acceptance by those who broadly feel or understand, as a result of their own participation, the general lines of homonomous responsibility within which decisions are being made. *Here* is prime material of what may be called personal leadership,[44] the integrated leadership of character.

In personal leadership through planning activities is the germ of the final victory of character over the Cartesian "common sense" personality split between fact-finding and value-judgment, between research and morality, currently common in administrative organization. Democratic administration may thereupon come into its own, relieved of the formalities of the past. As time goes on and experience piles up, as there is an accumulation of experimental product from scientific mediation, the leadership of character will become ever more assured. With each new elegant solution to a moral problem the leadership job of the executive will be eased. An elegant solution, a created bargain vicariously promulgated, becomes a possession of the race. It is an idea-artifact, a skill distillate from human experience. And it serves the usual refined function of instruments of control, permitting the less skilled (in that particular area) to assume the control normally belonging with know-how but now built into the instruments. Like the dam, the atomic pile, and the commercial fertilizer, moral instruments as skill-distillates deliver control into the hands of relatively uninstructed individuals.

THE ROUTINE PART OF LEADERSHIP

In addition to the primary job of creative purpose-making, the leader is faced with more or less pressing decisions. The primary job leads to decisions that should be made as slowly as the process of creative bargaining and scientific mediation requires. The second relates to decisions that may have to be made without full pause for participation. There is a third category. Besides decisions that should wait and those that cannot wait are those, constituting far the greater number, that need not wait. An important part of leadership is involved in the job of directing routine.

In an administrative organization, problems that do not need the leader's unique perspective should not, as a rule, be allowed to claim his attention. (Except, that is, as he is seeking them out for purposes of fuller understanding or control.) This rule of thumb can be used to provide another slant on administrative routine—as it looks from above, from each position looking down. Routine, from the leader's vantage, amounts to arranging for someone else to make the decisions that do not need the leader's unique perspective.

Some of routine leadership involves the re-presentation of achieved integration. The leader must be an expert in imparting what has been called "vicarious participation," in directing information into education. Conservative drag is obviated by elegant solutions only through an educational process. Plans are efficiently put into effect only when orders are seen not to do violence to demands for participation. Leadership is responsible to demonstrate to those involved that "orders" are compatible with and progressive within the lines of homonomous responsibility. Executive decisions must follow in implementation of plans as so far wrought. They, nevertheless, remain, in the larger sense, within the bounds of the planning process because, however imperceptibly, they modify it in a progression of continual evolution, as a general rule.

A plan is never finished. There should be continuous back and forth relay between vicarious participation and direct participation. The talent of leadership is to couch orders in the use of responsible ideas so that, when and as needed, processes of direct participation can be reactivated in the cause of social test or in the achievement of new levels of integration. It is the reliability of administration with a vital planning program that its leadership enables relief—as the leadership of authority cannot—from total and continual direct participation.

Accumulations of vicarious experience can, in addition to furnishing assurance for the leadership of character, become nuclei around which routine accumulates. Routine in this sense is correlative to habit, a structured substitute for purpose. Habit, for example, pinch hits for the purpose that raises hand to mouth in eating or puts foot in front of foot in walking. Routine is an analogous sort of administrative habit, institutionalizing purpose. As anyone who has had to relearn to walk will testify, knowing-how on some level (rational, kinesthetic, muscular) is a necessary forerunner to habit. Democratic administration and its democratic leader must insist upon a conscious level of knowing-how and a self-corrective basis to the nodes about which routine settles.

THE ENGAGING OF EXPERTISE

As traditionally viewed, the function of expertise also is routine. The leader and the expert are sorted into two diverse categories and an impressive story is told to the effect that the expert should be "on tap but not on top." And for the most part this maxim has been justifiable. The expert has been a store of knowledge—a human filing cabinet. In many cases his chief value has been in saving time, computer-like, by having information arranged and at hand.

The expert has been relegated to the position of mere fact-gatherer also in part because of the accentuation of vision differences that come with specialization. Much has been said about the recent political naiveté of the atomic scientists—their innocence in the face of human intentions. But this is not unusual. It is the sort of fault inherent in all specialization. It is why there is a basic good sense in the tradition that puts the specializing expert "on tap." A scientific élite would be no better than a military or any other élite; it would be no less self-deceived. As a matter of fact, it is possible for whole administrative agencies to be afflicted with the bias that attaches to specialization. As Harold C. Havighurst points out,

> The specialized knowledge acquired by the members of an agency who are constantly studying the problems arising within a narrow jurisdictional area, sharpens the *perception* of public need. The formulation of objectives and programs gives rise to a zeal for accomplishment which tends to dim the merit of the objections raised by the individuals affected.[45]

Here is a continual threat to the democratic potential in administration. The individuals affected—the material, subject-matter, citizen scientists (championed in chapter 5)—are vitally important and must not be left out. Programs must be rounded out with broad brush strokes of human intention, the latter taking precedence in government over special expertise or the narrow intentions embedded in it.

The position of the expert as somebody apart, not to be trusted in things political, can, however, be corrected—by developing the understanding that everyone is a specialist. The expert is only more so. This gives proportionate position to the subject-mater scientist and promises the possibility of integrative union of points of view.

Traditional theory of administrative organization is biased in behalf of the expert.[46] It emphasizes division of labor, unitary supervision (that is, only one boss for each man), separation of special staff services, coordination on functional basis (that is, each supervisor coordinating a small group of individuals doing the same thing). The product tends to illustrate the self-fulfillment of theory. So far as theory has effect it encourages, through each one of these devices, the perpetuation of thought, habit, and attitude favoring the separatism of special expertise, and discourages the growth of generalists and the generalist point of view. Under the influence of this thinking and these administrative devices, the specialist is more likely to be rewarded in his early years while the generalist has no place in which to make a start. The generalist tends to be eliminated before he begins, or the man with generalist potential and penchant is made cynical, if he is not converted by the preponderance of organizational pattern. It would appear that one of the important challenges to leadership is to revise organization structure so as to provide support for theory of scientific mediation, and in the process question the validity of each one of the practical maxims around which work-ways are structured.

Follett has said that the role of the expert is not knowledge of speciality but insight into the relation of a specialty to the whole.[47] When this sort of insight arrives—probably art-aided—the division between expert and leader *begins* to disappear. The expert should indeed not be "on top," just as the leader or the generalist should not be "on top." On the other hand, neither should he be simply "on tap" as if he were only a reservoir of knowledge.

To be sure, knowledge can be tapped. But knowing cannot—it must rather be "engaged." To the extent that the expert becomes involved in scientific mediation and his specialty leads him from simple intention studies (e.g., origin-destination studies, land use projections, time and motion studies, space and location analyses) to fact changing and interest integrating (through seeing and feeling the position of other people, incorporating it as his own, and then creating a new position by integrating the conflicting views), to that extent he becomes a generalist. The remoteness of the standard consultant arrangement is what is to be avoided.[48] It is through intimate relating of the expert within administration—in leadership *and* in routine—that truce is arranged between knowledge and power[49] and the unity of knowing and doing called "functional power" is achieved.

AVOIDING UNPRODUCTIVE CONFLICT

Another part of the routine to which the executive, who in this may be the leader, must attend may be described as the eliminating or avoiding of unimportant or insignificant conflict. This involves many things and many talents. It involves, for example, parcelling out work, dividing up labor so that things that can be handled separately do not get in each other's way; establishing unity of command so that where things are interdependent they can be considered together; planning organization so that independent parts will not be so small as to cause artificial conflicts (as has happened in multi-jurisdictional metropolitan areas); seeing that speech is free so that repressed minor differences will not pile up to erupt later in exaggerated form; setting up procedures so that the public or clientele and the personnel may receive expected, efficient, and equal treatment. Perhaps most important, however, it involves the task of putting across to the personnel of the organization a perspective that is broad enough to induce them to be concerned with their Selves instead of their selves—so that they themSelves may be able to cope with the more private conflicts that arise and may become prepared to participate more creatively in the more public ones.

Most people are capable enough, in the limited terms of physical and mental ability, to do the job for which they were hired. Conversely, very few hold their jobs on the basis of ability alone. More often than not difficulties arise from personal (moral) differences. The great majority of dismissals are due to incompatibility, to personality conflict or "maladjustment." True, there are personality types to be avoided, people who because of immaturity or grating characteristics should quite simply be placed in jobs well removed from interpersonal contact. And there are characteristics, such as desire to be responsive or efficient, that are to be sought in administrative personnel. It does not seem, however, that the clash of personalities and the resultant organizational disruption can be very adequately handled or avoided through careful personnel selection. It remains somewhat doubtful that extensive screening of recruits is either very possible or particularly advisable. With one person out of six in the civilian labor force employed by government, it is hard to expect government personnel to vary greatly from a cross section of the American people. Involved also is the wisdom of excluding at the outset the individual who is "unadjusted." Private industry cannot be expected, except in occasional instances, to accept this broader responsibility for humanity because, from the narrow partial perspective of product orientation, it is more economical to pick the right man for the job than to motivate and train a likely prospect and face possibilities of organizational disruption.[50]

The not too distant future will see a retirement of misfits in capitalist work-ethic America—before Communism anywhere achieves its "from each according to his ability." When population is brought under control and productive capacity is relieved of the need to meet expanding markets, attention will turn to planning for leisure and reducing work loads and work weeks. As a part of the effort at improving the work situation, it will be found convenient, after the most enlightened rehabilitation efforts have failed, to pension the misfit and immature rather than endure their ravages on orderly organization. This will happen as a relatively painless extension of the poverty program or its successor. It will have the important and valuable corollary virtue of permitting diehard individualists and dedicated artists and thinkers to "retire" on subsistence level allotment—giving society tremendous return, the return of a leisure class, a double return because the small investment is first paid for by the benefit of clearing the work-way of awkward obstacles.

In the meantime, personnel systems should be putting positive emphasis on the kind of a role that various jobs demand be played—rather than on matching personality type to work type.[51] This, again, is the transactional approach. Personality changes in changed situation and a man's probable behavior in a new position is apparently better gauged by observing present personnel playing the role that goes with the job situation than by studying personality traits.

As utopia approaches and there is less work per person to be done, there will be freer mobility in and out of jobs. (Society should never again get trapped in the inhuman failure of chance-"controlled" organization that makes some people do all the work while others remain unusefully unemployed.) Civil service regulations, which originally began as antidotes to political patronage and have since tended toward featherbedding protectionism, will develop a welcome fluidity. When survival is guaranteed, union protectionism will follow out the trend already begun —converting from protection of individuals to protection of a situation, a category, a pattern in the organization of society, and pointing toward a new sectionalism or political pluralism. The leadership of Character in personnel planning will then become possible—homonomous chief executive responsibility for personnel administration independent of both independent civil service commission and partisan political influence.[52]

It is undoubtedly true that "the real job is always done by two fellows who call each other by their Christian names and trust each other. To interfere with this process just to get the record right is to put the cart before the horse." [53] The executive's organization chart can be destructive when taken too seriously. It must sometimes be judiciously disregarded in the interest of avoiding the precipitation of unproductive conflict.

On the other hand, the leader cannot assume a strict "hands off" policy with regard to the informal organization that crisscrosses his chart. He must assume, as part of his devotion to freedom of speech, the job of protecting the individual, the non-conformist, when workways degenerate to group methods of exacting "adjustment." Though there are, obviously, motives that cannot be tolerated, the leader does not want a "properly motivated" crew—even if it were scientifically possible to recruit one. The motivation he chiefly needs of others, or needs to inspire in others, is an homonomous responsibility.

Wages are artificial in the same sense as are other financial institutions and technological achievements: they are man-made arrangements. They are social means of coercion, or control, as the case may be. So long as technological innovations continue to be introduced by the unprocessed push of the radical bent, at the private or semi-private decision of auton-

omous (even conscientious) individuals or groups, so long as the technological forces let loose in society remain uncontrolled, wages will
continue to be felt, however dully, to be bribes (perhaps disguised as
rewards or as signs of status) for the circumvention of conservative
drag, devices of social coercion rather than control. At the back of the
minds of employees and employers—private or governmental—remains
the awareness that neither group has been able to devise protection
against the uncontrolled forces astride in the world.[54] The sense of
bribery will remain until a guaranteed living frees the work situation
from the coercion of obeisance to survival.

Administrative leadership in the realms of personnel management
must accordingly recognize that work today is seldom completely voluntary, and must eschew the hope of organizing "morale" to attain the
purity of identification with organization. No matter what energy is
pumped into public relations or what "science" is brought to selection
in recruiting,[55] a full measure of free, uninhibited commitment will not
flourish so long as wages are felt, even remotely, to be coercive. The
public administrator steps out of his proper leadership role into the
businessman's role of salesmanship every time he turns to problems of
morale under these imperfect conditions—as unfortunately he nevertheless frequently must. Under the American economic system this distinction between salesman and leader cannot be avoided. Whereas the public
administrator *can* be free to commit himself to the public interest, the
private administrator has been constrained (under the established rules
of the economic game) to pursue, as a goal of his daily employment, the
profit or interest of a private group or of his own self. Following Galbraith's analysis, it appears, however, that the rules of the economic game
are being bent, in the large corporations, by a controlling "technostructure" more intent upon technical and professional performance and
achievement, and the approval of its peer groups, than upon stockholder
profits.[56] Thus, in a part of the private sector there seems to be room for
the growth of a broader (if not a public) interest, and of a corresponding
leadership—though stockholder profit remains an ultimate consideration.
To the exent that the administrator must justify coercive institutions, he must turn from techniques of free speech to those of publicity.
But to the extent that men are free he will never succeed and the lingering sense of involuntary service will remain. Wholehearted commitment to organization may never be possible in any case because of the
partial character of organizations, the division of labor itself—because
organization nowhere engages the whole of a man.

The fact that man is a creature of society, a product of group development, does not imply sanctity of any special grassroots or shirt-

sleeve group relationship. Tampering with association is a part of group functioning itself—whether rising from invisible interpersonal springs of group behavior or from the radical bent of member or leader. As a matter of fact, horizons have so expanded and social perceptions so sharpened that for many purposes the group is as wide as the population. Loyalties to work groups, professions, churches, economic classes— even families—are notably fluid. For example, a labor union is thought of by its members more as an agency to help them than as something of which they are a part[57]—a perception quite at variance with popular stereotype.

Reluctance to reach down through the crust of group relationships to deal directly with character and intention tends to perpetuate power relationships and prevent the continuing adaptation that assures the functionalizing of power. An understanding of this has been implicit in American federalism with its insistence that government rest on people instead of on states. The real focus of control must be at the point where intentions are raw. Correspondingly, an important administrative organizing principle is to keep decision as close to intention as possible. While informal organization must be tenderly treated, it must also be carefully led, reaching through to its "voting" members to guide the whole group on to homonomous responsibility. The source of functional power the administrator wishes to tap is not far beneath the sheath of group loyalties. While social habits (workways, efficiencies, etc.) are embodiments of intention, purpose, the processes of change must always reach through them to the ingredients of power—individual values, wants, aims, feelings, ideals, purposes. . . . All of which is simply to say that one of the most important tasks of the administrator is to help employees be flexible enough to see the need for change and to follow through with necessary actions.[58]

Personnel leadership devising to avoid insignificant conflict will seek to transform personnel policy into personnel planning. As this is done through the elimination of status and the promotion of the new free speech, "adjustment" will give way to integration (except where pathological or immature behavior is involved); the organization chart will bend to permit particular jobs to grow and regroup in relation to character growth and transactional transformation of workways;[59] emphasis will shift from technique and patterns of hierarchy to character and behavior; and the "right" to hire and fire will become an aspect of homonomous responsibility, a control element of operative personnel planning. In place of the dubious science in recruitment screening through psychological testing for character qualifications, will be a mediatory method that can scientifically investigate intentions through the resolving of problems and the creating of purposes. A positive emphasis on *making* the good will displace the negative approach of avoiding what is known or thought to be bad or of recruiting the ready-made good. Personnel planning will become essentially a participative process of Self-selecting and of Self-relating *in work*. (Incidentally, involving related treating of the many relevant elements now so frequently handled separately: job evaluation, abilities of employees, work conditions, possibilities for advancement, prevailing wages, production costs, cost of living . . .)

Twentieth century elaboration of the role of government in technological societies has highlighted the special problem of creative personnel. The need for creativity is increasingly recognized, especially in scientific, moon-shooting areas, but also in other activities as well—even in local government. Along with recognition has come a modicum of overdue respect. Recognition has followed in no small part from the turmoil stirred up within administration by creative personnel—perhaps in greater part than it has come from the need of organization for the service of creativity. And so there has been a tendency to treat the problem of creative personnel as a problem of disruptive influence. It is defined as one of "managing" creative personnel in order to reconcile the revolutionary with stable society. In the context of creative bargaining, however, the problem becomes one of *leading* creative personnel. It becomes normal rather than special—a part of perpetual revolution. The simple change in perspective will ease the situation and immediately permit creative release as conservative drag—which is not at all stability —is integrated with the radical bent in a conservative institution.

Leadership itself should come under the purview and review of personnel planning. There is an important distinction between groups the members of which choose a leader to help formulate and further their purposes, and groups whose members are hired along with the leader. But the personnel situation in democratic administration encompasses both of these categories. Except in a very formal sense, the personnel chart of democratic administration is open-ended, merging into the broad base of the population, and the leader is chosen neither by votes nor by outside appointment but by a method embodied in a plan to the improvement of which his responsibility is pledged.[60]

The leader is *representative* of the people through the plan. It is through the plan that administration opens out to rope relevant publics into direct participation in first instance, and subsequently projects out to involve broader populations in vicarious participation. In a very real way leadership thus opens out to guide both the citizen and his elected "representatives." In the contemporary world the leader must tread a mighty careful course, the tight rope of one who would be a political leader without becoming a partisan, preparing a political program for a governor or a city council without becoming identified with any of the invidious and sometimes despised senses of "politics," without being committed to particular programs in such a way as to be exposed to partisan abuse.[61] Statesman is the name sometimes given this pure stature when sometimes attained. Through skilled leadership of character in reliance on the whole-human operation of the planning process, the leadership that had been missing in the over-rationalist theories of legislative democracy[62] is supplied in the quiet and rounded way of administrative democracy.

SUMMARY

While personnel planning may be routine in inception, concerned to smooth the way by unobtrusively resolving some of the less socially significant conflicts, it very soon spills over into other sorts of planning as well—for example, budget planning, interdepartmental coordination. Indeed, it is a very organic part of the whole of whatever can be called "comprehensive planning." Its involvement with wages, its concern for leadership, and its opening out onto the population, these three factors in themselves are enough to proclaim its broader orientation. It affects and reflects the culture of the entire population. The routine of personnel is thus a preliminary to the planning of social control and to the creation of the public interest, the public intending.[63]

The routine procedures which leadership is called upon to bring to order, to compose into ordered relationships, and particularly the habits, institutional and personal, created in personnel planning, are the *sine qua non* of scientific mediation. The success of leadership in matters of routine is in insuring the public interest by establishing a stable basis from which scientific mediation may set forth as a matter of course— almost as a routine procedure itself. Only from the groundwork of Self control, of character development in open-ended planning and open-ended institutions, can leadership derive the functional power to inaugurate effective measures in the direction of strategic social control.

The leader's charge is to become Character, to bring responsibility back into the governmental process—homonomous, intentional, mature responsibility for the control of human conduct. Through perfecting the skills of the new freedom of speech, placing truth in the context of process, he will arrive at a new level. He will be able to begin taking full leverage off the freedom of speech fulcrum in quest of a new governing that means control.

Cloture

CHAPTER EIGHTEEN

The Politics of Truth

> . . . *the people, indeed they are entitled*
> *to order in the state, but man is*
> *entitled to truth; it is this that he*
> *serves by his piety, and when he shall*
> *achieve perception then the new kingdom*
> *will be created, the kingdom within*
> *the law of perception, the kingdom*
> *graced by its power to ensure creation.*
>
> HERMANN BROCH,
> *The Death of Virgil.*

BY THE VERY NATURE OF WHAT IT DEALS WITH, THIS BOOK cannot come to an end. Neither summary nor conclusion is possible. Nevertheless, a stop must be put to it for practical reasons. So, in grinding to a halt we are constrained to a final effort to relieve the open end with a generous portion of clarity, following out the aim a number of times piously announced: the relentless responsibility of being objective, of exerting maximum effort to the end that men understand one another. The broad implications of the politics of truth for the general patterns of government still need attention; and a rapid recapitulation may serve, at the peril of oversimplification, a useful job of selective emphasis.

SOCIAL CONTROL AND "COMPREHENSIVE" PLANNING

Personnel planning, organization planning, production planning, financial planning, even "public relations" planning—all these and many others are interrelated and interdependent. Their comprehensive coordination is the final achievement, the utopian achievement of the political science of public administration. Obviously there must be nothing autonomous about staff or auxiliary functions and services. They must be integrated into the "comprehensive" planning process. In particular the broadened perspective of the staff official, as against the narrowed outlook of the operating or line official, should be exploited to the fullest—at the same time that the detailed experience of the operating official, as against the lack of acquaintance with operating problems on the part of the staff official, is likewise exploited.

Administrative operations should not be structured, as is sometimes suggested, so as to reflect the values and the facts of society as they enter into the formulation of policy alternatives. Rather should leadership attempt to structure organization so that the diverse habits of line and staff and the diverse facts and values of society may rub elbows and strike sparks of creative conflict. The public interest is effectively insured by procedure only when procedure is busy making and remaking the public interest out of the teeming problems of transactional situations, making it over into public intending.

The sparks struck in the important area of creative bargaining between line and staff may be the very ones that will set off the chain reaction of a moral science. Strategically located staff officials may, because of their broad perspectives, succeed in becoming the first "pure" scientists of scientific mediation.[1] A weather eye should perhaps be kept on the convener in the Bureau of the Budget,[2] the national mediators in the National Mediation Service, the Regional Coordinators of the Department of the Interior, or even the international civil servants of UNESCO, parole and probation officers, medical social workers. . . . Wherever expert mediation has command of facts and the skill to sort out what is real perception from what is stereotype, inherited illusion and elaborated fancy, and thus succeeds in disintegrating partisanship—there is where the promise of a science of mediation is brightest.

Paul H. Appleby has said:

> There must be in [the departmental] level something that can't be so simply and definitely organized, something that must function on a reciprocal, intuitive basis, reflecting department-wide acquaintance on the part of successively smaller groups reaching up to the secretarial apex. . . . [The] process of coordination and integration is not one that can be readily described, but must be in considerable degree something that grows. It is for the lack of such growth that governments resort to arbitrary methods and to fragmentizing the jobs into specialized responsibilities that create stresses requiring subsequent managerial revolutions.[3]

On the other hand, Charles E. Merriam points out that "congestion and overcentralization are among the very gravest diseases of the body politic, and judgment and foresight are indispensable if they are to be averted."[4] From combining these two contrasting statements emerges the thought that as coordination grows it must develop within itself the seeds of decentralization. This growth need, however, not be so "organic," so animal-like, so much a matter of blood and bones that it must remain indescribable. Some deliberate, thinking, judicious leadership toward decentralization is called for. "Comprehensive" planning must contemplate zones or areas of independent initiative.

Coordinated control is not constituted by aggregating specific controls that have been separately made through the working out of field or local plans.[5] Rather, it comes through the process of its own planning effort of which specific controls may be considered transactional elements. But, as "comprehensive" plans for coordinated control are achieved, it may well turn out, indeed, it very probably will, that selected specific controls are intentionally excluded—and that the agencies creatively involved in their development and in their continuing promulgation and perfection may be accorded corresponding independence. Reality may turn out to be so pluralistic[6] that, in place of the total global or national planning sometimes envisioned, extensive decentralization may be the order of tomorrow. The latest advances in technology may already have made this possible. Orchestration of intention through scientific mediation may make adequate public intending also possible. The fact remains that we do not now know the limits and tolerances, the apathies of reality. They will be discovered or created through "comprehensive" planning that intentionally investigates the improvement of intentions (the temporal dimensions of purposes and apathies) and the yield of coordinated or specific controls in terms of improved satisfactions.

FORTUNATE FEDERALISM

In the meantime, the time and place to start are here and now. The balance of power is here and will not resolve into planning overnight. And, it is yet possible that, as Horace Fries says, "reality may, after all, prove to be *too* pluralistic, giving rise to some conflicts which are inherently irresolvable."[7] Any success in setting manipulators to compete with one another, any governmental assistance to the development of countervailing power (for example, assistance to labor with the Wagner Act and the Fair Labor Standards Act, to the farmer with price support and acreage restriction, to investors with the Security Exchange Act),[8] any administrative achievement in playing pressure groups against each other—such corrections of imbalances of social pressures tend to expand the area in which men may act relatively free of restraint. They encourage extension of bargaining so that it may be creative beyond compromise. When balance quiets down to stalemate, it may provide the lull out of which can break the rush of creativity that ends in creative bargaining. One of the virtues of large administrative departments is that, in the process of minimizing the influence of pressure groups by playing one against the other, they serve to focus conflict—intensifying it at that point instead of letting it grow to become uncontrollably intense (coercive) at a subsequent focal point—thus opening the way for creative bargaining. Such maneuvering is almost impossible when different departments operate in separate halves of the conflict area.[9]

There is a special danger in overmuch decentralization—a threat to stabilization of responsibility. Authority is a very tenacious holdover, out of whose limitations we shall have slowly to work our way. Over the centuries it has, as a part of status, been deeply engrained in human nature. Gradual growth to homonomous responsibility will accordingly be an arduous process. Excessive decentralization must, it would seem, serve to delay the development of this mature responsibility. If independent administrative units are too small, too local, or too restricted in scope, they are likely to have horizons too narrow to contain the vistas necessary for an homonomous responsibility. If their concerns, their problems are so parochial that they are surrounded by public apathy instead of what is felt to be significant conflict, occasion is not at hand for growth beyond autonomy or constraint as the case may be. Inconvenience and humiliation will be suffered as the easy alternative to the ardors of conflict, much less creative bargaining. An agency must be big enough and perform a broad enough function before it will produce a climate that can encourage the kind of professional tendencies that are conducive to homonomous responsibility. There is great danger of lack of democracy today where government is small and almost entirely amateur.[10] And there is a great deal of wisdom in the feeling of many people that, distant though it is, the federal government is the most democratic part of the federal system.

The question of the concentration or diffusion, the centralization or decentralization of government will, however, not be consciously and deliberately resolved until allegiance to homonomous responsibility is much further developed than it is at present. Meanwhile, there is in America the fortunate circumstance of a federalism that is, as a principle, "characterized by a tendency to substitute coordinating for subordinating relationships or at least to restrict the latter as much as possible; to replace compulsion from above with reciprocity, understanding, and adjustment, command with persuasion, and force with law." [11] It is also, as a practice, characterized by a kind of limited pluralism that persistently resists tendencies toward over-compartmentalization of social habit in government, in administration. Federalism is clearly an advantage, an excellent starting point for administrative democracy. It is a stabilizing influence in the balancing of social pressures. It restrains or qualifies both centralization and decentralization, leaving open the potential play of creativity while limiting the effective range of authority. Homonomous responsibility is its implicit promise.

SEARCH FOR PATTERN IN UTOPIA

Administrative democracy is, without a doubt, utopian—not, however, in the sense of disembodied dreaming, but in the sense of ideal possibility. If it is well founded, it is well founded in a *search* for adequate definition of reality. It is just beginning, starting with the realities that are beginning to be understood about human nature as apparent first from experiments in the psychology of perception. There will be a long way to go before patterns can be definitively set, in any sense. A series of progressive approximations, as understanding of human nature is progressively improved, should be the present expectation.

The implication is clear that, as legislative policy accommodates administrative planning, there will, at the point of utopia, be a shift in the constitutional "division of powers." As legislative democracy matured it was hedged about with theories that have now become fundamentally untenable, based as they were in first instance on faulty understanding of human nature—the "representative" theory of perception. Most sadly inadequate were the theory and also the institution of democratic leadership. What there was did not involve reciprocal leader-led relationships. It was ineffective, no more "organic" than a market place relating of disembodied minds, through a public opinion approach to free speech. As administration develops a way with functional power, the vision of the overriding purpose of government as the creating of purpose through planning processes based on the skills of the new free speech may be expected to "catch on." And as it does, personal leadership through administrative organization will replace the eclectic leadership that follows the unrelated or chance-related swings of summations of unprocessed, pre-purposed votes. It will culminate in fully purposed plans far beyond compromise.

Legislatures will not wither away, however. Rather will their functions be more and more clearly seen to take a turn culminating from tendencies already quite apparent. For all the questioning in the courts of the delegating of legislative authority, such delegation is already on its way toward explicit institutional acceptance. As negotiation and creation are more and more given over to administration, legislatures become more and more oriented toward the business of review and ratification.

It is not, however, to be expected that legislatures will become "rubber stamps." In administrative democracy they will use the two "powers" Luther Gulick assigns them—veto over major policy and the right to audit and investigate[12]—to accomplish a number of vital functions.

■ They will serve as steady organizers of stalemates so that creative, purpose-full resolutions may arise. They do this now, unsystematically.

■ Following out the legislative reluctance to act without concurrent approval by all relevant minorities (John C. Calhoun's concurrent majority), they will insist upon widespread agreement, as a regular prerequisite to legislative acceptance of a plan, program, or proposed problem solution. Thereby they will be exacting from the public executive creative coordination of public intention. In this connection, legislatures will play an important role in identifying proper scope, identifying the range of activities that must be brought together in a social experiment that seeks the public good, insisting on universalization when the success of experiment depends on universalization—for example, broadening flood control planning to include social welfare, aesthetic, and pollution control considerations—accepting less when less is enough. The legislature will also play a key role in sorting out areas of strategic control, separating them from areas of lesser social significance that do not need formal political attention.

■ They will supervise the institution of free speech, insisting not on lack of restraint but on relevance and completeness, on the objectivity of being sure we understand one another. As they grow into full acceptance of homonomous responsibility of maturity themselves, they will insist on expertise in governmental performance and abundance of participation. (See pp. 315, 320, above.)

■ They will suprintend the enforcement of the new understanding of political obligation, directing the government's traditional monopoly of the use of physical force against the unregenerate who fail or refuse to mature to an acceptance of homonomous responsibility. In a sense this is an obverse of the function of insisting on concurrence. It is the delicate job of determining what behavior does not warrant participation.

Many senior legislators have amassed backgrounds of valuable experience and in some cases have developed excellent staffs.[13] There are not infrequent opportunities for legislative-administrative confrontation on common ground with comparable expertise. Administrative democracy will expect much closer, less jealous, more forthright and direct give-and-take (freedom of speech) between politicians and administrators. There will be continued mutual respect: for the legislator, on the one hand, for his final say and his judgment of people; for the administrator, on the other hand, for his expertise and his "command" of method of agreement, his artistry in scientific mediation. Separate functions will continue to be stressed, however, and the potential creativity in difference urged. In particular, the administrator will be kept out of partisan politics, not only because it is alien to his procedures, and because he must guard against partisan pressure to admit the logically irrelevant into processes of deliberation, but because his influence already has special weight in matters of highest policy. In place of suspicion a trust should arise, growing out of common devotion to a democratic method of knowing and a developed leadership of character.

RECAPITULATION

Under twentieth century conditions, particularly the conditions brought about by technological development, exclusive identification of democracy with representation and majority rule is no longer possible. When the administrative way of life begins to eclipse the legislative way of life in scope and importance, it is time to look not only at what it does but at what it can and should do, and to see if it can be made specifically democratic.

Traditional thinking about democratic political institutions has been grounded in what are now understood to have been erroneous accounts of human nature. This book has accordingly sought to base a theory of democracy appropriate to the administrative age in recent experimental findings in the psychology of perception and to establish the developing "transactional" understanding of the human condition (begun by John Dewey and Arthur F. Bentley) in place of the discrete individualism that heralded the advent of representative institutions and still hedges our thinking about government.

More's *Utopia* appears to have been based on actual observations of human nature as it showed itself in ancient Peru.[14] In contrast, administrative democracy looks forward to a progressively improving understanding of human nature and pretends only to a beginning understanding of some of its implications as uncovered by experimental investigation. It is thus intimately allied with what has been found to be the most reliable way of knowing—scientific inquiry.

But government, politics, is preeminently a moral enterprise; it deals in purposes and conflicts of purposes. Science also deals in purposes and conflicts of purposes—usually in an unscientific way. Science, the experimental way of knowing, can however be deliberately extended to include experimental inquiry into the purposes of the knowers involved. It is possible then to identify the "master" science, moral science (political science), as that which deals experimentally with human purposes, with intentions, by instituting changes (on purpose change of purpose) and observing consequences. To become a viable way of knowing, to achieve results, such science must necessarily be democratized because experimental handling of purposes can be achieved only as a third ("citizen," "subject-matter") scientist joins the traditionally distinguished pure and applied scientists, that is, only as the purposer participates in the experimental changing of purposes.

The product of scientific inquiry is *knowing how* to gain ever more satisfactory results. As this is achieved in physical science, men attain control over environment. In such knowing is a "functional" kind of power that can be applied without magic, without doing violence to nature. As such *knowing how* is achieved in moral (democratic) science, men will attain control over themSelves, social control made up of contributory Self-controls. They will learn how to make social power "functional" so that it is neither spur nor carrot but instead is companion to the changing nature of the human being-doing.

Representative democracy has, for the most part, marked its success with struck bargains, with compromises balancing coercive powers of conflicting interests. Participation has been celebrated in the vote, an algebraic summation of unrelated or chance-related (uncontrolled) opinions of discrete individuals. Administrative democracy organizes for the possibility of creative bargains characterized by participation that intentionally integrates conflicting purposes by the creation of new and improved purposes which are then embodied in plans for coordinated action. Administrative democracy becomes a creative way of *making* public intention—not a way of finding public interest.

As *knowing how* is achieved through a scientific approach (called "scientific mediation") to this process of purpose changing, the furious activity of direct participation is permitted to subside, much of it to be displaced by vicarious participation through validated knowings. The leadership of character within public administration is made possible. And government is enabled, through creative planning processes grounded in the Self-controls of citizen scientists, to achieve functional power for strategic social control.

Here then is the conservative utopia par excellence, the truth-tuned democracy, the universal utopia toward which all government ultimately points, the kinetic utopia of self-correction. Government, aspiring to social control through the gradual development of functional power, becomes a democratic agency of moving equilibrium in times of change. And it attains its simplicity, sorting out the pigpile of technological complexity, through leadership with vision.

If he is truly to lead, the leader must lead forth in truth. Scorning preoccupation with explanation he must play bird dog, point ahead with hypothesis. The larger and deeper secrets of moral and political life may well remain hidden until political democracy is comprehensively reorganized for the pursuit of truth. Reconstruction in democracy that perfects the politics of truth will, however, involve a parallel reconstruction of social inquiry. It will be marked by a merging of the structures of inquiry and politics.

The politics of truth begins the moment politics is understood to be more than an arena in which to apply discovered truths and more than a field for dispassionate, "objective" observation. It begins when politics is recognized, in its broadest sense, to be a process in which moral truth is made. Deliberate and self-conscious alliance of politics with truth makes an unbeatable combination. The politics of compromise will slowly fall by the wayside. In an age when democracy seems to be slipping away because government is too complex, too big, the truth can again make men free. A citizen science that must insist on democracy as the condition of the advancement of learning in political-social-moral matters, will assure the democratic character of the politics of which it becomes a part. The process of government seeking social control through the functional power that is based on the knowings-how of citizen Self-control becomes inescapably a democratic politics of truth.

HOW TO ACHIEVE PAINLESS CIVIC SURGERY*

by Herman L. Danforth

Traffic engineers have done an outstanding job of squeezing maximum use from horse-and-buggy street layouts, but a saturation point is reached where major street widenings and new street connections—involving proper acquisition—are the only answer. Major improvements are frequently deferred because of reluctance to undertake the unpleasant —but necessary—civic surgery.

* * * *

A number of ambitious proposals have been advanced (and rejected) to solve Rockford's major traffic headaches. Subsequently a more modest plan, with expandibility to meet foreseeable needs, found general acceptance. This is the basis for a number of current projects, but it was readily apparent that any basic traffic improvements required major surgery.

One segment of the plan provides for carrying primary north-bound traffic by the extension of Ninth Street, part of an existing one-way couple. This was selected as one of the early projects. Three moving and two parking lanes, plus reasonable allowance for sidewalks, indicated a seventy-foot right-of-way. It was found that certain relatively high-value property could be avoided without sacrificing good alignment. Otherwise little attention was paid to existing improvements or property lines in locating the new connection.

After preliminary surveys and staking of the approximate street line (a precise survey was not considered feasible at this stage) appraisals were secured by contract with the local Real Estate Board. Appraisals were made of each entire parcel affected, together with a net appraisal of the portion required for street purposes.

The next step consisted of selecting and contracting with realtors for negotiating for acquisition of property. It was felt that the importance of this step warranted careful consideration, which resulted in the selection of two local realtors, William F. Franzen and Harley E. Swanson, who

---

*Condensed from *Street Engineering*, I (January, 1956), pp. 46-47; by permission of the publisher.

proposed to work on the project jointly. The smoothness with which negotiations were subsequently carried out indicated that a wise choice had been made.

The contract with the negotiators was drawn up on a lump sum basis for all necessary work, including legal services such as checking titles, rendering opinions, drawing option papers and being available for consultation with the negotiator and seller's attorney. Some difficulty was experienced in arriving at a basis for such a figure. No realistic relationship between number of parcels or percentage of appraised value could be readily established. The problem was finally approached from two angles, the realtor's estimate of time and expense, and comparable acquisition costs on previous projects, payment having been made on a per diem basis.

Another problem was specifying performance, recognizing that if all reasonable efforts at negotiation failed, condemnation proceedings could not be anticipated and provided for in the contract. A great deal necessarily depended on the integrity and ability of the negotiators. As it turned out, all property was acquired at the appraised price without condemnation or overt threat thereof. Furthermore, by placing responsibility with one agency, a minimum amount of time was required for coordination by the engineering department and no loose ends were left hanging.

* * * *

There appear to be two common attitudes on the part of the public. At one extreme is the property owner who assumes that if part of his property must be taken for street purposes, the City will take it and there is little or nothing he can do about it. He has a hazy conception of what recompense, if any, he may receive. A street improvement involving his property is, to him, somewhat akin to a cyclone or flood or other natural disaster. At the other extreme is the cagy owner who feels that all he need do is hold out long enough and he will get a real bonanza. To get the public improvement through, the City will have to meet his price, however unreasonable it may be.

It is important at the outset to have a clearly stated and well understood policy regarding payment for property to be taken. The public official has a dual obligation—to the public as a whole and to the citizen as an individual. His obligation to the public at large is to pay no more than a fair and reasonable price for property, but not necessarily the least price for which it might be acquired. If it is determined that a property is "worth" eighteen thousand dollars, it might be acquired for seventeen after the owner has satisfied himself that he could get the eighteen thousand only at the cost of having his own appraisal made and paying legal fees to fight the case in court. The additional amount he stands to get may well be less than what it would cost to fight. To take advantage of this situation in the name of public interest is a failure to recognize the equal obligation to the individual and may also result in unnecessarily delaying vitally needed improvements.

Furthermore, it goes without saying that a "one price" policy is most essential. There may be a strong temptation to shade the original offer a few hundred dollars to push over the last few "tough ones". Go right ahead—provided you never expect to have to acquire right-of-way again.

Appraisal and negotiation should be treated as distinct operations, and should be carried out, in any particular project, by different individuals or firms. Both, however, had best be done by thoroughly qualified real estate appraisers, if possible, who preferably should be local residents well established and respected. The negotiator is in a far better position to approach the owner with an appraisal made by someone else than with his own figure. He should, nevertheless, be thoroughly familiar with the basis for the appraised figure in order to explain to the owner how the price was determined. If the negotiator is not in accord with the figure that has been established, he should review it with the appraiser with a view to adjustment or request a reappraisal *before* he first approaches the owner.

The negotiator should be selected with the greatest care. He is the key man. Consider his assignment. You are asking him to buy a particular piece of property from a particular individual (the owner) for a pre-established price. It calls for a high degree of tact, patience, and just plain downright good salesmanship. The negotiator should be willing to go out of his way to advise the owner of his legal rights and in regard to incidental pertinent matters that appear insignificant to the negotiator, but may be most troublesome and seemingly important to the owner. In thus being helpful, the negotiator may well expect to make six or more calls for every piece of property acquired. Unnecessary antagonism can and should be carefully avoided; condemnation or overt threat of condemnation is rarely necessary or warranted.

If the work is to be done right by a properly qualified person, an adequate fee must be allowed. It is reasonable to expect to pay the equivalent of his average normal hourly earnings, which may be substantial for a top-flight man. It is also likely to prove least expensive in the long run.

Set a deadline. This may be established already by the construction program, but when possible, fairly generous time allowance should be made. The owner must be given time to consider the offer, to consult with his attorney or friends, to find a place to which to move, and to make the many other arrangements being forced on him. But a firm deadline, say six months from the start of negotiations, is usually necessary to nudge along those who would otherwise procrastinate or stall indefinitely.

Various arrangements may be made at the option of the owner. He may elect to sell his entire lot, or only the portion required for actual street right-of-way. Again, if there are improvements, he may choose to sell these or retain them with the provision that he move or remove them within a stipulated time. It is sometimes feasible for a group of neighbors to agree among themselves to exchange or consolidate remnants, individually unusable, selling the City only that property required for street purposes.

In the matter of appraisals, it is well to know ahead of time what you may expect to receive. The appraisal can be an impressive-looking form with the value of land and improvements inserted and attesting to the fact that the appraisal was prepared by a realtor qualified to make appraisals. Or it can be a three- or four-page document giving not only the final figures, but full data on which they are based. Insist on the latter and you and your negotiator will have firm ground on which to stand.

If it should be necessary to resort to condemnation, the courts will properly hold that a "fair" price should be paid. This is commonly defined as the price a willing purchaser would pay to a willing seller. This is sound in theory, but rather hypothetical and of little practical usefulness in establishing a figure. For this reason, the appraisal must be based on something more readily measurable. Most commonly considered are purchase price (if property has traded hands recently), replacement cost less depreciation (for improvements), comparative sales, capitalized revenue (for income property) and assessed valuation. A "fair" price is established with due consideration of the figures determined by all approaches which may apply. It is to be noted, however, that the appraised value still rests on the judgment of the appraiser. If brought to court, the "fair" value there determined rests on the judgment of the jury, the appraiser's substantiating data constituting evidence and the opinion of the appraiser being in the nature of expert testimony.

Real estate appraisers are apt to be specialized, residential, commercial and industrial property presenting somewhat different appraisal problems. It is wise to select a specialized appraiser if any substantial amount of property is involved or if special problems are anticipated.

Some appraisal problems are apt to give particular trouble. One of these frequently encountered in business district fringe areas is weighing present value with existing residential improvements as against potential or speculative land value for commercial use. The owner will probably figure his price as the two added together, and it may take some explaining to get it across that it must be either one or the other.

Another problem, not so much of appraisal as of selling, arises from the fact that sentimental value cannot legitimately be recognized. The bed-ridden widow in the ancestral home can be tough, and don't think it can't. Situations of this sort might well be taken into account right from the beginning.

The idea is sometimes expressed to the effect that property for major improvements should be purchased secretly or options secured before any announcement of the proposed project is publicized. This sounds good, and may work well in private business, and even possibly in the case of large governmental units, but it is most difficult to conceive how it is practically possible under the close scrutiny usually accorded the City Hall. Even with the best intentions and possibility of bargain prices, the public servant who follows this practice is open to charges of "secret deals" and insinuations of municipal chicanery.

The theory of excess condemnation crops up, too. The principle is for the City to buy all land adjoining the improvement in order to sell it at a profit when the project is completed. It is probable that in many cases taxes, maintenance, liability on the unused property and other incidental costs during the time such property may be held will offset possible gain. Where the proposed improvement is of obvious local benefit, it may be beter to assess a portion of the cost under special assessment or local improvement procedure.

It is hoped that these observations may be of some benefit. Cities of all sizes are finding it increasingly necessary to revise their street pattern to handle today's traffic, and frequently the individuals responsible find little in their training or experience to help them in approaching the problem of property acquisition. But once they get their feet wet, having waded in with their eyes open, it's not too bad.

Appendix B

BIBLIOGRAPHY
OF THE WRITINGS OF
HORACE S. FRIES

(1902-1951)

1927
"Mr. Broad's Analysis of the Perceptual Situation," University of Wisconsin. Unpublished Ph. M. thesis.

1929
"Some Attitudes and Considerations and a Biological Argument for Epiphenomenalism," *Journal of Philosophy*, 26, pp. 626–34.

1932
"The Law of Man," *New Humanist*, 5, pp. 29–31.

1933
(with Shigeto Tsuru) "A Problem in Meaning," *Journal of General Psychology*, 8, pp. 281–84.

1934
"The Development of Dewey's Utilitarianism," University of Wisconsin. Unpublished Ph. D. dissertation.

"On a Naturalistic Religion," *New Humanist*, 7, pp. 22–27.

1935
"Life and the Philosophers," *New Humanist*, 8, pp. 105–106.

"The Spatial Location of Sensa," *Philosophical Review*, 44, pp. 345–53.

"The Uncertainty Principle," *Campus Bulletin*, Lawrence College, Appleton, Wisconsin, 8 (January 19).

1936
"The Appeal of Communism," *New Humanist*, 9, pp. 97–102.

"Educational Confusion Confounded," *Journal of Social Philosophy*, 1, pp. 169–74.

"The Functions of Whitehead's God," *Monist*, 46, pp. 25–58.

"On an Empirical Criterion of Meaning," *Philosophy of Science*, 3, pp. 143–51.

"On the Meaning of Intelligence," *Educational Administration and Supervision*, 22, pp. 29–50.

1937
"The Method of Proving Ethical Realism," *Philosophical Review*, 46, pp. 485–502.

"Skimming the Surface" (review of *Educating for Democracy*, a Symposium), *Social Frontier*, 4, 32–33.

"Social Science and Human Values," *Journal of Social Philosophy*, 3, pp. 54-58.

1938

"Method in Social Philosophy," *Journal of Social Philosophy*, 3, pp. 325–41. [According to a note in an unpublished manuscript, Fries subsequently departed from the view expressed in this article.]

"Needed: An Educational Experiment," *Social Frontier*, 5, pp. 87–88.

Review of *The Dewey School* by Katherine Camp Mayhew and Anna Camp Edwards, *Journal of Educational Research*, 31, pp. 626–27.

Review of *The Ideal School* by B. B. Bogoslovsky, *Journal of Educational Research*, 31, pp. 625–26.

1939

"Physics: A Vicious Abstraction," *Philosophy of Science*, 6, pp. 301–08.

Review of *Logic: The Theory of Inquiry* by John Dewey, *Common Sense*, 8, pp. 26–27.

1940

Review of *The TVA Labor Relations Policy at Work* by Judson King, *Wisconsin State Employee*, 9, 10ff, and *Journal of State and Local Employees*, 4, p. 19.

"Some Democratic Implications of Science in Scientific Management," *Advanced Management*, 5, pp. 147–53.

1941

"Can Science Be Unified Humanistically?" *Humanist*, 1, pp. 142–45.

"Humanistic Spooks," *Humanist*, 1, pp. 61–62.

"Idols or God," *Journal of Liberal Religion*, 3, pp. 92–95.

Review of *Biography of the Gods* by A. E. Haydon, *Humanist*, 1, p. 22f.

"Science, Ethics, and Democracy," *Journal of Social Philosophy*, 6, pp. 302–25.

"Virtue Is Knowledge," *Philosophy of Science*, 8, pp. 89–99.

1942

"Against the Neo-Thomists: In Defense of the Angelic Doctor," *Antioch Review*, 2, pp. 236–51.

"The Gods Live Again" (review of *Biography of the Gods* by A. E. Haydon), *Journal of Social Philosophy and Jurisprudence*, 7, pp. 271–75.

"On the Unity and Ethical Neutrality of Science," *Journal of Philosophy*, 39, pp. 225–34.

"Science and the Individual," *Antioch Review*, 2, pp. 591–611.

"William James ... Jan. 11, 1842. Philosopher of the Practical," *Humanist*, 2, pp. 20–23.

1943

"Ethical Objectivity through Science," *Philosophical Review*, 52, pp. 553–65.

"Hartshorne vs Ely on Whitehead," *Journal of Liberal Religion*, 5, pp. 96–97.

"Liberty and Science" (review of *The Machiavellians, Defenders of Freedom* by James Burnham, *Public Administration Review*, 3, pp. 268–73.

"On Managerial Responsibility," *Advanced Management*, 8, pp. 45–48.

Review of *Man Stands Alone* by Julian S. Huxley, *Ethics*, 53, pp. 147–48, and *Humanist*, 3, pp. 41–42.

"World Revolution Number Five," *Antioch Review*, 3, pp. 425-37.

1944

"Is Democratic Collectivisim Possible?" *New Leader*, 27, p. 26 (August 12).

"Humanism and Agnosticism," *Journal of Liberal Religion*, 6, pp. 4–8.

"On the Unification of Science," *American Journal of Economics and Sociology*, 3, pp. 193–200. [Adapted from "Can Science Be Unified Humanistically?" 1941.]

Review of *The Future of Education* by Porter Sargent, *Progressive* (November 20).

Review of *Vitalizing Liberal Education* by Algo D. Henderson, *Progressive* (August 14).

"Science and the Foundations of Freedom," *Journal of Philosophy*, 41, pp. 113–26.

"The Theology that Obstructs Science," *Humanist*, 4, pp. 17–22.

"Wisdom Hath Builded Her House" (review of *The Uses of Reason* by A. E. Murphy), *Humanist*, 4, pp. 37–40.

1945

"Mediation in Cultural Perspective," *American Journal of Economics and Sociology*, 4, pp. 449–60.

"A Methodological Consideration," *Journal of General Psychology*, 33, pp. 11–20.

Review of *Fate and Freedom* by Jerome Frank, *Progressive* (June 5).

Review of *Humanism and Human Dignity* by Luther W. Stalnaker, *Crozer Quarterly*, 22, pp. 281–82.

"Scientific Mediation—Tool of Democracy," *Antioch Review*, 5, pp. 388–401.

"The Teaching of Dogmatic Religion in a Democratic Socity," *American Journal of Economics and Sociology*, 4, pp. 193–210.

"Towards a Naturalistic Religion," *Crozer Quarterly*, 22, pp. 301–307.

1946

"A Methodological Consideration," *Journal of Educational Research*, 39, pp. 321–27. [Summarized from same title, 1945.]

"On the Origin of Communication," *American Journal of Economics and Sociology*, 5, pp. 411–14.

1947

"Science, Causation and Value," *Philosophy of Science*, 14, pp. 179–80.

"Varieties of Freedom: An Effort toward Orchestration," in *Freedom and Experience*, ed. Sidney Hook and Milton R. Konvitz (Ithaca: Cornell University Press), pp. 3–24.

1949

"Dewey's Theory of Method," *New Leader*, 32, special section, p. 7 (October 22).

Review of *Humanism as a Philosophy* by Corliss Lamont, *Crozer Quarterly*, 26, pp. 368.

Review of *Modern Man's Conflicts: the Creative Challenge of a Global Society* by Dane Rudhyar, *Crozer Quarterly*, 26, p. 154.

1950

"Contributing to World Confusion" (review of *Authority and the Individual* by Bertrand Russell), *New Leader*, 33 (March).

"Educational Foundations of Social Planning," in *Essays for John Dewey's Ninetieth Birthday*, ed. Kenneth D. Benne and William O. Stanley (Urbana: University of Illinois, Bureau of Research and Service, College of Education), pp. 59–73.

"Logical Simplicity: A Challenge to Philosophy and to Social Inquiry," *Philosophy of Science*, 17, pp. 207–28.

Review of *Evolution and the Founders of Pragmatism* by Philip P. Wiener, *Philosophy of Science*, 17, p. 357.

1951

"Art, Science and Socialism," *Socialist Call*, 18, pp. 2, 5 (February 23).

"Educational Opportunity" (review of *The Human Community* by Baker Brownell and *Small Town Renaissance* by R. W. Poston), *Progressive Education*, 28, pp. 103–104.

"The Experimental Approach to Socialism," *Socialist Call*, 18, pp. 2–3. (February 9).

"Five Suggestions," *Transformation: Arts, Communication, Environment —A World Review*, 1, pp. 107–109.

"John Dewey's Philosophy," in *Papers in Honor of John Dewey on his Ninetieth Birthday, October 19–20, 1949* (Madison: University of Wisconsin, School of Education and Department of Philosophy), pp. 38–40.

"Perception and Value Inquiry," *American Journal of Economics and Sociology,* 11, pp. 19–32.

"Philosophy for Social Inquiry" (review of *Philosophy and the Social Order* by George R. Geiger), *American Journal of Economics and Sociology,* 10, pp. 431–36.

" 'To Sail Beyond the Sunset,' " *Educational Theory,* 1, pp. 23–34.

1952

"Is the Psi-Function Description 'Complete'? A Layman's Question," *Philosophy of Science,* 19, pp. 166–69.

"Situational Quality," *Progressive Education,* 29, p. 163.

"Social Planning," in *The Cleavage in Our Culture,* ed. Frederick Burkhardt (Boston: Beacon Press), pp. 81–104.

Unpublished

Fries' unpublished manuscripts are deposited in the library of the Wisconsin State Historical Society in Madison.

Notes

Chapter One

1. Bernard J. James, "The Issue of 'Power'," *Public Administration Review*, XXIV (1964), 47.

2. The Speaker of the House was removed from the Rules Committee in 1910. The privilege of selecting standing committees was restored to the House in 1911.

3. For example, M. P. Follett, *The Speaker of the House of Representatives* (New York: Longmans, Green, 1896).

4. 1911 was also the year when Commons divested the House of Lords of effective policy control, reducing its function to delaying action, and thus clearing the way for granting leadership to the Cabinet. Cf. Don K. Price, "The Parliamentary and Presidential Systems," *Public Administration Review*, III (1943), 317–34.

5. Among such inventions also must be included improved techniques for administering large organizations.

6. "The democracies must learn to manage better the complex civilization which machines make mandatory.... You can't use machines without creating complex units of administration.... I don't believe our civilization can endure and prosper unless at the same time we become cleverer and cleverer at how we manage these agglomerations of machines and the intricate social organization that results from them." Lyndall Urwick, "Experiences in Public Administration," *Public Administration Review*, XV (1955), 250.

7. Woodrow Wilson, "The Study of Administration," *Political Science Quarterly*, II (1887), 204.

8. At the same time, according to Eugene Rabinowitch, science "saved capitalism, just as the laboring masses were getting ready to revolt against its iniquities, by increasing productivity until capitalists were not only able, but eager, to supply the masses with enough goods for satisfactory living. Capitalism has lost out in the parts of the world where this transformation from scarcity to plenty of goods has not come in time." *Bulletin of the Atomic Scientists*, XIX (October, 1963), 13.

9. Wilson, "The Study of Administration," p. 204.

10. *Ibid.*

11. *Ibid.*, 209–10.

12. Which is, in another sense, correct indeed; except that, if it is truly good, it is democratic and thus incompatible with dictatorship.

13. Wilson, "The Study of Administration," p. 218. Italics his. Note the stark mind-body dualism projected into the State as MAN writ large. Compare John Stuart Mill, *Representative Government* (New York: D. P. Dutton, 1910), p. 196.

14. Wilson, "The Study of Administration," p. 220.

15. One of Wilson's concerns, in denying that there are democratic or authoritarian aspects to administration, was to encourage learning from the administrative experience of Europe, particularly from Germany, in face of popular fear of foreign institutions.

16. "Mr. Rowland Egger's remarkable review of *A Bell for Adano* emphasizes the point that an administrator who has a fundamental appreciation for the value and

dignity of man acts in a certain way. [*Public Administration Review,* IV (1944), 371–76.] Major Joppolo is a 'good man,' and in governing the village of Adano he provides a 'democratic administration.' This suggests that it has been a mistake to declare that the principles of administration apply under any form of government and to assume that administration (or governance) is not concerned with political theory." Donald Morrison, "Public Administration and the Art of Governance," review of *Case Reports in Public Administration, Public Administration Review,* V (1945), 85.

Chapter Two

1. Graham Wallas, *Human Nature in Politics* (London: Constable & Co. Ltd., 1948), 4th edit., p. 199. (First published 1908.)

2. The Greek and Christian tradition had already placed definite entities (soul, mind) within the human body as passive observers of the passing scene, and had thereby provided a later age with a convenient dumping-ground for everything that could not be interpreted in terms of geometry and mechanics. The break came when wetness was denied to be a property of water and established as a quality in the mind of the perceiver. See John Herman Randall, Jr., *The Making of the Modern Mind,* revised edition (Boston: Houghton Mifflin, 1940), p. 268.

3. "It is interesting that while we think of the highest administrative class in this country or in England in terms of the policy-framing authority that it possesses, in Mexico the element of personal relationship between ministerial and department heads and their immediate subordinates is the decisive criterion in legally defining this top group in the bureaucracy." William Ebenstein, "Public Administration in Mexico," *Public Administration Review,* V (1945), 108.

4. This over-rational assumption as found in the working ranks of politics was emphasized by Robert E. Park: "One reason that electioneering seems a queer business is probably due to the fact that the candidate attempts to deal with the electorate in accordance with the democratic assumption that every voter is a rational human being, quite capable of acting wisely, independently, and in the public interest, if only he is afforded the temporary protection and seclusion of a voting booth. He discovers, however, that most men are timid, irrational, and sentimental creatures, controlled by all sorts of personal interests and irrational affections and antipathies." "Social Planning and Human Nature," *Publications of the American Sociological Society,* XXIX (1935), 21.

5. "[Pavlov] made the blunt observation that if a dog salivates in response to the presence of meat on his tongue, and if that is a physiological process, the process ought to be just as truly physiological when the dog salivates to the sight of meat two feet away. Why insert a spook in the latter case and not in the former? To answer this, he just eliminated a couple of feet of rigid Newtonian space from his investigational background; and incidentally he did that long before Einstein gave the rest of us the tip." Arthur F. Bentley, *Inquiry into Inquiries* (Boston: Beacon, 1954), p. 122.

6. See Bertrand Russell, *Selected Papers of Bertrand Russell* (New York: Random House, 1927), pp. 310-11. "Contrary to the view of Berkeley and other philosophers, it is vision rather than touch that appears to be the developmentally precocious and dominant source of perceptual information . . . if anything, vision 'teaches' touch, rather than the other way around." John H. Flavell and John P. Hill, "Developmental Psychology," *Annual Review of Psychology,* XX (1969), 1–56.

7. Carl J. Friedrich pictures the following progression: (1) mercantilist consolidation of administrative services into a bureaucracy, (2) subjection of the bureaucracy to the controls of a constitutional system, (3) democratization of constitutionalism. See his *Constitutional Government and Democracy* (Boston: Ginn, 1941), pp. 20, 29.

8. It is interesting to speculate on the following progression: (1) the circle of the ancients ➤ Plato's cyclical theory of history, (2) Newton's straight line ➤ doctrines of progress, (3) space-time geodesics ➤ ???. Does it culminate (for the time) in purpose, in character?

9. *Human Nature and Conduct* (New York: Holt, 1922), pp. 26–27.

10. "Some Thoughts on the Meaning of the Word Democracy," *Human Relations*, III (1950), 175–86.

11. *Ibid.*, p. 176. All italics are his.

12. *Ibid.*, p. 180.

13. *Ibid.*, pp. 180–81. Joyce Cary arrives at an almost identical conclusion: "All relations between human beings in a free world require continuous adjustment. Every moral situation is unique and needs a special answer.... It is just because the free creative world, in which we live, presents to us a continuous novelty of event that personal integrity is of such enormous importance. It is our only criterion of value. Our trust is given to certain leaders because their honor, their character, are the only things we can trust." "Political and Personal Morality," *The Saturday Review*, XXXVIII (December 31, 1955), 6, 31.

14. See, for example, E. Pendleton Herring, *Public Administration and the Public Interest* (New York: McGraw Hill, 1936), pp. 7–8. C. Wright Mills makes this interesting analysis: "Neither party has a political vocabulary—much less political policies—that are up-to-date with the events, problems and structures of modern life. Neither party challenges the other in the realm of ideas, nor offers clear-cut alternatives to the electorate. Neither can learn nor will learn anything from classic conservatism of Mr. Kirk's variety. They are both liberal in rhetoric, traditional in intention, expedient in practice.... Within each party and between them there is a political stalemate. Out of two such melanges, you cannot even sort out consistent sets of interests and issues, much less develop coherent policies, much less organize ideological guidelines for public debate and private reflection. This means, for one thing, that 'politics' goes on only within and between a sort of administrative fumbling. The fumbles are expedient. And the drift that they add up to leads practically all sensitive observers to construct images of the future that are images of horror." "The Conservative Mood," *Dissent*, I (1954), 29.

15. Schuyler C. Wallace, *Federal Departmentalization: A Critique of Theories or Organization* (New York: Columbia University Press, 1941), p. 234.

16. Wallace S. Sayre, "Trends in a Decade of Administrative Values," *Public Administration Review*, XI (1951), 1–9.

17. Charles S. Hyneman, *Bureaucracy in a Democracy* (New York: Harper, 1950).

18. Cf., for example, Robert H. Dahl, "The Science of Public Administration: Three Problems," *Public Administration Review*, VII (1947), 1-11; Arthur W. Macmahon, "The Administrative State," *Public Administration Review*, VIII (1948), 203-11; Herman Finer, "Administrative Responsibility in Democratic Government," *Public Administration Review*, I (1941), 335–50.

19. Paul H. Appleby's view is very persuasively presented in any of his books: *Big Democracy* (New York: Knopf, 1945), *Policy and Administration* (University of Alabama Press, 1949), or *Morality and Administration* (Baton Rouge: Louisiana State University Press, 1952).

20. Which is not to say that they do not understand well the business of pleasing people and of engineering reelection through superficial display of representation.

21. If disturbed by the usage of the word "conservative," please see Chapter 9.

22. On the federal scene, too, the control thus exercised by administrative bodies may well eclipse in effect the ability of the legislature to promote or even discover its own intent. See Dwight Waldo's description of the importance to our World War II effort of administrative acceptance of Keynesian economic theory, in his

Perspectives on Administration (University of Alabama Press, 1956), pp. 21–22. The belief that Congress is assuming a supervising and investigating character in place of its former policy-making function has been expressed from many quarters.

Chapter Three

1. Arthur E. Morgan, *Nowhere was Somewhere* (Chapel Hill: University of North Carolina Press, 1946).

2. John Dewey, *Logic: The Theory of Inquiry* (New York: Henry Holt & Co., 1938).

3. John Dewey and Arthur F. Bentley, *Knowing and the Known* (Boston: Beacon Press, 1949). See Bentley's last published article, "The Word 'Transaction'," *The Humanist*, XVII (1957), 17–21, for a concise statement of this approach. An interesting hint at later use of the word is found in this passage from Emerson: "It was not, however, found easy to embody the readily admitted principle that property should make law for property, and persons for persons; since persons and property mixed themselves in every transaction." "Politics," *The Essays of Ralph Waldo Emerson* (New York: Random House, Inc., 1944), p. 335.

4. Perhaps best represented in Franklin P. Kilpatrick, ed., *Explorations in Transactional Psychology* (New York University Press, 1961). See also Hadley Cantril, ed., *The Morning Notes of Adelbert Ames, Jr.* (New Brunswick: Rutgers University Press, 1960).

5. Bentley, "The Word 'Transaction'," p. 21.

6. Dewey and Bentley, *Knowing and the Known*, p. 108.

7. Hermann Broch, *The Death of Virgil* (New York: Pantheon Books, Inc., 1945), p. 29, Tr. by Jean Starr Untermeyer .

8. P. W. Bridgman, *Reflections of a Physicist* (New York: Philosophical Library, 1955), pp. 152–53.

9. John Dewey, *Human Nature and Conduct* (New York: Henry Holt & Co., 1922), p. 14.

10. Dewey and Bentley, *Knowing and the Known*, p. 138.

11. Arthur S. Eddington, *The Nature of the Physical World* (New York: Macmillan Co., 1928), p. xiv.

12. It would possibly be more sensible in the long run to discard "reality" altogether as a term hopelessly tainted by mind vs matter delusions. "What difference can it make to the physicist whether 'ideas', 'concepts', 'minds' really 'exist' or not, or whether anybody else thinks they exist or not? He has long since overcome his old imagined dependence on the 'reality' of physical objects as a necessary presupposition for scientific work." Arthur F. Bentley, *Inquiry into Inquiries* (Boston: Beacon Press, 1954), p. 139.

13. *Ibid.*, p. 352. For another description of this same experiment see Semour Robins, "Perception and Man-Made Environment," *The Humanist*, XVII (1957). See also P. W. Bridgman's philosophical comments in *Reflections of a Physicist*, Chapter 8. Ames' original description may be found in "The Rotating Trapezoid," in Kilpatrick, ed., *Explorations in Transactional Psychology*, pp. 222–56.

14. Robert Livingston, "Perception and Commitment," *Bulletin of the Atomic Scientists*, XIX (February, 1963), p. 16. That perceived size of objects depends on more than the size of the retinal image is by now reliably established. [See Edwin G. Boring, "The Perception of Objects," in Herschel W. Leibowitz, *Visual Perception* (New York: Macmillan, 1965), pp. 67–85.] Both heredity and learning are involved. The Honi phenomenon [Warren J. Wittreich, "The Honi Phenomenon: A Case of Selective Perceptual Distortion," in Hans Toch and Henry Clay Smith, eds., *Social Perception* (Princeton: D. Van Nostrand Co., 1968), pp. 73–83.] and other related

studies have shown that some objects (some faces, for example) are perceived with remarkable stability or constancy by given individuals, despite distorted retinal patterns, whereas others are not. Explanations vary. Experiments in the realms of sound have demonstrated that here too, as would be expected, culture, or the "subjective" aspect of the perceiver, participates in the very first fashioning of the sensory data of perception. See Richard M. Warren and Roslyn P. Warren, "Auditory Illusions and Confusions," *Scientific American*, CCXXIII (December, 1970), pp. 30-36

15. Walter Lippmann, *Public Opinion* (New York: Penguin, 1946), p. 61. Cf. Richard Neutra's emphasis on the importance of physiological structurings. *Survival through Design* (New York: Oxford University Press, 1954). Reliable information on the effects of culture on perception is coming in from all directions. See Marshall H. Segall, Donald T. Campbell and Melville J. Herskovitz, *The Influence of Culture on Visual Perception* (Indianapolis: Bobbs-Merrill, 1966).

16. Richard L. Gregory, "Visual Illusions," *Scientific American*, CCXIX (November, 1968), 75.

17. Michael Polanyi, "Passion and Controversy in Science," *Bulletin of the Atomic Scientists*, XIII (1957), 116. Note the quotation from Isak Dinesen on page 135, above.

18. See Lewis Cope, "Brain Research Points Way to Brighter Future," *Minneapolis Tribune*, December 30, 1968, p. 15.

19. Ralph W. Gerard, "How the Brain Creates Ideas," in Sidney J. Parnes and Harold F. Harding, eds., *A Source Book for Creative Thinking* (New York: Charles Scribner's Sons, (1962) p. 120.

20. Livingston, "Perception and Commitment," p. 18.

21. *Ibid.*

22. See below, pp. 84–87, for elaboration on the meaning of "objective".

23. Ian Stevenson, "Schizophrenia: What we are Finding Out About our Worst Mental Illness," *Harper's Magazine*, CCXV (August, 1957), 63. See also *Sensory Deprivation*, ed. Philip Solomon [and others] (Cambridge: Harvard University Press, 1961), and Duane P. Schultz, *Sensory Restriction: Effects on Behavior* (New York: Academic Press, 1965). The technique I have described was developed by J. C. Lilly and reported in his "Mental Effects of Reduction of Ordinary Levels of Physical Stimuli on Intact, Healthy Persons," *Psychiatric Research*, V (1956), 1–9. S. Howard Bartley generalizes from the results of many variously designed experiments in sensory deprivation or perceptual isolation, concluding that they give evidence of the deterioration of cognition and motivation. *Principles of Perception*, 2nd ed. (New York: Harper and Row, Publishers, Inc. 1969), p. 419.

24. Hadley Cantril, Adelbert Ames, Jr., Albert H. Hastorf, William H. Ittelson, "Psychology and Scientific Research," *Science*, CX (1949), 519. "In current ways of talking, an observation is an organism's 'act'. For us, in contrast, it is the existence—the very phenomenal presence—of a sight-seen, which is not a 'function' of anything." Bentley, *Inquiry into Inquiries*, p. 146.
The difference between separation and distinction is well illustrated by Francis M. Myers: "The front end and the back end of a horse are not the same. But if one insists that the only way to distinguish them is to chop the horse in two, he will no longer have a horse. It is the same with fact and value in the process of knowing." *The Warfare of Democratic Ideals* (Yellow Springs, Ohio: Antioch Press, 1956), p. 63.

25. "While sights-seen, etc., are ... established in an evolutionary setting, this setting itself is an outgrowth of knowledge, and this very 'knowledge' arises directly out of the sights-seen, etc., which provide its materials." Bentley, *Inquiry into Inquiries*, p. 144.

26. For descriptions of this experiment see Franklin P. Kilpatrick, "Two Processes in Perceptual Learning," *Journal of Experimental Psychology*, XLVIII (1954), 362–70,

and William H. Ittelson, *The Ames Demonstrations in Perception* (Princeton: Princeton University Press, 1952).

27. Leibowitz, *Visual Perception*, p. 22. Richard Held and Melvin Schlank have demonstrated that self-produced movement (resulting in "re-afferent" visual stimulation) rather than passive movement is necessary for learning new eye-hand coordination under unusual, systematically disarranged conditions. "Adaptation to Disarranged Eye-Hand Coordination in the Distance-Dimension," in *ibid.*, pp. 91–95.

28. Ross L. Mooney in Parnes & Harding, eds., *A Source Book for Creative Thinking*, p. 319. Cf. Bartley, *Principles of Perception*, 2nd ed., p. 453. In turn, it should be pointed out, dispelling illusion is sometimes a matter of relearning. We do not yet know the extent to which the perceptions that are so hard to change were learned in the first place.

29. Herman Melville, *Typee* (New York: International Readers League, 1944), p. 255.

30. See below, Chapter 13.

31. Hadley Cantril, "The Nature of Social Perception," *Transactions of the New York Academy of Sciences*, Series 2, X (1945), 145.

32. Priscilla Robertson, "On Getting Values Out of Science," *The Humanist*, XVI (1956), 169.

33. "The problem of perception is the problem of how a living being goes about its transactions with its environment so as to make emergent life possible." Ross L. Mooney, "A Conceptual Model for Integrating Four Approaches to the Identification of Creative Talent," in Parnes & Harding, eds., *A Source Book for Creative Thinking*, p. 78.

34. Robert L. Fantz, *Scientific American* CCIV (May, 1961), 66–72. It promises to be very interesting to watch as the line is drawn between the perceptual abilities developed by the species and those left to post-natal learning. Depth perception by means of light and shadow cues is apparently not innate. [Eckhard H. Hess, "Shadows and Depth Perception," *Scientific American*, CCIV (March, 1961), 138–48.] There seems also to be an interesting in-between category of "innate" abilities that do not show up in infants, but only with maturation.

35. *Newsweek*, LXV (February 15, 1965), 56–57.

36. Dewey, *Human Nature and Conduct*, pp. 232–33.

37. Cantril *et al*, "Psychology and Scientific Research," p. 518.

38. Quoted by Bentley in *Inquiry into Inquiries*, p. 154. Dewey says names (e.g., "man") are used to "call attention to features of a situation." They are "tools for directing perception or experimental observations." Introduction to *Universe* by Scudder Klyce (Winchester, Mass.: S. Klyce, 1921), p. iii.

39. See Hoyt L. Sherman, Ross L. Mooney, and Glenn Fry, *Drawing by Seeing* (New York: Hinds, Hayden & Eldridge, 1947); Hoyt L. Sherman and others, *Report on the Visual Training of the Varsity Football Team and the Varsity Basketball Teams* (Columbus, Ohio: Ohio State University, March 1, 1949.)

40. Horace S. Fries, "Perception and Value Inquiry," *The American Journal of Economics and Sociology*, XI (1951), 21.

41. See below, pp. 266–69. Pattern seems to be involved at the very heart of learning as carrier and coordinator of information. It is also instrumental in increasing perceptual discernment and in expanding the temporal span of apprehension—even unto simultaneous grasp of the whole composition of a symphony. See James J. Gibson, *The Senses Considered as Perceptual Systems* (Boston: Houghton Mifflin, 1966), p. 270.

Chapter Four

1. Josiah Royce, quoted by William James, "On a Certain Blindness in Human Beings" in *Essays of the Past and Present*, ed. Warner Taylor (New York: Harper & Bros., 1927), p. 159. The capital S in Self comes from the original.

2. Theoretically, as Max C. Otto points out, morality is even conceivable when the conflicting desires are entertained by one and the same man. *Things and Ideals* (New York: Holt, 1924), p. 116.

3. Robert E. Park, "Social Planning and Human Nature," *Publication of the American Sociological Society*, XXIX (1935), 26.

4. Horace M. Kallen, "Morals", in *Encyclopedia of Social Sciences*, ed. Edwin R. A. Seligman (New York: Macmillan, 1933), X, 645.

5. Robert Redfield, "The Folk Society," *American Journal of Sociology*, LII (1947), 299. "To primitive man, the moral and the physical universe are one and the same thing, and a rule is both a law of nature and a principle of conduct." Jean Piaget, *The Moral Judgment of the Child* (Glencoe, Illinois: Free Press, 1948), p. 340. Cf. Ernest Cassirer, *An Essay on Man* (Garden City, New York: Doubleday, 1953), Chapter VII. The constructed type for an ideal folk society is also set forth in Horace Miner, "The Folk-Urban Continuum," *American Sociological Review*, XVII (October, 1952), 529–37 and Gideon Sjoberg, "Folk and 'Feudal' Societies," *American Journal of Sociology*, LVIII (November, 1952), 231–39.

6. James H. Breasted, *The Dawn of Conscience* (New York: Scribner's, 1947), pp. 38–42. Lewis Mumford suggests that Breasted "overlooked the amicable, non-predatory practices of the neolithic village, where forbearance and mutual aid prevailed, as they do generally within pre-'civilized' communities. Breasted saw ... the increased ethical sensitiveness of the ruling classes, ready to relieve the poor peasants from the gross bullying and unconscionable robbery practiced too often by their superiors. But he did not ask how a dominant minority had gained the position that enabled them to exercise such arbitrary powers." [*The Myth of the Machine* (New York: Harcourt, Brace & World, Inc., 1966), p. 214.] As a matter of fact, records of such early history are so tenuous that their chief value is possibly that of myth. At any rate, it is the development of *reflective* morals (or the myth of their development) that is of interest here. In this one plausible story, they come not out of primitive forbearance and mutual aid but from a civilization which appears to have lost these and to have had to create a substitute in *thinking, reflecting*, terms.

7. *Ibid.*, p. 19.

8. *Ibid.*, p. 145. Italics his.

9. *Ibid.*, p. 19.

10. *Ibid.*, p. 168. When these ethical recognitions or visions seep down to the lower classes they become a consolation for the poor and wretched. Sacerdotalism enters to obviate the leveling implicit in the logical (Aristotelian) demands of such an ethic.

11. *Ibid.*, p. 216.

12. Ralph Waldo Emerson, "Politics," in *The Essays of Ralph Waldo Emerson* (New York: Random House, 1944), p. 343. "That which all things tend to educe; which freedom, education, intercourse, revolutions, go to form and deliver is character." *Ibid.*, p. 342.

13. Compare Gordon W. Allport, *Becoming* (New Haven: Yale University Press, 1955), p. 64.

14. Otto, *Things and Ideals*, p. 105.

15. Such was Bosanquet's opinion. Bernard Bosanquet, *Some Suggestions in Ethics* (London: Macmillan, 1919), Chapter IX, "Stupidity."

16. It is interesting to speculate on the control effected by divergent interpretations of the meaning of freedom. See below pp. 66–67.

17. The word "chance", as used here involves a denial of the Automatic Market, the General Will, the Mind of Society, the Destiny of Man, and indeed, any reification of Society.

18. See John Dewey, "Authority and the Individual," in *Intelligence in the Modern World*, ed. Joseph Ratner (New York: Random House, 1939), pp. 343–63.

19. See Thomas H. Huxley, *Evolution and Ethics, and other Essays* (New York: Appleton, 1920), p. 57.

20. Freedom is further analyzed in chapters 13 and 16, responsibility in chapter 15.

21. Ashley Montague, *On Being Human* (New York: Henry Schuman, 1950), pp. 44–45. Compare P. W. Bridgman, *Reflections of a Physicist* (New York: Philosophical Library, 1955), pp. 70–71.

22. Roger Ernle Money-Kyrle, *Psychoanalysis and Politics* (New York: W. W. Norton, 1950).

23. Alfred Adler, *Social Interest: A Challenge to Mankind* (New York: Putnam's, 1938), pp. 282–83.

Chapter Five

1. "And let us not forget that this human love, which science recognizes as an essential attribute of the species and indicates to us as the basis of a natural morality, this love on whose account we ought never to despair of mankind however alarming its future may look, was constantly necessary, and still is, to the advance of science itself. For if there had been nothing but cold logic and insensitive reason, science would never have come into existence. One might even, with a slight flamboyance, go so far as to say that there is no science entirely devoid of conscience, for there is no science without love. By what would the scientist be carried forward and upheld, if not by the strange 'passion for knowledge'?" Jean Rostand, *Can Man Be Modified?* (New York: Basic Books, 1959), p. 103.

2. Charles Frankel, *The Case for Modern Man* (New York: Harper, 1955), pp. 132–33.

3. Julian Huxley, "The Science of Society," *Virginia Quarterly Review*, XVI (1940), 356.

4. See Max Wertheimer, *Productive Thinking* (New York: Harper, 1945), pp. 168–88. See also Joseph Ratner, ed., *Intelligence in the Modern World* (New York: Random House, 1939), pp. 108–09.

5. John Dewey & Arthur F. Bentley, *Knowing and the Known* (Boston: Beacon, 1949), p. 134. Italics theirs.

6. This is a distinction made by Horace S. Fries. See his "Logical Simplicity: A Challenge to Philosophy and to Social Inquiry," *Philosophy of Science*, XVII (1950), 216–17.

7. Quoted by Hadley Cantril, Adelbert Ames, Jr., Albert H. Hastorf, and Wm. H. Ittelson, "Psychology and Scientific Research," *Science*, CX (1949), 521.

8. *Ibid.*, p. 495. "The conditional relationships we abstract out of a total situation and except for which the situation would not exist do not exist in their own right. Nor is there any adequate intellectual explanation of their existence. These conditional relationships or aspects of a total phenomenon … the scientist calls 'variables.' … Variables that provide the bases for standards are purely the creations of man, enabling him to formulate an abstract, common, determined phenomenal world. The variables employed in any scientific research are based on intuitive judgments and in any concrete investigation depend upon the way in which the investigator has formulated his problem."

9. "If the natural scientists attempt to abstract themselves from direct concern for human welfare in their special investigations, on the grounds that it might divert or prejudice their efforts, that is itself an evaluation of their aims, their tasks, and the best ways of fulfilling them. It is, in other words, not an exclusion of evaluations, but an insistence that evaluations be appropriate to the matter at hand. And that, in general, it seems to me, is not essentially different from the integrity of workmanship that we ask from a mechanic, a butcher or an artist." Francis M. Myers, *The Warfare of Democratic Ideals* (Yellow Springs, Ohio: Antioch Press, 1956), p. 208. Dewey, however, makes an important distinction: "The soundness of the principle that moral condemnation and approbation should be excluded from the operations of obtaining and weighing material data and from the operations by which conceptions for dealing with the data are instituted, is, however, often converted into the notion that all evaluations should be excluded. This conversion is, however, effected only through the intermediary of a thoroughly fallacious notion; the notion, namely, that the moral blames and approvals in question *are* evaluative and that they exhaust the field of evaluation. For they are *not* evaluative in any logical sense of evaluation. They are not even judgments in the logical sense of judgment. For they rest upon some preconceptions of ends that *should* or *ought* to be attained. This preconception excludes ends (consequences) from the field of inquiry and reduces inquiry at its very best to the truncated and distorted business of finding out means for realizing objectives already settled upon. Judgment which is actually judgment (that satisfies the logical conditions of judgment) institutes means-consequences (ends) in *strict conjugate relation* to each other." *Logic: The Theory of Inquiry,* (New York: Holt, 1938), p. 496. Italics his.

10. C. H. Waddington, *The Scientific Attitude*, revised ed. (London: Penguin, 1948), p. 112.

11. Jean Rostand, *The Substance of Man* (New York: Doubleday, 1962), p. 78.

12. Cf. Edgar Zilsel, "The Genesis of the Concept of Scientific Progress," in *Roots of Scientific Thought*, ed. Philip P. Wiener & Aaron Noland (New York: Basic Books, 1957), pp. 251–75. A. C. Keller, commenting on "Zilsel, the Artisans, and the Idea of Progress in the Renaissance," *ibid.*, pp. 281–86, contends that the genesis of the idea of progress had a broader base than the artisans alone. However this may be, it should be pointed out that a scientific ideal of progress as elaborated by Zilsel to include:

> (1) the insight that scientific knowledge is brought about step by step through contributions of generations of explorers building upon and gradually amending the findings of their predecessors; (2) the belief that this process is never completed; (3) the conviction that contribution to this development, either for its own sake or for the public benefit, constitutes the very aim of the true scientist

is not very compatible with the idea of inexorable, relentless progress found to abound at times in social thinking. There is a world of difference between an idea and an ideal. The latter adds human effort, purpose, direction. It is melioristic.

13. J. Robert Oppenheimer, "Physics in the Contemporary World," in *Great Essays in Science*, ed. Martin Gardner (New York: Pocket Books, Inc., 1957), pp. 197–98.

14. Cf. S. E. Toulmin, "Crucial Experiments: Priestley and Lavoisier," in *Roots of Scientific Thought*, p. 491.

15. Henry Margenau, *Open Vistas* (New Haven: Yale University Press, 1961), p. 12.

16. James B. Conant, *On Understanding Science* (New York: Mentor, 1951), p. 23. Italics his.

17. C. S. Peirce's description of matter as "mind hide-bound with habit" remains to haunt us. So does the thought hazarded by Julian Huxley that mental activities

may inhabit lifeless matter at such a low level of intensity that they cannot be detected, becoming evident only as intensely concentrated in what we call a brain, an analogy being to electricity which, while abounding in nervous systems and nature, was recognized, until recently, only in the charge of the electric eel. See his *Living in a Revolution* (New York: Harper, 1942). Will it some day make sense to think of physical laws as habits of mindless matter paralleling description of human habits as institutionalizations and refinements of intention?

18. See above, pp. 19–21.

19. Clarence Edwin Ayres, "The Gospel of Technology," *American Philosophy Today and Tomorrow,* ed. Horace M. Kallen & Sidney Hook (New York: Lee Furman, 1935), p. 25.

20. Cantril *et al,* "Psychology and Scientific Research," p. 521. Italics theirs. They suggest: "The myth that 'science is objective' may tend to be fostered in most cultures today in an attempt to preserve whatever status quo exists by giving it scientific blessing."

21. Frankel, *The Case for Modern Man,* p. 138.

22. See Leonardo Olschki, "Galileo's Philosophy of Science," *Philosophical Review,* LII (1943), 355.

23. Dewey and Bentley, *Knowing and the Known,* p. 327.

24. Cf., for example, Huxley, "The Science of Society."

25. Werner Heisenberg, *Physics and Philosophy* (New York: Harper 1958), p. 81.

26. Max Born, *Physics and Politics* (New York: Basic Books, 1962), p. 51.

27. P. W. Bridgman, *Reflections of a Physicist* (New York: Philosophical Library, 1955), p. 315.

28. "Ways and means must be discovered of making value judgments themselves the subject matter for scientific inquiry." Cantril *et al,* "Psychology and Scientific Research," p. 521.

29. Graham Wallas, *Human Nature in Politics* (London: Constable, 1948), p. 76.

30. Robert E. Park, "Social Planning and Human Nature," *Publication of the American Sociological Society,* XXIX (1935), 22–23.

31. The first steps from "the objective" into "the subjective" are well shown in Peral H. M. King's description of a training program for linking in the hosiery industry where it was found necessary to hire a psychologist in order to delve below the surface of objective job analysis (time and motion study) into subjective analysis of the kinesthetic and perceptual aspects of the job. ["Task Perception and Interpersonal Relations in Industrial Training: Part II," *Human Relations,* I (1948), 373–412.] Here is the testimony of a group of psychologists: "Psychology runs the risk of retarding its discovery of new bases for psychological standards through the use of bases for standards employed successfully in the past by the physical sciences. . . . By refusing to place firm reliance on standards whose bases are necessarily subjective, psychology sometimes complacently throws out some of the most important problems with which it should be concerned." Cantril *et al,* "Psychology and Scientific Research," p. 518.

32. This topic is expanded below: pp. 124–27, 147–48, 157, 215.

33. John Dewey, *Human Nature and Conduct* (New York: Holt, 1922), p. 235.

34. Dewey in Ratner, ed., *Intelligence in the Modern World,* pp. 315–25.

35. Cf. A. C. Crombie, "From Rationalism to Experimentalism," in Wiener & Noland, ed., *Roots of Scientific Thought,* pp. 125–30.

36. Donald Morrison, "Public Administration and the Art of Governance," review of *Case Reports in Public Administration, Public Administration Review,* V (1945), 84.

37. Dewey in Ratner, ed., *Intelligence in the Modern World,* pp. 316, 951.

38. See below pp. 200–208, 235–70.

39. Compare Horace S. Fries, "A Methodological Consideration," *The Journal of General Psychology*, XXXIII (1945), 11–20.

40. See Toulmin, "Crucial Experiments: Priestley and Lavoisier," pp. 481–96. See also Conant, *On Understanding Science.*

41. Ratner in *Intelligence in the Modern World*, p. 124. Italics his.

42. Einstein himself clung to the idea of determinism, as did Planck. Here is what Max Born says: "Determinism presumes that the initial state is given with absolute precision. Given the smallest margin of uncertainty, there will be a point in the development of events from which prediction will become impossible. The concept of absolute precision of physical measurements is obviously absurd, a mental abstraction created by mathematicians to simplify the logic of their systems of thought. It belongs as little to physics as do all other statements which are in principle not verifiable—for example, absolute simultaneity in the theory of relativity, or the rotation period of an electron in Bohr's atomic theory. The principle of elimination of empirically meaningless statements ... is a heuristic idea, which has proved its worth in all parts of modern physics." *Physics & Politics*, p. 34. Sir Arthur S. Eddington explains that "Anything which depends on the relative location of electrons in an atom is unpredictable more than a minute fraction of a second ahead. ... The break-down of an atomic nucleus, such as occurs in radio activity, is not predetermined by anything in the existing scheme of physics. All that the most complete theory can prescribe is how frequently configurations favoring an explosion will occur on the average." ["The Decline of Determinism," in Gardner, ed., *Great Essays in Science*, p. 253.] Which is to say that the future is never entirely determined by the past; it is sometimes practically determined.

43. "Sometimes people say that this atomic theory is characterized by the fact that we cannot observe a system without disturbing it. But that is not quite right. It is not the disturbance which makes the trouble; it is the fact that the means of observation would be frustrated as a means of observation if we tried to take account of the disturbance which we are making." J. Robert Oppenheimer, "Analogy in Science," *The American Psychologist*, XI (1956), 132.

44. It appears to this writer that the epistemological leap back into subject-object (body & soul; individual freedom & social power; physical & moral; matter & life) dichotomies through the analogical device of emphasizing correspondence to the physicist's partition between system and measuring tool—as put forward by Bohr in his extrapolation of complementarity into methodology and limitation of knowledge —has by no means been warranted by experiment—or even by observational evidence, for that matter. It remains to be seen whether and to what extent complementarity has a place in the realm of purpose. The principle of complementarity may serve as an eye-opener in bringing about understanding of human behavior by helping in the reevaluation of such dichotomies as freedom vs causality. But cues and analogies from the physical sciences are only a start, needed perhaps to help social science catch up and set an even keel. In the end we should be prepared to see physical science find its well-springs in social science—the discipline that can get within its subject-matter. (See below, pp. 125–27.) The quantum theory also contains the insight that 'the observer must somehow be included in the system.' Cf. Bridgman, *Reflections of a Physicist*, p. 152.

45. See, for example, Dewey, *Logic: The Theory of Inquiry*, Chap. 22.

46. "The parallelogram of forces, like all the 'exact' devices of science, is without temporal significance. That they escape all implication of time is indeed the mark of their 'exactness'." C. O. Weber, "Scientific Method and Moral Concepts," *Journal of Philosophy*, XXII (1925), p. 298.

47. Oppenheimer, "Analogy in Science," p. 134. " 'Prediction' is a misleading term when used to designate the basic test of scientific truth. What the scientist actually

employs in the laboratory (even in the field of astronomy, though not so obviously here) is concrete transformability. That principle, theory, or 'law' is dignified as scientific which best promotes the actual attainment or control of concrete transformations.... And 'results' and 'production' mean *controlled transformations*. If the social scientist wishes to learn from the nature sciences how to assure objectivity, he will try to test his principles and theories on the rock of concrete social-human transformations." Horace S. Fries, "Liberty and Science," *Public Administration Review*, III (1943), 271–72. (Italics his.)

48. Dewey, *Logic: The Theory of Inquiry*, p. 456. Italics his.

49. Logically, at least, the same pattern obtains where the change affects the conditions of observation instead of the subject-matter under inquiry, because observer, conditions of observation and subject-matter are all merely aspects of the transaction of inquiry. "If you perform specified gymnastics with a telescope at the proper time, you will see an eclipse."

Chapter Six

1. On free speech, see Chapter 16 below.

2. Erich Fromm, "The Psychology of Normalcy," *Dissent*, I (Spring, 1954), 142.

3. Notice how much more tenacious the idea of charity is than are the much less moral ideas of the philosopher's stone, the Northwest Passage, or the elixir of life—once also very powerful controls and inspirations behind human behavior.

4. There was a bit of experimentation that took place in Ancient Greece. Archimedes of Syracuse, as the originator of the experimental science of mechanics, was the most outstanding exception to the practice of limiting inquiry to observation—until the time of Galileo.

5. See above, p. 40.

6. See below, pp. 224–25.

7. Herbert A. Simon, for example, believes that "we are in time going to have theory in management—theory of the kind that predicts reality, and not the kind that is contrasted with practice." "Modern Organization Theories," *Advanced Management*, XV (October, 1950), 4. Horace S. Fries counters, "If ... science is merely a method for increasing the accuracy of prophecies about the future, then at very best we can use it ... only to try to prepare ourselves for an adjustment to the inevitabilities of fate." "Liberty and Science," *Public Administration Review*, III, (1943), 271.

8. The impossibility of the smug status arrogated by Malinowski-The-Agnostic: "Let us work for the maintenance of the eternal truths which have guided mankind out of barbarism to culture, and the loss of which seems to threaten us with barbarism again. The rationalist and agnostic must admit that even if he himself cannot accept these truths, he must at least recognize them as indispensable pragmatic figments without which civilization cannot exist." Bronislaw Malinowski, *The Foundations of Faith and Morals*, Ridell Memorial Lectures, 1934–1935 (London: Oxford University Press, 1936), last page. People have thought before that the truth would destroy civilization.

9. In contradiction to such cynical pronouncement as this: "To gain the material support necessary to expand social science as *science* ... the social scientist must gain the support of the man of affairs. And how can he do this but by convincing the man of affairs that his work holds out promise of greater success in the conscious manipulation of social forces and the 'mass mind.' " Reinhard Bendix, quoted by Andrew Hacker, "The Specter of Predictable Man," *Antioch Review*, XIV (1954), 195.

10. Perhaps the modern fashion could be productively used here, describing purpose in terms of field.

11. This analysis of the idea of causality as deriving from the imposition of social organization on nature is indebted to Julius P. Weinberg's analysis in a Freshman Forum lecture, University of Wisconsin, WHA Radio broadcast, May 22, 1958. Compare Ernst Mach on the idea of cause as an intrusion of mind into nature: *The Science of Mechanics: A Critical and Historical Account of Its Development*, trans. Thomas J. McCormack, 6th ed. (La Salle, Ill: Open Court, 1960), p. 580.

12. F. R. Moulton, "Influence of Astronomy on Science," in *Readings in the Physical Sciences*, ed. Harlow Shapley, Helen Wright, and Samuel Rapport (New York: Appleton-Century-Crofts, Inc., 1948), 87.

13. It is to be doubted that "cause and effect" is the last anthropomorphism, the last intrusion of mind into matter, or, as some would say, the final expression of *hubris*. As Dampier suggests, there is a larger, more general pattern:

> The regularities of science may be put into it by our procedure of observation or experiment. White light is an irregular disturbance, into which regularity is introduced by our examination with prism or grating; an atom can only be examined by gross interference which must disturb its normal structure; Rutherford may have created the nucleus he thought he was discovering. Substance vanishes, and we come to form, in quantum, waves, and in relativity, curvature. The form or pattern of the picture of nature we are accustomed to is one we most easily accept for new ideas, and because they are taken into it they become 'laws of nature'—subjective laws which have grown out of the subjective aspect of physical knowledge. Thus the epistemological method leads us to study the nature of the accepted frame of thought. We can predict *a priori* certain characteristics which any knowledge must have, merely because it is in the frame, though physicists may rediscover its characteristics *a posteriori*.

> And so with the mathematics we use—they are not in our scheme of physics till we put them there. The success of the operations whereby mathematics can be introduced depends on the extent to which our experiences can be related to each other. Mathematically the process needed is contained in what is called the Theory of Groups and Group Structure.

Sir William Cecil Dampier, *A History of Science* (Cambridge University Press, 1949), pp. 491–92.

The following passage attributed to Anaximander indicates that an earlier age was more candid in its mixing of the moral into the physical. "Into that [infinite and eternal primary substance] from which things take their rise they pass away once more, as is ordained, for they make reparation and satisfaction to one another for their injustice according to the ordering of time." From Werner Heisenberg, *Physics and Philosophy* (New York: Harper, 1958), p. 60.

14. See Summary to Chapter 7, pp. 140–42.

15. Arthur Stanley Eddington, "The Decline of Determinism," in *Great Essays in Science*, ed. Martin Gardner (New York: Pocket Books, 1959), p. 261. Italics his.

16. Compare Henry Margenau's discussion of the difference between freedom and chance as "choice supervening upon chance." *Open Vistas* (New Haven: Yale University Press, 1961), p. 213.

17. "The most comprehensive units in personality are broad intentional dispositions, future-pointed. These characteristics are unique for each person, and tend to attract, guide, inhibit the more elementary units to accord with the major intentions themselves. This proposition is valid in spite of the large amount of unordered, impulsive, and conflictful behavior in every life. Finally, these cardinal characteristics are not infinite in number but for any given life in adult years are relatively few and ascertainable. This fact should encourage psychodiagnosticians to seek

methods more appropriate than some they now employ." Gordon W. Allport, *Becoming* (New Haven: Yale University Press, 1955), pp. 92–93.

18. Norman Cameron, "A Biosocial Approach to Ethics," in *The Cleavage in Our Culture*, ed. Frederick Burkhardt (Boston: Beacon, 1952), p. 129. Italics his.

19. Eduard C. Lindeman, "Child Labor and the Community—a Note on New Procedures for Social Research," *Social Forces*, IV (1926), 774.

20. There are great opportunities for dialectical subtleties behind this analysis of coercion and control. For example, is a man controlled by fear (instead of knowing) when that fear turns out to be right? Or is it still coercion? Is he coerced when what he knows is wrong? Or is that still control? The answer, of course, lies in the transactional matrix where watertight compartmentalization of emotion and thought is denied.

21. See above, pp. 68–70.

22. Roger Ernle Money-Kyrle, *Psychoanalysis and Politics* (New York: W. W. Norton, 1950), p. 66.

23. Jean Rostand, *The Substance of Man* (New York: Doubleday, 1962), p. 41.

24. See Ralph Schwitzgebel, *Streetcorner Research; An Experimental Approach to the Juvenile Delinquent* (Cambridge, Mass.: Harvard University Press, 1964).

25. Carl R. Rogers, "A Therapist's View of the Good Life," *The Humanist*, XVII (1957), 299. Abraham Maslow is making a notable contribution to this idea of maturity in his attempts to clarify the meaning of psychological health. See esp. his "Self-Actualizing People: A Study in Psychological Health," in *The Self: Explorations in Personal Growth*, ed. Clark E. Moustakas (New York: Harper, 1956), pp. 160–94.

26. Robert Roessler, "A Psychiatrist's View of Morality," *The Humanist*, XVIII (1958), 333.

27. *Ibid.*, p. 335.

28. See above, fn. 43 to p. 96.

29. Cf. James L. McCamy, *Science and Public Administration* (University of Alabama Press, 1960,) pp. 173–75.

30. P. W. Bridgman, *Reflections of a Physicist* (New York: Philosophical Library, 1955), pp. 143-44

31. See below p. 218.

32. Lee R. Steiner, "Why Do People Consult the Occult?" *The Humanist*, XIX (1959), 30.

Chapter Seven

1. Attempts at mathematical treatment for purposes of prediction and control succeed only in portraying a curious world of fantasy. See, for example, L. S. Shapley and Martin Shubik, "A Method for Evaluating the Distribution of Power in a Committee System," *American Political Science Review*, XLVIII (1954), 787–92. This is again an expansion of the theory of games. The appropriate comment is again:

> "To play is to let purpose wander free;
> Who play with purpose court insanity."

Now is not the time to cut short such efforts, however. They should rather be judiciously encouraged so that we may the sooner assess their limits.

2. Carl J. Friedrich, *Constitutional Government and Democracy* (Boston: Ginn, 1941), p. 19.

3. T. V. Smith, "Power: Its Ubiquity and Legitimacy," *American Political Science Review*, XLV (1951), 693. Italics his.

4. Harold D. Lasswell and Abraham Kaplan, *Power and Society* (New Haven: Yale University Press, 1950), p. 75.

5. James K. Feely, "An Analysis of Administrative Purpose," *American Political Science Review*, XLV (1951), 1071.

6. Shapley and Shubik, "A Method for Evaluating the Distribution of Power in a Committee System," p. 787.

7. Charles E. Merriam, *Political Power*, Part II of *A Study of Power* by Harold D. Lasswell, Charles E. Merriam, and T. V. Smith (Glencoe, Ill.: Free Press, 1950), p. 7.

8. Max Weber, *From Max Weber, Essays in Sociology*, ed. & trans. H. H. Gerth and C. Wright Mills (London: Routledge & Kegan Paul, 1948), p. 180.

9. *Ibid.*, p. 78.

10. Lasswell and Kaplan, *Power and Society*, p. 75.

11. Smith, "Power: Its Ubiquity and Legitimacy," p. 693.

12. "We find in ourselves a power to begin or to forbear, continue or end several actions of our minds, and motions of our bodies, barely by a thought or preference of the mind ordering, or, as it were, commanding the doing or not doing such a particular action." John Locke, *Essay Concerning Human Understanding*, Chapter XXI, Section 5.

13. E. g., Peter Drucker, "The New Philosophy Comes to Life," *Harper's Magazine*, CCXV (August, 1957), 36–40.

14. For comprehensive analysis of the failings of this approach to power see my *Sin and Science* (Yellow Springs, Ohio: Antioch Press, 1956).

15. See George W. Stoking's criticism of *American Capitalism: The Concept of Countervailing Power* by John Kenneth Galbraith, in his review in *American Political Science Review*, XLVIII (1954), 230.

16. "Those who wish a monopoly of social power find desirable the separation of habit and thought, action and soul, so characteristic of history. For this dualism enables them to do the thinking and planning, while others remain the docile, even if awkward, instruments of execution. Until this scheme is changed, democracy is bound to be perverted in realization." John Dewey, *Human Nature and Conduct* (New York: Holt, 1922), p. 72.

17. See Friedrich, *Constitutional Government and Democracy*, p. 17; Hallowell, "Politics and Ethics," p. 653; Odegard, *Sin and Science*, pp. 122–23.

18. Luigi Barzini, Jr., "The Real Mafia," *Harper's Magazine*, CCVIII (June, 1954), 40, 42. Italics added.

19. Isak Dinesen, *Out of Africa* (New York: Random House, 1937), p. 375.

20. Compare Gordon W. Allport's comments on ego-extension, *Becoming* (New Haven: Yale University Press, 1955), p. 45. Note how easy it is for America to focus on a new Frontier—Mars, the latest property-surrogate push—making room for the expansion of the Self in the glory of the space program. How much easier it is to spend billions of work days and hundreds of billions of dollars expanding the Self among the stars, than to expend moral resources expanding among other Selves in non-coercive fellowship.

21. John Kenneth Galbraith, *The New Industrial State* (Boston: Houghton Mifflin, 1967). Galbraith's wisdom traces back to Berle's thesis of "separation of ownership and control" in Adolf A. Berle, Jr., and Gardiner C. Means, *The Modern Corporation and Private Property* (New York: Macmillan, 1932).

22. Robert E. Park, "Social Planning and Human Nature," *Publication of the American Sociological Society*, XXIX (1935), 27.

23. See above, pp. 16–18, 66–67.

24. See above, pp. 5–6.

25. For example, controlling the use of land through strategic location and timing of highways and sewers. Compare Merriam's use of the term "strategic control" in *Political Power.*

26. "To make the State absolutely sovereign, the repository of an abstract social will, is to make it frankly utopian, to remove it from all contacts with the actualities of human existence.... On the other hand, to reduce the State to the level of the other elements of institutional life is to deprive it of that unifying function which constitutes its ultimate claim on existence. That is precisely the mistake made by all theories that would organize the State along functional lines: the industrial State satisfied a need of human nature only so far as man is an economic being; the Guild Socialist State satisfied many specific human needs, but it has no contribution to make to the indivisible moral life of the whole man." Joseph Carson, Jr., Review of *The Ethical Basis of the State* by Norman Wilde, *Journal of Philosophy,* XXII (1925), 356.

27. David B. Truman, *The Governmental Process* (New York: Knopf, 1951), p. 24.

28. John Dewey, "Creative Democracy—The Task Before Us," in *The Philosophy of the Common Man,* ed. Sidney Ratner (New York: G. P. Putnam, 1940), p. 91.

29. See above p. 58.

30. "... (when both [man] and [woman] are attending to the *agreeableness* of their activity *to the other*) the conduct is called *cooperation.* ... When more than two persons are engaged in that mutually-regarding activity, the combination is called a *democracy.* ... In cooperation each one of the at least two parts of the machine (team) which is working, substantially contains in itself a secondary personality (or structure) that is a duplicate in miniature of the reacting part (and so on in regress) so that the reactions of the reacting parts are known simultaneously with its own actions.... To put it in every day terms, we know we can feel our own actions and at the same time feel roughly (inaccurately) how the reactions of our partner will subsequently affect *him;* and we can thus work together." Scudder Klyce, *Universe* (Winchester, Mass.: S. Klyce, 1921), pp. 210–11. Italics his.

31. "In theory, democracy should be a means of stimulating original thought, and of evoking action deliberately adjusted in advance to cope with new forces. In fact it is still so immature that its main effect is to multiply occasions for imitation. If progress in spite of this fact is more rapid than in other social forms, it is by accident, since the diversity of models conflict with one another and thus give individuality a chance in the resulting chaos of opinions." Dewey, *Human Nature and Conduct,* pp. 65–66.

32. Robert K. Merton, quoted by Harold Orlans, *Utopia, Ltd.* (New Haven: Yale University Press, 1953), p. 302.

33. Cf. David Easton, *The Political System* (New York: Knopf, 1953), Chapter 5; *Varieties of Political Theories* (Englewood Cliffs, N. J.: Prentice Hall, 1966), p. 147.

Chapter Eight

1. See below, pp. 186–87.

2. See below, p. 166.

3. See above, pp. 24–25.

4. Mary P. Follett, *Creative Experiences* (New York: Longmans, Green, 1924), p. 134.

5. Gordon W. Allport, "The Psychology of Participation," in *Human Factors in Management,* ed. Schuyler Dean Hoslett (New York: Harper, 1946), p. 259. Gordon W. Allport, *Becoming* (New Haven: Yale University Press, 1955).

"The etiquette and the public spirit that are necessary to make institutions of free discussion and consent work must come out of the habitual personal experience of men and women with these institutions. And they can only have this experience if they have the chance to participate meaningfully in the work of social groups that have some independent power and are doing something important." Charles Frankel, *The Case for Modern Man* (New York: Harper, 1955), p. 204. Cf. also Douglas McGregor, "Conditions for Effective Leadership in the Industrial Situation," in Hoslett, ed., *op., cit.,* pp. 47–48, for a similar understanding of participation.

6. "Participation, as opposed to peripheral motor activity, sinks a shaft into the inner-subjective regions of the personality. It taps central values. Thus in studying participation the psychologist has an approach to the complete person." Allport, "The Psychology of Participation," p. 263.

7. See above, pp. 49–52.

8. The frailty of attitude (the electoral system of majority rule) is most evident in countries where it is not buttressed from below by an established participative process. The Latin American coup d'état republics are cases in point.

The representative vote did not come about until bifurcation into subjective vs objective, until the notion of opposition of group interests had grown up. See Ewart Lewis, "The Contribution of Medieval Thought to the American Political Tradition," *American Political Science Review,* L (1956), 470.

9. See above, pp. 65–66.

10. David B. Truman, *The Governmental Process* (New York: Knopf, 1951), p. 218.

11. Robert A. Dahl, *Preface to Democratic Theory* (Chicago; University of Chicago Press, 1956), p. 145.

12. *Ibid.*

13. Elton Mayo, *The Political Problem of Industrial Civilization* (Cambridge, Mass.: Harvard University Graduate School of Business Administration, 1947), p. 13.

14. Cf. Dwight Waldo, "Development of Theory of Democratic Administration," *American Political Science Review,* XLVI (1952), 89, and Reinhard Bendix, "Bureaucracy: The Problem in Its Setting," *American Sociological Review,* XII (1947), 501.

15. Robert Tannenbaum and Frederick Massarik, "Participation by Subordinates in the Managerial Decision-Making Process," *Canadian Journal of Economics and Political Science,* XVI (1950), 416–18.

16. Woodrow Wilson, "The Study of Administration," *Political Science Quarterly,* II, (1887), 208.

17. See Charles P. McCormick's two books: *The Power of People* (New York: Harper, 1949) and *Multiple Management* (New York: Harper, 1938), and Thomas R. Reid, "Multiple Management Re-examined," *Advanced Management,* VIII (1943), 60–63.

18. See H. H. Carey, "Consultative Supervision and Management," *Personnel,* XVIII (1942), 286–95.

19. See Clinton S. Golden and Harold J. Ruttenberg, *The Dynamics of Industrial Democracy* (New York: Harper, 1942).

20. Everett Reimer, "Magic and Science in Human Relations," a review of books, *Public Administration Review,* XII (1952), 208.

21. A. A. Imberman, "Personalities in Labor-Management Conflicts," *Advanced Management,* XV (December, 1950), 19–20. See also William H. Whyte, Jr., *Is Anybody Listening?* (New York: Simon & Schuster, 1952).

22. Mayo, *The Political Problem of an Industrial Civilization.*

23. "From the sixteenth century onwards we began a rapid descent from a real civilization toward the mere cultures—the types of social organization that change and pass, leaving only historic traces." *Ibid.,* p. 20. "The Medieval idea of the co-operation of all is the only satisfactory source of civilized procedure." *Ibid.,* p. 23.

24. Cf. Reinhard Bendix and Lloyd H. Fisher, "The Perspectives of Elton Mayo," *Review of Economics,* XXXI (1949), 312–19. My reading of Mayo agrees more closely with Bendix and Fisher than with George C. Homans, "Some Corrections," *ibid.,* pp. 319–21.

25. Gouldner has very similar comments to make about Philip Selznick. Alvin W. Gouldner, "Metaphysical Pathos and the Theory of Bureaucracy," *American Political Science Review,* XLIX (1955), 496–507.

26. Roscoe C. Martin, *Grass Roots* (University of Alabama Press, 1957), p. 18.

27. John D. Lewis, "Some New Forms of Democratic Participation in American Government," in *The Study of Comparative Government,* ed. Jasper B. Shannon (New York: Appleton-Century-Crofts, 1949), pp. 172–73.

28. Cf. Selznick's comments on TVA's "cooptation" of local groups. Philip Selznick, *T.V.A. and the Grass Roots* (Berkeley: University of California Press, 1949).

29. Lehman, for example, testifies that "UNRRA can not aid effectively in reliev-ing distress in its full mission if it does not nurture and in the end develop the active and participating collaboration of all or, at least, most of the United Nations. ... Some of these [advisory] committees have been used effectively both to gain the technical knowledge of the delegates of the several nations represented and to increase the total collaboration of each nation in the work of UNRRA." Herbert H. Lehman, "Some Problems in International Administration," *Public Administration Review,* V (1945), 96–97.

30. See Chester Bowles, "OPA Volunteers: Big Democracy in Action," *Public Administration Review,* V (1945), 357.

31. Arthur F. Bentley ran into such difficulties in his early book, *The Process of Government* (University of Chicago Press, 1908). Hadley Cantril bravely begins Chapter 5 of *The "Why" of Man's Experience* (New York: Macmillan, 1950) by including bodily activity, intellectual activity, and the activity of making value-judgments all under the category of action. But then he reverts, unannounced, to the old definition in terms of motion. From "we experience a value attribute in the action of making the judgment" on p. 79, he turns to "any judgment we have must end in action if it is to become part of us" on p. 80.

32. George H. Mead, "Scientific Method and the Moral Sciences," *The Interna-tional Journal of Ethics,* XXXIII (1923), 241.

33. See above, pp. 68, 119.

34. See below, pp. 186–87.

Chapter Nine

1. This is, I take it, equivalent to what Gordon W. Allport calls "propriate striv-ing." See his *Becoming* (New Haven: Yale University Press, 1955), pp. 47–51.

2. Automatic resistance to change is well illustrated in the material with which L. Coch and J. P. R. French, Jr. experimented: "Overcoming Resistance to Change," *Human Relations,* I (1948), 512–32. Their evidence supports the conclusion that par-ticipation is superior to representation as a way of overcoming resistance to change. They add the very interesting note that the representatives of an experimental group overcame their resistance at about the same rate as the group they repre-sented, but slower than the members of a participative group. *Ibid.,* p. 522.

3. See below, pp. 226–27.

4. One of Kurt Lewin's most famous experiments demonstrated that people who dislike particular foods and refuse to be persuaded to eat them will change their eating habits, independently of their dislikes, when they participate in a group discussion and decision to change food habits. Cf. Kurt Lewin, "Group Decision and Social Change," in *Readings in Social Psychology*, ed. T. Newcom and E. Hartley (New York: Holt, 1947), p. 334. Allport concludes: "A person ceases to be reactive and contrary in respect to a desirable course of conduct only when he himself has had a hand in declaring that course of conduct to be desirable. Such findings add up to the simple proposition that people must have a hand in saving themselves; they cannot and will not be saved from the oustide." Allport, Gordon W. "The Psychology of Participation," in *Human Factors in Management*, ed. S. D. Hoslett (New York: Harper, 1946), p. 259.

5. Treatise on Grace, Part I of Second Part, Question 109, Art. 6, *Summa Theologica*.

6. Cf. Eric Hoffer, *The Ordeal of Change* (New York: Harper & Row, 1963), pp. 12–13. See David S. Brown, "The Key to Self-Help: Improving the Administrative Capabilities of Aid-Receiving Countries," *Public Administrative Review*, XXIV (1964).

7. Cf. Hadley Cantril, *The "Why" of Man's Experience* (New York: Macmillian, 1950), p. 166.

8. See above, p. 56.

9. What has here been called conservative drag might well, by expanding on Allport's basic terminology, be called "propriate conservatism." The conservatism of the man obviously to be hurt by a proposal might likewise be termed "peripheral conservatism" were it not for the fact that immediate hurt usually involves the "proprium" at some stage, even though money, property, respect, or some other such is generally the primary concern.

10. See above, pp. 68, 119.

11. See above, p. 44.

12. See above, pp. 85, 152–53, and note 12 to p. 199.

13. See above p. 82.

14. See below, p. 180.

15. Cf. Horace S. Fries, "Social Planning," in *The Cleavage in Our Culture*, ed. Frederick Burkhardt (Boston: Beacon, 1952), p. 82.

16. See above, p. 82.

17. See A. J. Carlson, "Science and the Supernatural," Pamphlet of The American Humanist Association, January, 1964, p. 4.

18. Scientific enterprise does not differ from the rest of life as much as we might wish to think. In particular the readiness of scientists to accept the overturn of established theories by the evidence of simple contradictory experimental evidence is not so facile as commonly supposed. Old ideas can be as well entrenched in scientific minds as in any others. See James B. Conant, *On Understanding Science* (New York: Mentor, 1947), p. 48.

19. C. Wright Mills, "The Conservative Mood," *Dissent*, I (Winter, 1954), 27.

20. See above pp. 150–51. Channeled into tentative group experiment (instead of individual or mass action) the radical bent can become the start of a new cycle of rounded experience.

21. This, of course, does not mean that analogy must be therefore discarded as guide, nor that either creativity or analogy must be dropped as tool of inquiry. Cf. Robert Oppenheimer, "Analogy in Science," *The American Psychologist*, XI (1956), 127–35.

22. Charles E. Merriam, *The Role of Politics in Social Change* (New York: New York University Press, 1936), pp. 98, 99.

Chapter Ten

1. Without attempting to track down intellectual indebtedness—a feckless activity at its best—we may list among the persons influenced by Follett's thought: Metcalf, Urwick, Ordway Tead, Harleigh Trecker, John Gaus, Horace Fries, Morris Llewellyn Cooke.

2. Except for the work of John Gaus, the contributions of later writers that may be said to stem from Follett's thinking have been more in the nature of quoted theme plus variations. And Urwick, for all his appreciation and commentation, clearly misunderstands some of Follett's most firm and fundamental assertions. Contrast, for example, his remarks on "consent" in his "The Problem of Organization," *Bulletin of the Taylor Society and of the Society of Industrial Engineers*, I (1935), 164, with Follett's comments in *The New State* (New York: Longmans, Green, 1918), pp. 21, 180–81.

3. Mary P. Follett, *Dynamic Administration*, ed. H. C. Metcalf & L. Urwick (London: Bath Management Publications Trust, 1941), p. 297.

4. The casual American reader would find her way of thinking unfamiliar and therefore fuzzy. While much of her talk in terms of "principles" is a heritage from the Scientific Management movement, much else—the General Will, the state as the fulfillment of the individual, the socialization of natural rights, freedom as the capacity of becoming our real selves in community with others—either derives from or coincides with the school of English Idealists. "If a political philosophy has to be understood to be a social force as well it cannot afford to remain in the realm of vagueness and near-mysticism. It is characteristic of idealism, and it has contributed to so much misunderstanding of its message, that it sometimes exhibits a quality of tone which is uncharitably described as priggishness." Adam B. Ulam, *Philosophical Foundations of English Socialism* (Cambridge: Harvard, 1951), p. 26.

5. See Follett, *The New State*, pp. 52–57 (against Teleological ethics); 137–47 (chapters entitled "Democracy not 'Liberty' and 'Equality,'" and "Democracy Not the Majority."); 210 ("What we need above everything else is clear thinking.... Take care of your thinking and your morals will take care of themselves.")

6. See *ibid.*, p. 21; Follett, *Creative Experience*, pp. 197–210; and Follett, *Dynamic Administration*, pp. 210–29.

7. See Follett, *The New State*, pp. 60–68, 137, 21 ("There is no such thing as the 'individual,' there is no such thing as 'society'; there is only the group and the group-unit—the social individual.")

8. See Follett, *Creative Experience*, pp. xii, 179–94.

9. See Follett, *The New State*, pp. 307–08.

10. "The truth is that the same process which creates all else creates the very purpose. That purpose is involved in the process, not prior to process, has far wider reaching consequences than can be taken up here. The whole philosophy of cause and effect must be rewritten." *Ibid.*, p. 57.

11. "Control must be generated by the activity which is to be controlled." Follett, *Creative Experience*, p. 224. See also Follett, *Dynamic Administration*, pp. 183–209; Mary P. Follett, "The Illusion of Final Authority," *Bulletin of the Taylor Society*, XI (1926), 246–49; and Mary P. Follett, "The Process of Control," in *Papers on the Science of Administration*, eds. L. Gulick & L. Urwick, 161–69. Urwick describes her "control" as a "self-generated control [that] does not coerce. It is neither spur nor carrot." Urwick, "The Problem of Organization," p. 169.

12. See Follett, *Creative Experience*, pp. 53–77.

13. Harry A. Overstreet, Review of *Creative Experience* by M. P. Follett, *Journal of Philosophy*, XXII (1925), 500.

14. Follett, *The New State*, p. 64.

15. *Ibid.,* p. 288.

16. *Ibid.,* pp. 159–60. "The most significant progress ... Miss Follett sees in substituting for the old ideas of 'business as trading and managing as manipulating,' the newer conception of business as 'an opportunity for individual development through the better organization of human relationships,' and of management as exercising 'creative ability in contribution to organization,' " Henry C. Metcalf, "Introduction," in *Business Management as a Profession,* ed. Henry C. Metcalf (Chicago: A. W. Shaw, 1927), pp. 6–7.

17. Follet, *New State,* p. 93.

18. *Ibid.,* p. 33.

19. "As progress is through the release and integration of the action tendencies of each and every individual in society, way should be provided for such activity to take place normally." Follett, *Creative Experience,* p. 224.

20. See Follett, *Dynamic Administration,* pp. 30–49.

21. I realize that Waldo once said that she put "great—perhaps too great—emphasis upon avoidance and resolution of conflict." Waldo, "Development of Theory of Democratic Administration," *American Political Science Review,* XLVI (1952), p. 96. But it is not at all clear that he had at that time read her *Creative Experience.*

22. Cf., for example, Follett, *New State,* pp. 21, 180–81.

23. Follett, *Creative Experience,* p. 198.

24. Follett, *Dynamic Administration,* p. 210. On p. 211 Follett refers to the inverted practice in the business world of "consent of the governors," where the department heads OK the plans of their underlings. This practice, of course, is not unknown in public administration. The consent system, however, has the same fault whether public or private, inverted or erect.

25. *Ibid.,* p. 219.

26. *Ibid.,* pp. 185–86.

27. *Ibid.,* p. 204. Circular Behavior is the basis of integration. (*Ibid.,* p. 105.) Follett sometimes used the word "coordination" in place of "integration," particularly in some of her later lectures where she apparently felt that it was easier to use a familiar term approximating her meaning than to go through a lengthy essay in definition.

28. Follett, *Creative Experience,* p. 156.

29. Follett, *Dynamic Administration,* p. 30.

30. Follett, *Creative Experience,* p. 301. Italics hers.

31. Follett, *Dynamic Administration,* p. 31. Sometimes she breaks the first into two categories: (1) voluntary submission, or self-sacrifice, and (2) struggle and victory of one side. *Creative Experience,* p. 156.

32. Follett, *Dynamic Administration,* p. 32. Italics hers. Lindeman describes a continuum of discussion results ranging from acquiescence to assent to compromise to consent to integration. "In this scale of qualitative values it is assumed that acquiescence in a solution accepted but unchanged by discussion is the lowest form of conclusion, whereas integration, the social invention of a wholly new solution, represents the highest form of result or emergence. Integration is considered a creative mode of resolving differences since it not merely gives security to all interests but utilizes these very differences as the dynamic elements in an inventing, creating enterprise." Eduard C. Lindeman, "Discussion," in *The Encyclopedia of Social Sciences,* ed. Edwin A. R. Seligman (New York: Macmillan, 1931), V, 167. See also Eduard C. Lindeman, *The Democratic Man,* ed. Robert Gessner (Boston: Beacon, 1956), pp. 56–62.

33. Follett, *Dynamic Administration,* p. 32. Because of Follett's indebtedness to the British Idealists, the following passage from Bosanquet is interesting: "A

hundred million people are resolved to march south at a given hour on given narrow roads; and another hundred million to march north on the same roads at the same time. Nobody need be devilish on either side. They do not want a collision; they *merely* want to do *exactly* what they have set their hearts on doing. But a frightful collision must ensue. Then, of course, when they are on the roads, and can see no way round, they will become devilish. Of course there is always a way round, if we look out for it in time. But stupidity prevents us. Nations are not alert, not sensitive to the minds and needs of other nations; they do not realise where others want to go and why; nor how their own direction can be modified in harmony with the others', and yet none of their really essential aims be sacrificed. They are not at all clear, perhaps, what are their own essential aims. *Their social arrangements do not permit a distinct vision of them.*" Bernard Bosanquet, *Some Suggestions in Ethics* (London: Macmillan, 1919), pp. 243–44. Last italics mine.

34. Follett, *Dynamic Administration*, p. 35.

35. "Conference and Compromise," *New Republic*, LXI (1929), 364–65.

36. Waldo, "Development of Theory of Democratic Administration," p. 96.

37. Follett, *New State*, p. 335.

38. Follett, *Dynamic Administration*, p. 219.

39. *Ibid.*, p. 229.

40. Lindeman, *The Democratic Man*, p. 60.

41. The point is that the segregated, selective, interest-oriented association of today revels in the narrowing fraternity of specialized function and compartmentalized knowledge. Cf. Follett, *New State*, p. 195. Difference, for her, is not the key to individuality but an aspect of creative activity. *Ibid.*, p. 63.

Follett's messianic participationism is very similar in tone and excitement to G. D. H. Cole's. She, however, takes firm exception to the "functional representation" of Guild Socialism because "it leaves the representative assembly as a mere registering and coordinating body," instead of a creating body. Follett, *Creative Experience*, p. 246.

42. Ralph Waldo Emerson, *The Essays of Ralph Waldo Emerson* (New York: Random House, 1944), p. 335.

43. Cf. Roscoe C. Martin, *Grass Roots* (University of Alabama Press, 1957) and *The Cities and the Federal System* (New York: Atherton, 1965).

Defenses of the neighborhood will be found in Baker Brownell, *The Human Community* (New York: Harper, 1950), and Arthur E. Morgan, *The Small Community* (New York: Harper, 1942). Lindeman on discussion is very similar to Follett on neighborhood groups. While what he says is much the same, he seems more stable about it, less rah-rah participate! Cf. Lindeman, *The Democratic Man*, pp. 94–103. Bosanquet also has a similar neighborhood concept. Cf. Ulam, *Philosophical Foundations of English Socialism*, pp. 53–54.

44. See L. Coch and J. P. R. French, "Overcoming Resistance to Change," *Human Relations*, I (1948), 512–32. Experimental studies have shown, particularly, that "it is easier to change ideology or cultural habits by dealing with groups rather than with individuals." Lewin in Kurt Lewin; Ronald Lippitt & Charles Hendry; Alvin Zander; John R. P. French, Jr., *et al.*, "The Practicality of Democracy," in *Human Nature and Enduring Peace*, ed. Gardner Murphy (Boston: Houghton-Mifflin, 1945), p. 312.

45. Norman R. F. Maier, "The Quality of Group Decisions as Influenced by the Discussion Leader," *Human Relations*, III (1950), 156.

46. Cf. "So You Appointed a Committee," (Two Lessons in Group Dynamics), *Educator's Washington Dispatch* (Supplement, January, 1948).

47. Cf. Lindeman, *The Democratic Man*, p. 99.

48. *Ibid.*, p. 93. The superiority of the group is at least partly due to its efficiency

in evaluating suggestions and rejecting false ideas. Cf. Maier, "The Quality of Group Decisions as Influenced by the Discussion Leader," p. 156. This special talent of the group obviously carries special implications in respect to objectivity and the social test of truth. Maier also points out that (1) "all problems do not raise the issue of solution quality per se . . . cooperation and support of a plan may be more important than the nature of the plan," (2) "many problems that require technical knowledge, and seem to demand the services of an expert, may also involve facts that the expert may not have at his disposal," (3) "some problems are purely problems of attitude so that practically the whole subject matter for solution is in the group." *Ibid.*, pp. 157–58.

49. Cf. Follett, *New State*, p. 143.

50. Maier, "The Quality of Group Decisions," p. 157.

51. Cf. Lindeman, *The Democratic Man*, p. 93.

52. Cf. Lewin, "Group Decision and Social Change," p. 336.

53. Cf. *Ibid.*, p. 342. Follett calls this not a group but a crowd.

54. Thomas Huxley's belief that 'fear of the opinion of their fellows' and 'conventions of honour' are the greatest restrainers [*Evolution and Ethics, and other Essays* (New York: D. Appleton, 1929), p. 29.] and Bertrand Russell's belief that wise allocation of praise and blame is the key to producing a good community [*Selected Papers of Bertrand Russell* (New York: Random House, 1927), p. 266.] must be considered waning truths held over from the days of vigorous organic group life.

55. Lewin in "The Practicality of Democracy," p. 310.

56. Maier, "The Quality of Group Decisions," pp. 162–63.

57. *Ibid.*, p. 170.

58. Horace S. Fries, "On Managerial Responsibility," *Advanced Management*, VIII (1943), 47.

59. Follett, *New State*, pp. 85, 86.

60. *Ibid.*, p. 109.

61. *Ibid.*, p. 119n.

62. Cf. e.g., Follett, *Dynamic Administrations*, p. 228.

63. "We take to war because we do not have enough vitality, to religion because we do not have enough spiritual energy." Follett, *New State*, p. 103.

64. Follett, *Creative Experience*, p. 163. Cf. also her *Dynamic Administration*, p. 36.

65. See above p. 164, and below p. 227.

66. Cf. John M. Gaus, "Public Participation in Federal Programs," in *Democracy in Federal Administration*, ed. O. E. Conaway, Jr. (Washington, D. C.: U. S. Department of Agriculture Graduate School, 1956), p. 15, and, of course, John Dewey, *The Public and Its Problems* (Chicago: Gateway Books, 1946).

67. Follett, *Dynamic Administration*, p. 190.

68. Cf., for example, *ibid.*, p. 229.

69. Cf., for example, *ibid.*, pp. 218–19 on unifying the aims of employers and employees, and *New State*, pp. 79–80 on seeing the larger community, the larger loyalty.

70. *Ibid.*, p. 65. The truth in this "spirit craves totality" idea is more accurately represented by Gordon W. Allport's concept of "propriate striving." See his *Becoming* (New Haven: Yale University Press, 1955), pp. 47–51.

71. Cf., for example, Ernest Cassirer, *An Essay on Man* (Garden City, New York: Doubleday, 1953), pp. 109–12. Particularly striking is the likeness of Follett's view to Cassirer's description of primitive man's view of nature: "neither merely theoretical nor merely practical; it is *sympathetic*." *Ibid.*, p. 109. Italics his.

72. Follett, *Dynamic Administration,* p. 258.

73. Waldo suggests, "It is arguable that Mary Parker Follett was as much theologian as social philosopher." "Development of Theory of Democratic Administration," p. 85. Follett has her own distinctive variety of pluralism equated with her distinctive interpretation of federalism: "(1) Sovereignty ... is the power generated within the group—dependent on the principle of interpenetration [integration]. (2) Man joins many groups—in order to express his multiple nature. These two principles give us federalism." (*New State,* p. 296.) "I have no medieval idea of mediate articulation, of individuals forming groups and groups forming the nation.... The members of the nation are to be individuals, not groups." (*Ibid.,* p. 256.) "I go to the polls to express the multiple man which the groups have created." (*Ibid.,* p. 292.) "The relation of neighbors one to another must be integrated into the substance of the state." (*Ibid.,* p. 257.)

74. See above pp. 96–97. It brings to mind a magazine story in which a time traveler accidentally stepped off the observation platform while visiting the age of dinosaurs. He crushed a small leaf with his foot, but upon returning to the hour he had left, he found that as a result of his slip a fascist revolution had swept over the land. It is a cause-and-effect mysticism in which each happening, no matter how paltry, has unending repercussions in a chain reaction echoing forever down the halls of time.

Follett's world-view of compounded wholeness built up by a Gestalt relating of relations is strikingly similar to the tight world of the absolute determinist where every occurrence has a cause. "The truth is that the same process which creates all else creates the very purpose. That purpose is involved in the process, not prior to process, has far wider consequences than can be taken up here. The whole philosophy of cause and effect must be rewritten." *New State,* p. 57.

75. Robert Oppenheimer, "Analogy in Science," *The American Psychologist,* XI (1956), 133.

76. Avery Leiserson, "The Study of Public Administration," in *The Elements of Public Administration,* ed. Fritz Morstein-Marx (New York: Prentice Hall, 1946), p. 44.

77. Follett's position is that "we verify through the process of creating," *Creative Experience,* p. 143.

78. "Unless we can have ends in view without experiencing them in concrete fact, no regulation of action is possible." John Dewey, *The Quest for Certainty* (New York: Minton, Balch, 1929), p. 151.

79. Follett, *Creative Experience,* p. 31. She is not entirely consistent in her denial of vicarious experience. See her usage on p. 245, *ibid.*

80. *Ibid.,* p. 150. Cf. *ibid.,* p. 198.

81. *Ibid.,* p. 150. Italics hers.

82. *Ibid.,* p. 21.

83. *Ibid.,* Chapter I.

84. *Ibid.,* pp. 212–17.

85. This may be a primarily American phenomenon. See Allport, "The Psychology of Participation," pp. 253–65, in which the motor orientation of American psychology is analyzed.

86. Follett, *Creative Experience,* p. 137.

87. See above, pp. 159–60.

88. Graham Wallas once wondered "whether, now that men lived in the larger world of knowledge and inference, rather than in the narrower world of sight and hearing, a patriotism of books and maps might not appear which should be a better guide to life than the patriotism of the village street." *Human Nature in Politics* (London: Constable, 1948), p. 271.

89. Wood's apt interpretation of Follett. See Arthur Evans Wood, "The Social Philosophy of Mary P. Follett," *Social Forces*, IV (1926), 767.

90. Follett would probably finally agree if confronted with a direct question. As a matter of fact, the extreme motor set she subscribes to is practically untenable—in evidence whereof are her self-contradictions. After discarding vicarious experience she says that "the core of the problem of responsibility is ... how to make people share vicariously in their representative's activity." (*Creative Experience*, p. 245.) While declaring that "the only way to change our characters is by *doing* things," (*Ibid.*, p. 143. Italics hers.) she is writing a book.

91. See above, pp. 134–35.

93. See above, pp. 56–57.

93. John M. Gaus, "The Authority of Organized Knowledge," *Public Administration Review*, II (1942), 167. Italics added. "Clarity of statute objectives and allocation of resources, common operating assumptions across all bureau and department lines as to common elements such as land use, for example, and department personnel familiar by experience with the relating of special expert knowledge to the variety of local conditions, seem to me the basic public participation in program making." Gaus, "Public Participation in Federal Programs," p. 18.

94. For example, *Creative Experience*, p. 187 and "The Illusion of Final Authority."

95. Follett, *Dynamic Administration*, p. 297. Also in her "The Process of Control" where she scrambles the succession. They are "classic" because so frequently culled from her writings for particular comment: for example, Gaus, "The Authority of Organized Knowledge," p. 166; Urwick, "The Problem of Organization," p. 167.

96. Follett, *Dynamic Administration*, p. 204.

97. *Ibid.*, p. 267.

Chapter Eleven

1. Even T. V. Smith. Sometimes his compromise or sportsmanship democracy seems almost to comprehend "integration," as in the following passage: "Moralists, by the very impotence of their method to effect monism, beg the question of agreement. When what they beg is not bequeathed, moralists are at an impasse. The politician cannot beg the ambiguous question; he must *create* an acceptable answer. So it is that the moralist's extremity becomes, willy-nilly, the politician's opportunity." "Power: Its Ubiquity and Legitimacy," *American Political Science Review*, XLV (1951), p. 697. Italics his. His principle of legitimacy seems to be a very generalized statement of "integration." *Ibid.*, pp. 701–02.

2. Karl Mannheim, *Freedom, Power and Democratic Planning* (New York: Oxford University Press, 1950), p. 203. He acknowledges indebtedness for the term "integrative behavior" to H. N. Anderson ["Domination and Social Integration in the Behavior of Kindergarten Children and Teachers," *Genetic Psychology Monographs*, XXI (1939), 287–385] and to D. W. Harding ["The Custom of War and the Notion of Peace," *Scrutiny*, IX, No. 3 (1940) and *The Impulse to Dominate* (London: 1941)]. Sara E. Southall is another observer who noticed "integration" in passing: "The ability to integrate ideas, especially when they seem to be unalterably opposed, is an art which needs to be cultivated. The first step in such an effort must be a readiness to listen to the other fellow's side and to refrain from forming ideas so rigid and inflexible that they cannot be changed. There is no place for inflexible thinking in industry today. The creative approach is essential to achieving, in the public interest, a proper balancing of the interests of stockholders, customers, and employees. It is even more essential in the area of collective bargaining." *Industry's Unfinished Business* (New York: Harper, 1950), p. 39.

3. Otto adds: "Ingenious philosophic speculation might even find in this adjudicating process a key to unlock the mystery of all that exists and occurs." Max

C. Otto, "Professional Philosophy and the Public," in *Philosophy in American Education*, by B. Blanchard, C. Ducasse, C. W. Hendel, A. E. Murphy, and M. C. Otto (New York: Harper, 1945), p. 160.

4. It is not meant to imply that Follett misunderstands this inner dynamics: "We make two mistakes in regard to purpose when we are considering social process," she says, "we try to substitute an intellectualistic purpose for that involved in the situation, or when the purpose appears from out the activity, we think, by some strange mental legerdemain, that that was the purpose which had been actuating us all along." (*Creative Experience*, p. 82.) Her vacillation on this latter point is due to two things: (1) a looseness in some of her illustrations of integration, and (2) overgeneralization in description of the original purposes involved in conflict. One of her illustrations (*Dynamic Administration*, pp. 199–200), for example, involves the "psychological aspirations" of a man and the "economic integrity" of his father—very generalized descriptions of original patterns of purpose. Both of these are satisfied in her description of the integration, with an emergent value added: "a better social policy." A more adequate description would show new patterns of specific purposes satisfied *in* emergent values.

5. When "the larger systems of propriate striving," when purposings central to character are involved in conflict, interests, instead of being suppressed, may evaporate. Cf. Gordon W. Allport, *Becoming* (New Haven: Yale University Press (1955), pp. 85–86. When this happens we have an objectivizing process—the reverse swing from internalizing.

6. Max C. Otto, "Creative Bargaining," *The Standard*, XXXVII (1951), p. 268, and Max C. Otto, *The Human Enterprise* (New York: F. S. Crofts, 1940), p. 148. Compare this list with Lindeman's seven steps in discussion ("Discussion," in *The Encyclopaedia of Social Sciences*, ed. Edwin A. R. Seligman (New York: Macmillan, 1931), vol. V, pp. 166–67, and with Tufts' three processes involved in "distributing the apple" and his "moral method" (James Hayden Tufts, "The Moral Life and the Construction of Values and Standards," in *Creative Intelligence* by John Dewey *et al.* (New York: Holt, 1917), pp. 394, 407.

7. Allport, *Becoming*, p. 30. Allport identifies this tendency as Comte's "law of affective evolution." Even Elton Mayo claims that "there is evidence everywhere that as general education advances, the desire for personal freedom from dictatorial injunction is increased" and places in evidence Jean Paget's studied conclusion that "The infant develops from a morality of constraint to a morality of cooperation." *The Political Problem of Industrial Civilization* (Boston: Harvard University Graduate School of Business Administration, 1947), pp. 3–4.

8. Max C. Otto, "War and Moral Progress," *The Progressive*, XIII (September, 1949), p. 5.

9. See Hadley Cantril, "The Nature of Social Perception," *Transactions of the New York Academy of Science*, Series 2, X (1948), p. 150.

10. Follett, *Creative Experience*, p. 301.

11. See above, pp. 56–57.

12. Again in the sense of "I am *determin*ed to see this through." "We cannot, coming into something new, deal with it except on the basis of the familiar and the old-fashioned. The conservatism of scientific enquiry is not an arbitrary thing; it is the freight with which we operate; it is the only equipment we have.... The criterion of truth must come from analysis, it must come from experience, and from that very special kind of objectivity which characterizes science, namely that we are quite sure we understand one another and that we can check up on one another." Robert Oppenheimer, "Analogy in Science," *The American Psychologist*, XI (1956), pp. 129–30.

13. See above, pp. 85, 152–53, 168.

14. Walter Lippmann, *Public Opinion* (New York: Penguin, 1946), p. 309. Follett:

"Every man has *his* interests; at those points his attention can be enlisted. At those points he can be got to take an experimental attitude toward experience." *Creative Experience*, p. 230. Italics hers.

15. Cf. Eduard C. Lindeman, *The Democratic Man*, ed. Robert Gessner (Boston: Beacon, 1956), p. 170.

16. Cf. Otto, "Creative Bargaining," p. 267 and Follett, *Dynamic Administration*, p. 203. Cf. also Winnicott's similar plea for resolving political cleavages by internalizing the struggle, pp. 24–25, above.

17. James H. Breasted, *The Dawn of Conscience* (New York: Scribner's 1947), p. 395.

18. Allport, *Becoming*, p. 86n. Allport's italics quoting Sigmund Freud, *The Problem of Anxiety* (New York: Norton, 1927), pp. 82f.

19. Otto, "Creative Bargaining," p. 266.

20. Jean Rostand, *The Substance of Man* (New York: Doubleday, 1962), p. 189.

21. John Dewey, *Human Nature and Conduct* (New York: Holt, 1922), p. 143.

22. P. W. Bridgman, "Error, Quantum Theory, and the Observer," in *Life, Language, Law*, ed. Richard W. Taylor (Yellow Springs, Ohio: Antioch Press, 1957), p. 131.

23. Will Durant, on "This I Believe," Edward R. Murrow, Commentator. Columbia recording SL 192.

24. "There is only one test for the value of wants: their confronting or conflict, but conflict constructively conceived, not as resulting in adjustment, mere adjustment, but as opening the way for integration." (Follett, *Creative Experience*, p. 260.) "Social ends are not preexisting things but eventual things." (*Ibid.*, p. 42.) "Values are 'eventual things'." (*Ibid.*, p. 172.) "Look for purpose in 'so far' integrated behavior." (*Ibid.*, p. 81.) "Think of personality ... as 'so far integrated behavior'." (*Ibid.*, p. 207.)

25. Norbert Wiener, "Science, Monkeys, and Mozart," *The Saturday Review*, XXXVII (November 20, 1954), 48.

26. Charles Frankel, *The Case for Modern Man* (New York: Harper, 1955), p. 150.

27. Cf. George R. Geiger, *Towards an Objective Ethics* (Yellow Springs, Ohio: Antioch Press, 1938), p. 43.

28. Max Wertheimer, *Productive Thinking* (New York: Harper, 1945), pp. 168–88.

29. Otto, "Creative Bargaining," p. 268.

30. See Chapter 13 for comments on the important play of art in connection with form, memory and objectivization.

31. See above, pp. 69–70.

32. James B. Conant, *On Understanding Science* (New York: Mentor, 1951), p. 48.

33. Which is also, of course, change—a change from change or a change of change.

34. For an example, see "So You Appointed a Committee" (Two Lessons in Group Dynamics), *Educator's Washington Dispatch*, Supplement, January 1948.

35. Mannheim, *Freedom, Power, and Democratic Planning*, pp. 230–31. I find it impossible to go along with Mannheim's division of humanity into definite types of personality structure—except tentatively or provisionally. (Which is perhaps all that he is really asking.) Personality constantly changes as purposes, values, and intentions change. That a summation of these changes should become discernible at some clear point of accumulation *as a change in type*, seems to me highly doubtful.

36. The idea of creative bargaining as politics even squares with T. V. Smith's

powerful definition: "Politics is, by historic derivation, the undisputed king of all that is in serious dispute among men" [Smith, "Power: Its Ubiquity and Legitimacy," p. 697.] and with Meyerson and Banfield's definition: "When there is a conflict, real or apparent, between the ends of different actors (or within the end-system of a single actor) and not all of the conflicting ends can be realized, an *issue* exists and the actors whose ends conflict are parties to the issue. . . . *Politics* is the activity (negotiation, argument, discussion, application of force, persuasion, etc.) by which an issue is agitated or settled." [Martin Meyerson and Edward C. Banfield, *Politics, Planning and the Public Interest* (Glencoe, Illinois: Free Press, 1955), p. 304. Italics theirs.]

37. For example, Hans Morgenthau: "To know with despair that the political act is inevitably evil, and to act nevertheless, is moral courage." Quoted by Walter E. Sandelius, "Reason & Political Power," *American Political Science Review,* XLV (1951), p. 704.

38. The compromise meaning of "politics" is clearly evident in such a comment as the following by Mary Follett: "If the heads of departments confront each other with finished policies, agreement will be found difficult. Of course they then begin to play politics, or that is often the tendency." ["Process of Control" in *Papers on the Science of Administration,* ed. L. Gulick & L. Urwick (New York: Institute of Public Administration, Columbia University, 1937), p. 164.] According to her, "Many men despise politics because they see that politics manipulate, but make nothing. If politics are to be the highest activity of man, as they should be, they must be clearly understood as creative." (*The New State*, p. 7.) Her conclusion is reinforced by Sandelius' opinion: "We miss the most vital side of political reality when we confine our observations to what might be called the underside of politics, the *how of conflict,* and and [sic] do not attend sufficiently to the *how of the creative, and at times sacrificial, fulfillment of the human being himself;* which is to say, to those deeper aspects of the political which are *in fact* of a spiritual nature." ("Reason and Political Power," p. 715. Italics his.)

How is T. V. Smith's idea of democracy as middle class skills borne out in our institutions—if politics (that is, compromise) manipulates but makes nothing? See his *The Promise of American Politics* (University of Chicago Press, 1936), pp. 223–44.

39. Mannheim, *Freedom, Power and Democratic Planning,* p. 205. He adds that already "in the sphere of morality and religion, it is considered enough to come to an agreement on externals only, and essentials are no longer considered. This is why democracy has become so unattractive for people who yearn for a purpose to which they can be devoted."

40. From Herbert Spencer's *First Principles,* quoted by Max Otto in "Creative Bargaining," *The Standard,* XXXVII, March 1951, pp. 266–67.

41. Boris Pasternak, *I Remember* (New York: Pantheon Book, 1959), p. 44. Taken somewhat out of context from a description of artistic activity.

42. See above, p. 61.

Chapter Twelve

1. Jacques Maritain's, for instance: *Principes d'une Politique Humaniste* (New York: Maison Francais, 1944), pp. 71–80, or *Education at the Crossroads* (New Haven: Yale University Press, 1943), pp. 92–93.

2. See above, p. 65.

3. See above, pp. 118–20.

4. See above, p. 138.

5. C. Wright Mills, "On Knowledge and Power," *Dissent*, II (Summer, 1955), 205.

6. This is not at all Mills' moral. He does not use the understanding of power and functional power developed in this book. He accordingly reverts to a rationalist position: "Only when mind has an autonomous basis, independent of power, but powerfully related to it, can it exert its force in the shaping of human affairs." *Ibid.*, p. 212.

7. See *ibid.*, p. 205.

8. See above, pp. 63–64.

9. Horace S. Fries, "Social Planning," in *The Cleavage in Our Culture*, ed. Frederick Burkhardt (Boston: Beacon, 1952), p. 97. The other four are listed on p. 197, above.

10. *Ibid.*, p. 95.

11. Horace S. Fries, "Perception and Value Inquiry," *The American Journal of Economics and Sociology*, XI (1951), 25. See above, p. 45.

12. Horace S. Fries, "Logical Simplicity: A Challenge to Philosophy and to Social Inquiry," *Philosophy of Science*, XVII (1950), 220. As Henry Margenau says, scientific theories "strive for a maximum of logical fertility." *Open Vistas* (New Haven: Yale University Press, 1961), p. 12. "Indeed, *understanding* itself, scientifically conceived, is an operational affair. To aim at understanding is to aim at the continual improvement of both the abstract and concrete ideational instruments of investigation. The scientist understands water, hydrogen, and oxygen to the extent that he can operate successfully with and upon them. The absract concepts which are the *stuff* of scientific explanation (which are often confused with the stuff of nature and even supernature) designate in generalized terms the *operations* which are necessary or possible to arrive at certain specified *concrete* consequences under specified conditions. A scientific hypothesis is an experimental plan, and a scientific theory is a tentative way of life in the laboratory." Horace S. Fries, "Science, Ethics, and Democracy," *Journal of Social Philosophy*, VI (1941), 310. Italics his.

13. Fries, "Perception and Value Inquiry," p. 24.

14. Fries, "Logical Simplicity," p. 215. As Fries explains, "applied mathematics before Galileo (except for Archimedes, et al.) was the technological application of theorems previously demonstrated. Experimental science, on the other hand, is the application in physical controls of *demonstration* itself." *Ibid.* Italics his. Cf. also Horace S. Fries, "World Revolution Number Five," *The Antioch Review*, III (1943), 430.

15. John Dewey and Arthur F. Bentley, *Knowing and the Known* (Boston: Beacon, 1949), p. 319.

16. Fries assumes that "human thinking emerges in an effort to realize aims more adequately." Fries, "Logical Simplicity," p. 221.

17. Horace S. Fries, mimeographed clarification of a passage on p. 14 of "A Methodological Consideration," *The Journal of General Psychology*, XXXIII (1945), 11-20.

18. The "pure" scientist, in Fries' words, "wants the concrete transformations to be interrelated by symbolic operations in such a way that a change of one abstraction tends to involve a change throughout the system. The relation which accomplishes this is *implication* or the closely related quantitative relation of *equivalence*. Thus the outcome of an experiment shaped by one hypothesis tends to throw light on the other physical transformations interrelated by the abstract system. For example, a discovery of the way light bends as it passes the sun may throw light on the nucleus of the atom—that is, of all atoms. The employment of the abstractions of experimentation for the sake of improving them is the meaning of the

significant definition of science as self-corrective inquiry." ("A Methodological Consideration," p. 12. Italics his.)

Under the heading of "logical simplicity," Fries gives extended consideration to the interrelation of abstractions. Simplicity results when two or more logically independent sets of concepts are joined in a simpler or more unified statement. A prototype is found in the unification of Einstein's concepts which form a more tightly woven implicative set, incorporating "all the principles of the Newtonian set in a *logically simpler* or *more unified* set of 'very convincing assumptions'." ("Logical Simplicity," p. 215. Italics his.) "Simplicity," Fries says, "operates as a test of adequacy in inquiry when the controlling aim is the improvement of the conceptual tools themselves.... It would then be that property in virtue of which the reflexive use of the [conceptual] tools on themselves brings about their own improvement." (*Ibid.*, p. 219.)

19. Sir William Cecil Dampier, *A History of Science* (Cambridge University Press, 1949), 4th edition, p. 36.

20. "The scientist does not aim at *finality*.... He aims at generality, to be sure, but he also tries continually to find exceptions to his 'laws,' and theories. Neither mystery nor paradox is involved in this situation if we are willing to think of all the experimental abstractions, 'laws,' theories, equations, as tools or instruments. The aim at improvement of the abstractions then becomes the use of the abstract instruments for the sake of improving them. The instruments themselves are instruments of concrete control. To improve an instrument we look for places where it will not work: we look for exceptions. But as scientists we try to construct them so that one failure to achieve control tends to throw light on the other instruments. Hence the aim at abstract solidarity or operational generality. The engineer can neglect this second aim since his concern is primarily practical." Fries, "A Methodological Consideration," p. 12. Italics his.

21. Fries, "Logical Simplicity," p. 221.

22. Mary P. Follett, *Creative Experience* (New York: Longmans, Green, 1924), p. 135.

23. Cf. Fries, "Logical Simplicity," p. 220.

24. Fries, "A Methodological Consideration," p. 12.

25. Dewey in Dewey and Bentley, *Knowing and the Known*, p. 327.

26. Rather than barrenly admit to mysticism with the assertion added that this is a mysticism of a special sort: one that will evolve into meaning when scientific effort has been applied. This is the mysticism Read Bain describes as consisting of "the awe and wonder generated by a vivid, personalized experiencing of the imperfectly understood." "Mysticism & Humanism," *The Humanist*, XVII (1957), 288.

27. See comments above on thinking as acting, pp. 159–60, 190.

28. See Gordon W. Allport's comments on "propriate striving," in *Becoming* (New Haven: Yale University Press, 1955), pp. 47–51. See also Charles M. Hardin's review of *Becoming* (*American Political Science Review*, L (1956), 541–43) relating Allport's work to political science.

29. Cf. Fries, "A Methodological Consideration," p. 15.

30. *Ibid.*, p. 13.

31. See above, pp. 104–105, 134.

32. Eduard C. Lindeman says much the same thing in the following passage, though his terminology varies from that I have been using: "The key word of democracy is participation.... Social action is in essence the use of force or coercion. The use of force or coercion is justified only when the force is democratic and this means that it must be derived from intelligence and reason." *The Democratic Man*, ed. Robert Gessner (Boston: Beacon, 1956), p. 167.

33. Horace S. Fries, "Scientific Mediation: Tool of Democracy," *Antioch Review,*
V (1945), 399.

34. "Assume an unsatisfactory social situation. Let those best informed about
the concrete, discoverable features of the situation confer with experts about the
various special aspects involved. Let them agree tentatively upon the formulation
of the problem for a possible way of resolving the conflict. *Let the formulation be
made in the interest of improving the instruments of planning,* by using as a
criterion of success the resolution of this and subsequent actual difficulties. The
tentatively suggested solution constitutes a social plan. Let this plan, this hypothesis, be put to work to observe its consequences in the way of resolution as a test
of planning instruments. Eventually the planning instruments will come to constitute the abstract subject-matter of the social sciences. These instruments will continue to designate concrete operations to be performed within our social insitutions
to achieve certain specified concrete consequences. The abstractions will constitute
the *stuff* of the explanations of the social world, and these explanations will doubtless be found to be as relative and changing and progressive as our explanations
of nature. For all we know to date, these operations will become as firmly established in natural causal connections as are the operations now possible in the
nature sciences. Eventually, as with the nature sciences, laboratories may emerge;
that is, relatively isolated areas designed to simplify the problem of scientific control." Fries, "Science, Ethics, and Democracy," pp. 309–10. Italics his.

35. Cf. Fries, "Social Planning," p. 93.

36. See above, p. 112.

37. In Fries' words, the *"concrete* material or 'subject matter' [of this experimental
science] is the realm of human interests and all their natural causal connections
with other biological and social factors." ("Scientific Mediation," p. 399. Italics his.)
"As a moment of an ongoing self-corrective enterprise, an hypothesis is not an
isolated idea. It gets parts of its directive authority from a more comprehensive
theory or outlook. Else when it conflicts with other hypotheses it will breed mutual
interference rather than a correction of the theory and a modification of the hypothesis in the light of the difficulty. Consequently as the body of relevant experimental knowledge grows and as the experimental field becomes more complicated,
these guiding ideas or hypotheses give rise to an *abstract* subject-matter of planning principles or social theory. The crucial difference from the contemplative
theory is that the function of theory in science is to guide the manipulation of practical concrete realities." ("Science, Ethics, and Democracy," pp. 312–13. Italics his.)

38. See above, p. 113.

39. Fries, "A Methodological Consideration," p. 14.

40. The "unique practical differences" that Fries doesn't consider "serious for the
application of control concepts" ("Social Planning," p. 95.) are in fact to be controlled by intention.

41. Fries, "Logical Simplicity," p. 223.

42. Fries, "A Methodological Consideration," p. 15. Cf. also Fries, "Scientific
Mediation," p. 399.

43. "Democracy is to the social realm what science is to the physical, namely, an
unending series of experiments with no certain outcomes promised in advance."
Lindeman, *The Democratic Man,* p. 65.

44. Fries, "Social Planning," p. 98.

45. See above, p. 126.

46. Horace S. Fries, "Liberty and Science," *Public Administration Review,* III
(1943), 272.

47. "The objection to the idea of social experimentation rests its case upon the
claim that scientific control of human beings is out of the question. Now such con-

trol is doubtless out of the question (except possibly by means of hypnosis) when conceived to be necessarily an extraneously imposed affair of which the 'elements,' in this case we human beings, must be kept in ignorance. But unless *knowing* is conceived as an unnatural social phenomenon, there is obviously no justification for such a notion of control. For, on the other hand, if we may assume that social-causal relations are involved among humans who know something about what they are trying to do, then there is every reason for attempting a rational type of social scientific control. And such control, until tried and found wanting, is presumably feasible." Horace S. Fries, "Some Democratic Implications of Science in Scientific Management," *Advanced Management*, V (1940), 1949. Italics his.

48. Cf. John Dewey, *Human Nature and Conduct* (New York: Molt, 1922), p. 235.

49. Cf. Fries, "Scientific Mediation," p. 390.

50. See above, p. 164.

51. See John M. Gaus, "The Authority of Organized Knowledge," *Public Administration Review*, II (1942), on Follett's contribution to organized knowing. Metcalf and Urwick refer to the adoption of a previous solution to a previous comparable problem as illustration of what Follett means by "integration." (Metcalf and Urwick in Mary P. Follett, *Dynamic Administration*, ed. H. C. Metcalf & L. Urwick (London: Bath Management Publications Trust, 1941), p. 34n.) And Follett herself specifically refers to such a situation in one of her examples of "integration." (Follett, *Creative Experience*, pp. 157–58). Such indication of the acceptability of "elegant solutions" opens the door to vicarious experience and to a recognition of its efficiency, and affords intimations of the possibility of a moral science.

52. See below p. 287, where it is suggested that the word "authority" should be dropped from use except in historical reference.

53. Cf. Fries: "Social Planning," p. 95; "A Methodological Consideration," p. 19; "Logical Simplicity," p. 225.

54. Fries, "Liberty and Science," p. 273. "The habitual reliance on the authority of experimental procedure . . . reshapes the interests of the inquirer by incorporating his interests within it. It does not of itself narrow human interests. Where science as method is employed only in a narrow range of activities (as is generally the case today with the nature scientists), the range of interest is necessarily narrow. But even within the most specialized area of creative research, these interests are amazingly rich. As the method becomes broadened through experimental planning to include an attack on all problematic situations, all interests would be reshaped and broadened. Variety and even conflict of interests would no longer be a threat to authority and security but, in virtue of a comprehensive self-corrective method for the more satisfactory resolution of social conflicts, would be found to be an undisguised blessing." *Ibid.*

55. Fries, "Logical Simplicity," p. 225.

56. From the "deliberate effort to change the interests of conflicting parties." Fries, "Scientific Mediation," p. 396.

57. See above, pp. 163–66.

58. Robert Oppenheimer, "Analogy in Science," *The American Psychologist*, XI (1956), 130. See above, note 12 to p. 199.

59. See above, p. 170.

60. " . . . those experts in administration who are willing to put their faith in the strength of a union of science with democracy are increasing. At a certain point the number will be sufficient to bring to pass a change of social direction, and a self-corrective society will be developing." Fries, "Some Democratic Implications of Science in Scientific Management," p. 150.

61. Fries, "Science, Ethics, and Democracy," pp. 216–17.

62. Fries, "Some Democratic Implications of Science in Scientific Management,"

p. 150. Also Horace S. Fries, "Ethical Objectivity through Science," *Philosophical Review*, LIII (1943), 563–64.

63. I do not find in Fries' writing *specific* recognition of the vicarious leavening of arduous participation through knowing as it has been developed above.

64. Cf. Fries, "Liberty and Science," p. 272.

65. See above, p. 138.

66. Horace S. Fries, "On Managerial Responsibility," *Advanced Management*, VIII (1943), 47.

67. Cf. Harold C. Havighurst, "Technology and Political Organization," *Advanced Management*, VIII (1943), p. 50.

68. See above, pp. 134–35.

69. Cf. Charles E. Merriam, *The Role of Politics in Social Change* (New York: New York University Press, 1936), p. 131.

70. The ultimate test being the quality of the reality created. Cf. Fries, "Perception and Value Inquiry," p. 31.

71. See above, p. 95.

72. See above, p. 81.

Chapter Thirteen

1. Horace S. Fries, "Science, Ethics, and Democracy," *Journal of Social Philosophy*, VI (1941), 313.

2. Cf. Horace S. Fries, "Perception and Value Inquiry," *The American Journal of Economics and Sociology*, XI (1951), 31.

3. Horace S. Fries, "Logical Simplicity," *Philosophy of Science*, XVII (1950), 211. Mary Follett, *Creative Experience* (New York: Longmans, Green, 1924), p. 105.

4. Roger Fry. Quoted by Susanne K. Langer, *Philosophy in a New Key* (New York: Penguin, 1948), p. 166.

5. Cf. Barbara Wooton, *Testament for Social Science* (London: Allen and Unwin, 1950), p. 162, and Herbert Read, *The Grass Roots of Art* (New York: Wittenborn, Schultz, 1949), p. 15.

6. James H. Breasted, *The Dawn of Conscience* (New York: Scribner's 1947), pp. 44. Cf. also André Malraux, *Le Musée Imaginaire de la Sculpture Mondiale* (Paris: La Galerie de la Pléiade, 1952), 19–25. Tufts advances the proposition "that art production is prior to art appreciation, and is its cause rather than its effect." James Hayden Tufts, "On the Genesis of the Aesthetic Categories," *The Decennial Publications of the University of Chicago*, First Series, III, Part 2 (1903), p. 8.

7. Albert E. Wiggam, *The New Decalogue of Science* (Indianapolis: Bobbs Merrill, 1922), p. 205.

8. *Ibid.*, p. 215.

9. See above, p. 43. Cf. Fries, "Perception and Value Inquiry," p. 23.

10. *Ibid.*, p. 26.

11. Joseph Conrad, Preface to *The Nigger of the Narcissus* (1897). Italics his.

12. Cf. John Dewey in *Intelligence in the Modern World*, ed. Joseph Ratner (New York: Random House, 1939), pp. 320–23.

13. See above, pp. 45–46.

14. John Dewey, *Human Nature and Conduct* (New York: Holt, 1922), pp. 155–56.

15. Mary P. Follett, *Dynamic Administration*, ed. H. C. Metcalf and L. Urwick (London: Bath Management Publications Trust, 1941), p. 202.

16. "We shall see every moment the passing of one concept into another but

always through the perceptual." Mary P. Follett, *Creative Experience* (New York: Longmans, Green, 1924), p. 143.

17. Horace S. Fries, "Social Planning," in *The Cleavage in Our Culture*, ed. Frederick Burkhardt (Boston: Bacon, 1952), p. 101. Italics his. Cf. Van Meter Ames, "Aesthetic Experience," in *Essays in Philosophy*, eds. T. V. Smith and W. K. Wright (Chicago: Open Court, 1929), p. 249, and Tufts, "On the Genesis of the Aesthetic Categories," p. 13.

18. See above, pp. 200–202.

19. Follett, *Creative Experience*, p. 105.

20. Cf. Philip F. A. Seitz, "Anxiety," *The Humanist*, XIX (1959), 93–103.

21. Horace Kallen, *Art and Freedom*, 2 Vols. (New York: Duel, Sloan & Pierce, 1942), p. 31, vol. I. Italics his.

22. T. V. Smith, *The Promise of American Politics* (University of Chicago Press, 1936), pp. 223–84.

23. William James, "On a Certain Blindness in Human Beings," in *Essays of the Past and Present*, ed. Warner Taylor (New York: Harper & Brothers, 1927), pp. 158–59.

24. See Chapter 16.

25. Robert Louis Stevenson, "The Lantern-Bearers," in *Essays by Robert Louis Stevenson*, ed. William Lyon Phelps (New York: Charles Scribner's Sons, 1918), p. 314.

26. See above, p. 77–78.

27. Ames, "Aesthetic Experience," pp. 238, 242.

28. Fries, "Perception and Value Inquiry," p. 25, and "Social Planning," p. 100.

29. *Ibid.*, p. 101. (Italics his.)

30. "If our awareness of the change in an external event is to be considered at all functional in nature, then the subjective sense of surety accompanying the perception must be of primary psychological significance." Hadley Cantril, Adelbert Ames, Jr., Albert H. Hastorf, William H. Ittelson, "Psychology and Scientific Research," *Science*, CX (1949), 496.

31. Peter Drucker, "The New Philosophy Comes to Life," *Harper's Magazine*, CCXV (August, 1957), 37. "The visual impression does not yield its full content, since it can offer this only to the mind that becomes one with what it sees, thus breaking down the rigid subject-object antithesis.... It is to this synthetic discipline that biology, in its autonomous aspect, belongs; its function is fulfilled when it offers its mite towards the ultimate fusion of metaphysical and scientific thinking." Agnes Arber. Quoted by Alfred P. Stiernotte, "Scientists as Philosophers," *American Scientist*, XLII (1954), 654.

32. Cf., for example Gunnar Myrdal, *An American Dilemma* (New York: Harper, 1944), esp. Appendixes, and Robert S. Lynd, *Knowledge for What?* (Princeton University Press, 1939).

33. Attributed to Robert Penn Warren by John Ciardi, "How Does a Poem Mean?" Opening Address at the Annual Conference on the Teaching of English, delivered at the University of Wisconsin, Madison. July, 1958.

34. John Ciardi, *How Does a Poem Mean?* (Boston: Houghton Mifflin, 1959). "One sees a wizard of a poet tossing his words in the air and catching them and tossing them again—what a grand stunt! Then suddenly one may be astonished that the poet is not just juggling cups, saucers, roses, rhymes and other random objects, but the very stuff of life. And discovering that, one discovers that seeing the poet's ideas flash so in the air, seeing them performed under such control, is not only a reward in itself, but a living experience that deepens every man's sense of life. One finds himself more alert to life, surer of his own emotions, wiser than he would have

been without that experience.... *the unparaphraseable and undiminishable life of the poem lies in the way it performs itself through the difficulties it imposes on itself. The way in which it means is what it means." Ibid.*, p. 670. Italics his.

35. Fries, "Logical Simplicity," p. 218.

36. *Ibid.*

37. Albert Einstein, *Essays in Science* (New York: Philosophical Library, 1933), p. 12.

38. Michael Polanyi, "Passion and Controversy in Science," *The Bulletin of the Atomic Scientists*, XIII (1957), 115.

39. *Ibid.*

40. *Ibid.*

41. *Ibid.*

42. Henry Margenau, *Open Vistas* (New Haven: Yale University Press, 1961), pp. 77–101. Cf. also Max Born, *Physics and Politics* (New York: Basic Books, 1962), pp. 25–31.

43. See above, p. 201.

44. "If the first step in the understanding of a business problem is an understanding of what constitutes the field of control, the second is an understanding of the process of passing from one field of control to another. Perhaps no one thing will have a greater effect on business management than a realization of the importance of this, for then anticipation will not mean forecasting alone; it will mean far more than predicting the next situation. It will mean more than *meeting* the next situation, it will mean *making* the next situation." Mary P. Follett, "The Illusion of Final Authority," *Bulletin of the Taylor Society*, XI (December, 1946), p. 249. Italics hers.

45. Leonard B. Meyer, *Emotion and Meaning in Music* (University of Chicago Press, 1956), pp. 35–38.

46. Edvard Grieg. Letter to his parents. Quoted by David Monrad-Johansen, *Edvard Grieg* (Princeton University Press, 1938), p. 127.

47. Cf. Meyer, *Emotion and Meaning in Music*, pp. 87–91.

48. *The New Oxford History of Music*, Vol. I, ed. Egon Wellesz (London: Oxford University Press, 1957), p. 341. The proportions of the Pythagorean tetrachord strictly carried out in practice produced a tonality persistently rejected as uncomfortable by the human ear. Reconciliation of the demands of the ear with those of mathematics, begun by Didymus in 60 A.D., was completed by Ptolemy in 130 A.D. There was some interest in practical musical theory in Greece after Pythagoras: Aristoxenus and others.

49. A. C. Crombie, "From Rationalism to Experimentalism," in *Roots of Scientific Thought*, ed. Philip P. Wiener & Aaron Noland (New York: Basic Books, Inc., 1960), p. 131.

50. James Travis, *Miscellanea Musica Celtica* (Brooklyn, N. Y.: Institute of Mediaeval Music, 1968). It is not improbable that other traditional forms of primitive part singing existed in other parts of Europe.

51. See D. F. Tovey's article "Rhythm" in *The Encyclopedia Britannica*, 11th ed. Of the late fourteenth century French secular motet, Willi Apel says, "Not only is ...the harmonic basis infinitely more vague—not to say, weak—than it is in Palestrina, but also the characteristic fuzziness of the rhythmic structure often renders seemingly obvious distinctions impossible of application. For example, there are not a few instances in which it would be difficult to say whether we are dealing with parallel thirds or parallel seconds." *French Secular Music of the Late Fourteenth Century* (Cambridge, Mass.: Mediaeval Academy of America, 1950),

p. 12. According to theories of the "Mensuralists," plainchant originally had distinctive and repetitive rhythmic patterns.

52. See "Modes, Musical," in *The Encyclopedia Britannica*, 1969. Too much should not be made of these distinctions. The Lydian mode with characteristically flatted fourth degree produced something very close to the Ionian mode, and the Aeolian with characteristically raised seventh degree was much like the minor mode.

53. Galileo's father, Vincenzo Galilei, was a proselytizing music scholar, redoubtable champion of the new monodic style of composition in which one part predominates, contrasting with the style of the madrigal and motet. The monodic movement, in emphasizing the solo voice, helped turn attention toward the vertical harmonic structure of the accompanying voices and their function in heightening the emotional interest of the text. The next move was to turn more direct and undivided attention to harmonic progression from chord to chord, developing a harmony strong enough to control otherwise unprepared discords employed for expression of emotion. Near successors of the monodists established the modern key system. Less well known than Monteverdi, Gesualdo, a generation earlier, is perhaps even more significant.

54. W. C. Dampier, *A History of Science* (Cambridge: Cambridge University Press, 1949), p. 491.

55. Alfred North Whitehead, *Science and the Modern World* (New York: Mentor Books, 1949), p. 33.

56. A system of harmony based on the interval of the third apparently developed early in the Celtic corner of medieval European culture. By the twelfth century, Celtic harp music already used systematically dissonant harmonies and complex chords built up of a series of thirds. The nature and extent of the influence of Celtic harmony is still a matter of speculation. [See Travis, *Miscellanea Musica Celtica*.] Who knows, perhaps Druidic overtones heralded the revolution in hearing. The interval of the third occurs in primitive music, but here even fourths and fifths are difficult to identify when they do occur. [See *The Encyclopedia Britannica*, 1969, "Music, Primitive."] They may be more the product of accident or error than design, far from providing a basis for tonal harmony. Other cultures (far eastern, near eastern, African) permit sounding of various notes (principally the fourth, fifth and octave) simultaneously with the melody, as a means of occasional decoration, but this is merely a heterophonic device and not harmony in the accepted meaning of the word. [See *The New Oxford History of Music*, Vol. 1, pp. 279, 471.]

57. Alfred Mann, *The Study of Fugue* (New Brunswick, N. J.: Rutgers University Press, 1958), p. 4. There is increasing doubt that very many ears found the major third harsh at this late date. Anonymous IV (c. 1275) records the exception in the Westcuntre where the third was considered an "excellent consonance." [See *The New Oxford History of Music*, Vol. 2, ed. Dom Anselm Hughes (London: Oxford University Press, 1955), p. 351.] The third was in frequent use and may have been considered theoretically "imperfect" more than it was thought "harsh."

58. Travis, *Miscellanea Musica Celtica*, p. 31.

59. D. F. Tovey, "Music," in *Encyclopedia Britannica*, 11th ed.

60. H. H. Stuckenschmidt, *Arnold Schoenberg* (New York: Grove Press, Inc., 1959).

61. Henri Poincaré, "Mathematical Creation," in *Readings in The Physical Sciences*, ed. Harlow Shapley, Helen Wright, Samuel Rapport (New York: Appleton-Century-Crofts, Inc., 1948), p. 241.

62. John Dewey, *Freedom and Culture* (New York: G. P. Putnam's Sons, Inc., 1939), p. 150. See also his *Art as Experience* (New York: Minton, Balch, 1934), pp. 344–49.

63. John Galsworthy, "The Creation of Character in Literature," *The Bookman*,

LXXIII (1931), 568–69. "The novel, through its delineation of character, represents the values in personality that are being sought by everyone who is in the process of evolving a social self." Ames, "Aesthetic Experience," p. 246.

64. Lionel Trilling, *The Liberal Imagination* (Garden City, N. Y.: Doubleday, 1953), pp. 214–15.

65. Cf. Fries, "Perception and Value Inquiry," p. 27.

66. *Ibid.*, pp. 25–26.

67. H. J. Muller, "Man's Place in Living Nature," *Humanist*, XVII (1957), p. 13.

68. "The notion of the importance of pattern is as old as civilization. Every art is founded on the study of pattern. Also the cohesion of social systems depends on the maintenance of patterns of behaviour; and advances in civilization depend on the fortunate modification of such behaviour patterns. Thus the infusion of pattern into natural occurrences, and the stability of such patterns, and the modification of such patterns, is the necessary condition for the realization of the Good." Alfred North Whitehead, *A Philosopher Looks at Science* (New York: Philosophical Library, 1965), p. 21.

69. Reminiscent of the primitive pre-Celtic Irish custom of eating portions of human corpses to perpetuate or transfer the virtues of the deceased. Cf. Julius Pokorny. "The Origin of Druidism," *Annual Report of the Smithsonian Institution, 1910* (Washington, D. C.: USGPO, 1911), p. 590. The experiments involving transfer of learning through RNA transplant are described in Isaac Asimov, *The New Intelligent Man's Guide to Science* (New York: Basic Books, 1965), p. 777.

70. Poincaré, "Mathematical Creation," pp. 239–40. Italics his.

71. Figurate numbers ran through a great range of complexity from triangular numbers, ⁚· , to square numbers, to hexagonal numbers, ⁝⁚ , to stellate numbers, ⁖· ·

72. Herbert Read, *The Grass Roots of Art* (New York: Wittenborn, Schultz, 1949), pp. 18–21.

73. See Alvin L. Schorr, "The Physical Environment and Social Problems," *American Institute of Planners 1946 Proceedings*, pp. 141–45.

74. Fries, "Logical Simplicity," pp. 216–17. See also Henry Margenau, *The Nature of Physical Reality* (New York: McGraw Hill, 1950), pp. 96-100.

75. Sir Arthur Stanley Eddington, "The Decline of Determinism," in *Great Essays in Science*, ed. Martin Gardner (New York: Pocket Books, Inc., 1957), p. 256.

76. See Fries, "Logical Simplicity," p. 217.

77. *Ibid.*, pp. 219–22.

78. Reference is again to the Flash Technique training. See above, p. 51.

79. Ciardi, *How Does a Poem Mean?*

80. See above, p. 164.

81. Cf. Fries, "Social Planning," p. 103.

82. To supplement "the subjective sense of surety accompanying [a] perception" which Cantril *et al* believe to be "of primary psychological significance." "Psychology and Scientific Research," p. 496.

83. See above, pp. 84–86, 199–200.

84. Fries, "Logical Simplicity," p. 225.

85. *Ibid.*, p. 226.

86. See, for example, Koyré's analysis of Galileo's original approaches as deriving from deep philosophical and theological speculation. Alexandre Koyré, "Galileo and the Scientific Revolution of the Seventeenth Century," *The Philosophical Review*, LII (1943), 333–48.

Chapter Fourteen

1. Neil MacNeil and Harold W. Metz, *The Hoover Report, 1953-1955*, p. 299. Quoted by James W. Fesler, "Administrative Literature and the Second Hoover Commission Reports," *American Political Science Review*, LI (1957), 144.

2. Ordway Tead, *The Art of Leadership* (New York: McGraw Hill, 1935), p. 51.

3. John M. Gaus, "A Quarter Century of Public Administration," *Advanced Management*, V (1940), 179.

4. Elton Mayo, *The Human Problems of an Industrial Civilization* (Boston: Harvard University Graduate School of Business Administration, 1946). One of the most notable things about Mayo's account of his experiment is the complete change in pace, tone, temper when he steps from the detailed methodology of his laboratory to the not-yet-scientific area of his conclusions.

5. Morris Janowitz's study of the Wehrmacht in World War II now confirms (if confirmation is needed) the fact of the primacy of group cohesion over ideological motivation, giving further evidence of the social and political penchant of the rational animal. E. A. Shils & Morris Janowitz, "Cohesion and Disintegration in the Wehrmacht in World War II," *Public Opinion Quarterly*, XII (Summer, 1948), 280–315.

6. Compare Ordway Tead, *The Art of Administration* (New York: McGraw-Hill, 1951), p. 3.

7. Cf. Paul H. Appleby, *Policy and Administration* (University, Alabama: University of Alabama Press, 1949), p. 17.

8. Herbert A. Simon, *Administrative Behavior* (New York: Macmillan, 1945), p. 72. Lyndall F. Urwick, *The Pattern of Management* (Minneapolis: University of Minnesota Press, 1956), p. 9.

9. Horace Fries says the supposition that the objective of management is predetermined "must be rejected. For as regards democracy, the legislative functions ... are no longer extraneous to administration; and if democracy means participation, then the objectives of management ... *should not* be extraneously determined. ... As regards science, the only 'predetermined objective' of experimental procedure is the resolution of the actual difficulties in such a way as to improve continually the instruments for resolution. The division of labor within the experimental enterprise does not follow extraneously imposed objectives. The objectives themselves change and develop from the development within science." "Some Democratic Implications of Science in Scientific Management," *Advanced Management*, V (1940), p. 151. Italics his.

10. This use of the word "proprietary" differs, of course, from traditional usage.

11. Philip Selznick, "An Approach to a Theory of Bureaucracy," *American Sociological Review*, VIII (1943), 49.

12. Peter F. Drucker, *The Practice of Management* (New York: Harper, 1954), p. 392.

13. See above, pp. 160–61.

14. Cf. Eduard C. Lindeman, *The Democratic Man*, ed. Robert Gessner (Boston: Beacon, 1956), pp. 56–62.

15. See above, p. 91ff.

16. See above, pp. 186–87.

17. John Dewey, *Human Nature and Conduct* (New York: Holt, 1922), pp. 40–41, 42. Italics his. Also compare his treatment of habit on pp. 172–80.

18. F. W. Taylor, "Shop Management," p. 99, in F. W. Taylor, *Scientific Management* (New York: Harper, 1947), a collected edition of a number of Taylor's works, each separately paged. Quoted by Urwick, *The Pattern of Management*, pp. 11–12.

19. See above, pp. 168–69.

20. See above, pp. 68, 119, 161.

21. Cf., for example, Mary P. Follett, "The Illusion of Final Authority," *Bulletin of the Taylor Society*, XI (1926), 246; Paul H. Appleby, *Big Democracy* (New York: Knopf, 1945), p. 100; and *Morality and Administration* (Baton Rouge: Louisiana State University Press, 1952), p. 100.

22. See Urwick, *The Pattern of Management*, Chapter 2.

23. See above, p. 336ff.

Chapter Fifteen

1. See above, pp. 57–60.

2. Actually, action in accord with viable folkways might not at the time be felt to be coercive. (See Chapter 3.) There must, however, be a level—in social realms as there is in environmental realms—of bumbling ignorance below which attempts at control become coercive.

3. See above, p. 58.

4. Jean Piaget, *The Moral Judgment of the Child* (Glencoe, Illinois: Free Press, 1948), p. 335. Cf. Ashley Montagu, *On Being Human* (New York: Henry Schuman, 1951), p. 86.

5. Gordon W. Allport, *Becoming* (New Haven: Yale University Press, 1955), p. 74.

6. *Ibid.*, p. 72.

7. *Ibid.*, p. 73.

8. See above pp. 122–24.

9. See above pp. 113–15.

10. See above, pp. 84–86, 199–200.

11. Walter Lippmann, *Public Opinion* (New York: Penguin, 1946), p. 309.

12. Piaget, *The Moral Judgment of the Child*, p. 337.

13. See above p. 65.

14. "It would appear to be more than coincidental that countries with this family system [strong family group; decisions on authoritarian basis by the oldest active family members] complain of lack of individual initiative and pioneering spirit and of nepotism in both business and government." Chester L. Hunt, "Cultural Barriers to Point Four," *The Antioch Review*, XIV (1954), 162.

15. See Chester I. Barnard, Review of *Bureaucracy in a Democracy* by Charles S. Hyneman, *American Political Science Review*, XLIV (1950), 1001–03. He criticizes the "hoary maxim" that "authority must be commensurate with responsibility" from another, though complementary, point of view.

16. Cf. John M. Gaus, "The Responsibility of Public Administration," in *The Frontiers of Public Administration* by John M. Gaus, Leonard D. White and Marshall E. Dimock (University of Chicago Press, 1936), pp. 25–44.

17. *Ibid.*, p. 31.

18. Fritz Morstein-Marx, "Administrative Responsibility," in *Public Management in the New Democracy*, ed. Fritz Morstein-Marx (New York: Harper, 1940), pp. 232–33.

19. *Ibid.*, p. 232.

20. *Ibid.*, pp. 230–31.

21. This view is supported, for example, by Carl J. Friedrich, "The Dilemma of Administrative Responsibility," in *Responsibility*, Nomos III, ed. Carl J. Friedrich

(New York: Liberal Arts Press, 1960), p. 194; *Constitutional Government and Democracy* (Boston: Ginn, 1941), Chapter 19; and "Public Policy and the Nature of Administrative Responsibility," in *Public Policy*, eds. C. J. Friedrich and E. S. Mason (Cambridge, Mass.: Harvard University Press, 1940), p. 14; by Gaus, "The Responsibility of Public Administration," p. 39; by Reinhard Bendix, "Bureaucracy and the Problem of Power," *Public Administration Review*, V (1945), 204–05; by Arthur A. Maass and Lawrence I. Radway, "Gauging Administrative Responsibility," *Public Administration Review*, IX (1949), 191–92; by Fritz Morstein-Marx, "Administrative Responsibility," in *Public Management in the New Democracy*, ed. Fritz Morstein-Marx (New York: Harper, 1940), p. 249; and by T. V. Smith, "Professional Work as an Ethical Norm," *The Journal of Philosophy*, XXII (1925), 365–72.

In contrast, Herman Finer emphasizes the pitfalls of professionalism as insurer of responsibility in "Administrative Responsibility in Democratic Government," *Public Administration Review*, I (1941), 335–50. See also Kenneth S. Lynn, ed. *The Professions in America* (New York: Houghton Mifflin, 1965) based on the Fall 1963 issue of *Daedalus.*

22. York Willbern, "Professionalism in the Public Service: Too Little or Too Much?" *Public Administration Review*, XIV (1954), 16. Willbern maintains that "professionalism, in getting 'out of politics,' is merely substituting for the open and often earthy politics of an uneducated electorate and its all too human leaders the concealed but sanctified politics of a priesthood." *Ibid.*, p. 17. The secretive and esoteric aspects of professionalism are apparent in the tendency of municipal consultants to write reports as if their final recommendations derived their validity from the professional status of the writer, neglecting therefore to show how the conclusions were reached, where the data came from, what formulas were used, in short, how the conclusions can be independently checked.

23. Cf. *ibid.*, p. 18.

24. "Perhaps, if we can professionalize our generalists before the professionalization of our specialists has fully crystallized, in a particular jurisdiction or area, then the separatism with which the professions have tried to protect themselves from the unprofessionalized politicians can be tempered." *Ibid.*, p. 20. See *Report of the Committee on Qualifications of Planners* (London: His Majesty's Stationery Office, 1950), esp. pp. 47–62, for an excellent discussion of generalist characteristics.

25. Dennis O'Harrow, "No Time for Softness," *American Society of Planning Officials Newsletter*, XXXI (January, 1965), p. 3. O'Harrow explains that the public official, conversely, has the positive duty of listening, especially to citizens who honestly differ from him.

26. See Lyle E. Craine, "The Inner Directed Field Man," review of *The Forest Ranger* by Herbert Kaufman, *Public Administration Review*, XX (1960), 227–30.

27. Milton J. Esman, "Administrative Stability and Change," *American Political Science Review*, XLIV (1950), 949.

28. Morstein-Marx, "Administrative Responsibility," p. 250.

29. Gaus, "The Responsibility of Public Administration," p. 38.

30. Eduard C. Lindeman, *The Democratic Man*, ed. Robert Gessner (Boston: Beacon, 1956), p. 170.

31. Luther Gulick, "Political and Administrative Leadership," *Public Management*, XLV (November, 1963), 245.

32. Quoted by Gaus, "The Responsibility of Public Administration," p. 38.

33. "In science authority emerges from procedures whose results all can respect. Without a structured legitimate will, the enterprise of the sciences escapes anarchy and secures the discipline of an authority that all can accept without loss of human dignity or intellectual self-respect. A cooperating organization can operate successfully without a commanding hierarchy. Is this a special case of human behavior, or

does it have implications for public administration?" Norton E. Long, "Public Policy and Administration: The Goals of Rationality and Responsibility," *Public Administration Review*, XIV (1954), 25. The same idea is expressed by John Dewey in *Intelligence in the Modern World*, ed. Joseph Ratner (New York: Random House, 1939), pp. 343–63.

34. John M. Gaus, "The Authority of Organized Knowledge," *Public Administration Review*, II (1942), 167. It should be noted, in addition, that the publicity forced on the public administrator by the public character of his work can be an important incentive to objectivity.

35. See above, pp. 200–202.

36. There are other reasons, too, for refusing to review lower decisions. See the fine list compiled by Barnard, Review of *Bureaucracy in a Democracy*, pp. 1002–03.

37. Cf. Hadley Cantril, *The "Why" of Man's Experience* (New York: Macmillan, 1950), p. 152. "Responsibility to the situation" and "authority of the situation" are alternative possible descriptions *provided* the moral, creative, developing, and knowing contents of the situation are recognized. Lindeman pictures it: "To bring truth out of error, to change ugliness into beauty, to distinguish good from evil, to rear harmonies out of discords, to exchange freedom for bondage—these are the methods by which values are created." *The Democratic Man*, p. 202.

38. Cf. Lyndall F. Urwick's insistence on the importance of integrity as "the most vital of all the qualifications for the individual charged with the responsibility of leading a group of his fellows." *The Pattern of Management* (Minneapolis: University of Minnesota Press, 1956), p. 19 *et seq.*

39. See above, pp. 160–61.

40. On power, see Chapter 7 above, especially pp. 132–34.

41. See above, pp. 226–28.

42. Piaget, *The Moral Judgment of the Child*, pp. 339, 340.

43. Lippmann, *Public Opinion*, p. 222.

44. See above, pp. 122–24.

45. "Responsibility is the analogue in politics and society of objectivity in intellectual affairs." Charles Frankel, *The Case for Modern Man* (New York: Harper, 1955), p. 203.

46. "The Conflict between Maturity and Organization," *Public Management*, XLIII (November, 1963), 262. (Digest of an address presented by Chris Argyris at the Third Annual Public Relations Institute, at Cornell University.)

47. Friedrich, *Constitutional Government and Democracy*, p. 21.

48. See above, pp. 18–19.

49. See above, pp. 30–32.

50. See above, fn. 18 to p. 220, pp. 265–66.

51. Cf. Horace S. Fries, "Social Planning," in *The Cleavage in Our Culture*, ed. Frederick Burkhardt (Boston: Beacon, 1952), p. 103.

52. See above, pp. 70–71.

Chapter Sixteen

1. Francis M. Myers, *The Warfare of Democratic Ideals* (Yellow Springs, Ohio: Antioch Press, 1956), p. 236.

2. See Charles P. Curtis, *The Oppenheimer Case* (New York: Simon & Schuster, 1955). See also Jerome Frank's comments on the SEC experts as aides to judicial decision-making. "The Place of the Expert in a Democratic Society," *Philosophy of Science*, XVI (1949), 24.

3. E. C. Lindeman, "Discussion," in *The Encyclopedia of Social Sciences,* ed. Edwin A. R. Seligman (New York: Macmillan, 1931), V, 167.

4. See above, pp. 19–21.

5. On public opinion, see above, pp. 23–24, 149–150.

6. See above, p. 19, pp. 247–52.

7. Cf. Myers, *The Warfare of Democratic Ideals,* p. 237.

8. Max C. Otto, "Speech and Freedom of Speech," in *Freedom and Experience,* ed. Sidney Hook and Milton R. Knovitz (Ithaca: Cornell University Press, 1947), p. 84.

9. Sometimes called "privacy," as in opposition to the persistence of the Jehovah's Witnesses.

10. On administration as embodiment of public interest, see above, pp. 292–94, 297–98.

11. This, I think, can be said in the face of the firm truth contained in the humor of John Masters' off-hand hyperbole: "Scientists are nothing like as keen on knowledge for its own sake as they pretend, and a chap who produced a sure disproof of the Quantum Theory, or some other current fad, would likely wake up sharing a bottle of formaldehyde with a coelacanth." "The Abominable Snowman," *Harper's Magazine,* CCXVIII (January, 1959), 30.

12. Victor Cohn, "Science Races Man's Mind," *Minneapolis Sunday Tribune,* December 22, 1963, Sec. F, p. 1.

13. See Chapter 8.

14. Max C. Otto, *Natural Laws and Human Hopes* (Denver: Alan Swallow, 1953—second edition), pp. 48–49.

15. There is another full field for comment in the selling of politicians to the public by public relations experts. See Stanley Kelley, Jr., *Professional Public Relations and Political Power* (Baltimore: Johns Hopkins, 1956).

16. *Public Management,* XLVII (January, 1965), 18–19.

17. See above, pp. 111–12.

18. "Suburbanites Cast Their Votes for City Planning, *Architectural Forum,* CXIX (December, 1963), 84–85.

19. See above, pp. 205–206.

20. See above, pp. 225–26.

21. See above, pp. 133–34.

22. Donald W. Smithburg, "Public Administration and the Behavioral Sciences," Paper delivered at the 1953 annual meeting of the American Political Science Association, (mimeographed), p. 15.

23. Jean Piaget, *The Moral Judgment of the Child* (Glencoe, Illinois: The Free Press, 1948), pp. 327–55.

24. See above pp. 65–66.

25. See above p. 66.

26. Cf. William B. Shore, "Developments in Public Administration," *Public Administration Review,* XVIII (1958), 360.

27. William H. Whyte, Jr. found that no one was listening to the weighty gabble of management philosophizing. [*Is Anybody Listening?* (New York: Simon & Schuster, 1952).] But this is aside from the problem of status. It is a case of apathy normal to the situation where a propaganda barrage is sensed.

28. Henry S. Dennison, Review of *Dynamic Administration,* by M. P. Follett, *Advanced Management,* VII (1942), 144.

29. Cf. Otto, *Natural Laws and Human Hopes,* p. 58.

30. Someone asked the other day why there were so many great men (out of such a small population) in America at the time of the Constitution. Having just come from a visit to Monticello, I replied that it was because they lived so far apart in those days that in order to communicate they had to write long coherent, explanatory letters to each other. Making for themselves a freedom to speak through carefully culturing a skill of objectivizing thoughts, feelings, etc., they not only grew to greatness themselves but bequeathed a political freedom to the whole nation.

31. Myers, *The Warfare of Democratic Ideals*, p. 233.

32. Piaget, *The Moral Judgment of the Child*, p. 347.

33. See above, p. 206.

Chapter Seventeen

1. See above, pp. 15–21.

2. The reader is again asked to bear in mind that key terms are used with refined meanings.

3. See above p. 275.

4. Cf. Wallace S. Sayre, "Trends in a Decade of Administrative Values," *Public Administration Review*, XI (1951), 5. Norton Long, too, asserts that Simon and his school are in danger of setting up a new division between politics and administration. But, unfortunately, he accepts Simon as science and says this won't do because administration is concerned with values, with *reflecting* values: "Values are the essence of politics. Ergo, politics is not a science." "Public Policy and Administration: The Goals of Rationality and Responsibility," *Public Administration Review*, XIV (1954), 23.

5. Cf. Luther Gulick, "Politics, Administration, and the New Deal," *The Annals of the American Academy of Political and Social Science*, CLXIX (1933), 66.

6. Cf. Luther Gulick, "Political and Administrative Leadership," *Public Management*, XLV (November, 1963), 246.

7. Similarly, the autonomy achieved by means of professionalization in such fields as highway engineering, education, or public welfare may very usefully serve to afford protection from "vulgar" politics until such time as they can be integrated into the moral whole of government. Note the use of physicians to administer great state hospitals to avoid "spoils."

8. It might be said that the city manager movement's continuing success lies in the avenue it opens to planning by rising above the "partisanship" and compromise penchant of the local politician.

9. Lyndall Urwick and many others to the contrary notwithstanding. See his "The Function of Administration," in *Papers on the Science of Administration*, eds. L. Gulick and L. Urwick (New York: Institute of Public Administration, Columbia University, 1937), p. 119.

10. This may be a direct quote from a talk by Paul Opperman before the Chicago Chapter of the American Institute of Planners, June 4, 1958.

11. See above, p. 222.

12. John M. Gaus, "The Authority of Organized Knowledge," *Public Administration Review*, II (1942), 167.

13. See John Osman, "Cities Can Help by Transforming Urban Energy," *Public Management*, XLVII (March 1965), 50–57.

14. See above, pp. 292–94, 297–98.

15. See above, pp. 122–24, 285–86.

16. See Richard May, Jr., "The Urban Renewal Project Plan—A Medium for Social Change and Advance," *Pratt Planning Papers*, II (November, 1963), p. 2.

17. See, for example, Karl Mannheim, *Freedom, Power, and Democratic Planning* (New York: Oxford University Press, 1950), pp. 201, 230.

18. Cf. Milton J. Esman, "Administrative Stability and Change," *American Political Science Review*, XLIV (1950), 950.

19. "Institutions evolve workways which new members acquire, perhaps unconsciously, and this inheritance substitutes, to a considerable degree, for individual knowledge about how to carry on the institution. There is wisdom in these workways, as well as much that is archaic." Report of Paul H. Appleby's address on "Institutional Decision-Making" at the 1955 annual conference of the New York Metropolitan Chapter of the American Society for Public Administration in *ASPA Newsletter*, V (May, 1955). Cf. also Donald W. Smithburg, "Public Administration and the Behavioral Sciences." Paper delivered at the 1953 annual meeting of the American Political Science Association. (Mimeographed.) p. 13.

20. See above, pp. 278–80.

21. Eduard C. Lindeman, *The Democratic Man*, ed. Robert Gessner (Boston: Beacon, 1956), p. 56.

22. Pp. 312–13.

23. Lyndall Urwick, "Experiences in Public Administration," *Public Administration Review*, XV (1955), 250.

24. See above, pp. 169–170.

25. There are important exceptions to this.

26. Cf. *Public Administration Review*, XXV (June, 1965), 138.

27. See Alvin W. Gouldner, ed., *Studies in Leadership* (New York: Harper, 1950), pp. 23–45.

28. Gouldner seems to be approaching a transactional investigation of leadership when he suggests viewing it in terms of the "leadership corps of a group" instead of the personality characteristics of individuals. See *ibid.*, pp. 44–45.

29. See C. Wright Mills, "On Knowledge and Power," *Dissent*, II (Summer, 1955), 210.

30. Ordway Tead, *The Art of Leadership* (New York: McGraw Hill, 1935), p. 20.

31. See above, pp. 247–52.

32. Cf. Paul J. Brouwer, "The Power to See Ourselves," *Harvard Business Review*, XLII (1964), 156–65.

33. See above, p. 138.

34. See above pp. 132–34. "The essence of leadership lies not only in the initiative which dictates largely the experience of the group, but in the ability which transforms that experience into power." Mary P. Follett, "What Type of Central Administrative Leadership is Essential to Business Management as Defined in this Course?" in *Business Management as a Profession*, ed. Henry C. Metcalf (Chicago: A. W. Shaw, 1927), p. 363.

35. Mary P. Follett, *Dynamic Administration*, ed. H. C. Metcalf and L. Urwick (London: Bath Management Publications Trust, 1941), p. 92.

36. See above, p. 277 *et seq.*

37. Lindeman, *The Democratic Man*, p. 124. Compare Norman R. F. Maier and Allen R. Solem, "The Contribution of a Discussion Leader to the Quality of Group Thinking: The Effective Use of Minority Opinions," in *Group Dynamics*, ed. Dorwin Cartwright and Alvin Zander (Evanston, Illinois: Row, Peterson, 1953), pp. 561–72.

38. See above, pp. 205–206.

39. Cf., for example, Lyndall F. Urwick, *The Pattern of Management* (Minneapolis: University of Minnesota Press, 1956), pp. 23–29.

40. "Responsibility obtains when decision or choice is made in the fullest possible concrete, imaginative awareness of the human consequences which the decision involves. In such a decision the individual realizes, in regard to the situation in hand and in so far as available means of inquiry make possible, what his choice will do to persons affected (including himself) in terms of all their interests. The circumstances may, of course, be urgent. In this case the individual may not be able to take all the time he would like for antecedent reflection about the alternative consequences of his decision. But if the decision is responsible in such circumstances, the individual will have a definite interest in, or concern for, the ensuing consequences, even though they may turn out to be different from what was anticipated." Horace S. Fries, "On Managerial Responsibility," Advanced Management, VIII (1943), 47.

41. See above, pp. 198–200.

42. See above, pp. 200–202.

43. Cf. Gordon W. Allport, *Becoming* (New Haven: Yale University Press, 1955), p. 76.

44. "The final proof of [management's] sincerity and seriousness is uncompromising emphasis on integrity of character.... In appointing people to top positions integrity cannot be over-emphasized. In fact, no one should be appointed unless management is willing to have his character serve as the model for all his subordinates." Peter F. Drucker, *The Practice of Management* (New York: Harper, 1954), pp. 157–58.

45. Harold C. Havighurst, "Technology and Political Organization," *Advanced Management*, VIII (1943), 52. Italics added.

46. Robert T. Golembiewski, "Specialist or Generalist?: Structure a Crucial Factor," *Public Administration Review*, XXV (June, 1965), 135–41.

47. Mary P. Follett, *The New State* (New York: Longmans, Green, 1918), p. 64.

48. Although consultants are very handily "used" by administrators to divert the wrath of publics with whom they have been unable to establish sufficient communication to make their proposals palatable. There is no à priori reason why consultants could not be as sensitively involved as administrative personnel. And sometimes they are, particularly in the field of city and county planning.

49. Cf. Mills, "On Knowledge and Power," p. 207. "The problem is to relate specialists and men of action in such a way that the decision makers cannot protect themselves from new ideas and fresh viewpoints, and the specialists will occasionally have something relevant to contribute to the decision making process." Wayne A. R. Leys, *Ethics for Policy Decisions* (New York: Prentice–Hall, 1952), p. 361. See also above pp. 278–79.

50. Michael Creedman, "Psychologists Help More Firms to Raise Employes' Efficiency," *The Wall Street Journal*, October 19, 1964, p. 1.

51. Frank Sherwood, "The Role Concept in Administration," *Public Personnel Review*, (January, 1964).

52. Cf. Frank P. Zeidler, "Mobilizing to Meet Municipal Manpower Challenges," Pamphlet of the Public Personnel Association, adapted from an address before the 1963 Central Regional Conference of the Public Personnel Association in Detroit, Michigan.

53. Urwick, "Experience in Public Administration," p. 247.

54. "The decision as to when, where, and how to introduce a technological change is a social decision, affecting an extraordinary variety of values. And yet these decisions are made in something very close to a social vacuum. Technological

innovations are regularly introduced for the sake of technological convenience, and without established mechanisms for appraising or controlling or even cushioning their consequences." Charles Frankel, *The Case for Modern Man* (New York: Harper, 1955), p. 198.

55. Cf. A. A. Imberman, "Personalities in Labor-Management Conflicts," *Advanced Management*, XV (December, 1950), 19–22.

56. See John Kenneth Galbraith, *The New Industrial State* (Boston: Houghton Mifflin, 1967).

57. John J. Flagler, "Collective Bargaining in the Public Service—Developments and Trends." Address given to the Minnesota Chapter of the American Society for Public Administration, January 23, 1964.

58. See above, p. 139.

59. I am reminded of the classic "elegant solution" to the circular or "parasol" assembly problem set by a human bottleneck: see Norman R. F. Maier, "The Quality of Group Decision as Influenced by the Discussion Leader," *Human Relations*, III (1950), 155–74.

60. The enlightened TVA personnel policy should be mentioned in this connection. See Judson King, "The TVA Labor Relations Policy at Work," Bulletin No. 192-A, rev. ed., The National Popular Government League, April 19, 1940.

61. See Arthur W. Bromage, "Managers Become Oriented to Human Values," *Public Management*, XLVII (October 1965), pp. 256–60.

62. See above, pp. 18–19.

63. Follett says the problem of management is "obtaining control through effective unities." *Dynamic Administration*, p. 207.

Chapter Eighteen

1. See above, p. 218.

2. See Earl Latham, "Executive Management and the Federal Field Service," *Public Administration Review*, V (1945), 27.

3. "Organization for Overhead Management," *Public Administration Review*, II (1942), 64.

4. Charles E. Merriam, *The Role of Politics in Social Change* (New York: New York University Press, 1936), p. 128.

5. Compare Mary P. Follett, "The Illusion of Final Authority," *Bulletin of the Taylor Society*, XI (December, 1926), 247–49.

6. See above, pp. 96–97, 188, 215.

7. "Scientific Mediation—Tool of Democracy," *Antioch Review*, V (1945), 400. Italics his.

8. See Ray Ginger, "Business and Government," *Antioch Review*, XIV (1954), 22.

9. See Schuyler C. Wallace's excellent analysis of the pros and cons, a few large departments vs many small departments and agencies. *Federal Departmentalization: A Critique of Theories of Organization* (New York: Columbia University Press, 1941).

10. Cf. Roscoe C. Martin, *The Cities and the Federal System* (New York: Atherton, 1965), and *Grass Roots* (University of Alabama Press), 1957; Donald S. Strong, Review of *Community Power Structure: A Study of Decision Makers*, by Floyd Hunter, *American Political Science Review*, XLVIII (1954), 236; Georges Langrod, "Local Government and Democracy," *Public Administration*, XXXI (1953), 25–34.

11. Max H. Boehm, "Federalism," in *Encyclopedia of Social Sciences*, VI, p. 169. See also Jennie M. Turner, "Democracy in Administration," *American Political Science Review*, XVII (1923), 229.

12. Luther Gulick, "Politics, Administration, and the New Deal," *The Annals of the American Academy of Political & Social Science*, CLXIX (1933), 66. Cf. also Harold C. Havighurst, "Technology and Political Organization," *Advanced Management*, VIII (1943), 55. The continued systematic thrust of Congress in the direction of periodic review is clearly evidenced, for example, in Title VI of the 1968 Intergovernmental Cooperation Act, PL 90–577. Note also the increasing respect Senators are according membership on the Government Operations Committee. Senator Eugene J. McCarthy is said to have explained his 1969 move from Foreign Relations to Government Operations by quoting Marshall McLuhan, that "operations is policy."

13. And don't forget the Wisconsin Legislative Reference Library.

14. See Arthur E. Morgan, *Nowhere Was Somewhere* (Chapel Hill: University of North Carolina Press, 1946).

Index

Absolutism, 8, 10

Accountability, of administrators, 158. *See also* Responsibility

Action: defined, 38; and perception, 46; and purpose, 47; distinguished from participation, 157; includes thinking, 190; purpose as, 222–23. *See also* Doing

Active: indistinct from passive, 159

Actors: atomic, 38; and participation, 152. *See also* Individualism

Adler, Alfred, 72

Administration: democracy in, 5, 8; as a way of life, 6–7, 273; growth of, 6–8; Woodrow Wilson's view, 8–10; not politically neutral, 10; democratic vs. autocratic, 11; deficiencies in developing nations, 12; center of political theory, 147; using bargain-compromise methods, 154–55, 297; as balancer, 155; promises for participation, 174; business, 186, 276; democratization of, 228; democratic-scientific, 231; natural setting for creative bargaining, 231; principles of, not validated, 274; convergence with moral science, 280–82; proximate goals of, 281; responsibility in, 302; relation to legislature in utopia, 358–59. *See also* Theory

Administrative state: modern, 7; Egyptian, 58

Administrator. See Leader

Adversary system: and freedom of speech, 307. *See also* Judiciary

Advertising: abuses freedom of speech, 104, 311, 314, 315, 327

Aesthetic experience, 61, 241, 266

Aesthetic models: in planning, 333

Aesthetics: and specialization of function, 17; and problem formulation, 79; and Greek science, 88; beginning of creation, 207; and perception, 237; and invariance, 249; a doing, 261; and simplicity, 266; in social test, 268; mentioned, 61, 77, 139, 191. *See also* Art

Aesthetic sensitivity: precedes art, 261

Africa, 9, 11

Agreement, 231; process of, 32; methods of, 100; thru science, 101. *See also* Creative bargaining; Integration

Aggressiveness, 122

Agriculture, U. S. Department of, 156, 157, 159, 314

Aid: foreign, 12; economic, 165

Aims: distinguished from interests and intentions, 222, 224

Allegiance: an attribute of purpose, 209

Allport, Gordon W., 152, 198, 201, 216, 285, 378n13, 384n17, 388n6, 390n4

American Institute of Planners, 292

Ames, Adelbert, Jr., 40, 45, 323

Ames, Van Meter, 244

Analogy, 113

Anonymity: of urban life, 182

Anonymous IV, 407n57

Anthropomorphism, 113–14

Apathy: and participation, 6–7, 161; health in, 156; and partial problems, 156; and government, 186–87; as a lasting integration, 187; structured in organizations, 187; enabled by institutions, 278; and planning, 334; mentioned, 103, 136, 148, 150, 167, 182, 188, 333

Appleby, Paul H., 29, 354

Appreciation, 242; follows creation, 239, 261

Aquinas, St. Thomas, 165

Architect, 243

Architecture, 253

Aristocracy of the concerned, 148

Aristotle, 106, 159, 299

Art: service of, 46; and purpose, 47, 200, 235–39; of celebration, 236; and moral progress, 236; and evolution, 236–37; for art's sake, 238; and a disturbing concern, 238; and sensitivity to relations, 238; and the death of vigilance, 239; and objectivity, 239; precedes appreciation, 239; and knowing, 239; excuse for skill, 240; freedom's champion, 240–41; service to science, 243–44; new feel for con-

64, 232, 278, 416n54. *See also* Artifacts; Machines

Technostructure, v, 136, 347

Teleological ethics: start of, 61; temporary success, 63; and coercion, 63; ethical obsolescence, 63–64; and responsibility, 71, 286; breaking loose from, 104–05; shaken by change, 134; and politics, 137; mentioned, 74, 76, 142, 224, 278, 302, 328. *See also* Custom; Morality

Telephone experiment, 312, 322, 335

Television: contemptuous of public, 313

Teller, Edward, 252

Tenure: blocks group functioning, 27

Test, public: and objectivity, 85; in experiment, 92; of hypothesis by applied scientist, 126; of purpose in democracy, 140; and majority rule, 148; of a tool, 221; of purpose, 221–22; of functional power, 231; by quality, 227, 266–69; and art, 266–69; complexity of, 268; and freedom of speech, 310, 314; via skills, 324; and leadership, 338, 340; use of the minority in, 340; and the group, 393n48

Theory: needed for self-government, 13–14; as guide, 13, 25, 30; of administration to lead political theory, 15, 26, 147; after-the-fact political, 25, 36; promise in administrative, 28; effect in social control, 35–36; integrating function of, 36; as tool, 36, 91, 126; and perception, 36; vs. practice, 74; logical fertility of, 83; perfectible, 83; use of change in, 89; as instrument of control, 91; control by and over experiment, 92–93; as tool of pure and applied scientists, 126; complexity of administrative, 272; self-fulfillment of, 343. *See also* Science, Experimental method of; Concepts

Thermodynamics, 97

Thinking: as transaction, 44; and perceiving, 44–47; and evolution, 45, 72; vs. doing, 87; is action, 190. *See also* Concepts; Ideas; Theory

Third scientist: job of, 126; in scientific mediation, 225–26. *See also* Scientist, citizen

Time: reality of, 96, 202; denied by cause-and-effect, 96; held together by purpose, intention, 102, 115, 122, 127, 281; in physics, 102; and creativity, 150; irreversible in social affairs, 171; shown in creation, 202; and error, 203; and expectation 250; music and, 251; bound by art, 268; and freedom, 328. *See also* Continuity

Timelessness: of cause and effect, 96; of mathematics, 97

Tolerance: in reality, 79, 102; of scientific method, 83, 301; for moral abuse, 102, 105, 127, 167; political virtue of, 169, 171–72. *See* Uncertainty; Reality, imprecision of; Indeterminism; Disjunction

Tools: ideas as, 45, 53, 92, 217, 245; use in science, 89; knowhow built in, 91; abstract, of control, 91, 94, 218, 220; as mediators in control, 92; purposes as, 116, 221–23; test of, 221. *See also* Science, Experimental method of; Hypothesis; Theory

Totality, 187, 194

Tovey, D. F., 256

Tragic cycle, 173

Transaction: defined and analyzed, 37–39; painting as, 41; and integration, 50; science as, 77–80; of observation, 111; basic to control, 117; incompleted, 119; and participation, 151; of choosing, 166; and conservative drag, 175; and Follett, 178; and group life, 185; formalized in creative bargaining, 211; and invariance, 248; and aesthetics, 261; and responsibility, 290; and freedom of speech, 309–10; and skill, 324; and planning, 332; as defining context of leadership, 337–38; mentioned, 6, 65, 87, 101, 102, 116, 126, 134, 160, 161, 167, 274, 275

Transfer: of pattern, 249

Trapezoid experiment, 40

Travis, James, 406n50, 407n56

Trecker, Harleigh B., 195, 391n1

Trial and error, 93; not appropriate to moral affairs, 104; contrasted with moral science, 105. *See also* Chance

Trilling, Lionel, 260

Truman, David B., 138, 153

Trust: thru knowing, 191; of facts, 200; and vicarious experience, 227; on the job, 346

Truth: of science has falsified truth of government, 4; creation of, 14; politics of, 14, 142, 148, 280, 361; marketplace theory, 17, 24, 28, 307; from legislative deliberation, 19; test